Forensic Practice in Criminal Cases

Other titles available from Law Society Publishing:

CLSA Duty Solicitor's Handbook (2nd edn)
Andrew Keogh
1 85328 975 2

Criminal Defence (2nd edn)
Roger Ede and Anthony Edwards
1 85328 830 6

Criminal Justice Act 2003
Andrew Keogh
1 85328 877 2

Drinking and Driving Offences
Jonathan Black
1 85328 851 9

Immigration Advice at the Police Station (2nd edn)
Rosie Brennan
1 85328 747 4

All books from Law Society Publishing can be ordered through good book-shops or direct from our distributors, Marston Book Services, by telephone 01235 465656 or email law.society@marston.co.uk. Please confirm the price before ordering.

For further information or a catalogue, please telephone our editorial and marketing office on 020 7320 5878.

Forensic Practice in Criminal Cases

LYNNE TOWNLEY

Barrister

and

ROGER EDE

Solicitor and Deputy District Judge

The Law Society

The views expressed in this publication should be taken as those of the authors only unless it is specifically indicated that the Law Society has given its endorsement.

The authors have asserted the right under the Copyright, Designs and Patents Act 1988 to be identified as authors of this work.

Crown copyright material is reproduced with the permission of the Controller of Her Majesty's Stationery Office

© Lynne Townley and Roger Ede 2004

ISBN 1 85328 821 7

Published in 2004 by the Law Society
113 Chancery Lane, London WC2A 1PL

Typeset by J&L Composition, Filey, North Yorks
Printed by Antony Rowe Ltd, Chippenham, Wilts

Contents

Foreword

The demand for forensic science by the criminal justice system in England and Wales grows rapidly, spurred on by developments in science and technology and a desire by investigators to provide courts with ever more reliable forms of evidence.

The new opportunities which science provides require criminal justice practitioners to be aware of what is possible and to know enough about the skills and processes involved to take full advantage of what is on offer and ensure the integrity of the evidence which is gathered as a result.

The increased use of forensic evidence by the prosecution also requires a greater understanding of forensic practice by the defence. Miscarriages of justice can result not only from poor police and prosecution practice but also from sloppy work by the defence.

Professional testimony is now vital in many cases and the role of the forensic practitioner as an impartial, objective and competent witness is essential to ensuring a just outcome.

The Council for the Registration of Forensic Practitioners has been working with forensic practitioners and forensic evidence in court to enable courts and the public to be confident about the competence of forensic science experts.

That is why I welcome this informative and challenging book which will have something new for even the most experienced practitioners. It will help lawyers, the police and the courts to improve their understanding of forensic practice and enable them to work better with forensic practitioners. At a time when criminal practice is becoming even more complex, this is a practical guide to the uses, strengths and limitations of forensic evidence, covering forensic investigation, the different areas of forensic expertise, working with forensic practitioners and forensic evidence in court.

Professor Evelyn Ebsworth, Chairman, Council for the Registration of Forensic Practitioners; chemist; former Vice Chancellor of Durham University.

Acknowledgements

The authors wish to thank the following for their contribution to this book.

Traffic Accident Investigators
The chapter was compiled by James Keenan LCGI MITAI. Past Chairman of the Institute of Traffic Accident Investigators (ITAI); Chairman ITAI Grades Assessors; Edexcel External Examiner, Forensic Accident Investigation course, De Montfort University, Leicester.

Veterinary Science
This chapter was written and contributed by Professor John E Cooper, DTVM, FRCPath, FIBiol, FRCVS and Margaret E Cooper, LLB, FLS. Comparative Forensic Services, PO Box 153, Wellingborough, Northants, NN8 2ZA. UK Email: **NGAGI@compuserve.com** – overseas Email: **NGAGI@vetaid.net** (pathological and other investigations of all species).

The authors would like to thank the following for granting interviews on their specialisms and further, giving of their time to review the resulting chapters.

Computer crime
Professor David I Bainbridge, BSc, LLB, PhD, CEng, MICE, MBCS, Barrister, Professor of Law, University of Aston, Birmingham.

Contact traces
Professor Andrew Stoker Fawcett BSc, PhD, CChem, FRSC, Forensic Science Consultant (physical and chemical evidence in criminal cases).

DNA, blood and hair
Dr Elizabeth M. Wilson BSc, PhD, CBiol, MIBiol, Forensic Scientist.

Facial Mapping; CCTV; Video and Image Enhancement
Kenneth A Linge, BA, MSc, FBIPP, Forensic Photographic and Imaging Consultant, DABS Fingerprinting/Forensic Ltd (Tel./Fax: (01376) 573406).

Fingerprints
Ron Cook, FFS, RFP, MIAI, DipNEBSS; Fingerprint Consultant, R W Cook and Associates Ltd/DABS Fingerprints/Forensic Ltd, PO Box 6342, Kelvedon, Colchester, CO5 9PX.

Christopher McEvoy, BSc, BA (Hons) (Law), Fingerprint Consultant, Metropolitan Police Service, New Scotland Yard 1965–2002. Former Secretary to the National Fingerprint Service Project Board.

Firearms
Brian Arnold, Head of Firearms Section, Forensic Science Service, Metropolitan Laboratory 1973–2001.

Fire Investigators
Dr Roger Berrett, BSc, PhD, Forensic Science Consultant Fire and Explosion Investigation, 9 Heron's Croft, Weybridge, Surrey KT13 0PL (Tel. (01932) 859430).

Footwear Impressions and Instrument Marks
Professor Andrew Stoker Fawcett BSc, PhD, CChem, FRCS, Forensic Science Consultant (physical and chemical evidence in criminal cases).

Forensic Accountancy
Toni Pincott LLB, FCA, Forensic & Investigations Services Partner, Grant Thornton Asset Management Ltd, Grant Thornton House, Melton Street, Euston Square, London NW1 2EP.

Forensic Anthropology
Dr Sue Black OBE, BSc, PhD, Consultant Forensic Anthropologist, Human Identification Centre, Department of Forensic Medicine and Science, University of Glasgow, Glasgow G12 8QQ.

Forensic Archaeology
Prof John Hunter BA, PhD, FSA, FSAScot, MIFA, Professor of Ancient History and Archaeology, Department of Ancient History and Archaeology, University of Birmingham, Edgbaston, Birmingham B15 2TT.

Forensic Linguistics
Professor Malcolm Coulthard, Department of English, The University of Birmingham, Edgbaston, Birmingham B15 2TT.

Sue Blackwell, Department of English, The University of Birmingham, Edgbaston, Birmingham B15 2TT.

Forensic Odontologists
Dr David A Lewin BDS, Dip F Od (LHMC), Forensic Odontologist.

Dr Freddie Martin BDS (Univ Edin), Dip F Od (LHMC), Forensic Odontologist, for further information see *www.dentalidentification.com*

Forensic Pathology
Professor J Crane MB, BCh, FRCPath, DMJ (Clin et Path), State Pathologist for Northern Ireland and Professor of Forensic Medicine at The Queen's University of Belfast.

Forensic Physicians
Dr Michael A Knight LLM (University of Cardiff), DMJ (Clin), Senior Police Surgeon for Suffolk, Honorary Secretary of The Association of Forensic Physicians.

Forensic Psychiatry/Psychology
Anthony R Ostrin LLB (Hons), MCIT, MILT, Solicitor Advocate, a President of the Mental Health Review Tribunal and a legal assessor to the General Medical Council.

The authors wish to thank Professor Robert Bluglass CBE, Consultant Forensic Psychiatrist for granting them an interview.

Dr Eric Shepherd, Chartered Forensic Psychologist, Investigative Science.

Questioned documents
The authors wish to thank the questioned document examiner who advised on this chapter.

Toxicology
Dr Nikolas P Lemos BSc (Hons), MSc, PhD, MRSC, Head, Forensic Toxicology Service, St George's Hospital Medical School, University of London.

Stephen J Collier BSc, Cert Ed, AMIMI, AIRTE, Certified Drug Recognition Evaluator, National Drug Recognition Training Unit, Northamptonshire Police.

The authors would like to thank the following for their help:

Diana Bailey MSc; Matthew Brotherton MA (Cantab), Barrister, Law Reporter – The Consolidated Council of Law Reporting; Dr J Chanhan BDS (London); Dr Chris Davies MA, DPhil, RFP; Stephen Dawson, District Judge, Thames Magistrates' Court; Dr Angela Gallop BSc, DPhil, CBiol, FIBiol, FRSA, CEO of Forensic Alliance Ltd, Member of the Governing Council of the CRFP and President of the Forensic Science Society; Jane Hickman, Hickman & Rose, Solicitors, London; Alan Kershaw, Chief Executive, Council for the Registration of Forensic Practitioners; Robert Kite DipH&S, MA, MIOSH, Health and Safety Loss Management Consultant; Dr Simon Smith MBBS; Martin Thurston; Dr V Thyagarajan MBBS, MS; Andrew Vi-Ming Kok, Barrister; Peter Whent LLB, Barrister; Dr Paul N Williams, International Marketing Director, Lion Laboratories Ltd.

Abbreviations

ACPO	Association of Chief Police Officers
ACPOS	Association of Chief Police Officers (Scotland)
ACU	area crime unit
AFP	Association of Forensic Practitioners/Association of Forensic Physicians
AO	arresting officer
APS	Association of Police Surgeons (now the AFP) (see **para. 22.9**)
ARA	Assets Recovery Agency
AS	asset summons number
BAFO	British Association for Forensic Odontology
BAFS	British Academy of Forensic Science
BAHID	British Association for Human Identification
BCU	basic command unit
BISFA	International Bureau for the Standardisation of Man-Made Fibres
BMA	British Medical Association
BPA	blood-spatter pattern analysis
BPS	British Psychological Society
BS	British Standard
CCJU	Crime and Criminal Justice Unit [Home Office]
CCRC	Criminal Cases Review Commission
CCTV	closed circuit television
CICB	Criminal Injuries Compensation Board
CID	Criminal Investigation Department
CITES	Convention on International Trade in Endangered Species of Wild Fauna and Flora
CJ	criminal justice
CMA	Communications Management Association
CMD	Crime Management Department
CNS	central nervous system
CODIS	Combined DNA Index System

CPIA	Criminal Procedure and Investigations Act 1996
CPD	continuing professional development
CPS	Crown Prosecution Service
CRFP	Council for the Registration of Forensic Practitioners
CRS	crime reporting system
CSC	crime scene co-ordinator
CSI	crime scene investigator
CSM	crime scene manager
CTM	contact trace material
CV	curriculum vitae
DC	detective constable
DC	DNA confirmed marker
DCI	detective chief inspector
DCR	divisional control room
DCM	divisional crime manager
DETR	Department of the Environment, Transport and the Regions
DF	DNA failure marker
DFHID	Diploma in Forensic Human Identification
DFO/Dip F Od	Diploma in Forensic Odontology
DfT	Department for Transport
DI	detective inspector
DIR	drug influence recognition
DMJ	Diploma in Medical Jurisprudence
DMJ (Odont)	Diploma in Forensic Dentistry
DNA	deoxyribonucleic acid
DOH	Department of Health
DP	DNA profiled marker
DPP	Director of Public Prosecutions
DRE	drug recognition expert
DRO	drug recognition officer
DRT	drug recognition training
DS	detective sergeant
DT	DNA taken flag
DTI	Department of Trade and Industry
ECHR	European Convention on Human Rights
ECLM	European Council of Legal Medicine
ESDA	electrostatic detection apparatus
FCR	force control room
FDB	Forensic Anthropology Data Bank
FDR	firearms discharge residues/fire data report

FIT	field impairment tests
FME	forensic medical examiner
FOA	first officer attending
FSAG	Forensic Science Advisory Group
FSP	forensic science provider
FSS	Forensic Science Service
FUG	footmark user group
GBR	graduate basis for registration
GC	gas chromatography
GLP	good laboratory practice
GPR	ground penetrating radar
HMIC	Her Majesty's Inspectorate of Constabulary
HOLMES	Home Office large major enquiry system
HRA	Human Rights Act
HSRA	Homicide Stranger Rape and Abduction
ICAF	Institute for Communications, Arbitration and Forensics
ICT	information communication technology
IO	investigating officer
IRB	incident report book
ISO	International Organisation for Standardisation
ITAI	Institute of Traffic Accident Investigators
JOPI	Joint operational instructions
LCN	low copy number
LFEPA	London Fire and Emergency Planning Authority
LSC	Legal Service Commission
LSD	lysergic acid diethylamide
MCU	major crimes unit
MCS	major crime scene
MDMA	'ecstasy'
MDT	mandatory drugs testing
MG	Manual of Guidance for the Preparation, Processing and Submission of Files
MIRA	Motor Industries Research Agency
MIRSAP	Major Investigation Incident Room Standardised Administrative Procedure
MLP	Multilocus probes
MMJ	Master of Medical Jurisprudence
MRCVS	Member of the Royal College of Veterinary Surgeons

MS	mass spectrometry
MSP	microspectrophotometry
MtDNA	mitochondrial DNA
NAFIS	National Automated Fingerprint Identification System
NAMAS	National Accreditation of Measurements and Sampling
NCOF	National Crime and Operations Faculty
NDNAD	National DNA Database
NMPH	National Missing Persons Helpline
NRFE	National Register of Forensic Experts
NRT	nicotine replacement therapy
NTCSSCI	National Training Centre for Scientific Support to Crime Investigation
NTT	National Taxing Team
NVQ	national vocational qualification
OIC	officer in charge
OIS	operation information management system
PACE	Police and Criminal Evidence Act 1984
PAW	Partnership for Action Against Wildlife Crime
PC	police constable
PCP	phenylcyclohexylpiperidine ('angel dust')
PCR	polymerase chain reaction
PDH	plea and directions hearing
PNC	police national computer
POLSA	police search adviser
PRG	police research group
PS	police sergeant
RCCJ	Royal Commission on Criminal Justice 1993
RCPath	The Royal College of Pathologists
RDS	Research, Development and Statistics [Home Office Directorate]
RFLP	restrictive fragment length polymorphism
RFP	registered forensic practitioners
RI	refractive index
RSC	Royal Society of Chemistry
RSS	Royal Statistical Society
RTA	Road Traffic Act
RV	meeting points
SA	scientific adviser
SFST	standard field sobriety tests

SFO	Serious Fraud Office
SGM	second generation multiplex
SICAR	shoeprint image capture and retrieval
SIDS	sudden infant death syndrome
SIO	senior investigation officer
SLP	single locus probe
SNP	single nucleotide polymorphisms
SOC	scene of crime
SOCO	scenes of crime officer
SSD	scientific support development
SSM	scientific support manager
SSUs	scientific support units
STR	short tandem repeat
TIAFT	The International Association of Forensic Toxicologists
TLC	thin layer chromatography
TMS	traffic master systems
TNT	trinitrotoluene
TRL	Transport Research Laboratory
TSU	technical support unit
UFSE	Using Forensic Science Effectively
UKAS	United Kingdom Accreditation Service
UNDCP	United Nations Drug Control Programme
WHO	World Health Organisation

Table of cases

Table of statutes

Table of secondary legislation, codes of practice and European legislation

European legislation

SECTION A

Crime Scene Investigation, Forensic Examination, and Presentation of Findings

CHAPTER 1

Forensic evidence: its nature, uses, types and importance

1.1 INTRODUCTION

This book is written principally for lawyers who defend and prosecute, and judges and magistrates who try criminal cases. That is why it is written by lawyers. But it will also be of interest to students of forensic practice, police officers, other investigators and anybody else who works with or takes an interest in the criminal justice system. References to police procedures relate mainly to the larger forces in England and Wales.

A forensic practitioner is someone who uses professional, especially scientific, skills to progress an investigation and the aim of this book is to describe forensic practice: the increasing importance of forensic investigation; who the key players are; what their roles are; what they are capable of doing; which scientific techniques are used; how this contributes to the forensic investigation; how it may be used in court; and the part it plays in the criminal justice process. Section A deals with the nature of a forensic investigation and Section B with the specific areas of forensic expertise which may be utilised.

It is intended to help lawyers to understand the types of forensic investigation which should be carried out; how investigations can go wrong; what further investigations need to be (and can be) carried out; what documentary records of the investigation should exist (or may be missing); and how to instruct and make the greatest use of a forensic scientist to provide or challenge scientific evidence. Scientific evidence is not a special type of evidence. Its strength and reliability should be evaluated in the same way as any other evidence.

1.2 AVAILABILITY OF PHYSICAL EVIDENCE

From time-to-time things go wrong. This may be because proper procedures have not been followed, there is a lack of training and skills, a forensic investigation was not carried out (or only partially carried out), a wrong assumption was made or hypothesis was adopted at the beginning of the investigation, or evidence has been lost, disregarded or contaminated. The forensic scientist's contribution may have been hampered by limited information and/or material for analysis from the investigator.

Historically, there has been concern about the weak forensic scientific knowledge of some police officers who have lacked awareness of forensic science and scientific support. There has been a corresponding risk that potentially significant evidence has not been located, identified or evaluated. The even-handedness of investigations has been called into question by officers who considered that it was unnecessary and not cost-effective to take and submit samples for the purpose of testing the reliability of the prosecution case rather than adding to it.

Many people are not aware that forensic scientists rarely visit crime scenes, that scenes of crime officers (SOCOs) (now also referred to as crime scene investigators (CSIs)) sometimes receive only minimal briefing by the first officer attending (FOAs) and investigating officers (IOs) or that the SOCO may be directed to collect only fingerprints or evidence which may yield DNA. Some police officers and SOCOs would argue that such briefings add little to their knowledge of the scene. Others have said that this lack of communication and/or limits placed upon the search result in a crime scene examination which lacks a proper focus.

It is important for lawyers and courts to be aware that in-force testing has not always been externally validated. Evidence can be contaminated by improper packaging, handling or storage; the chain of custody may not be apparent and a forensic finding may have been made on the basis of the barest information from the police, exposing it to the possibility of a different interpretation should further information be forthcoming. Any of these possibilities may have a bearing upon a particular case and require consideration and investigation.

For every investigation that is incompetent there are many more which are not but people who work within the criminal justice system must be alert to the possibility of incompetence, because of the special weight which courts give to forensic evidence and the risk of miscarriages of justice occurring, convicting the innocent and/or allowing the guilty to go free. Forensic science is not a compulsory or usual part of a lawyer's training.

1.3 THE IMPORTANCE OF PHYSICAL EVIDENCE

With a decline in the importance of the interview as a means of obtaining prosecution evidence, there is a move in the police service to make investigation a more specialised task and for investigators to be more impartial in their reasoning. This was given a push by the heavy criticism of the police for the botched investigation in the Stephen Lawrence case in 1993, the introduction of the Criminal Procedure and Investigations Act 1996 (CPIA) and its Code of Practice and the implementation of the Human Rights Act 1998 (HRA).

The Macpherson Inquiry into the Stephen Lawrence investigation found that it lacked command, direction, organisation and proper documentation, such as a crime scene log showing the decisions made and the actions taken. The inquiry concluded that the Metropolitan Police needed to be better trained and more thorough in carrying out investigations. A columnist in *Police Review* (5 March 1999), wrote 'in the aftermath of the Macpherson indictment, one of the pressing priorities must surely be to fundamentally review criminal investigation'.

The CPIA challenges the police to be even-handed in an investigation, rather than just focusing on collecting evidence to convict an existing suspect. It requires the police, in conducting an investigation, to pursue all reasonable lines of enquiry, whether these point towards or away from the suspect. The government explained that this provision: 'should help to ensure that relevant material is not overlooked. It also provides statutory backing for what is already regarded as good investigative practice.'

The HRA has caused the police to audit their criminal investigative procedures to ensure that they comply with the European Convention on Human Rights (ECHR), such as the right to a fair trial (art.6). Interference with certain rights (such as the right to liberty and security of person (art.5) and the right to respect for private and family life (art.8)), is permissible but only in accordance with law. This has necessitated the introduction of a statutory framework of authorisation and supervision of certain police operations and the formulation of clear operational guidelines which investigators must follow. This has required the police to re-examine, systematise, and document their actions and has increased their accountability and the scrutiny of and control of their investigations.

At a conference 'Justice for All' presented by the Forensic Science Society, the Council for the Registration of Forensic Practitioners (CRFP) and the Expert Witness Institute in April 2003, Sir David Philips, formerly Chief Constable of Kent and President of the Association of Chief Police Officers (ACPO) now Director of the Centre for Policing, spoke of the need for better educated investigators, people who were recruited to carry out that skilled task, with a better feel for professional standards and ethics, rather than promoting investigators from the ranks of those who were recruited to fulfil general police duties. At an earlier conference on disclosure, commenting on the fact that the CPIA had opened police investigations up for close review by the defence, he said that police investigators needed to be at least as well educated as those defence lawyers who would attempt to pull the investigations apart.

1.4   USES OF PHYSICAL EVIDENCE

Evidence used to prosecute a case may be live testimony (including the witnessed accounts of an incident), documentary or physical evidence.

Whenever there is a crime scene: a place (including entry and exit points); an object (e.g. a vehicle); a person (suspect/victim), there is the potential for the recovery of physical evidence. The prosecution case will sometimes rely heavily upon forensic evidence. When this occurs, a jury will often find this scientific evidence compelling and place great trust in it. There is no compulsory accreditation scheme for forensic practitioners (although this has been addressed to some extent by the establishment of the CRFP: see **Chapter 10**). There are no minimum standards, no minimum qualifications, and no set procedures that have to be followed.

Physical evidence may include material items present at the crime scene. The importance of physical evidence, the 'silent witness' that 'does not forget' increases as the unreliability of confession evidence, eye witness and other witness testimony is better understood, and police evidence is not so readily believed as it used to be. Witnesses are increasingly reluctant to give evidence, identifications and admissions are regularly challenged, and so courts look for more objective and reliable sources of evidence instead.

The ACPO Crime Committee Homicide Working Group in *Scientific Support and Forensic Science in Homicide Investigations* (1999) states:

> the role of Forensic Science is just as important in providing information and intelligence as it is in providing evidence to support a prosecution. This means that Forensic Science must be considered at the earliest stages of an enquiry and the Forensic Scientist must be regarded as a member of the investigative team.

Many police investigations used to be reactive. A suspect would be arrested and investigators would then search for evidence to link the suspect to the offence. Now many investigations are proactive instead. The discovery of contact trace material (CTM) such as blood or semen or a fingerprint, footmark or earmark leads, through the use of a database such as the National DNA Database (NDNAD), or the National Automated Fingerprint Identification System (NAFIS), to an identification and the investigation and arrest of the offender.

1.5 TYPES OF PHYSICAL EVIDENCE

Physical material may:

- provide information about an offender;
- establish the identity of a victim or suspect;
- link a suspect with a scene or a victim;
- lead to a suspect admitting a crime in interview;
- eliminate a suspect;
- establish that a crime has been committed;
- establish the sequence of events;

- rule out lines of enquiry;
- validate a suspect or witness's account;
- suggest a possible defence;
- corroborate verbal witness testimony;
- establish when death occurred;
- link a crime with other crimes.

This is achieved through:

- scene examination;
- the collection of physical evidence;
- laboratory examination;
- laboratory analysis;
- scientific interpretation of results;
- scientific advice to the investigative team;
- use of databases (such as NDNAD and NAFIS).

Physical material includes:

- impressions: fingerprints, tool marks, footwear marks, fabric impressions, tyre marks, oil drips, bite marks;
- biological material (often referred to as 'human contact traces'): blood, semen, saliva, hair, teeth, nail scrapings, bloodstain patterns, DNA;
- trace evidence: accelerants, paint, glass, plastic and textile fibres;
- firearms: weapons, gunpowder patterns, gunshot residues, casings, projectiles, fragments, pellets, wadding and cartridges;
- questioned documents.

The importance of the material will depend upon its context within the case (what it is necessary to prove). It may be material which is used to identify an offender (such as DNA, fingerprints, footwear marks or earprints); or link an offender with a crime scene (such as glass, fibres or toolmarks) with varying degrees of certainty.

Some form of physical material can be found at the majority of crime scenes. This has been quantified in relation to burglary scenes where physical evidence has been found at 40 per cent of crimes (Forensic Science Service (FSS) Annual Report 2000–01).

The significance of CTM (fibres, glass and paint are dealt with in **Chapter 16**, and DNA, blood and hair in **Chapter 17**) was first recognised almost 100 years ago. In 1910, Dr Edmund Locard, the director of the first crime laboratory, working at the University of Lyons, formulated his exchange principle: with contact between two items, there will be an exchange. When any person comes into contact with an object or another person, a cross-transfer of physical evidence occurs. Thus criminals always leave something behind at the scene of the crime which was not there before and, similarly, carry away with them something that was not on them when they arrived.

Material left on the victim or at the scene is examined for biological, physical or chemical characteristics which are peculiar to the suspect. The clothing and property of the suspect is examined for the presence of materials characteristic of the scene or the victim. Different types of crime leave different types of CTM.

The ability to analyse DNA is by far the most significant breakthrough in crime detection since the introduction of fingerprints. Offenders may leave samples of their DNA at crime scenes. DNA can be obtained from most bodily fluids or tissue and the current method of analysing DNA gives a 'discriminating power' in excess of one in a billion, on average. This means that the DNA profile of the defendant, on a random basis, is likely to match only 1 person in a billion. As technology develops, the smallest amounts of tissue or fluid can be examined for DNA. The NDNAD User Group's evaluation of the use of DNA found that DNA was essential in 73 per cent of cases where an identification resulted in a solved crime.

Spending on forensic science has more than doubled in the three years to 2002, largely due to the increased use of DNA. Providing that government funds remain available, this growth should continue with new technological advances enabling evidence to be obtained from ever smaller amounts of material and new equipment advances such as portable DNA and fingerprint analysis devices which will enable fingerprint marks and DNA samples to be checked at the scene against a database.

New areas of forensic investigation are also available as a result of the use of technology to interrogate telephones and computers. Every time a person uses a mobile telephone there is a digital trace of that person's whereabouts and what they said; every time that a computer is used, the hard disk retains an impression of what the person did; closed circuit television (CCTV) cameras and Traffic Master Systems (TMS) record the movements of a person or a vehicle and if a crime has been committed it is often possible to find out who was in the vicinity at the time. Another new forensic tool is the use of national databases in relation to specific serious crimes, such as the Homicide Stranger Rape and Abduction (HSRA) database which can link similar features and geographical patterns.

Table 1.1 Types and uses of physical material at crime scenes

The traces of physical material left behind after a crime often play a crucial role in helping the investigator to reconstruct the past.

Fingerprints (including palm prints and bare footprints) and *DNA* are the best evidence to place an individual at the scene of a crime. Using DNA analysis, blood and seminal fluid can be matched back to an individual with a high degree of probability. *Ear* and *lip prints* are regarded by some as a dubious form of forensic evidence and by others as an exciting new opportunity.

Bite marks are frequently found in sexual assaults and can be matched back to the individual who did the biting, either physically or through the DNA in the saliva.

Natural fingernails have individual striations on them. A broken finger-nail found at a crime scene can be matched to the individual it came from.

Handwriting samples can also be matched back to the individual who produced them, when compared with known examples of the suspect's handwriting. *Questioned documents* can also be processed for fingerprints.

Bullets and casings found at the crime scene can be positively matched back to a gun or ammunition in the possession of a suspect.

Toolmarks can be positively matched to a tool in the suspect's pos-session or through the suspect's fingerprints. They can also be used as a means of linking crime scenes. A scene mark database can be compiled for intelligence purposes.

Shoeprints and *tyre tracks* can be matched positively to a pair of shoes or tyres in the suspect's possession. A footwear impression will show the size of the shoe, tread pattern and degree of wear. To tie it in with a par-ticular shoe the scientist will look for a specific wear pattern (determined by the wearer's way of walking), random damage (a cut, for example), or a stone in between the tread.

If a polaroid photograph of the shoeprints or tyre tracks is supplied, it may be used to tell investigators what type of shoes or tyres to look for. Investigators can be given intelligence information regarding the make and model of a shoe they should be looking for.

Fracture matches can positively link broken pieces of glass at the scene with pieces found in the possession of the suspect through a 'physical fit'. For example, headlight fragments found at the scene of a 'hit and run' could be positively matched to a broken headlight on a suspect vehicle.

If a root sheath is attached to a *hair* then DNA analysis can show that the hair came from a certain percentage of the population to which the suspect belongs. If there is no root sheath, then a microscopic analysis can show that the hair has the same characteristics and is similar to the suspect's hair. In addition, mitochondrial DNA from the shaft can be compared.

Fibres can be identified as being of the same type and colour as those found on the suspect's clothes, at the suspect's address or in the suspect's vehicle; the number of matching fibres found on the suspect's clothing, the number and type of each different fibre at the scene and how representa-tive of them the fibres found on the suspect's clothing will be assessed (the absence of fibres might be significant).

Paint can be said to be the same type, colour and chemical composition as paint found on a tool or in some other way in the possession of the suspect. Paint layer structure is often considered to be unique.

Glass fragments from a crime scene can be shown to have the same characteristics as glass found on the suspect. Glass fragments found on a person's clothing or shoes will be examined to determine the refractive index and composition and then matched with those from the scene of the crime. The distribution of the fragments and the surface on which they are found (they cling to different surfaces for different periods of time), may be significant.

Oil stains on a person's clothing following a 'hit and run' can be compared with the oil on the underside of a car. The sequence of different oils put into the car's sump can produce an oil stain which is as individual as a fingerprint.

REFERENCES

Police Review, 5 March 1999.

ACPO Crime Committee, Homicide Working Group (1999) *Scientific Support and Forensic Science in Homicide Investigations*.

CHAPTER 2

Forensic investigation: the people involved in the investigation of the scene

A call is made to the force control room (FCR), with information from a police officer, the victim, a witness or another member of the public. The FCR assesses the call, screens the request and determines the response. The management response to the crime and the forensic resource deployed as a result will be largely determined by the level of seriousness of the crime.

The FCR will route a call about low level or volume crime (such as low level assaults, criminal damage, theft and burglary) to the divisional control room (DCR) in the basic command unit (BCU). Calls about medium serious or serious crimes will be routed instead to the duty Criminal Investigation Department (CID) operational officer in the Crime Management Department (CMD) at force HQ.

If the alleged crime is, for example, a fight taking place in a public house, the DCR may contact the uniform relief or shift (uniformed officers on patrol on foot or in a car) and ask officers to attend the scene. Alternatively, if the alleged crime is a burglary and the offender has left the scene, the DCR may contact the crime desk of the BCU instead. The crime desk will screen the request, determine the response and decide what resource will be deployed. This may be to send a uniformed beat crime officer, a volume crime scene examiner, a crime scene attender, or crime scene analyst to the scene.

A new approach is for a uniformed officer (the first officer attending (FOA)) to be contacted first in relation to every reported crime and for him or her to decide the next course of action.

If the alleged crime is of medium seriousness, the duty CID operational officer will contact the area CID team (also called the area crime unit (ACU)). If it is of high seriousness, the duty CID operational officer will contact the major crime unit (MCU) or S10 team instead. The area CID team is a pool of CID officers based in a regional office. They will deal with a medium serious crime such as a suspicious death, an attempted murder, a serious assault, an attempted rape, or an aggravated burglary. The MCU is based at force HQ and is a pool of CID officers who will investigate all serious crimes, such as murders, rapes involving violence, and serial rapes.

Figure 2.1 illustrates the organisation of resources and routing of information in a large force

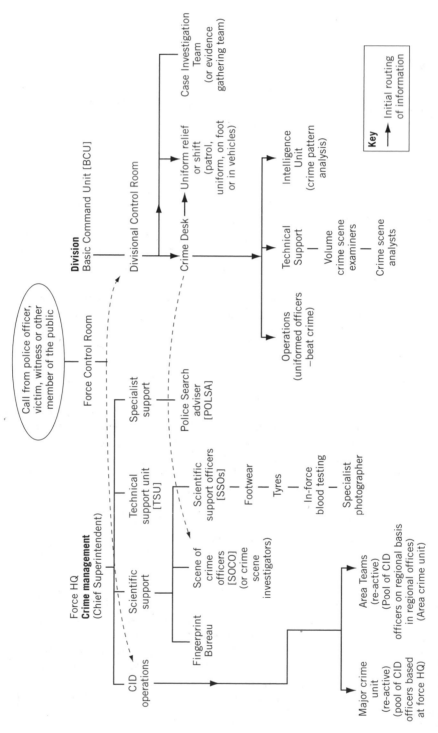

Figure 2.1 Police organisation in a large force

Call from police officer, victim, witness or other member of the public

Force HQ
Crime management
(Chief Superintendent)

CID operations

Scientific support

Technical support unit [TSU]

Specialist support

Fingerprint Bureau

Scene of crime officers [SOCO] (or crime scene investigators)

Scientific support officers [SSOs]

Footwear

Tyres

In-force blood testing

Specialist photographer

Police Search adviser [POLSA]

Major crime unit (re-active) (pool of CID officers based at force HQ)

Area Teams (re-active) (Pool of CID officers on regional basis in regional offices) (Area crime unit)

Division
Basic Command Unit [BCU]

Force Control Room

Divisional Control Room

Crime Desk

Case Investigation Team (or evidence gathering team)

Uniform relief or shift (patrol, uniform, on foot or in vehicles)

Operations (uniformed officers –beat crime)

Technical Support

Volume crime scene examiners

Crime scene analysts

Intelligence Unit (crime pattern analysis)

Key
→ Initial routing of information

12

2.1 LOW LEVEL OR VOLUME CRIME

If the offence is low level or volume crime, such as burglary, stolen vehicles or thefts from vehicles, the general standards for dealing with this across the criminal justice system are lower than for crimes of high seriousness and the standard of forensic investigation and skills levels reflect this. However, under pressure from government, the employment of volume crime scene examiners and the routine collection of DNA at volume crime scenes has significantly increased the number of offenders who are detected.

It is unlikely that the FOA will be expected to conduct the search for physical evidence. The FOA will contact the crime desk which will make management decisions about the use of resources to investigate the crime. It may allocate a crime scene attender or crime scene analyst. It will sometimes allocate a scenes of crime officer (SOCO). But these people will not be deployed contemporaneously and will be relatively remote from the investigation carried through by the FOA. There will be little or no dialogue regarding the investigation between them and the FOA.

2.1.1 Crime scene attenders/assessors

In some forces crime scene attenders/assessors examine the scenes of volume crime, e.g. burglary. These are uniformed officers who are trained to conduct a detailed search. They are not SOCOs. Where they consider it worthwhile, they can request the deployment of a SOCO (although many forces deploy a SOCO immediately). They typically assist in the operation of the crime desk.

2.1.2 Volume crime scene examiners

Volume crime scene examiners were originally called vehicle crime scene examiners, but it soon became clear that they could also be sent to other scenes such as burglaries. They focus on limited areas of activity in volume crime, principally looking for fingerprints and blood, and their work is closely supervised. Promising individuals are groomed to progress to wider SOCO activities.

2.1.3 Case investigation team

If a suspect is arrested and detained, the FOA will hand the investigation over to the case investigation team (also called the evidence gathering team) which will continue and complete the investigation.

2.1.4   First officer attending (FOA)

The FOA's knowledge of the potential for and the value of trace evidence may be poor and, to make matters more difficult, much trace evidence is barely visible. He/she may overlook or destroy important evidence. Trace evidence can easily be destroyed or contaminated.

In at least one small force in which SOCOs are a scarce resource and the force area is large, uniform patrol officers are trained to carry out SOCO duties, at the time of the initial search of the crime scene. In this case, the FOA assesses the situation to determine how the offender and victim may have behaved at the scene.

Where an FOA is expected, or is directed, to search this must be systematic and fully recorded. Where equipment is available, photographs should be taken and video recordings made.

Where the FOA makes a sketch or drawing of his or her pattern or approach to searching and of locations or objects, he or she must ensure that the drawing bears the officer's details and signature, and the date, time and place of production. The FOA gives a reference to the drawing, using the officer's initials and a number (referring to its place in the sequence of exhibits collected by the officer), and ensures there is an appropriate entry, including the exhibit reference, in the officer's pocket book concerning the production and collection of the sketch or drawing.

The FOA should also: note ambient conditions; take appropriate measures to preserve physical evidence, e.g. bagging up, sealing and assigning reference numbers to physical evidence recovered from the scene or removed from the suspect; mark off any traces, imprints, impressions and trace evidence noted within a location or outside; and later hand over exhibits and items found at the scene, or in the possession of the suspect, and taken by the FOA.

The FOA should make written hand-over notes, briefing the SOCO and investigating office (IO) with a fuller account of the FOA's preliminary investigation and subsequent actions by the FOA and others, details of the FOA's availability to give the SOCO or IO a verbal briefing or to answer any queries.

The lack of a hand-over briefing is less crucial when the SOCO is briefed by the crime desk, who will pass on information the crime desk have managed to obtain about the scene from the victim; the SOCO is able to talk to the victim and other witnesses at the scene; or there were no witnesses to the scene and the FOA has little information to brief the SOCO with.

The FOA will lodge an incident report on the force computer system which will be picked up by the divisional crime manager (DCM) who will task officers with actions to be carried out.

2.2 CRIMES OF MEDIUM SERIOUSNESS

If the alleged crime is of medium seriousness, the DCR will contact the uniform relief or shift and ask officers to attend the scene to carry out a 'holding exercise' until area CID can attend. Uniformed officers will attend rapidly to secure the scene and await the arrival of officers from the area CID team.

2.2.1 Area CID officers

In the area CID team, a detective sergeant (DS) or detective inspector (DI) will make a management decision about the use of resources: what expenditure will provide a reasonable return on investment.

The area CID team is made up of detectives (constables, sergeants, or a combination). DSs are deemed to fulfil a supervisory role, but in effect constables and sergeants work as relative equals. Officers from the area CID team attend the scene, summon and task SOCO and other support staff, e.g. the forensic physician or an external forensic science provider.

Area CID officers carry out both the preliminary and the continuing investigation, i.e.

- commencing an actions log;
- initial crime scene processing;
- CCTV of public places;
- video security systems – in commercial and private premises;
- conducting searches for physical evidence – assisted by uniform shift officers, with the possible assistance of a police search adviser (POLSA) officer;
- where applicable, liaising with the SOCO – in respect of assessment of the crime scene, identification of actual and potential marks, and other contact trace material (CTM);
- making pocket book entries;
- opening a crime report form;
- where applicable, tasking the forensic physician or hospital staff to conduct an examination of the victim or the suspect;
- contacting other medical practitioners and relevant professionals able to provide information, on the victim and the suspect;
- fingerprinting and taking samples from the suspect;
- selecting and making a case for submission of items for forensic testing.

2.2.2 Scenes of crime officers

SOCOs advise IOs and senior investigating officers (SIOs) about gathering, collecting and analysing physical evidence.

A high proportion of SOCOs are civilian support staff (85 per cent of staff inside scientific support units (SSUs), including fingerprint bureaux are civilian). Police officers employed as SOCOs may find it easier to integrate fully with those involved in the investigative process.

SOCOs:

- assess the crime scene;
- control the crime scene;
- systematically examine, and interpret the crime scene;
- identify the location of, and assess the quality of, physical evidence, specifically any form of CTM:
- keep a record of his or her searching;
- note ambient conditions, i.e. source and level of any illumination, the weather, temperature;
- record the scene – in note form and graphically – identifying the location of physical evidence i.e.

    - make a record of each item of evidence identified – a description, including a note of measurements and markings; who found it, where, when;

- take photographs;
- make video recording;
- make drawings;
- make notes;
- make sketches;
- take measurements concerning the layout of, and any specific locations within, the scene and the vicinity and the locations of: the victim, marks, imprints and impressions, trace evidence, items;
- are alert to, and making a record of, any form of negative evidence, e.g. something which was missing which should have been, or could have been reasonably expected to be, present;
- collect evidence;
- take control samples of material at the scene for comparison with CTM later found on the suspect;
- complete forms;
- prepare reports and statements of evidence;
- advise investigators and their supervisors on forensic scientific matters – particularly appropriate testing;
- provide intelligence – linking scenes or crimes together.

The SOCO will record the scene visit and list material recovered from the scene and samples submitted on the force computer system, together with any intelligence obtained. This information is accessible by all officers and will be attached in the force data warehouse to any other information already held about that crime on the system.

SOCOs do not have the level of expertise of forensic scientists. Scene examination by forensic scientists is rare and they are only called out in the most serious or complex cases.

2.2.3 Forensic physicians

Forensic physicians (also called forensic medical examiners (FMEs) or police surgeons) are medical practitioners who conduct forensic work, ranging from those in full-time practice as forensic physicians to those who only occasionally carry out forensic work. This is specialised work and there are courses which newly appointed medical examiners can attend, if they so wish. Forces are able to make attendance a condition of employment with the period before attendance regarded as probationary. The Association of Chief Police Officers (ACPO) has rejected this. Research found that forces in large rural areas are unwilling to risk losing medical examiners by making such requirements of them. The Association of Forensic Physicians (AFP) has sought to make membership a condition of employment as a medical examiner.

There is a move to establish a basic level of competence for forensic physicians. It should also be possible soon for forensic physicians and paediatricians to be independently assessed for registration with the Council for the Registration of Forensic Practitioners (CRFP) in one of the following sub-specialties:

- general forensic work;
- sexual offence examination (adults);
- sexual offence examination (children);
- child abuse and neglect.

The forensic physician conducts two principal types of examination:

- forensic examinations, which may assist the police in gathering evidence in a case (how 15 per cent of his/her time is spent);
- forensic tasks, such as blood testing suspected drink drivers (which takes up five per cent of his/her time), and assessing the fitness of prisoners to be detained or interviewed (occupying 80 per cent of his/her time), which may have a bearing on the admissibility of evidence obtained during interrogation.

The quality of the service provided by forensic physicians to police forces was found to be variable by the Audit Commission in its study 'The Doctor's Bill: The Provision of Medical Services to the Police'. There is no standard approach to recruitment, contractual arrangements or quality assurance. The majority of forensic physicians are general practitioners who combine this work with their own patient list. Many police stations have inadequate facilities for examining detained people. There is no standard format for recording a doctor's instructions to a custody officer. See **Chapter 22** for further information about the role of the forensic physician.

A forensic paediatrician uses their skills to assess a child's condition and give an opinion on the reasons for it. This process is evidence based: a medical diagnosis is made, accessing the vast body of available medical information whilst assessing its validity, i.e. the credibility of its source.

It is possible for the forensic paediatrician to refer to studies which show the probability of an injury resulting from an accident rather than from abuse. The forensic paediatrician's findings are considered in the context of the other information available, such as the child's growth and development history.

For example, through reconstruction (such as working out bath scald patterns using dye in bath water to mark the skin and comparing that to the pattern of a burn) and a knowledge of child development, it is possible for the paediatrician to assess whether the child's injury was caused by a forced immersion or by the child accidentally falling in the bath.

2.3   CRIMES OF HIGH SERIOUSNESS

If the alleged crime is of high seriousness, the standards worked to, the personnel involved, and the skills employed are much higher than for other crimes. Investigations at this level are intense and the actions of those involved are closely scrutinised. Every appropriate forensic resource will be deployed in the investigation of the crime and there are no financial limits on any work that may advance the investigation.

The duty CID operational officer will contact the MCU.

2.3.1   Senior Investigating officer (SIO)

An SIO is informed and is appointed to head the investigation.

The SIO controls the enquiry with a management team. Information is stored through an incident room using a computer system: Home Office large major enquiry system (HOLMES).

The SIO should be of sufficient rank, normally DI/detective superintendent and have received appropriate training and experience to fulfil that role. The SIO is the principal decision-maker in the investigation and is responsible for ensuring that all decisions are properly catalogued in the policy file and that each entry is endorsed with a signature.

The SIO will decide, in consultation with the incident management team and exhibits officer, which exhibits will be submitted for forensic examination.

In the absence of the SIO, control and direction of the investigation is the responsibility of the deputy SIO, normally a DI/detective chief inspector (DCI).

The *Major Investigation Incident Room Standardised Administrative Procedures (MIRSAP) Manual* is published by ACPO. It ensures that the evidence and data collected during the course of a major investigation are gathered in a uniform way by police forces throughout the UK.

The SIO will involve the scientific adviser (SA) in the early stages of the investigation to maximise the use of forensic intelligence and ensure that the SA has a good understanding of the investigative requirements at all stages of the investigation including:

- general scope and priorities;
- scope of the forensic examination;
- priorities of the forensic examination;
- evidential expectations/requirements;
- time scales;
- financial implications;
- communication channels;
- prompt notification of any changes in direction/tactics/priorities.

2.3.2   Scientific support department (SSD)

The CMD at force HQ will have an SSD with a fingerprint bureau, SOCOs, POLSA officers, specialist scientific officers, specialist photographers, and a technical support unit (TSU) at its disposal.

THE SCIENTIFIC SUPPORT MANAGER (SSM)

The SSM is responsible for the SSD, ensuring that resources are available to respond to the demands of all investigations. The SSM manages the scientific support resources and services; provides scene management, coordination and operational advice; and is consultant/adviser on forensic science matters to the force. He or she will consider the benefits of new technology and the practical implications for the force of new legislation.

Across the country, HMIC found that 60 per cent of SSMs are civilian and 40 per cent are police officers appointed to the role for varying periods of tenure.

The SSM will ensure that the department's work is geared to the needs of the force and helps to deliver divisional objectives. For example, street robberies or distraction burglaries may be prevalent and a push is made to detect the offenders; or government targets are set for persistent young offenders. The SSM will consider how forensic techniques can be used to obtain best evidence in such cases and will prioritise SOCO work and material being sent to external laboratories for examination to increase detections and speed these cases through the system.

The SSM is the SIO's main source of advice on, and interpretation of, physical evidence or CTM. Together the two are responsible for directing and coordinating the collection of forensic information (photographs, drawings, video recordings) and CTM.

2.3.3 Exhibits officer

The exhibits officer records and safeguards all property recovered by any means during the course of an enquiry, including items obtained by forensic scientists or SOCOs. They should be forensically aware and fully conversant with methods of recovery, correct packaging procedures, and safeguarding of evidence. They are responsible for control, continuity and security of exhibits. To avoid cross-contamination, the exhibits officer will not attend more than one crime scene in the same case or come into contact with any suspect.

The ACPO Crime Committee Homicide Working Group in 'Scientific Support and Forensic Science in Homicide Investigations' states that the exhibits officer should be involved in all forensic and enquiry briefings, and in conferences with counsel. He/she must also be fully trained in all the issues associated with disclosure and work closely with the disclosure officer in relation to all aspects of forensic material.

It summarises the roles and responsibilities of the exhibits officer as follows:

- record all items of property coming into police possession during an enquiry;
- ensure all items received have been properly searched and any contents recorded separately;
- maintain a full and up-to-date record of exhibits and their movements;
- ensure exhibits are correctly packaged, labelled and securely stored;
- preserve, for SOCO (when necessary), exhibits for forensic and/or fingerprint examination;
- where there is no SOCO involvement (e.g. drugs or fraud seizures) complete forensic laboratory submission forms and obtain relevant statements from those seizing/transporting exhibits;
- liaise with the SIO;
- maintain liaison with specialists, e.g. forensic scientists, pathologists;
- ensure compliance with disclosure rules;
- ideally should remain with the enquiry from crime scene to court;
- attend court for the entire trial.

2.3.4 POLSA officers

POLSA officers are trained to a high level in the processes of searching. They lead trained uniformed teams and are deemed to be the experts in searching. They keep full records of their searching (documentary, illustrations and, as necessary, video recordings or photographs); survey the scene, noting its dimensions and adjoining entry and exit areas; and adopt searching methods suited to the scene.

2.3.5 Specialist photographers

Specialist photographers are not found in all forces. They are essentially 'professional' photographers, producing high quality photography and video-images, where necessary using non-routine techniques and specialist equipment.

2.3.6 Technical support unit (TSU)

The TSU will provide technical support comprising: the use of devices enabling visual or audio surveillance (which may or may not record); emitting a signal enabling the tracking of objects to which they are attached; or enabling the interception of communications.

Overall responsibility is generally vested in an officer of detective superintendent rank.

2.3.7 Crime scene coordinator (CSC)

In a complex enquiry, a CSC will be appointed. The CSC may be a police officer or a civilian. Depending upon the scale of the investigation the crime scene manager (CSM) may also fulfil the responsibilities of the CSC. The CSM is responsible for the cross-flow of information between specialist and SIO investigation teams and the CSM's duties include ensuring that all staff attending a crime scene are briefed and debriefed; chairing meetings at which forensic exhibits and issues are discussed (these should be attended by either the scientist attending the scene or the SA); laboratory/forensic liaison; and ensuring that any forensic information is communicated to the interview coordinator and officers interviewing suspects – since this will necessarily affect the overall interviewing strategy.

2.3.8 Crime scene manager (CSM)

In major enquiries, such as homicide, management of the crime scene is the responsibility of one or more CSMs who advise about the requirement for specialist services and manage all key aspects of the scene examination (techniques; personnel; contamination; continuity; examinations) – ensuring the agreed strategy is delivered. They should be able to demonstrate the standards of performance developed through the European Commission (EC) funded OISIN programme.

The CSM should normally be a senior or experienced SOCO. He/she is responsible for all matters relating to the examination of a crime scene. Their primary role is to identify, secure, protect, and recover all potential forensic contact evidence from all crime scenes.

The ACPO Crime Committee Homicide Working Group in 'Scientific Support and Forensic Science in Homicide Investigations' advise that to establish clear objectives and priorities, the SIO must ensure that the CSM is fully aware of the crime circumstances and an agreed action plan put into effect. Open channels of communication and regular briefings are essential between the CSM and the SIO.

MIRSAP states that the importance of the CSM cannot be over-emphasised. The forensic science process begins at the crime scene and the examination of the scene, 'driven by any available criminal intelligence and directed to solve investigators' problems' is the most important first step.

MIRSAP states that the CSM (in conjunction with the SIO) takes full responsibility for:

- establishing control at the scene, and the position of cordons;
- liaison with the SIO or nominated representative by regular briefings which should be fully documented;
- advising the SIO on the value of having a forensic scientist and other experts attend the scene;
- in the initial stages of the investigation, contributing to the SIO's analysis of the scene, evidence and any material bearing upon its interpretation, establishing investigative priorities including event chronologies and the parameters and objectives of forensic enquiries;
- coordinating the scientific examination of the scene;
- advising on and fully briefing other experts required;
- instigating search procedures in the area;
- advising and assisting trained search teams;
- coordinating the search of each scene by forensic, CID, and POLSA;
- health and safety risk assessments;
- applying agreed systematic trace evidence recovery techniques;
- preparing for the development of new scenes;
- speedy submission of key exhibits to the FSS;
- ensuring the continuity of exhibits from the scene;
- with SIO, developing and agreeing laboratory submission policy;

- appointing officers to individual crime scenes and ensuring that no cross-contamination is possible;
- in complex cases involving multiple crime scenes or offenders, a CSM should commence a contamination log to ensure that this aspect is managed very well and to demonstrate at any subsequent trial that no contamination was caused by the police;
- all documentation relating to the scene examination;
- arranging Home Office pathologist in conjunction with SIO;
- advising the SIO on all available forensic avenues of enquiry and overseeing these.

FORENSIC SCIENCE SERVICE SPECIALIST ADVISERS (FSS SAs)

In a major investigation, SIOs may be advised by SAs provided by the FSS. Their role is to liaise with the SIO as soon as possible after the commencement of an enquiry, to provide advice about how best to exploit any forensic opportunities offered. Their involvement continues through the investigation and to court if necessary.

The FSS may deploy FSS SAs to forces. There was a 10 per cent rise in the use of the FSS's major crime service (MCS) by police forces in 2000–2001 over the year before. Complex major investigations are aided by the contribution of SAs, experienced forensic scientists acting as consultants to SIOs.

The SA assists the SIO by devising how investigative needs can be met, planning the actions, progress chasing within FSS laboratories, and maintaining a forensic overview in conjunction with a member of the enquiry team.

The SA has considerable experience in the investigation of major enquiries and an up-to-date knowledge of the range of forensic science and other services that are available and may be useful.

The SA will also maintain awareness in the force of the FSS and its capability to deliver external scientific support services and, where these are being delivered in a particular case, acting as a communication and liaison link between the police involved in the case and the scientist 'on the bench'.

In keeping with this intermediary role delivered by a generalist, as opposed to that of the 'hands on' scientist conducting the specialist examination, the prime role of the SA is communication. He or she may be requested:

- to work with the SIO to ensure the FSS provides cost-effective and timely service to meet the requirements of the investigation;
- to provide advice and coordinate the FSS response.

However, where the SA has a particular scientific specialism, experience and expertise applicable to the case in hand, he or she may be requested to go beyond this communication role and to bring this specialism to bear.

Because forensic science is most likely to make major contributions when all the available options have been assessed, early forensic advice is considered essential. Whilst this comes from the SSM who makes arrangements for handling and processing the scene, it will often be desirable for the SIO to obtain early advice from the SA deployed to the force who is able to speak as a generalist forensic scientist.

The ACPO Crime Committee Homicide Working Group in 'Scientific Support and Forensic Science in Homicide Investigations' describes the role of the SA as follows.

> The SA will, wherever requested to do so, work with senior investigators in major incidents to ensure that the FSS provides a cost-effective and timely service which meets the needs of the SIO at all stages of the investigation.

The SA will have a broad knowledge of forensic science, experience of the investigative process, and an understanding of relevant legal issues. They will be committed to the investigation, have an understanding of the differing needs of SIOs, and have good communication skills. They will also have an awareness and understanding of the specific needs of the forces they serve.

Responsibilities of the SA are to:

- Agree terms of reference with the SIO.
- Open a policy book to contain:
  - the terms of the agreement;
  - relevant sources of information (SIO, SSM, etc.);
  - notes on meetings and agreed actions relating to the incident, including any staging of examinations and deadlines/time-scales;
  - records of outcomes.

- Brief all scientists involved re case circumstances and any changes which may occur during the course of the investigation.
- Act as single point of contact within the FSS for the SIO.
- Attend force briefings and management meetings when requested to do so.
- Assist the SIO with selection, potential and prioritisation of FSS. Facilitate all appropriate forensic science support both by the FSS and other scientists where there is agreement to do so.
- Coordinate all work associated with the case submitted to the FSS.
- Keep the SIO informed of any significant scientific findings/developments or problems (including timeliness).
- Attend scene(s) as an adviser if requested to do so.
- Call upon specific expertise within the FSS to support the investigation at the scene with the agreement of the CSM and SIO.
- Respond to requests for advice rapidly (within 30 minutes if contacted by radio pager).
- Write a linking report where appropriate.

In 1998 Forensic Alliance Ltd came on to the scene, taking a different approach to the SA role, providing lead scientists to perform many of the same functions whilst also leading the scientific investigation within the laboratory.

NATIONAL CRIME AND OPERATIONS FACULTY (NCOF)

The National Crime and Operations Faculty (NCOF) has been established as a centre of excellence to support major crime investigations. As a national resource, the NCOF is able to harness the experience gained from many major enquiries and provide an operational service offering advice, guidance and if necessary direct support to an SIO.

NCOF liaison officers are deployed to facilitate SIOs in their strategic and tactical management of a murder investigation. They maintain close liaison with SAs, NCOF consultant scientists, and offender profilers. This ensures a timely response to emergent forensic issues, including second opinions, advice on procedures, devising or revising strategy, and tactics. Where the requirement emerges for unusual expertise to assist the investigation the NCOF researches and identifies potential candidates.

2.3.9 Pathologist

In a homicide case, the examination of the deceased will begin in detail at the crime scene. MIRSAP states that there should be a team approach involving the SIO, a pathologist on the Home Office list, the CSM, and a forensic scientist if necessary. The body is a crime scene and there will usually only be one opportunity to recover evidence, particularly minute debris. When the body has been removed, the team should plan the post mortem.

For reasons of continuity of evidence, a police officer should accompany the body to the mortuary. Further work at the crime scene may be postponed until the outcome of the post mortem is known. See **Chapter 23** for further information about the role of the forensic pathologist.

REFERENCES

ACPO Crime Committee Homicide Working Group (1999) *Scientific Support and Forensic Science in Homicide Investigations*.

Audit Commission (1998) *The Doctor's Bill: The Provision of Medical Services to the Police*.

Ede, R. & Shepherd, E. (2000) *Active Defence*, 2nd edn, Law Society Publishing.

CHAPTER 3

Forensic investigation: police organisation, training and awareness, and the process of identifications

Many suspects are investigated and arrested as a result of an identification through a DNA, fingerprint or footmark match. In Section B we examine the forensic techniques involved in this in some detail and consider how the identification is made and how reliable it is. But what are the systems in place for the collection of this evidence in the first place? What are the constraints on collecting it, such as a lack of training, awareness and resources? And what are the processes involved in searching for matches?

There are some crime scenes where contact trace material (CTM) is available but not collected, perhaps because the scene was not visited or the CTM was missed. On other occasions, CTM is collected from crime scenes but not submitted for examination because the investigator does not consider that it will advance the investigation. This has implications for all parties, if as a result, potential evidence is not made available either to convict or eliminate a suspect.

Unless the crime is extremely serious (such as murder, rape involving violence, or serial rape, where the forensic response is an unlimited one – as long as it may get results), an objective judgement has to be made about what amounts to a proportionate forensic response to the crime committed. The issue is not whether every crime should result in a 'no effort spared' investigation – as that would clearly not be possible – but whether forensic resources are engaged when they should be, used appropriately and whether the public gets value for money from the investigation. The amount spent on forensic resources and the application of science to the investigation of crime as a proportion of the overall amount spent by forces in England and Wales ranges between 1.6 per cent and 2.8 per cent.

3.1   MAKING USE OF FORENSIC SCIENCE

In 1996 the Association of Chief Police Officers (ACPO) and the Forensic Science Service (FSS) jointly published *Using Forensic Science Effectively* (UFSE) which was regarded as an opportunity for police forces to make more proactive use of forensic science and improve awareness in forensic science amongst investigative and operational officers. It was considered that a more professional and strategic exploitation of forensic science should have developed as a result. The Thematic Inspection Report, *Under the Microscope* published in July 2000 by Her Majesty's Inspectorate of Constabulary (HMIC) [ISBN 1–84082–501–4] was the first detailed inspection by HMIC of either scientific or technical support. It reported that the advice of UFSE had frequently not been acted upon and that the failure to respond was a product of ignorance of its contents. The HMIC was also concerned that forensic science was not championed by senior officers within forces.

In *Under the Microscope Refocused*, a revisit by HMIC to the investigative use of DNA and fingerprints since the 2000 report, the findings of the 1996 and 2000 reports were reiterated. The 2002 report concluded 'things are improving but sometimes too slowly'.

3.2 POLICE TRAINING IN FORENSIC INVESTIGATION

Forensic evidence can be critical in an investigation. A police officer decides which type of investigation should be carried out and officers need to be appropriately trained in order to make the right decisions. Police investigators are the first to attend and assess the crime scene and decide on the scientific and technical support required. It follows that they must have proper training in investigating a crime scene and their knowledge, skills and ability must be kept up to date.

In 1990, the Durham Police Authority created the National Training Centre for Scientific Support to Crime Investigation (NTCSSCI) to provide a forensic training service to police officers and support staff employed in forces in England, Wales and Northern Ireland. Most forces send their students to the NTCSSCI for an initial nine weeks' course to train them to be scenes of crime officers (SOCOs), called crime scene investigators (CSIs) by some forces to emphasise their investigatory role, or fingerprint officers. Later, they can take the Durham Diploma course which involves the completion of five units over two years whilst they remain in their job in the force. There is also a Forensic Science Society Diploma in crime scene investigation. By 2000, almost 1,000 students per year were attending residential courses at the NTCSSCI. Other forces, such as the Metropolitan Police, train in house at the Metropolitan Police Scientific Support College at Hendon.

Reports from the early and mid 1990s, such as UFSE and *Forensic Science and Criminal Investigation*, Tilley and Ford, Police Research Group (PRG) Paper 73, 1996, commented on the weak knowledge base of officers. In 1993 the Audit Commission report *Helping with Enquiries, Tackling Crime Effectively* said: 'One reason why detectives spend much of their time on less serious crime work is that uniformed officers lack expertise in some of the key tasks required at the scene of a crime.' In 1996 the PRG referred to a lack of awareness of forensic science within the police service. Also in 1996, UFSE stated that the knowledge base of forensic science of operational officers was inadequate and that there should be training for all such officers in physical evidence procedures which should be tested at regular intervals. UFSE surveyed the forensic awareness of operational police officers, SOCOs, and senior investigating officers (SIOs). Not surprisingly, SOCOs and SIOs were the most aware. They were followed by Detective Constables (DCs), Police Sergeants (PSs), Police Constables (PCs), and Detective Sergeants (DSs), in that order. The score of PCs and DSs was little better than would have been achieved by pure chance.

With the increasing use of, and reliance on, expert forensic practitioners by police forces, it could be argued that some lack of knowledge is not of overriding importance as long as officers know when to consult and call in the experts – SOCOs – in the force's Scientific Support Department (SSD).

But the fact that DNA is as likely to be obtained from a force examining almost all burglary dwelling scenes as one which selects for examination as suggested to HMIC in 2000 that first officers attending (FOAs), who were largely responsible for requesting a SOCO, were not very effective in identifying DNA productive scenes for examination by SOCOs. With tough targets from government to deal with burglary, some forces are moving away from letting the FOA select the scenes which a SOCO will atttend. Instead a SOCO will attend automatically, being informed about the offence by the crime desk at the same time as the FOA, while any physical evidence is still fresh.

UFSE recommended that all staff making resource decisions (e.g. in crime desks) should have sufficient awareness of scientific support to fulfil their duties. Four years later, in 2000, HMIC reported that a repetitive feature of their inspection was the lack of awareness amongst operational police officers and their supervisors of their role in the forensic science and technology process and how to fulfil it. There was no national policy that operational staff receive awareness training in forensic science and technology at regular intervals, and training for inspectors and sergeants, including national supervisory training for those ranks, had no input on scientific and technical support. HMIC found evidence that operational staff were rarely given awareness or refresher training, and lacked confidence to carry out this part of their daily duty. In all but one of the six forces visited by HMIC, SOCOs expressed concern about the forensic science knowledge base of police officers in general. HMIC also reported that the level of forensic awareness among intelligence officers was very poor. The government is supporting the training of FOAs, scientific support staff, and investigating officers in relation to the use of DNA.

To meet these criticisms and take a strategic approach to forensic investigation, ACPO has established the Forensic Training Strategy Group (FTSG) with the following sub-groups:

- Forensic Futures;
- Forensic Medicine, Pathology and Police Surgeons;
- Forensic Sciences Training;
- Forensic Intelligence and Evidential Standards;
- Scene Management;
- Performance Evaluation;
- Regional Forensic Science Groups;
- National Fingerprints Board;
- NDNA Database Board.

3.3   TRAINING AND MANAGEMENT OF SOCOs

Some forces have regarded forensic practitioners as add-ons to the investigation rather than fellow investigators brought in for a discrete purpose only, such as collecting the available evidence. UFSE reported that scientific support was usually managed separately from the investigative process and was rarely seen as an integral part of it. Consequently, communication with scientific support within forces was often poor and forensic practitioners were not always clearly focused on ways of supporting investigations. In addition, external forensic suppliers were not seen as part of the scientific support team and communication between forces and external suppliers was also poor.

HMIC reported that there was room for improvement in team working. They found that many SOCOs had no sense of belonging to the investigative teams in their basic command unit (BCU). Those located with Criminal Investigation Department (CID) officers or proactive teams either at BCUs or HQs, generally considered themselves to be better integrated and were more satisfied that there was productive communication.

HMIC considered that the role of SOCOs as investigators was ignored. Although forces viewed the provision of intelligence as a core role of the SOCO, they rarely if ever submitted intelligence to intelligence units and their scene reports were often not accessed either by investigating officers or intelligence units. The role of the SOCO was seen to be that of an evidence gatherer rather than an investigator. SOCOs often arrive at a crime scene after the investigating officer has left and speak to victims and others and can frequently be given further information relevant to the investigation. They should feed information, such as *modus operandi*, to the intelligence desk so that it is possible to link scenes by recognising methods used by individual criminals, as well as by fingerprints, footmarks, and DNA.

A number of reasons were given to HMIC for the rarity of investigators using the information provided by the SOCO:

- The quality of scene examination reports completed by SOCO was variable, sometimes confined to only a description of marks found or point of entry.
- Information from scene examination reports was sometimes not entered on crime information or recording systems in a timely manner.
- Scene examination reports were sometimes not being accessed by investigators.
- Very few formal links existed between SOCOs and investigators.

UFSE stated that SOCOs should be seen as investigators, supporting the investigation, as well as collectors. UFSE recommended that there should be an integrated approach to scientific activities in support of crime investigation, with SOCOs placed locally, close to investigators. UFSE stated that the provision of intelligence by SOCOs and scientific support units (SSUs) was central to successful crime investigation, and initiatives against target criminals should include greater use of scientific support. UFSE recommended that scientific activities should be driven by intelligence and directed much more proactively against, in particular, volume crime.

HMIC reported the lack of a common minimum standard of training and recommended that there should be a mandatory standard applied to SOCO and fingerprint staff, and those who deploy and use technical equipment. The training should be specific, for the specialist role, and also raise awareness of the specialist and generalist roles of others with whom they would come into contact. HMIC recommended that the police service must have in place: an effective national crime training strategy; a national training centre (centre of excellence) based at one or more sites; a nationally agreed training and development policy for specialist staff; and a national competency framework for each rank and role linked to the above.

In addition, HMIC recommended that the national strategy must provide an effective and complementary balance between: the training that specialist scientific and technical support staff receive; the basic knowledge, understanding skills and abilities that all police staff require to carry out their role (competences and competencies); and the awareness training that should be part of a programme of refresher training that every member of police staff receives.

HMIC found that the management of SOCOs was either the responsibility of the Scientific Support Manager (SSM) at HQ or devolved to BCU commanders. Irrespective of where management was vested, they found: day-to-day management of SOCOs was often poor with little policy to guide or set standards to achieve; there was no competency framework for SOCOs; there was no refresher or other training to minimum effective levels; there was an absence of meaningful appraisal even where SOCOs were intended to be within an appraisal scheme; and there was little opportunity for career development.

As a consequence of this apparent lack of concern for their management and development despite the fact that their expertise needs constant updating, SOCO and fingerprint staff often felt frustrated and undervalued.

HMIC welcomed the establishment of the Council for the Registration of Forensic Practitioners (CRFP) as a significant development in enhancing the status of scientific support practitioners within forces.

In line with a greater emphasis on management information, performance management and staff development in organisations generally, forces now organise development training and refresher courses for SOCOs, obtain statistics showing the number of DNA and fingerprint 'hits' per SOCO, and the proportion of those which result in identifications, and encourage SOCOs to develop areas of specialism ranging from blood distribution to entomology and forensic archaeology. As a career development tool and to provide the force with a degree of external validation, they also encourage SOCOs to obtain accreditation from the CRFP.

3.3.1 Training: collecting DNA

HMIC found that a wide variation in the rate of recovery of DNA existed between SOCOs in different BCUs and in the same BCU, suggesting a gap in skill, experience, and organisational arrangements.

3.3.2 Training: fingerprints

The training that SOCOs receive in this field is detailed in **Chapter 21**.

3.3.3 Training: footmarks

HMIC commented that the successful operation of a footwear system required FOAs to have received sufficient training to locate, evaluate and understand the forensic value of footwear marks. HMIC was concerned to find that the level of forensic awareness training in footwear marks given to front line officers was regarded by officers themselves to be minimal, and some officers had received no such training since their initial police training. As a result, footwear evidence did not feature as a high priority in the thinking of many officers as a method of detecting offences.

SOCOs on the other hand, HMIC found, were well trained and had a positive attitude towards footwear evidence but were frustrated by a lack of systems in force to properly capture and compare the evidence.

3.3.4 Training: surveillance

HMIC reported on the awareness of the provisions of the codes of practice under the Police Act 1997 for authorising the carrying out of surveillance, either in public places where confidential material was not sought, or in private places where confidential material was likely to be obtained. Awareness in most force Technical Support Units (TSUs) was very high amongst managers and staff, and in BCUs good at superintendent level but

31

poor at inspector level. Inspectors severely criticised the lack of input which they had received. Many uniformed inspectors had received no information and felt vulnerable as a result. Amongst BCU teams conducting proactive operations against volume crime, there was a lack of material available to personnel to assist them with the codes. Operational officers at constable level in BCUs had very poor knowledge of the codes and in many cases were unaware of their existence or of any changes affecting surveillance. Even at supervisory level knowledge of the codes was very weak, HMIC reported, with instances of sergeants being quite happy to authorise operations which under the codes required a superintendent's authority (observations of a known target in a public place). HMIC was concerned that forces ensure the integrity of evidence by adherence to the codes and the maintenance of standards.

3.4   LOW LEVEL SERIOUSNESS AND VOLUME CRIMES

It is not surprising that in a cost-conscious age, police investigators have a financial incentive not to use forensic science procedures unless they are a worthwhile investment, e.g. they are likely to identify the offender; better still if they will help to convict a persistent or serial offender. It used to be that police forces could submit anything they liked to the Home Office laboratories for examination without additional financial penalty for the force. This led to the scientists, rather than the police investigators, making decisions about what they should be examining, often without sufficient information about the case. Since the FSS became a government agency in 1991, the police have had to pay directly for work done, either on a block or case-by-case basis.

After the initial investigation, carried out as soon as possible after the offence, officers will consider what, if any, material should be submitted for examination, in what sequence ('if A, B and C don't produce a positive result, then D, E and F certainly will not'; or 'if A, B and C do produce a positive result, then D, E and F may not be needed' or 'we may be repeating ourselves with E and F'), taking into account how quickly results are needed and can be obtained and 'contextualising' the forensic investigation, i.e. making clear how significant it is within the context of the case as a whole.

HMIC received evidence from officers in some forces that forensic submissions were restricted by financial rather than evidential considerations. Whilst it is understandable that 'financial considerations' are a reason for the police not submitting evidence for forensic examination and analysis, in some cases forensic examination and analysis may be the most cost effective means of securing a conviction.

Low level seriousness and volume crime has been described as being 'cash-capped', i.e. of insufficient seriousness to merit expenditure on expensive forensic analyses. Perhaps a better way of explaining the situation is that investigations of these types of crimes will be limited to pursuing readily identifiable leads which are assessed as being likely to progress the investigation and lead to the identification of the offender, and where the cost of that is not disproportionate to the seriousness of the offence. About 75 per cent of crime scenes are visited by a police officer or a SOCO. The aim of the visit is primarily to obtain a fingerprint, footmark, or material which yields DNA – such as a cigarette end, hair, or blood. Other evidence, such as toolmarks, fibres, and broken glass, may provide a match with a suspect who has been arrested, but they can not produce an identification on their own. For that reason, glass or fibres are unlikely to be submitted on their own.

This means that the most productive scenes (stolen vehicles are twice as likely to produce an identification as a burglary, which itself is more likely to produce an identification than other offences) will almost always be visited; and that attention is paid to key parts of the investigation – those likely to yield the offender's DNA or fingerprints – such as a broken piece of dashboard in a stolen car, or blood at the point of entry in a burglary.

Crimes of low value seriousness and volume crimes routinely met with little or no forensic investigation in the past, faced with the situation that in about 85 per cent of investigations, police do not have a suspect at the outset of the investigation. In the early days of DNA, in the mid to late 1980s, an amount of material the size of a ten pence piece was required for examination which was labour intensive and expensive. In the first half of the 1990s, although it was possible to replicate a small crime stain, the result was of little use from an evidential point of view as it was not sufficiently discriminating. It was in the mid 1990s, around the time that the National DNA Database (NDNAD) was established in 1995, that scientific developments greatly boosted the discriminating power of DNA so that it became a powerful tool for identifying offenders. Further developments in the late 1990s, and the introduction of Low Copy Number (LCN) DNA in 2000, allowing profiling of minute amounts of DNA, have continued to increase its potency.

The Home Office sponsored Pathfinder project, a scheme between the FSS and selected divisions of the Greater Manchester Police and Lancashire Constabulary, was launched in June 2000. It assessed the effectiveness of applying enhanced forensic techniques to scenes of volume crime. It used a full range of forensic techniques, including the latest DNA technology, to maximise the recovery of forensic evidence from crime scenes, and used forensic intelligence databases to link suspects to crimes and identify serial offenders. Not surprisingly it confirmed that value could be gained from the effective use of forensic techniques, and that the availability of forensic evidence resulted in a higher proportion of guilty pleas.

The result of this is that volume crime is the area where there is the largest increase in police submissions to the FSS, with the number of burglary and vehicle crime case submissions increasing by 25 per cent in 2000–2001 over the previous year.

By July 2003 the NDNAD reached two million sample profiles from individuals. Most NDNAD matches relate to dwelling house burglaries (33.11 per cent), non-dwelling burglaries (32.69 per cent) and car crime (23.21 per cent). Other volume crime and serious crime make up the remainder. This explains why a search for physical evidence is particularly necessary in offences against property, particularly burglary.

HMIC also found that because they are charged for DNA services, forces restricted crime scene DNA submission for financial reasons. Costs for DNA analysis are obvious as an invoice is raised every time a submission is made, but fingerprint costs are hidden as part of staffing costs. They found one force where DNA submissions reduced dramatically towards the end of the financial year. This was in contrast to in-force means of detection such as fingerprints, which will be tried first as a means of obtaining an identification.

But the Home Office DNA Expansion Programme has made £182 million available to the police over a four-year period ending in 2004. This has lifted financial constraints on the submission of DNA suspect and crime scene samples by forces and enabled the routine use of DNA for volume crime scenes. In the revisit by HMIC in 2002, it was reported that the employment of volume crime scene examiners had substantially increased vehicle crime scene attendance, the recovery of DNA material, the workload of fingerprint bureaux and consequently the number of identifications.

If DNA expansion funding is not continued to support this forensic spending after the end of the period, the gap could not be met by police forces from existing budgets, and there is a risk of police practices reverting then to a more restrictive use of DNA.

HMIC found that activity was counted but its value was rarely assessed. Many forces were unaware of how many primary detections resulted from their DNA identifications, and very few had procedures for evaluating the benefits, in terms of detections or value for money, obtained from the identifications.

Sometimes, where there is evidence other than forensics which led to the suspect's arrest in the first place, an officer may be tempted to limit forensic investigations to evidence which supports the case against a suspect. The officer may be unwilling to spend time and money on collecting a wide range of samples which may only have the effect of negating the evidence which has already been collected, e.g. a car is stolen to carry out an armed robbery and is then abandoned; a suspect is arrested on foot nearby and the police take that person's clothing; the SOCO takes tapings from the car seats (sellotape strips to lift textile fibres and debris) and a match with fibres on the suspect is shown; if clothing was taken from all those who have legitimately used the car, not just from the suspect, it may reveal a fibre match with a legitimate user as well.

3.4.1 Management of submissions

It is important for officers to ensure that submissions are appropriate for the required examination, and that the examination will be of benefit to the investigation.

HMIC recommended that there should be clear criteria for decisions on laboratory submissions.

The cost to police of scientific investigations by the FSS is a significant factor in explaining why forensic scientists attend only about one in 500 crime scenes. UFSE found that SOCOs spent only between 20 per cent and 25 per cent of their time at crime scenes, although cost is not the reason for this. SOCOs spend time travelling to and from scenes; advising IOs about the significance and handling (collecting and packaging) of material recovered from suspects in detention, from searches of premises or from victims examined in police stations; and compiling notes and reports, and dealing with disclosure.

3.4.2 National DNA Database

Part IV of the Criminal Justice and Public Order Act 1994 amended the Police and Criminal Evidence Act 1984 (PACE), increasing the power of the police to take samples from detainees. Further extensive powers were given to the police in the Criminal Justice and Police Act 2001. These criminal justice (CJ) samples are checked against the NDNAD. Two samples are taken from the suspect and submitted to an approved forensic laboratory. The laboratory carries out DNA profiling for database purposes on one of the samples, and submits the profile to the custodian of the NDNAD for addition to the database. The other sample is stored by the laboratory on behalf of the submitting police force. The police also obtain samples from biological materials left at the scenes of crimes. Where there is no immediate suspect, those samples are submitted for analysis to an approved laboratory and the profiles are added to the NDNAD.

The traditional use of forensic science as a corroborative tool is being complemented by its use in providing information at the start of an investigation to help identify suspects. Each new profile added to the NDNAD is checked for matches against all other profiles held on the database. If a match is found between a crime scene and a CJ sample, it is reported as intelligence information to the police. If the police wish to use the match as evidence against a person, then a second or evidential sample is taken from the suspect. The CJ sample provides the intelligence leading to an arrest, and the sample taken from the suspect is the evidence for the court.

The Home Office funded DNA Expansion Project aims to increase the size of NDNAD to 2.6 million profiles by 2004, to match the size of the criminally active population and to establish an elimination database of frontline police staff.

3.4.3 National Automated Fingerprint Identification System (NAFIS)

For fingerprints (covered in more detail in **Chapter 21**), the NAFIS links all fingerprint bureaux in England and Wales, enabling forces to interrogate the system by searching prints found at a crime scene or taken from a suspect against a national database.

Crime scenes can often be linked if fingerprints relating to the same donor are found at different scenes. NAFIS have the facility to search between different crime scene marks.

Palm marks are recovered from 20 per cent of crime scenes examined, but there is no facility on NAFIS to speculatively search palm marks, although this may soon become available.

The majority of fingerprint bureaux (see **Chapter 21** for practice and procedure in fingerprint bureaux) are in the SSU headed by the SSM. The bureaux are headed by a bureaux manager and staffed by fingerprint experts, trainees, and support staff.

3.4.4 Footmarks computer systems

Footmarks are another source of identification (see **Chapter 15** for further information on footwear impressions). HMIC found different systems in operation to maximise recovered scene footmarks:

- the use of commercially manufactured computer systems such as SICAR (Shoeprint Image Capture and Retrieval), or software development within forces to run on existing hardware, e.g. SHOE-FIT (Surrey) and SHOEMARK (West Yorkshire);
- the use of locally developed manual or computer-based systems that tend to include individual methods of coding or data extraction;
- local collections of recovered scene marks usually held within scenes of crime offices. Individual scene marks are circulated to investigating officers and may be displayed at various sites within local police stations;
- the use in force of a qualified footwear expert.

While a suspect is in custody their footwear may be matched against recovered scene marks ('realtime systems'). Any matching footwear can then be seized as evidence. HMIC reported that in West Yorkshire staff can access lists of current scene marks on a database from various sites within the force, and an expert comparison made in-force whilst the suspect is in custody.

Alternatively, covert marks can be collected from prisoners who are released from custody with their footwear. Comparisons can then be confirmed later with an existing recovered scene mark (although the footwear pattern may change with subsequent wear), or with a scene mark recovered subsequently (when a further examination of the footwear will be required). In an example that we were shown, a person who was detained for disqualified driving ended up pleading guilty to a series of burglaries as a result of this procedure. Impressions of his footwear had been taken at the police station. They were found to match a footwear mark from a burglary scene. That mark was also found to match marks from a number of other burglaries. The police searched his home for evidence and not only found the shoe which had left the original mark but found another shoe which matched a mark left at the scenes of another string of burglaries.

The ACPO Footmark User Group (FUG) has assisted in the production of guidelines on footwear image capture relating to the taking of covert impressions from prisoners. A force may have a policy of taking covert marks, a prompt being generated to the custody sergeant to check that the investigating officer has taken footwear impressions, where appropriate, prior to the prisoner's release. The force analyst may nominate local offenders who are thought to be active burglars, and an entry made on the respective intelligence records with a marker indicating that a covert impression of their footwear is required if the opportunity arises.

3.4.5   SOCO attendance at crime scenes

Police forces have policies to prioritise SOCO attendance at crime scenes. HMIC came across the following range of policies:

- attendance in support of force and BCUs' policing priorities;
- blanket attendance at certain categories of volume crime, particularly residential burglary;
- SOCO attendance determined by the FOA (sometimes within preset policy parameters);
- SOCO attendance determined by crime desk staff;
- crime management sergeant determines against a matrix of intelligence and presumed solvability;
- assessment of burglary scenes by uniformed officers with particular training.

Force by force, chief officers determine scene attendance policy. Where the FOA or another police officer establishes SOCO attendance, that officer must be properly trained so as to determine the issue adequately. HMIC reported that most forces had screening policies on the use of SOCOs to maximise their efficiency, and avoid non-productive scenes, but these policies led to lost opportunities to tackle key offences of volume crime. In some forces, the attendance of SOCOs at motor vehicle crime was a rarity.

Some forces would deploy police officers with some forensic training to these scenes, although they are an expensive resource. In Northamptonshire, SOCO aides, trained in house, are employed to undertake low level examinations. HMIC reported that they gain substantially more identifications than SOCOs because of the highly productive nature of the crimes they examine, and recommend the appointment of scene of crime assistants to gather evidence regarding motor vehicle crime.

HMIC found no correlation between the percentage of recorded burglary dwelling scenes examined and the recovery rate of DNA or fingerprints per scene. This suggested that the preselection of scenes was not productive and that if all burglary scenes were examined the number of DNA samples and fingerprints recovered would increase proportionately.

In the revisit by HMIC in 2002, it was found that crime scene attendance and screening policies continued to present difficulty.

On the other hand, it may not be practical for SOCOs to visit the scenes of all crime, and decisions have to be made about which scenes are likely to yield most in terms of evidence and intelligence and which crimes are felt to be highest priority.

DNA and fingerprint evidence should be collected and submitted for examination quickly and once an identification has been made a follow up investigation should be conducted efficiently. Footwear marks need to be investigated quickly because the shoes that made the marks will change and may even be destroyed.

REFERENCES

ACPO & FSS (1996) *Using Forensic Science Effectively*.

Audit Commission (1993) *Helping with Enquiries, Tackling Crime Effectively*.

Her Majesty's Inspectorate of Constabulary (2000) *Under the Microscope*.

Her Majesty's Inspectorate of Constabulary (2002) *Under the Microscope Refocused*.

Tilley, N. & Ford, A. (1996) 'Forensic Science and Criminal Investigation', *Police Research Group Paper* (73).

CHAPTER 4

The process of examining the crime scene

4.1 THE COLLECTION AND ANALYSIS OF PHYSICAL EVIDENCE BY POLICE OFFICERS

Assessment of the crime scene involves constructing a theory about what might have happened, which is usually based on what witnesses or suspects say whilst at the scene or early on. This will then direct the search undertaken, the selection of samples and the tests to be undertaken. Investigators will draw necessarily reasonable inferences about what happened from the appearance of the crime scene and information from witnesses.

Investigators need to be objective, careful, thorough, and thoughtful. They must not leap to an immediate conclusion as to what happened based upon limited information as they can make incorrect interpretations as a result of preconceived ideas. They must resist the tendency to select the evidence which fits their expectations, and ignore or reject evidence that does not.

Instead, they should begin with several different theories about the crime, ruling any of them out only as a result of further information from the scene and from witnesses. They must recognise that assumptions may be made which prove to be wrong in the future. Investigators are trained to test their initial hypothesis. An investigator may visit a scene and make a hypothesis about what happened on the basis of the blood distribution. As witness statements are obtained, the investigator will need to test that hypothesis against what the witnesses said happened, and the investigator may then have to formulate a new hypothesis as a result.

Also, the investigator should guard against ignoring physical clues initially thought irrelevant which may become crucial later, and must look further than the evidence required to support or make out the initial prosecution case and look for evidence which may be useful later to support or undermine a defence.

Investigators need to speedily:

- assess the crime scene;
- protect the crime scene;

- preserve the crime scene with minimal contamination and disturbance of physical evidence;
- approach the crime scene as if that occasion is the only opportunity to preserve and recover physical evidence. There is usually only one chance to perform the job properly;
- recognise physical evidence;
- collect and submit physical evidence for scientific examination;
- preserve physical evidence with minimal contamination.

A crime scene examination in daylight is preferred unless the delay would result in a potential loss of forensic material.

The Forensic Science Service (FSS) publishes a basic forensic awareness video pack, *Think Forensic*, to inform junior officers who may find themselves in the position of being first officer attending (FOA). The pack features information regarding the preservation, collection and submission of evidence.

The Crime Scene Investigator (CSI) (**www.crime-scene-investigator.net**) website has many useful articles on crime scene investigation and some of the information below and in the following two chapters has been adapted from them (please see the references section at the end of this chapter).

A crime scene assessment of the offender's behaviour may be conducted to provide intelligence information and identify linked scenes.

4.2   THE SEARCH FOR PHYSICAL EVIDENCE

The scene should be well preserved by the caller (the victim or the reporter of the incident) to whom advice is routinely given about how to do this.

On arrival the FOA should engage in initial crime scene processing. The officer must get a visual picture, making a quick survey of the scene and its surrounding context to identify and assess:

- actual or potential approach and exit routes taken by the offender;
- point of entry and exit.

The FOA secures the scene; carries out a 'flash' search of the area to identify and locate physical material which could lead to the early arrest of suspects or gather vital information to speed enquiries; and ensures the integrity of potential evidence such as objects, marks, and traces.

The investigator systematically examines the scene and the vicinity, looking for anything which can be used to connect a victim to a suspect or a suspect to a victim or crime scene: marks, imprints, impressions and trace evidence, including actual items, with a potential evidential value. Contact trace material (CTM) is examined and analysed by the scenes of crime officer (SOCO). Types of material that the SOCO would look for include the following:

- Latent prints: contact of the friction ridge detail of either the hands or feet with a surface resulting in the transfer of 'sweat' from the ridges onto the contact surface, which is not readily visible.
- Marks, imprints and impressions: objects or materials that have retained the characteristics of other objects that have been physically pressed against them – comprising evidence left by a person, e.g. a mark or impression made by a tool, instrument, shoe, tyre or glove; and evidence left of a person, e.g. a fingerprint, thumbprint, palm print.
- Trace evidence: e.g. fibres, particles of metal, wood, glass and other materials; implements (including weapons), clothing, personal effects, dropped stolen property; potentially informative items such as a crumpled cigarette packet or a cigarette end; hair body tissue and body fluids, e.g. blood, secretions and excretions.

Locard's exchange principle at the scene is that the person or persons at the scene when a crime is committed will almost always leave something and take away something. This doctrine of exchange or transfer is based upon observations that:

- the perpetrator will take away traces of the victim and the scene;
- the victim or scene will retain traces of the perpetrator.

The principal aim of the forensic investigation is:

- to find, properly collect, and preserve any traces left at the scene;
- to locate matching materials on a suspect in order to provide objective evidence that he or she was present at the scene at the material time.

Certain evidence, such as shoeprints, can be fragile and easily destroyed or lost if not collected immediately. Some evidence will be destroyed by the offender if it is easily recognisable. But other evidence, such as trace evidence which results from the transfer of small quantities of material, such as hairs, textile fibres, paint chips, glass fragments or gunshot residue particles, will unknowingly be left behind or taken away by the offender.

The FOA or investigating officer (IO) assesses the scene accurately to identify the most effective use of SOCO and forensic scientist's effort in the identification and collection of CTM.

The FSS publishes a *Scenes of Crime Handbook*, a pocket guide to preservation, evidence recovery, and safety at scenes of crime.

Martin Gaule in *The Basic Guide to Forensic Awareness* lists the types of material which investigators will look for in volume crime, vehicle and burglary cases.

Vehicle crime – look for:

- discarded property;
- shoemarks (on paper mats);
- cigarette ends (for DNA);
- drinks containers (for DNA);
- half-eaten food or chewing gum (for bite marks or DNA);
- broken glass (control sample for later comparison);
- fibres attached to broken glass, seats, seat belts;
- instrument marks around damaged areas inside or outside;
- fingermarks (on interior mirror, removed interior bulb, discarded cassette cases or documents from glove compartment);
- blood around damaged areas;
- paint disturbed (control sample for later comparison with tool);
- paint from instruments.

Burglary – look for:

- discarded property;
- shoemarks (in earth, on refuse bin lids or other surfaces climbed onto or used to stand on);
- fibres (on edge of anything climbed over/foliage);
- cigarette ends (DNA);
- drinks containers (DNA);
- half-eaten food or chewing gum (for bite marks or DNA);
- paint disturbed (control sample for later);
- paint from instruments;
- broken glass (control sample for later comparison);
- instrument marks;
- blood (at point of entry or on discarded tissue, for DNA);
- fingermarks (around broken or forced window, opened drawers, disturbed property);
- knife moved from original location (fingermarks on knife or kitchen drawer).

4.3   INITIAL RESPONSE

The investigator notes the address/location, time, date and parties involved.

The investigator approaches the scene promptly but cautiously, being alert for discarded evidence. The entire area is scanned to thoroughly assess the scene and note any possible secondary crimes.

Observation is made of any people, vehicles, events, potential evidence and environmental conditions, particularly persons or vehicles leaving the crime scene. Potential victims, suspects and witnesses are identified.

4.4 IDENTIFYING, ESTABLISHING, PROTECTING, AND SECURING BOUNDARY

The investigator delineates the extent of the search area, takes control of the scene and ensures that it is secured.

Boundaries of the crime scene are defined and controlled to protect and secure the scene. The boundary should be greater than the crime scene and can later be reduced if necessary. A boundary around the scene must be marked off wherever possible, signalling to passers-by and those stopping to look that they must keep away and not enter the bounded area. The investigator extends the secured area if searching near the boundary has led to the discovery of potentially more physical evidence. An outer cordon will protect a wide area around the crime scene whilst an inner cordon protects the area of critical interest, such as a body or an abandoned vehicle. On arrival, the crime scene manager (CSM) will review the position of the cordons and extend or reduce them as necessary.

The investigator excludes the public, press and predatory animals from the scene, and prevents key individuals from leaving the scene. If officers are approached by any person asking questions about the crime, they should record details of the enquiries including the identity of the individual and the conversation taking place, in case the person making the enquiry is the offender who is trying to find out how the police are progressing.

The crime scene has traditionally been regarded as a physical location, e.g. the immediate area where the offence took place; a piece of land; an area within a street; a vehicle, a building or a specific room within a building; possible points and paths of entry and exit; and places where the victim or evidence may have been moved from or to. A crime scene may also include the victim, the suspect, all material places of contact between the offender and victim; those physical changes to a victim's body or clothing arising from the commission of the offence; any witness to be interviewed or eliminated from the investigation, and the homes of suspects, victims and witnesses.

Physical barriers (e.g. crime scene barrier tape) are set up and scene guards may be necessary.

Access to the scene is controlled and a log kept of everyone entering and leaving the scene, e.g. a medical examiner, paramedics, fire officers, their time of arrival and departure, and what they did at the scene.

There may be more than one scene, for example a body deposition scene may have a murder scene nearby.

Unauthorised people and animals are kept out. Bystanders are removed and other people are prevented from altering/destroying physical evidence.

A path of entry/exit to the crime scene and areas within the scene by authorised personnel is established using string (common approach path). The pathway should be examined first. Meeting points (RV points) are established.

Additional investigative resources are determined and requested.

The scene is not released until a final survey has been conducted. The completeness of the search will be discussed and checked. It will be ensured by the person in charge, who releases the scene, that all evidence is accounted for and that an inventory of the evidence (log) has been completed.

The time and date of the release of the scene is documented, including who released the scene.

4.5 SCENE WALK-THROUGH

A careful walk-through of the scene is conducted by the investigator in charge together with individuals responsible for processing the scene. This provides an overview of the entire scene, identifies any threats to scene integrity, and ensures protection of physical evidence.

The investigator makes a preliminary survey, evaluates what evidence is likely to be present and prepares a narrative description. This walk-through will enable a plan of the search to be formulated.

Preliminary documentation of the scene as observed is prepared. Written and photographic documentation provide a permanent record.

It is important to recognise what should be present at a scene but is not (it may have been removed by the offender); what appears to be out of place there (which may have been moved or left behind by the offender); and what looks contrived. This is described in a running narrative of the conditions at the crime scene.

Notes are made about possible entry and exit routes used by the offender.

Information is obtained from people who have entered the scene about its original conditions, and who has been at the scene.

4.6 AVOIDING CONTAMINATION

During the walk-through, the investigator in charge avoids contaminating the scene by using the established path of entry. An effort must be made to disturb things as little as possible. The floor or ground poses the greatest potential for contamination since this is where most evidence is found. The investigator will examine the ground on which they are about to tread first and place a marker at the location of any evidence as a warning to others.

There is a particular problem with not disturbing evidence if the investigator has to enter the crime scene to arrest an uncooperative suspect.

Investigators will wear special clothing and should keep their hands occupied or in their pockets to avoid leaving unwanted fingerprints.

A record should be made of any accidental or unavoidable contamination of the scene (widely defined, i.e. including the victim, the suspect, any witness), e.g. by touching first one person and then another; or any accidental or unavoidable disturbance of the scene.

People should not smoke, chew tobacco, use the telephone or toilet/bathroom, eat or drink, move any items, open windows or doors, touch anything unnecessarily, reposition moved items, litter or spit within the established boundaries of the crime scene.

There is always the risk of:

- the FOA destroying evidence by a vague and unprofessional approach to searching;
- the victim or others unwittingly interfering with evidence, e.g. following an initial desire to sort through the mess to find out what is missing, to engage in cleansing.

If police officers are not needed at the scene they should be kept out of it, otherwise there is a risk that they will grind evidence into the ground, smear a good fingerprint, or leave items at the scene which are later mistakenly thought to be of evidential value.

4.7 THE SEARCH

A 'line' or 'fingertip' search in a systematic specialised search pattern is carried out, depending upon the size and location of the scene. This will usually be conducted by trained uniformed officers supervised by a police search adviser (POLSA) officer supported by SOCOs;

- point-to-point – following a chain of objects that are obviously evidence;
- an ever widening circle – starting at a focal point of the scene or the centre of an area and working outwards, circling in a clockwise or counter-clockwise direction until the edge of the secured area is reached. The spiral is then reversed, working towards the centre or focal point (NB: although applicable to outside and inside, within a room account must necessarily be taken of size and contents);
- a sector search – the scene is subdivided into a chequerboard of segments with the victim or the building in the centre sector; each sector is searched as an individual unit;
- a strip search or grid search – applied to outside areas. First the area is searched up and down (in strips), then the area is searched back and forth (completing a grid coverage).

The Manual of Standard Operating Procedures for Scientific Support Personnel at Major Incident Scenes is published by the Association of Chief Police Officers (ACPO) Crime Committee. Authored by leading specialists in scientific support it draws together good practice from around the UK. The manual has a search/examination list:

Inside

- cupboards/wardrobes;
- between clothing;
- pockets;
- trouser turn-ups;
- unfold clothing;
- drawers;
  - under bottom;
  - outside back;
- under carpets;
- floorboards;
- new decorations/alterations;
- laundry baskets;
- clothing;
- towels;
- dishcloths;
- basins;
- sinks;
- toilets;
- baths;
- u-bends;
- cistern;
- drains;
- fireplaces;
- ashtrays;
- waste bins;
- washing machine;
- tumble dryer;
- dishwasher;
- roof space;
- diaries;
- computers;
- personal organiser;
- telephone accounts;
- bedding;
- underside of mattress.

Outside

- outhouses/sheds/garages;
- vehicles;
- drains;
- manholes;
- compost heaps;
- vegetation disturbance;
- soil disturbance;
- bonfires;
- fences/walls;
- vegetation;
- shrubs/trees;
- washing lines;
- roofs;
- dustbins (postpone collection from dustbins in the locality);
- workplace.

Transient or fragile physical evidence is identified and protected. Measures are effected to preserve/protect evidence that may be lost or compromised (e.g. protect from rain, snow, wind, footsteps, tyre tracks). During rain or snow conditions, water is diverted and tyre, shoe and other impressions covered with available boxes or cardboard (but preferably not polythene).

The investigator removes 'at risk' physical evidence to a safe place, i.e. removes:

- entire items of evidential value which are liable to inadvertent removal or destruction, or are of immediate investigative value, e.g. a cassette containing a video recording by a security camera; a weapon or tool; trace material which should be removed with tweezers and placed in a polythene bag;
- material, or an object, liable to irreversible change, e.g. in hot weather, a sample of putty containing marks; an item bearing a mark, such as a container of spread.

Each type of evidence has a specific value in an investigation. The value of evidence should be kept in mind by the investigator when doing a crime scene investigation. For example, 'best evidence' requires that more time should be spent collecting good fingerprints than trying to find fibres left by a suspect's clothing. Fingerprints can positively identify a person as having been at the scene of a crime whereas fibres could have come from anyone wearing clothes made out of the same material.

Personal notepads, diaries, personal organisers, palm top and other computer equipment, telephones (last number redial) and telephone answering machines (message store), and phone books are good sources of information.

All items are photographed before collection and noted in a photographic log.

The locations of evidence are marked on a diagram or sketch.

Evidence identification markers can be used to mark and illustrate items of evidence at a scene.

The investigator draws the attention of those remaining at the scene and others who will either be recommended to attend or will attend as a matter of course (e.g. the crime scene attender/analyst or SOCO) to physical evidence which has been marked off and protected.

Markers include identification marking stands: two-sided to three-sided plastic letters and numbers. They are used to reveal evidence which may not be seen in photographs, such as items obscured by surface covering. The marking is put in place after the scene has been photographed. Further photographs are then taken to document the scene with the identification markers in place.

Easily accessible areas in open view are focused on first, by conducting a cautious search when steps are taken to avoid evidence loss or contamination. This progresses to a vigorous search of possible out-of-view locations where items may have been hidden or concealed. Possible hiding places in difficult access areas should not be overlooked.

Indoors, on hard floors, if a flashlight is held about one inch from the floor and the beam is angled and fanned back and forth, so that it just sweeps over the floor surface and is almost parallel to the surface, evidence and shoe prints will show up.

The most transient or fragile evidence is documented, photographed, and collected first, down to the least transient or fragile.

The effectiveness of the search is continuously re-evaluated and the potential of any items found at or near the scene should not be overlooked.

A crime scene is three dimensional and includes what is above the investigator.

4.8 BRIEFING OF SOCOs

There must be proper communication between investigators and others conducting a search.

Every effort should be made by police officers to brief SOCOs adequately in order to ensure an effective examination of the scene for CTM.

Wherever possible the briefing of the SOCO should be verbal. They should always be informed of the arrest of a suspect. SOCOs believe a briefing prior to the scene visit is either essential or useful, with verbal briefings being the most effective.

Briefing of SOCOs by police officers is commonplace in major crimes. The SOCO typically arrives with the Criminal Investigation Department (CID) officers or when officers are still at the scene. The SOCO will discuss possible pieces of evidence and the uses to which they might be put. If the SOCO attends alone, he or she will be fully briefed before doing so.

In cases investigated by uniform officers, e.g. volume crimes:

- the officer has departed;
- SOCOs most commonly attend the scene 'blind':
  - with no background information;
  - at best with only sketchy information, e.g. some details available on the crime reporting system (CRS).

Lack of briefing can result in the SOCO conducting a 'routine' examination without specific focus on the details of the case, which are unknown to the SOCO.

Scene examination by SOCOs should be as comprehensive as possible.

- In the case of burglaries, with large numbers of scenes to be attended, scene examination focuses on a small number of evidence types. If there is a suspect then SOCOs will respond to a request for other specific forensic material.
- Some forces have a limited search policy, i.e. SOCOs are required to collect tangible CTM – fingerprints, footwear marks, blood/DNA if the offender bled – and to ignore other evidence such as particles, e.g. glass, fibres.
- Limited searches, i.e. those adopting a narrow focus concerning CTM, are generally thought to be undesirable by SOCOs who are worried that restricted scene examination practices or policies create the possibility of missing evidence which might either implicate or eliminate suspects.
- SOCOs are trained that prioritisation in scene examination is generally ad hoc.
- On average, SOCOs spend 70 per cent of their time searching for fingerprints and 30 per cent searching for other forensic evidence.

This situation of non-communication and SOCOs and IOs working independently of each other means that the two paths of investigation are not interactive except in the most major crimes.

If a forensic scientist is instructed to attend the scene, he/she will almost always try and attend the first briefing at the police station before going to the scene. All the possible leads come together during that briefing. At the scene, if it is still 'warm' the scientist may never get to see the senior investigating officer. Investigators will be out making investigations and will not be present at the scene to brief the scientist.

Videotaping the crime scene

- Make sure that battery is fully charged.
- Use a tripod when necessary and possible, to take more professional shots.
- The camera should have date and time videotape display functions.
- Use a title generator or leave 15 seconds blank at the beginning of the tape to add a title card.
- Check the lighting: is it daylight, artificial or a mixture?
- The scene should be marked and lit.
- People should be cleared from the camera range and those out of range should remain silent.
- Aim for quality not quantity.
- Do not stop the recording until the taping is complete.
- Move the camera slowly and pan past objects to record detail.
- Plan your pan.
- Take an exterior general view shot of the location first: a general overview of the scene and the surrounding area.
- Use wide angle before close up and extreme close up shots to establish the layout of the evidence and the relationship of the evidence with other evidence and parts of the scene to each other and to capture detail.
- Use close up and extreme close up shots to capture detail.
- When covering a long narrow section of a scene, such as a corridor or track, consider a slow zoom from a tripod rather than walking along it.
- If perspective has to change, for example you have to see behind objects, then a walking shot may be inevitable. Plan your shot route first, use as wide an angle as possible to minimise sway and judder and move as smoothly as possible.
- In small rooms or spaces, use a high angle shot from a corner.
- A high angle shot is also useful to show separation of objects on similar planes.
- Leave 15 seconds blank at the end of the taping to prevent the tape running into anything previously recorded.
- Transfer the tape to a high quality master tape which should be stored in a safe place.
- Copies can be made from the master tape.

Photographing the crime scene

- Use a camera with interchangeable lenses: 28mm wide angle, 55mm normal and a lens with macro capabilities (1:4 or better).
- Use an independent flash which can function at different angles and distances from the camera.
- Use print and/or slide colour film of up to 400 ISO.
- Begin with wide angle shots of the crime scene and surrounding areas.
- Show the overall layout of the crime scene and the spatial relationships of the various pieces of evidence to each other.
- Next shoot from medium range to show the relationships of pieces of evidence to other pieces of evidence or structures in the crime scene.
- Then take close up shots of individual key pieces of evidence.
- Where relative size is important, photograph the object, then include a ruler with and on the same level as the object being photographed.
- Take photos of spectators who are standing around watching the activities as the offender may return to observe the actions of the police or it may help to later identify a witness.
- Take notes of what is being photographed in each shot and what the photograph is aiming to show.

Sketching the crime scene

- A sketch is usually made of the scene as if the reader is looking straight down (overhead sketch) or straight ahead (elevation sketch) at the crime scene.
- A rough sketch is made first on graph paper in pencil with squares representing the distance involved.
- The directions are taken from a compass.
- Measurements are taken of the distances between objects and/or structures at the crime scene using a tape measure or other measuring device.
- The measurements are proportionally reduced on the rough sketch and the objects drawn in.
- Measurements should be double checked.
- Two measurements at right angles to each other or from two reference points will place the objects on the sketch.
- A final sketch is made later and the original rough sketch is retained.

4.9   TYPES OF SAMPLES

4.9.1   Reference samples

These would include material from a verifiable/documented source, which when compared with evidence of an unknown source shows an association or linkage between an offender and a crime scene and/or victim (e.g. a carpet cutting taken from a location suspected as the point of transfer for comparison with fibres taken from the suspect's shoes; a sample of paint removed from a suspect vehicle to be compared with paint found on the victim's vehicle following an accident; or a sample of the suspect's and/or victim's blood submitted for comparison with a bloodstained shirt recovered as evidence).

4.9.2   Control/blank samples

These could consist of material of a known source that presumably was uncontaminated during the commission of a crime (e.g. a sample to be used in laboratory testing to ensure that the surface on which the sample is deposited does not interfere with testing. For example, when a bloodstain is collected from a carpet, a segment of unstained carpet must be collected for use as a blank or elimination sample; or a sample taken from the scene to compare with a similar sample which may later be taken from the suspect).

4.9.3   Elimination samples

A sample of known source taken from a person who had lawful access to the scene to be compared with evidence of the same type (e.g. fingerprints from occupants, tyre marks or footprints from police or medical vehicles). One reason why the names of those people entering a crime scene are taken is in case investigators later need to collect fingerprints, shoes, fibres, blood, saliva or hair pulled from any of them.

4.9.4   Comparison samples

These are obtained from an unknown/questioned source. They may be:

- recovered crime scene samples whose source is in question (e.g. evidence left by suspects, victims);
- evidence that may have been transferred to an offender during the commission of the crime and taken away by him or her. This evidence can be compared with evidence of a known source and can thereby be linked to a person/vehicle/tool of a crime.

4.10 FINAL SURVEY

The investigator in charge conducts a walk-through at the conclusion of the investigation.

The crime scene is inspected visually.

All evidence collected at the scene is accounted for.

ACPO Crime Committee Homicide Working Group 'Scientific Support and Forensic Science in Homicide Investigations' stresses that at the conclusion of a crime scene examination the final briefing between the CSM and the senior investigating officer (SIO) is an all-important milestone, particularly before the scene is released. There is generally only one opportunity to examine a crime scene and a future re-examination may not be possible. The SIO should decommission the scene(s) in conjunction with the CSM and they may consider taking other independent experts' advice in relation to the examination of the scene(s) before doing so.

4.11 THE SUSPECT/VICTIM

The suspect/victim is also a crime scene. Once arrested or brought to the police station, he/she is taken to an examination room. A crime scene investigator (CSI) or IO or custody examiner will:

- comb his/her hair onto a clean sheet of paper;
- separately wrap his/her clothes and seal them in a brown paper bag (so that they can be examined for textile fibres and other traces);
- have a doctor take blood or other samples;
- have a doctor examine him/her for injuries which could be linked to commission of the offence.

Martin Gaule in *The Basic Guide to Forensic Awareness* lists potential samples which can be taken from suspects and victims:

- pulled head hair – control sample of hair or DNA;
- hair combings – fibre traces, glass particles, alien hairs;
- saliva – control sample;
- mouth (buccal) swab – control sample or DNA;
- facial swabs and nasal blowings – firearm residue traces;
- dental impressions – for comparison with bite marks;
- pulled pubic hair – control sample;
- pubic hair combings – traces of alien hair, fibres and vaginal debris;
- penile swabs – vaginal debris, lubricants;
- footprint impressions – comparison with bare footprints or linking to footwear inners;

- fingerprints – comparison with fingermarks;
- nail scrapings – fibre traces, hairs and blood;
- hand swabs – firearm residues, explosives residues, metal traces, trap markers and dyes;
- blood – DNA control, alcohol and drugs content;
- urine – alcohol and drugs content;
- footwear – comparison with shoemarks at scene, fibres, blood, glass and paint;
- gloves – comparison with glovemarks at scene, fibre control, paint and glass.

4.12 COMMUNICATING WITH THE SOCO

The IO will need to exploit forensic aspects further by speaking with the SOCO, the forensic 'expert', to establish:

- if, or when, the SOCO had attended or intends to attend the scene;
- the results of any attendance:
  - description and assessment of the scene;
  - the outcome of his or her search for forensic evidence, i.e. a list of CTM recovered;
- the location (at the scene) of any CTM recovered – preferably assisted by an explanatory drawing;
- the SOCO's assessment of recovered CTM;
- if the SOCO has not handed over the CTM to the IO, its present whereabouts.

4.13 FORENSIC PHYSICIANS

They may carry out the following:

- the examination of victims – particularly for physical examination and the taking of samples, e.g. in a case of alleged rape;
- the taking of blood samples from people suspected of driving whilst under the influence of drink or drugs;
- mental examination to identify the presence of psychiatric illness or psychological disorder.

4.14   COMMUNICATING WITH THE FORENSIC PHYSICIAN

Where the suspect is in custody the IO may liaise with the medical examiner in order:

- to request an immediate written report (for inclusion in the crime file) of the conduct and outcome of, and opinion upon, any examination of:

  - the body – which he or she certified as dead;
  - the victim;
  - witnesses – in order to exclude these as suspects;
  - the suspect;

- to request a list of samples taken;
- to take charge of samples taken – signing the doctor's notes to the effect.

4.15   MEDICAL EXAMINATION OF THE VICTIM

The examining doctor should be:

- comprehensively briefed as to the allegation;
- appropriately briefed about the prosecution case and the investigation conducted so far.

This should occur especially in cases of sexual assault.
   Such briefing allows the examining doctor:

- to place the victim's account in the context of the detailed police briefing;
- to take the samples appropriate to the alleged offence;
- to provide the IO or SIO with a fuller, more timely, written report, supported by a list of samples taken:

  - which informs the investigation at a crucial early stage;
  - which should be included in the crime file;

- to provide a comprehensive statement in due course – aided by the examiner's personal notes made during the examination.

4.16   TAKING OF SAMPLES FROM THE SUSPECT, AND SUBMISSION FOR ANALYSIS

Samples are taken by police officers and forensic physicians to eliminate the suspect or to corroborate suspicions by linking the suspect to scenes.
   The Forensic Science Service Evidence Recovery Systems produces a range of biological evidence recovery items for sale to law enforcement

agencies. These include a forensic medical examination kit developed in partnership with the Association of Forensic Practitioners (AFP) and ACPO. The kit is intended to be used by medical examiners in order that evidence can be recovered from either victims or suspects in cases of sexual assault. The medical examiner is provided with a number of self-contained modules, which are designed to assist in the recovery of certain evidence types. These are set out in the box below.

Documentation module containing

- kit information and sampling guidelines;
- examination forms (MEDX1A, 1B and 1C) to be completed by the medical examiner;
- APS (Association of Public Surgeons) Medical Aftercare leaflet;
- ACPO Good Practice Guide – help for those who have been sexually assaulted.

Couch cover module: one disposable couch cover

Body outline module: body diagrams for use by the medical examiner

Swab module for the recovery of body fluids from the examinee

- plastic shaft-sterile swabs with criminal evidence markings;
- adhesive labels;
- labelled tamper-evident bags;
- sterile water;
- container.

Hair sample collection module for the recovery of dried body fluids and foreign particles or fibres

- scissors;
- disposable forceps;
- comb;
- sheet of paper;
- labelled tamper-evident bags.

Alcohol/drug blood module for preserving and storing samples for analysis of alcohol, drugs and volatiles/solvents

- blood container with preservative and anticoagulant;
- outer plastic security container with absorbent padding;
- adhesive labels;

- labelled tamper-evident bag;
- alcohol free wipe;
- syringe;
- needle;
- plaster.

Alcohol/drug urine module for preserving and storing urine samples for alcohol and drug analysis

- urine collection vessel;
- urine container with preservative tablet;
- outer plastic security container with absorbent padding;
- adhesive labels;
- labelled tamper-evident bag;
- pair of disposable gloves.

Fingernail sample collection module for the preservation of trace evidence such as body fluids and fibres from underneath fingernails

- fingernail quills;
- sheets of paper;
- labelled tamper-evident bags;
- nail clippers.

Mouth collection module for the recovery and storage of semen from the mouth of the examinee

- containers;
- plastic shaft-sterile swabs with criminal evidence markings;
- adhesive labels;
- labelled tamper-evident bags;
- sterile water.

Disposable clothing module

- paper gown;
- paper pants;
- ground sheet for the examinee to stand on during examination.

DNA evidential module: a comb kit to obtain a non-intimate DNA sample

4.17   POST MORTEM (AUTOPSY)

The ACPO Crime Committee Homicide Working Group 'Scientific Support and Forensic Science in Homicide Investigations' gives the following advice:

> The examination of the deceased will identify critical information for the investigation and decision-making process. Importantly the examination should commence in detail at the crime scene and involve a team approach including the SIO, a forensic pathologist on a Home Office approved list, CSM, together with a forensic scientist if necessary. There should be a joint planned and sequential approach to the examination which may require a significant amount of work to be conducted before the body is removed to the mortuary. Every person charged with a homicide offence has the right to have their own pathologist examine the body. A defence pathologist may act for one or more of the defendants which reduces the number of examinations and may lessen the anxiety and trauma of the family of the deceased.
>
> There is sometimes a tendency towards haste in respect of the deceased. The body itself should be treated as a crime scene and there will usually be only one opportunity to recover evidence, particularly minute debris. It is therefore essential that each step is fully considered, agreed and documented.

At an appropriate stage when evidence retrieval from the body at the scene is concluded, the team should review actions undertaken, revisit if necessary and plan the post mortem. Continuity of evidence also applies to the deceased and an officer should accompany the body from the scene to the mortuary. In murder cases there is usually a second post mortem for the benefit of the defence. The SIO and CSM should ensure that appropriate representation is made at that event, including themselves in complicated or doubtful cause cases.

Unless there are any significant factors to consider, it may be better to suspend further work at the crime scene(s) until the outcome of the post mortem is known. Clearly, post mortem findings may radically alter the scene examination priorities initially identified, but it is important that there are clear communications between the CSM and the SIO at the post mortem relative to exchange of information.

Prior to the commencement of the post mortem a team briefing should take place to clearly identify the stages of evidence recovery and roles to be undertaken by each team member. Again pacing is important as undue haste can lead to exhibit confusion and unsatisfactory documentation. The planning process of a post mortem should include:

- team plan and agreement of actions to be undertaken;
- risk assessment of post mortem;
- body identification;
- limiting the number of personnel attending to an absolute minimum, i.e.

SIO, pathologist, mortuary technician, CSM, crime scene examiner – photography, crime scene examiner – notes/sketches, crime scene examiner – receiving/packaging exhibits, coroner's officer, forensic scientist;

- general photography of body;
- detailed photography of body (if required);
- establishing body grid reference;
- recovery of trace material from body and clothing *in situ*;
- gradual removal of clothing;
- recovery of trace material from naked body surface;
- detailed examination of naked body surface, particularly injuries;
- recovery of external body samples;
- quality audit progress;
- commencement of post mortem proper;
- recovery of internal samples;
- continuing photography as required;
- summarising findings: contextualise to the crime scene;
- ensuring post mortem exhibit continuity;
- considering repeat visit to view bruise development;
- closing team briefing.

It is important to note that the surface of the body may have incurred injuries such as scratches and bruises together with minute trace debris. It is good practice to 'grid' each area of the body as a template to ensure the detailed examination of the body surface.

A new technique pioneered in the UK by Forensic Alliance involves the systematic covering of the entire body of the victim with adhesive tape strips. This enables precise mapping of any textile fibres which could have come from a suspect, providing information not just about the contact but also about precisely how the contact occurred.

The SIO or their nominee should take an active interest in the progress of the post mortem and be encouraged to confer with the Home Office pathologist throughout the examination.

At the conclusion of the post mortem the critical known findings should be summarised and agreed. These findings will clearly have a significant impact on the future direction of the enquiry and their importance cannot be over-emphasised. SIOs should be aware that repeat examinations of the body following the post mortem may provide vital information as bruising and other marks on the skin develop. Specialist photography in these circumstances should be exploited and the pathologist should be asked to advise as to evidential value of further photographic work. It is also important that SIOs are aware of the body deteriorating.

In the case of Mrs Sally Clark, the Cheshire solicitor whose convictions for murder of her two infants were set aside by the Court of Appeal, Dr Alan Williams, the Home Office pathologist instructed by the Crown, performed a post mortem on the second child. A laboratory report indicated evidence of infection which may have been the cause of death. This report was not disclosed to the Crown Prosecution Service (CPS) or to the defence.

The Home Office has re-emphasised a requirement that forensic pathologists make all findings in the course of a post mortem examination, not just those which the pathologist believes in his/her opinion to be important, available to the CPS.

REFERENCES

ACPO Crime Committee, *Manual of Standard Operating Procedures for Scientific Support Personnel at Major Incident Scenes.*

ACPO Crime Committee, Homicide Working Group (1999) *Scientific Support and Forensic Science in Homicide Investigations.*

Crime Scene Response Guidelines are available online at **www.crime-scene-investigator.net/csi-articles.html**

Ede, R. & Shepherd, E. (2000) *Active Defence*, 2nd Edition, Law Society Publishing.

Forensic Science Service (as updated) *Scenes of Crime Handbook*, FSS.

Gaule, M. (2002) *The Basic Guide to Forensic Awareness*, New Police Bookshop.

Redmayne, M. (2001) *Expert Evidence and Criminal Justice*, Oxford University Press.

Ruslander, H., *Searching and Examining a Major Case Crime Scene*, available online at **www.crime-scene-investigator.net/csi-articles.html**

Schiro, G., *Collection and Preservation of Evidence, Examination and Documentation of the Crime Scene, Protecting the Crime Scene*, all available online at **www.crime-scene-investigator.net/csi-articles.html**

Thomas, P., *Video Guidelines for Evidence Scenes*, available online at **www.crime-scene-investigator.net/csi-articles.html**

US Department of Justice (2000) *Crime Scene Investigation: A Guide for Law Enforcement*, available online at **www.fbi.gov//hq/lab/fsc/backissu/april2000/twgcsi.pdf**

CHAPTER 5

Documentation of examination, removal, and submission of contact trace material (CTM) and other material and objects

5.1 DOCUMENTATION OF THE CRIME SCENE

The investigator should make extensive notes and not rely upon their memory. Investigators are advised that they cannot over-document the physical evidence.

Documentation should be double checked to detect inadvertent errors. If a crime scene is properly documented other people can use the information as part of the investigation and/or prosecution in court.

Written notes and reports should be done in chronological order and should only include facts, not opinions, analyses or conclusions; documenting what the person sees not what they think.

If the crime is of low level seriousness or volume crime, it does not require a fine grain detail record to be kept of the forensic response. The crime report will be the main document recording the actions which were taken. If the crime is of high level seriousness, a range of operational logs and management records will detail everything which took place. In ascending order of the seriousness of the crime, the records usually produced are set out below.

5.1.1 Incident report book or pocket book

The first officer attending (FOA) completes entries in their incident report book (IRB) or pocket book about his/her verbal exchanges with the victim, witnesses and the suspect and actions including bagging up, sealing and assigning reference numbers to physical evidence recovered from the scene or removed from the suspect.

The scenes of crime officer (SOCO) may make entries in a pocket book of information obtained from victims and witnesses.

5.1.2 The crime report

The crime report is a standardised form, the design of which varies greatly between forces. It is cumulatively completed by both police officers and civilian staff.

Despite differences in design, the content is common, is cross-referenced to the operation information management system (OIS), and contains data fields in respect of:

- type of premises/scene of crime, point of entry;
- type of offence;
- additional specific features, e.g. method of gaining entry, actions within, use of incendiary devices and accelerants, objects, marks and other contact trace material (CTM), victim attributes;
- details of SOCO: requested/attending scene;
- details of enquiries;
- enquiries at the scene, in the vicinity, potential outlets for stolen items, potential locations visited by suspect;
- actions: in serial number order, time and date, details of action including all persons involved (e.g. victim, witnesses, informants, officers, civilian staff), signature of person directing or effecting action.

Although the form is completed manually, the data fields constitute detail for inputting into the crime reporting system (CRS).

5.1.3 SOCO's report

Forces differ in the way SOCOs record the results of their scene examinations – ranging:

- from forces where there is no scene examination form, the results being recorded in a pocket book;
- to forces where SOCOs complete a very comprehensive pro forma which will necessarily require the officer to indicate which forms of searching/ examination were not carried out.

Most forces use broadly similar scene examination forms. Comprehensive and fully detailed accounts are a relative rarity. Because of this, the Association of Chief Police Officers (ACPO) and the Forensic Science Service (FSS) have recommended a national template with information that can be fed into the force's CRS.

A typical report will contain information about:

- name of SOCO;
- address of location examined;
- date of examination;
- registration number of vehicle examined;
- details of photographs taken.

This will be followed by a Y/N tick box section concerning:

- scene examined;

- fingerprints found;
- elimination prints taken;
- elimination kits left;
- photographer;
- footwear;
- forensic;
- DNA;
- toolmark.

For each item of scientific evidence:

- item number;
- exhibit number;
- details of the article;
- where it was recovered.

There may be an opened out diagram of a car and diagrams of points of entry on the report form, on which can be marked the position of fingerprints or forensic evidence, together with any supporting details.

5.1.4 Policy book

A SOCO will have a policy book or file in which he/she documents every decision they have made. It will detail the number of officers on the enquiry, the lines of enquiry and the parameters of any suspect, called the eliminating criteria.

5.2 THE CRIME FILE

This is opened to house:

- documentation (including: the crime report and enclosures; copies of forms, including the IRB; copies of printout from the OIS; witness statements; photocopies of pocket book or desk diary extracts; notes);
- a record of exchanges and correspondence with key individuals within the force, e.g. scientific support department (SSD), and external to the force, e.g. Crown Prosecution Service (CPS), forensic physician, forensic scientists.

5.2.1 Photographs of scene

The crime scene is photographed as soon as possible. First, the entire area is photographed before it is entered. This includes adjacent areas such as points of entry and exit. Victims, suspects, crowds and vehicles are photographed.

The entire scene is photographed progressively with overall, medium and close-up coverage.

Photography should be inclusive: something which has no apparent value at the time may later turn out to be significant.

Evidence items are photographed in place before they are moved, collected and packaged. Photographs should continue to be taken if the investigator is revealing layers of evidence which were not previously documented because they were hidden from sight.

When appropriate, a scale device is used for size determination in a second photograph. The area under a body should be photographed once the body has been removed. Although fingerprints developed at crime scenes may be photographed prior to them being lifted, other impressions are usually photographed before being cast.

Where photographs are taken for evidential purposes, all the negatives should be retained even if the photographs are subsequently not intended to be used as evidence. A record should be kept of the total number of exposures made and if a statement is provided, this information should be included in the statement (Joint Operational Instructions for the Disclosure of Unused Material (JOPI) 2003, Annex H8 (see **www.cps.gov.uk**, **para.9.4** and **Appendix 5**)).

5.2.2 Videotape

This may supplement photographs.

5.2.3 Photographic log

A photographic log and sketch are made to document the technical and descriptive information regarding the photographic process.

5.2.4 Diagram/sketch

- Documentation of physical evidence items, including conditions, locations and measurements showing size and distance relationships in the crime scene area;
- diagrams supplement photographs;
- a rough sketch is drawn at the scene and used as a model for a finished sketch;
- a sketch has the advantage that it can be drawn to leave out all the clutter that would appear in a photograph;
- a rough sketch will include:

    - the perimeter;
    - fixed objects, such as furniture;

- specific location;
- date;
- time;
- case identifier;
- preparer;
- weather;
- lighting conditions;
- scale or scale disclaimer;
- compass orientation;
- position of evidence;
- measurements;
- key or legend.

5.2.5 Latent print lift log

Documentation of the recognition, collection, marking and packaging of lifts made of latent prints discovered at the scene. All fingermarks lifted or photographed at the scene must be recorded, retained and made available to the disclosure officer (JOPI 2003, Annex H4).

5.2.6 Evidence recovery log

- Documentation of the recognition, collection, marking and packaging of physical evidence for administrative and chain of custody purposes;
  - who had contact with the evidence;
  - the date and time the evidence was handled;
  - the circumstances of the evidence being handled;
  - what changes, if any, were made in the evidence.
- the record should include:
  - exhibit number;
  - full description of exhibit;
  - time and date of recovery;
  - full description of where recovered.

This establishes that the items of evidence collected at the crime scene are the same as the evidence that is being presented in court. Number designations on a sketch can be coordinated with number designations on the evidence log.

Documents should include name or initials of the individual collecting the evidence, each person or entity subsequently having custody of it, agency and case number, victim or suspect's name, dates the items were collected or transferred and a brief description of the item.

Evidence identifiers may be tape, labels, containers and string tags used to identify the evidence.

Tags should contain the following information:

- description of item;
- case number or identifier;
- date;
- location of collection;
- collector's name and identifier;
- brand name;
- any serial number or garment information.

On the reverse side, every person who has responsibility at any stage for that exhibit must sign and date the label in sequence. Similar information should be labelled or marked on the outside of packaging.

5.2.7 Form MG FSS

The police provide the laboratory, as early as possible, with advance notice (using form MG (Manual of Guidance for the Preparation, Processing and Submission of Files) FSS) of their intention to submit an item for examination (some forces have their own forms). It contains details of surrounding circumstances affecting the case.

Documents and information which might be relevant to the examination, which subsequently come to light, should be dispatched to the laboratory either with form MG FSS or as soon as possible afterwards.

The form provides information on:

- officer-in-case or day-to-day contact details of another officer in respect of the case;
- proposed offence charged;
- for urgent and critical submissions only, the category of justification, i.e. young, offender, adult in custody, Police and Criminal Evidence Act 1984 (PACE) requirement, child victim of sexual abuse/violence, child witness, or other (at the request of the CPS);
- appropriate forms and documents submitted at the same time, e.g.

  - glass/fibre form;
  - sexual offences form;
  - firearms safety form;
  - toxicology form;
  - drugs/drive form MG DD/E;
  - technical defence form MG DD/D;
  - plans;
  - victim's statement;
  - voluntary statement, i.e. by suspect;

- photographs;
- scene examiner's (i.e. SOCO's) report;
- relevant additional documentation;

- subjects – for each subject: surname, forename(s), sex, date of birth (DOB), ethnic code, occupation, status (i.e. deceased, victim, suspect, subject for elimination), date and time of arrest;
- circumstances of incident;
- what is required to be established, stating the priority: 1 – urgent; 2 – critical; 3 – standard;
- listed items for scientific examination: for each item specifying:
  - item number;
  - exhibit number;
  - exhibit bag number;
  - description of items;
  - subject or location from which recovered;
  - date/time found/taken;
  - name of person seizing the item.

5.3 ENTRY/EXIT DOCUMENTATION

A log is kept of everyone entering and leaving the crime scene. The ACPO Manual of Standard Operating Procedures for Scientific Personnel at Major Incident Scenes recommends that the log contains the following information:

- time and date of visits and departure;
- details of visitor;
- reason and authority for visit;
- signature of visitor;
- details of loggist;
- details of hand-over between loggists.

5.3.1 The incident log

This is used to account for the presence and movements of personnel within a designated crime scene area, to provide continuity of exhibits and to prevent contamination. The log should be started immediately and kept by a designated officer.

The officer keeping the log must sign, date and time the log both at the commencement and conclusion of the task. The log should show:

- the name of the officer keeping the record;
- the name of the person entering or leaving the scene;
- date and time of each entry/exit;
- reason for entry.

To ensure consistency of standards in communication a standardised format should be used. This has been produced by the Home Office.

5.4   SCENE RELEASE DOCUMENTATION

Release of the crime scene. Documentation should record:

- time and date of release;
- to whom released;
- by whom released.

5.5   THE ACTIONS LOG

An action is a written instruction to an officer to carry out a particular line of enquiry. The action is in two parts: the instruction and the result. The allocation, carrying out and results of actions are recorded on a form, in a book or log, as an entry in a computer document, or electronically. If the crime is of low level seriousness or volume crime, the actions will be recorded mainly in the crime report.

If the crime is of medium or high level seriousness, area Criminal Investigation Department (CID) and Major Crimes Unit (MCU) officers will keep records of their actions and items likely to be offered as evidence. Given the larger scale of their enquiries, actions are recorded in an actions log, which may be a manuscript or computer record.

5.6   CRIME SCENE MANAGER'S (CSM's) LOG

This will contain the following details:

5.6.1   Reference details

- Incident;
- location;
- date;
- crime reference;
- SOC (scene of crime) reference;
- lab reference.

5.6.2   Personnel

- Scene manager and telephone number;
- senior investigating officer (SIO) and telephone number;
- exhibits officer and telephone number;

- incident room location;
- scientist and telephone number;
- Home Office pathologist and telephone number;
- SOCOs attending;
- fingerprint officers attending;
- photo/video officers attending;
- others attending: role/contact number.

5.6.3   Aide memoire

TO CHECK

- Position of cordons;
- common approach path;
- protection of scene;
- commencement of scene investigation;
- approach to scene searched and cleared;
- initial photos/video.

TO RECORD

- Other occupants;
- people expected;
- empty rooms/flats;
- people with access;
- sketch plan.

EXAMINE/RECORD

- Deceased;
- clothing;
- obvious injuries;
- heating details;
- general security;
- doors/locks;
- windows – catches/locks;
- curtains – positions;
- lighting/switches;
- meters and readings;
- telephone/answerphone/last number/incoming call/voice mail;
- disturbances internal/external;
- evidence of search;
- foreign items;
- areas of burning;

- blood patterns;
- tyre marks;
- footwear marks;
- fingerprinting;
- detailed photographs;
- weapon;

BODY

- Death certified;
- coroner's authority for removal;
- prepared for removal;
- photos;
- tapings;
- items;
- clothing;
- temperature;
- bag hands/feet.

SEARCH/EXAMINE

(See the list in **para.4.7** taken from the ACPO Manual of Standard Operating Procedures for Scientific Support Personnel at Major Incident Scenes.)

5.6.4   Initial scene assessment/examination

There will be space for a narrative description, with the date and time.

5.6.5   Plan of premises

This is on squared paper.

5.6.6   Record of actions/requests

- Number;
- action/request;
- time/date;
- complete.

5.6.7   Record of articles removed

- Area/room found;
- article recovered;
- officer finding;

- reference number;
- time found;
- notes/location.

5.6.8   Scene handover document

- Examination completed in agreement with senior investigating officer (SIO);
- signature CSM;
- signature SIO;
- time;
- date;
- location.

5.7   SCIENTIFIC SUPPORT COORDINATOR'S NOTES

- Incident information;
- address/location;
- date and time of examination;
- incident/SOC reference;
- examiner(s) details;
- incident description;
- plans;
- written description;
- completion of matrix (to avoid cross-contamination or loss of potential evidence).

5.8   MAJOR SCENE INCIDENT MATRIX

To avoid contamination of evidence by investigating officers and SOCOs visiting more than one crime scene, this labels different crime scenes (such as house, suspect, victim, vehicle) each label in a separate vertical column down the page and the names of the personnel involved in the investigation (such as SOCO, detective sergeant (DS), detective constable (DC) each in a separate horizontal row across the page. A tick to mark the person's visit to the scene is placed in the box formed by the vertical column and horizontal row

5.9   POST MORTEM EXAMINATION NOTES

Pathologists maintain their own notes and produce the exhibits which they have examined.

CHAPTER 6

The collection, removal and submission of forensic material for examination

In order that physical evidence is reliable and admissible:

- it must be correctly and securely packaged, i.e. in a sealed, referenced container which is appropriate to the character and properties of the item;
- where applicable it must be stored in appropriate ambient conditions;
- continuity must be assured, i.e. that from the moment of initial packing until removal by the scientific support officer or forensic scientist:

   - the item has been held under secure circumstances;
   - no individual has unsealed, removed to inspect or to handle, or caused others to remove or to handle (particularly the suspect) the item in question.

Good practice within forces will be to ensure that:

- there are appropriate and adequate containers, packages and equipment for packaging samples;
- there are adequate procedures for continuity, storage and preservation (including drying) of items;
- there is separation of victim and offender samples.

Documents record every person who has had custody of the evidence from the time it was found at the scene until it is presented in court. The police service and forensic suppliers have procedures to document the chain of custody. It is the individual investigator's duty to make sure these are followed.

The chain of custody must be established. A court will require the progress of an exhibit from the crime scene to its arrival at court to be fully accounted for by provable documentation. The court needs to know the identification of the custodian of evidence at each stage and of that person's awareness of the consequences of deficiency: the need to protect items from deterioration and contamination.

Continuity is fundamental to ensuring the integrity of an item of collected contact trace material (CTM). Integrity means the expectation by the forensic scientist who conducts the analyses that there has been no change, loss or addition, so that the item received is in precisely the same state as when it was collected at the scene (accepting the occurrence of natural physical changes such as desiccation, i.e. that blood dries and semen cracks and powders).

The police, civilian staff and external providers of services, and the prosecution have to demonstrate to the defence and the courts integrity in the process of collecting, recording and handling of physical evidence: that nobody, or nothing, affected, or was allowed to affect, the character of the item from the time of collection to the time of analysis.

6.1　COLLECTION OF EVIDENCE

The person collecting the evidence will initial the evidence or container of the evidence. Containers of evidence are sealed at the scene, labelled and dated. Most items of evidence will be collected in paper containers such as packets, envelopes or bags. They may have see-through windows so that the contents can be looked at without the need for the container to be opened.

Different types of evidence require different containers (e.g. porous containers such as paper bags or cloth bags, non-breakable; leak-proof containers such as glass jars or metal cans for liquids or vapours, crush proof).

Clean paper may be folded to be used to contain trace evidence.

Only large quantities of dry powder should be collected and stored in plastic bags.

If moist or wet evidence (such as blood) is collected in a plastic or paper container to prevent contamination of other evidence, it must be removed within two hours and allowed to completely air dry. Otherwise microorganisms will grow which can destroy or alter evidence.

Biohazard bags will be used as containers for materials that have been exposed to blood or other biological fluids (e.g. mucus, perspiration, saliva, semen, vaginal fluid, urine) that have the potential to be contaminated with viruses

Care is taken to handle the evidence as little as possible.

Items are packaged separately in closed and secured containers to avoid contamination or cross-contamination. Contamination is the unwanted transfer of material from another source to a piece of physical evidence. Cross-contamination is the unwanted transfer of material between two or more sources of physical evidence.

Lids of containers may be sealed or secured with adhesive tape to prevent minute particles from escaping and contaminating other evidence.

Electronically recorded evidence is secured immediately (e.g. answering machine tapes, surveillance camera videotapes, computers).

The Forensic Science Service Evidence Recovery Systems Unit (tel. 01257 224485; fax. 01257 234866) produces a range of evidence recovery items for sale to law enforcement agencies. Reputable commercial suppliers also provide the police with similar or the same equipment. These include:

- a firearms/explosives residue kit designed to collect discharge residues;
- accelerant tins: metal containers for the storage of liquid samples in cases of suspected arson;
- etching kit and electro-etch solution: equipment and chemicals to restore erased serial numbers and other marks from metal surfaces;
- gel footwear and fingerprint lifters for lifting footwear impression and fingerprints;
- footwear/tyre track impression casting kit;
- exhibit boxes;
- exhibit labels;
- poly bags with a printed Criminal Justice Act (CJA) exhibit label on the front;
- tamper-evident drugs evidence bags, uniquely numbered and with a printed exhibit label;
- bags for use in DNA kit submissions;
- tamper-evident swab evidence bags with a printed biohazard symbol, a unique number and a printed integral exhibit label;
- nylon bags for evidence suspected of containing fire accelerants.

6.2   SELECTING ITEMS FOR FORENSIC TESTING

The preparation of the case by the police for the prosecution has a substantial impact on the forensic science process because the police select items to be submitted to the Forensic Science Service (FSS) and other laboratories and supply information about the crime. Items are selected by the investigator for submission for in force testing or analysis by an external forensic supplier where there are prospects of evidence advancing the investigation and the expenditure is warranted. Investigating officers (IOs) should be advised by scenes of crime officers (SOCOs) on this matter. There is a move to keep a tighter control over submissions and in many forces the material is only submitted by and with the agreement of the Scientific Support Department (SSD).

In major crimes a core function of the crime scene manager (CSM)/scientific support manager (SSM) (a senior SOCO) is to advise the senior investigating officer (SIO) on CTM. The situation is more problematic in other offences.

The IO may have a wide range of material available for forensic testing. In each case the IO must answer the following questions:

- Is the probative value of the evidence already available to the investigation sufficient to implicate or eliminate the suspect? Is it anticipated to be so for charging, proceeding or court purposes?
- If the answer to the previous questions is no, and should a forensic examination be positive, will the total amount of evidence then be sufficient, or justify further enquiries?
- Are the costs involved justified in the light of the circumstances and force priorities?

The absence of sound advice, or any advice, to the IO is crucial. Budgetary constraints are a major source of tension, particularly since decisions are devolved in the majority of forces. IOs have to make (or to ask a superior officer to make) cost–benefit decisions as to what will, or will not, be subjected to forensic testing.

IOs must guard against a temptation to test only for corroboration and not for elimination as this creates the real risk of a decision not to submit for in-force testing or external analysis CTM which may well have eliminated a suspect or failed to corroborate suspicions which linked the suspect with the scene.

The IO considering submission of case material for external forensic analysis by the FSS or other provider:

- should always seek the advice of the SOCO, or the FSS or other provider, on the scientific potential of the material in question;
- will need to consult with a supervisor or manager, who will decide whether the proposed analysis, or analyses, of an item represents value for money.

In the case of fingerprints the IO must bear in mind:

- the position of any identified marks for a suspect regarding possible access;
- the suitability of relevant surfaces for retaining friction ridge detail;
- where appropriate, the history of a contact surface concerning ageing of ridge detail;
- the location of unidentified ridge detail which may assist for exclusion purposes;
- that the discovery of unidentified prints at the scene imply eliminator tests, i.e. the prints of officers who attended must be checked, as well as those of individuals who live at or have had access to the scene, in addition to the suspect.

6.2.1 Protocol for the supply by the FSS of forensic science services to the police and the Crown Prosecution Service (CPS)

- The police solely decide to send a particular item for analysis.
- The decision is made as soon as possible.
- The item should then be sent as soon as possible.
- Where there is doubt whether a proposed examination is capable of providing the information required, before any examination is commenced, the officer in the case seeks advice and receives assistance from contacts in the force Scientific Support Department (SSD) or the FSS.
- When submitting an item for examination to the laboratory the police use form MG (Manual of Guidance for the Preparation, Processing and Submission of Files) FSS containing details of surrounding circumstances affecting the case.
- The FSS is given information concerning a custody or other statutory time limit/court direction.
- The police provide the laboratory with any further information, which might be relevant to the examination, which subsequently comes to light.
- Documents and information should be dispatched to the laboratory either with form MG FSS or as soon as possible afterwards.
- The police decide on the priority of any work submitted for examination and mark the form accordingly.
- Not all work in one case requires the same degree of priority: the police should indicate when the results are required for each sub-set of work.
- Jobs are classified as urgent, critical, or standard. The definitions of the two non-standard categories are:

  - urgent: required to assist police in their investigation – delivery date and time to be agreed; critical: to be delivered in advance of a specified court date; standard: according to FSS turnaround times – to be notified and updated.
  - critical: youth offenders, adults remanded (or likely to be remanded) in custody, sexual abuse/violence towards children cases, child witnesses, and other cases where there is a risk of the case being stayed by court if results not given by specified date.

N.B. In practice scientists often advise by telephone or at case conferences.

The MG FSS only requires listing of those items submitted for analysis, not all those collected or seized by the police.

6.3   CONTAMINATION

An example of how evidence can become contaminated is packaging being opened by investigators wishing to examine the item or to show it to a suspect in interview as 'persuasive evidence', e.g. a police officer had two items of clothing out on her desk, one after the other. This provided an opportunity for contamination of the second item, belonging to the suspect, by fibres from the first, belonging to the victim. To avoid this happening, SSDs invest in paper packets, bags or envelopes with a see-through window.

If it is necessary to open a package to examine the exhibit, the examination should be conducted by a SOCO and the package resealed before being returned to the store. The statement form should refer to this process and the forensic science laboratory informed if the item is sent there for examination.

Other examples of how, despite training, evidence may be contaminated are:

- the placing of a hand or finger inside an exhibit bag;
- blood or semen is inadvertently transferred to other surfaces of an item, e.g. by folding items without separating the surfaces, so that the surfaces contact each other;
- a suspect being placed in a cell used by another suspect and sharing the cell blanket;
- a police officer having contact with both the victim and a suspect;
- a suspect being placed in the same vehicle which had transported the victim;
- shaking or disturbing an item of clothing which is not on its own;
- poking a finger through a stab or bullet hole in a given item or surface;
- scraping of a body part, clothing or item across a bloodstain;
- removing debris;
- more than one item being placed in one bag;
- insecure packaging, e.g. use of staples instead of adhesive tape;
- the first officer attending (FOA) coming into contact with both the victim and the suspect cross-contaminating the two, e.g. attending to the victim then arresting the suspect; arresting the suspect and then attending to the victim;
- the FOA failing to ensure that the same vehicle does not transport the victim and the suspect at different times;
- the same forensic examiner inspecting items from the suspect and the victim without decontamination in between;
- the same room in a laboratory being used to inspect items from the suspect and the victim without cleaning in between. Where possible, laboratories will keep separate rooms for suspect and victim material inspections;
- the same tools, such as a fibre collection kit, being used to collect trace evidence from the suspect and the victim.

There is no requirement for an IO to submit samples immediately for analysis. This could potentially create a situation where a sample is left in a refrigerator for so long that meaningful analysis cannot be, and is not, performed.

Detailed arrangements for the retention of case material by the FSS are set out in a Memorandum of Understanding on the Retention of Case Material agreed between the Association of Chief Police Officers (ACPO) and the FSS (referred to in the joint operating instructions (JOPI 2003, Annex I, 6.1).

The FSS in its Code of Practice requires staff to ensure that the integrity of items submitted to them is not compromised by contamination. Her Majesty's Inspectorate of Constabulary (HMIC) found that because of incorrect form filling by the sampling officer, criminal justice (CJ) bags were left unsealed to allow force DNA units to rectify errors prior to dispatch to the laboratories. HMIC commented that this raised issues concerning the integrity of the samples.

When inspecting the DNA units, HMIC found:

- lack of formal training for most staff;
- little evidence of written guidance or policies for staff reference;
- poor monitoring of error rates;
- little performance management information;
- administrative errors not rectified;
- inadequate dispatch or delivery service security arrangements;
- inadequate storage of samples.

Low copy number DNA (LCN DNA) profiles allow identification of a suspect from a minute amount of DNA. The latest technique using minute amounts of DNA is FSS SGM (second generation multiplex) Plus. Such minute amounts of material may be unreliable as evidence because:

- the swabbing of a complete surface for DNA, such as a steering wheel, produces a mixed profile and a situation where material is mixed with other material, so that the result is not sufficiently discriminating to produce an identification which is of evidential value;
- it is entirely possible for minute amounts of DNA to be transferred quite innocently:
  - from an individual to one or more people, e.g. by a sneeze, and for any one of these to transfer this DNA to a crime scene surface, be that an inanimate object or person;
  - from a suspect to a crime scene surface if measures have not been taken to ensure that contamination by the suspect does not occur after the offence.

CHAPTER 7

The forensic scientist

7.1 WHAT DOES AN EXPERT DO?

1. Educate: explain the situation to help the investigator or lawyer to understand the potential evidence and the alternatives available.
2. Evaluate: determine the significance of potential evidence in the circumstances of the case.
3. Test: conduct tests of items of potential evidence.
4. Experiment: conduct a series of experiments to prove or disprove a point.
5. Gather evidence: to help the party to build their case.
6. Other experts: locate and recruit other experts.
7. Report: provide a report of their findings.
8. Demonstrative evidence: produce material which helps to demonstrate or explain matters, such as maps, models and computer simulations.
9. Testify: give evidence about their findings and/or interpretation of other evidence.

7.2 WHAT QUALITIES DOES A LAWYER LOOK FOR IN AN EXPERT?

1. Compatibility: so that they get on with their professional client.
2. Presentation skills: so that they can explain their subject in an accessible and attractive way.
3. Education, degrees, training, publications and teaching: so that they not only meet the requirements of the task but are seen to be the equal of an expert instructed by the other party.
4. Specific knowledge: knowing enough already about the field in which they are instructed.
5. Practical experience: sufficient 'on the job' actual experience as well as the requisite academic qualifications and training.
6. Balance: being seen to be able to approach the task from either party's point of view.
7. Experience: being an experienced expert witness.

7.3 FORENSIC SCIENCE PROVIDERS

There are three suppliers of 'mainstream' forensic science services to the police. FSS provides comprehensive services and has about an 86 per cent of the total forensic science market. Forensic Alliance Ltd also provides comprehensive services with an 8 per cent market share. Most of the remaining share is provided by LGC Ltd (formerly the Laboratory of the Government Chemist), working in specific fields of DNA, toxicology, drugs and documents.

7.3.1 The Forensic Science Service (FSS)

The FSS provides a national service to the 43 police forces of England and Wales, the Crown Prosecution Service (CPS), Her Majesty's Customs and Excise, the Criminal Cases Review Commission (CCRC) and other agencies. It also provides services to the defence. In 2002–2003 its total income was £160 million, over 90 per cent of this derived from work for police forces.

Its stated vision in its 2001–2002 Annual Report is 'to realise the full potential of forensic science to contribute to a safer and more just society'. Its mission is 'to provide impartial forensic science services in support of the investigation and detection of crimes, the prosecution of offenders and the prevention, deterrence and reduction of crime'.

The FSS is based around the country:

London Forensic Science Laboratory	tel. 020 7230 6700
	fax 020 7230 6253
Birmingham Operations	tel. 0121 607 6800
	fax 0121 666 7327
Chepstow Laboratory	tel. 01291 637100
	fax 01291 629482
Chorley Laboratory	tel. 01257 265666
	fax 01257 274752
Huntingdon Laboratory	tel. 01480 450071
	fax 01480 450079
Wetherby Laboratory	tel. 01937 548100
	fax 01937 587683

General services are provided locally, with specialist expertise, such as firearms, questioned documents and Low Copy Number (LCN) DNA concentrated in particular laboratories.

The FSS has an agreement with the Association of Chief Police Officers (ACPO) that it will remain the principal supplier of forensic science services to the police. The police are classed by the FSS as a 'key strategic partner'. It is argued by those who support that position that access to the core volume business of the police forces gives the FSS the capacity to undertake research and development. This also ensures that the FSS does not turn any police work away and is able to carry out the labour intensive and less profitable work that other forensic suppliers choose not to do. Critics of this near monopoly complain that as a result of this agreement with ACPO, market forces cannot operate to provide strong competition and achieve best value for customers. They point to the fact that limited research work, other than into DNA, is carried out in FSS laboratories. In 2001–2002 its spend on scientific research was only £3 million, 2.5 per cent of its turnover, a very small investment for a science-based organisation.

The FSS charges for its services on an item-by-item, case-by-case or contract basis. Direct charging by the FSS sparked the development of a forensic science market which provides the competition to the FSS. Police do now shop around for forensic science services. In addition to their main competitors, Forensic Alliance and LGC Ltd (formerly the Laboratory of the Government Chemist), the Defence and Evaluation Research Agency specialises in explosives and there are also services provided by university departments, public analysts and private practitioners.

A major review of the FSS was completed in 2003, culminating in an announcement by the government that a decision had been made in principle to float the FSS as a public/private partnership. The future custodianship of the National DNA Database (NDNAD) is still to be decided at the time of writing.

The perception of the FSS by its customers is of an organisation which has adequately trained and qualified staff and which provides a service which consistently meets the required quality standard. That is very important when an error could cost a person their liberty. Although it is regarded as meeting timeliness requirements in major crime investigations it does not do so in cases of volume crime and there is some doubt about the extent to which it gives value for money. Police use non-FSS suppliers to challenge the FSS on cost and service.

FSS target turnaround times are:

Priority cases

Urgent	delivery date as agreed
Critical	42 days
Persistent young offenders	21 days

Non-priority cases

Drugs	35 days
Crime scene samples	14 days
DNA match confirmation	14 days

Attempts by the police to reduce the cost of forensic evidence lead to more forensic science analysis being conducted in-house. This brings a risk of the police sacrificing quality for cost and independence and less well-trained scientists undercutting the FSS and the independent sector.

7.4 TESTING MATERIALS IN FORCE

The Home Office recommended that forces should take on more testing in-force in order:

- to reduce the workload of forensic laboratories;
- to extend the scientific support officer's role;
- to obtain quick results for the police;
- to sift cases in-force so that only essential items are submitted to laboratories for analysis.

The range of testing should include presumptive testing of blood and of drugs. There must be adequate, specified arrangements for quality and performance control.

In-force testing should be subject to the same quality control procedures which should apply to an external forensic supplier (see below). An in-force laboratory may carry out basic screening for blood and semen. The laboratory will examine items for the presence of either of these. If the result is positive, the item will be sent to an external laboratory for further examination. The external laboratory later produces a report for the police, and in turn CPS, and a statement for court. This process saves the expense of having the external laboratory examine a number of items which do not contain a blood or semen stain. If the item has fragments of glass or fibres, the in-house laboratory will send it straight to the external laboratory so as not to disturb these. If the item has the appearance of being free of such particles, the in house laboratory will carry out the examination of it on a sheet of brown paper so that any debris from an item yielding a stain is retained.

A significant advantage of having an in-house laboratory carry out this work is that the officer can be told if blood or semen is present very soon after delivering the item for examination. If fingerprints are apparent from dusting a surface and do not need to be developed, the in-house fingerprint bureau can tell the officer equally quickly whether they match the suspect's prints. This information can then be put to the suspect in interview.

In a number of forces there is a tendency to take a positive presumptive test as fact and not to send it for external testing. This can lead to a case being built upon wholly mistaken evidence. If a presumptive test produces a positive result, the item should be sent to an external forensic scientist for secondary testing to confirm or disconfirm the result.

ACPO and the FSS have acknowledged that in addition to the inadequacy or absence of quality control of in force testing there were disadvantages to in force examination that are not readily identified:

- it may provide evidence which may be subject to attack in court due to lack of impartiality and deficiencies in scientific standards;

- when done incautiously, particularly for blood, it has the potential to destroy evidence.

7.5 QUALITY CONTROL OF THE FORENSIC SCIENTIST'S PERFORMANCE

All external forensic suppliers should have:

- the necessary level of expertise and experience to undertake the requested analyses;
- quality control and quality assurance procedures for the forensic analyses and the reporting of their scientists.

The laboratory should be regulated and accredited in respect of its fulfilment of quality criteria.

The United Kingdom Accreditation Service (UKAS) is recognised by the government for the National Accreditation of Measurements And Sampling (NAMAS). UKAS independently assesses and accredits calibration and testing laboratories to the NAMAS Accreditation Standard M10 and the NAMAS Regulation M11. Accreditation in accordance with this means that a laboratory meets the European Standard EN45001 and the International Standard ISO/IEC Guide 25. UKAS accredits for objective tests, i.e. one which having been documented and validated is under control so that it can be demonstrated that an appropriately trained staff member will obtain the same result within defined limits.

All the procedures and methods used by the scientist should be fully documented. Forensic science laboratories should normally have a comprehensive system detailing procedures to be followed and methods to be used.

Good practices specified by *Using Forensic Science Effectively* for the examination of items within the supplier's laboratory are:

- quality control procedures should be implemented, which include the routine testing of operators and equipment, with records kept;
- specific checks should be made by team leaders of the interpretation and quality of the statement;
- critical observations, i.e. unrepeatable or qualitative observations, should be confirmed in writing;
- there should be a handbook of authorised procedures and authorised operators, to be revised periodically;
- each research officer and assistant should have a personal competence record, based on assessment, authorising them to undertake work activities;
- there should be a clear record of actions requested of, and supervision of, assistants;

- the research officer's statement should deal with the manner in which tests were conducted and the use of assistants;
- a disclosable schedule should be kept which should include the name of the person who conducted each test referred to in the statement and whether an assistant performed some or all of the tests under the research officer's supervision;
- the databases and research necessary to allow interpretations of results should be subject to the same quality control procedures as other instruments and procedures;
- there should be a formal system of quality assurance, i.e. the testing of the whole system by blind and declared trials.

The forensic scientist should record every action undertaken by themselves and by every assistant or other person working on their behalf. This includes:

- telephone calls and written correspondence between the scientist and the party he/she is working for;
- lists of items for examination;
- any material gathered or generated in connection with the forensic examination;
- statements from witnesses;
- invoices;
- requests for attendance at court;
- notes to assistants or other colleagues about work being carried out;
- any information obtained in connection with the forensic examination whether this points towards or away from the suspect;
- all examinations carried out and tests undertaken, together with the results of any tests or calculations, whether positive or negative, and the interpretation of the results;
- any information generated during the course of the examination that might have an impact on the investigation;
- all fingermarks and any lifts or photographic negatives retained as the result of an exhibit having been examined;
- a fingermark which is determined to be of insufficient value to determine identity;
- the identity of the person eliminated from the enquiry where a fingermark is identified as belonging to a person having legitimate access;
- drafts of the final report;
- copies of the final report.

Significant decisions should be confirmed by a colleague to reduce error.

7.6   THE FORENSIC SCIENTIST'S REPORT

In the vast majority of cases the forensic scientist does not attend court and the prosecution rely upon their report. A forensic scientist should produce a witness statement which:

- contains the name and address of the scientist who compiled it and of the laboratory where the work was done;
- sets out the scientist's qualifications;
- lists the names of colleagues who undertook work and indicates the work they carried out;
- outlines the background of the case – as reported to the scientist;
- notes the questions posed by those commissioning the analyses;
- indicates which questions could not be answered;
- lists the exhibits examined and from whom they were obtained (so that the chain of continuity is maintained);
- gives an explanation of the tests undertaken;
- gives the results of the tests – frequently referring to the probability of matches examined in the light of statistical data and reported norms/ tabulated data;
- gives an opinion in the context of the circumstances as presented to the scientist as to:
  - the meaning of the results in terms of the questions posed;
  - the strength of the evidence – particularly that a given individual was somewhere or did something because of the co-presence of trace materials (with known distributions) and other circumstantial evidence.

The copy served upon the defence must be accurate, i.e. a photocopy of the original or an error-free print-out from the Home Office large major enquiry system (HOLMES).

REFERENCE

ACPO & FSS (1996) *Using Forensic Science Effectively*.

CHAPTER 8

The forensic scientist working for the prosecution

As well as access to the Forensic Science Service (FSS), Forensic Alliance, and the LGC (see **para 6.1**) the police service maintain a national register of specialists and also recommend reference to the Council for the Registration of Forensic Practitioners (CRFP) register. In addition, the National Crime and Operations Faculty (NCOF) run a 24-hour help desk and a senior officers investigation support service with regionally based liaison officers.

8.1   THE EXTERNAL FORENSIC SUPPLIER

In the case of submissions for analysis by an external forensic provider, the MG (Manual of Guidance for the Preparation, Processing and Submission of Files) FSS form must be submitted (see **Chapters 5** and **6** on documentation and submission of forensic evidence).

Police should provide external forensic suppliers with:

- full background information on the case – particularly witness statements providing accounts of what happened, when and how;
- items selected for analysis by the supplier – with a view to throwing light on the case;
- a list of all other items collected which might be analysed;
- questions which, it is hoped, forensic analysis will resolve.

The logic for such full communication is that the value of any item of contact trace material (CTM) depends upon the individual circumstances of the case. It enables the forensic scientist to choose and to plan the analyses appropriately and to consider alternative possible explanations for the findings.

The *Using Forensic Science Effectively* (UFSE) report identified the following criticisms by forensic suppliers:

- inappropriately formulated questions – some of which cannot be answered by forensic examination;
- bare minimum information;
- inappropriate or inadequate range or form of items for examination;

- the absence of a full list of items retrieved – which would provide information to allow advice on further tests of items which have not been submitted.

Given that there is insufficient understanding of what reasonably can be expected from various scientific procedures, it is not surprising that:

- police users are often not in a position to determine in advance the usefulness of analyses conducted by a forensic scientist;
- they ask inappropriate questions.

In respect of information provision, the more serious the case the more information is typically provided to the supplier. Much less information is given in low level seriousness or volume crimes.

Research found that witness statements were supplied in 37 per cent of serious and five per cent of volume crime cases. Based on these figures, in two-thirds of the serious cases sampled, forensic scientists were completely in the dark concerning the content of key witness accounts. But those we spoke to were used as a matter of routine to at least receiving the victim's statement.

8.2 THE ANALYSES UNDERTAKEN BY THE EXTERNAL FORENSIC SUPPLIER

The forensic scientist should examine items which are likely to throw light on:

- the questions posed by the police;
- other issues relevant to the case and the investigation.

The forensic scientist must be intellectually independent and scientifically objective. Some suppliers examine almost all, if not all, materials submitted for analysis. Some fail to assess or to indicate whether additional forensic analyses might be useful or are essential to the enquiry.

8.3 SELECTIVE SUPPLY OF INFORMATION AND MATERIAL BY THE POLICE

The police investigator, having decided what the scientist can do to assist the case, will not supply information to the scientist which the police investigator considers is not relevant to the enquiry which they want the scientist to conduct. And the scientist is not told what the police are holding back.

The police investigator has 'pigeonholed' the forensic scientist's contribution. The forensic scientist may chase more information and, depending upon the particular force, receive it from the police investigator, such as the victim's statement, the suspect's interview, or the defence statement.

8.4 COMMUNICATION BETWEEN THE FORENSIC SCIENTIST AND THE INVESTIGATING OFFICER (IO)

All forensic scientists are involved in providing evidence to help establish whether, and by whom, a crime has been committed, and information to help future investigations. They should interpret their findings, taking account of the circumstances of each case, to show how far they support alternative theories.

The forensic scientist should communicate verbally with the IO in respect of the detail, the outcome and the implications of requested analyses. Such conversations should take place both prior to and following the production of the scientist's statement.

The forensic scientist and the IO should make a record of the exchange – in the case of the officer this should be as a formal note, e.g. in a pocket book or a formal report, although a request to the police officer and the forensic scientist to disclose the content of their record of communication could well be expected to present individuals with some difficulties.

Seven years ago, in 1996, Tilley and Ford found that the forensic scientists had direct contact with the investigating officer in 44 per cent of the serious crime cases and 37 per cent of the volume crime cases. In other words, in over half the serious cases there was no dialogue between the forensic scientist and the officer in the case. This statistic surprised those we spoke to, who would expect a scenes of crime officer (SOCO) or forensic scientist to attend every police briefing, with the crime scene manager (CSM) or crime scene coordinator (CSC) making sure of this. The senior investigating officer (SIO) would normally wish to have forensic experts present to ensure that they are making the right decisions.

In an average case, the police investigator and the SOCO may spend 10 to 15 minutes at the outset in discussion with the scientist. But the scientist is often not given a picture of the case as it develops e.g. a knowledge of the defence case such as the defence case statement; and what the suspect said during interrogation. The fact that most communication, if at all, takes place towards the beginning of the case, means that the forensic scientist is reaching conclusions without the benefit of all the information which is available.

In contrast, when the defence instruct the scientist there is usually more personal contact between customer and scientist and more information about the case is supplied to the scientist.

There should always be an open mind about the possible lack of objectivity of a forensic scientist. At the time when the Court of Appeal was faced with a string of miscarriages of justice cases a decade ago, the reality then – which could apply now – was aptly described by Glidewell LJ giving the judgment of the court in *R.* v. *Ward* (1993) 96 Cr App R at 51:

For lawyers, jurors and judges a forensic scientist conjures up the image of a man in a white coat working in a laboratory, approaching his task with cold neutrality, and dedicated only to the pursuit of scientific truth. It is a sombre thought that the reality is sometimes different. Forensic scientists may become partisan. The very fact that the police seek their assistance may create a relationship between the police and the forensic scientists. And the adversarial nature of the proceedings tends to promote this process. Forensic scientists employed by the government may come to see their function as helping the police. They may lose their objectivity.

The Association of Chief Police Officers (ACPO) and the FSS have stated that the forensic scientist should be treated as a member of the investigative team. The scientist's professionalism is the guarantee that their findings are not compromised by their involvement in the process.

In the early stages of a serious crime enquiry the forensic scientist may be called upon to be the scientific adviser to the IO or SIO. It is one former Home Office forensic scientist's view that it is psychologically difficult, if not impossible, having tested the items collected and selected for analysis and been intimately involved in the case for the same scientist to then destroy the effect of those analyses, their outcome, and the scientist's opinion by proposing a contrary view. This is effectively 'expecting the hound who has just caught the hare to set to with a will to give it the kiss of life' (Stockdale, R., 'Running with the Hounds', *New Law Journal*, 7 June 1991).

The prosecution scientist has to resist the drive to look for supporting rather than contradictory evidence, and to regard evidence of better quality if it confirms their hypothesis. In an article 'Crime and the Flawed Expert' (*New Law Journal Expert Witness Supplement*, 28 February 2003), B. Mahendra writes about 'a new trend discernible amongst some doctors . . . to reflect personal crusades undertaken on behalf of some belief, the emphasis then being on driving some personal agenda rather than offering dispassionate diagnosis, treatment or opinion'.

Lord Justice Auld in his 'Review of the Criminal Courts' said: 'a forensic practitioner's overriding duty is to the court and the administration of justice and his findings and evidence must be presented fairly and impartially'.

At the conference 'Justice for All', Lord Falconer, Home Office Minister, said:

Experts must remain impartial even though they may be called upon to operate within an adversarial framework. It is not their role to win the case for a particular party, but rather to assist the court with objective evidence. It means acknowledging that there may be other possibilities, and being open when a conclusion is wrong or where technical errors have occurred . . ..

. . . If an expert has carried out experiments or tests which tend to disprove or cast doubt on his initial opinions, he or she is under a clear obligation to bring those results to the attention of the police or the prosecutors who are instructing him or her. Similarly, if an employer or regulating body becomes aware that an individual expert witness cannot be relied upon, they then have an obligation to disclose that to the police, prosecuting authorities and defence teams.

The prosecution scientist's objectivity and expertise may be difficult to review because a crime scene cannot be preserved. Some tests may completely destroy the exhibit so that it cannot be tested further by the defence.

But a defence or prosecution expert may be motivationally biased and show party allegiance. Either party can bias their experts during the pre-trial preparation and the defence are able to choose experts who best suit their case and, where the money is available, 'expert shop' by seeking opinions from one expert after another until a favourable one is found.

The FSS Code of Practice requires staff to be impartial by:

- being objective when considering items of evidence for examination;
- ensuring that conclusions based on these examinations are sound;
- ensuring that when opinions are given, reasonable possible alternatives are advanced, depending upon the information supplied.

It also requires staff to:

- report all relevant findings in advice and reports;
- comment on the strength of the evidence and any limitations.

Dr Ian Evett, consultant to the Chief Scientist at the FSS, told the 'Justice for All' conference that the classical view was that scientists from government laboratories provided evidence only from the prosecution perspective. The scientist would consider the defence case only to anticipate hostile cross-examination and how to deal with it. This has been replaced by the realisation that the scientist must also consider the probability of the evidence from the defence perspective and calculate the ratio of these determiners. If the probability of evidence from the prosecution perspective (if the prosecution case is right, what is the probability that I would have found that evidence?) is greater than that from the defence perspective, then the scientific evidence supports the prosecution case. If the opposite, then the scientific evidence supports the defence case instead.

Forensic practitioners registered with CRFP are obliged to adhere to its Code of Conduct (see **Appendix 3**) which requires findings and evidence to be presented in a fair and impartial manner.

REFERENCES

ACPO & FSS (1996) *Using Forensic Science Effectively*.

Ede, R. & Shepherd, E. (2000) *Active Defence*, 2nd edition, Law Society Publishing.

Mahendra, B. (2003) 'Crime and the Flawed Expert', *New Law Journal – Expert Witness Supplement*, 28 February.

Redmayne, M. (2001) Expert Evidence and Criminal Justice, Oxford University Press.

Stockdale, R. (1991) 'Running with the Hounds', *New Law Journal*, 7 June.

CHAPTER 9

The forensic scientist working for the defence

9.1 DEFENCE FORENSIC INVESTIGATION

No witness statement should be assumed to be incontrovertible fact, beyond challenge or question, and totally accurate simply because:

- it comes from a laboratory;
- it has been produced by a scientist;
- it is expressed in emphatic terms;
- it creates the impression of precision and irrefutability;
- the witness is prestigious.

Contrary to some popular beliefs, science is a highly uncertain endeavour:

- It does not deal in certainties, but probabilities.
- Expert evidence depends upon concurrence between scientists which may not last.
- Experts may disagree about the interpretation to be placed on agreed findings of fact.

Dr Christopher Hobbs, a consultant paediatrician, speaking at the 'Justice for All' conference, gave examples of how science can change with the publication of new research. Anal reflex dilation was previously regarded by paediatricians as the definitive test of sex abuse in children. But a later study showed that it was, in fact, common amongst normal children who had not been abused. Paediatricians thought that it was possible to determine the age of a bruise from its colour. Now it is accepted that colouring is unpredictable and that other factors besides age contribute to the colouring of a bruise.

In some cases the prosecution expert may be persuaded to revise his or her initial opinions, either because of new information or because the defence expert is able to spot the significance of some factor which the prosecution scientist has overlooked. Similarly, the evidence of a forensic physician, a clinician who examined or attended the victim or your client, or a forensic pathologist, are also open to question.

- No forensic analysis should be accepted without independent verification.
- The quality of work of individual scientists cannot always be assured.

Research for the Royal Commission on Criminal Justice 1993 (RCCJ) (Zander, M. and Henderson, P. (1992) *The Crown Court Study, – RCCJ Research Study No. 19*, HMSO) found that, in three out of four cases, scientific evidence went unchallenged and that over a half of those challenges were by cross-examination only. This is despite the fact that:

- the methodology used may be inappropriate;
- data handling and reporting may be erroneous;
- the scientist may lose sight of the context when asserting probability;
- opinions may be unfounded.

The value of the defence forensic work is illustrated by the fact that, in another research study for the RCCJ (Steventon, B. (1992) *The Ability to Challenge DNA Evidence*, RCCJ Research Study No. 9: HMSO) 43 per cent of defence experts who provided an independent analysis of the evidence stated that their conclusions differed from those of the prosecution's expert. Of defence lawyers who consulted an expert, 94 per cent felt that they had been assisted by that expert, either in the evaluation of the case and the advice they gave the client or in presenting the case in court.

Instances occur where the report has been entered into the Home Office large major enquiry system (HOLMES) database and errors have been introduced by the indexer inputting the data. Hence the printout provided to the defence gives a false picture in respect of the erroneous detail.

Research for the RCCJ (Roberts, P. and Wilmore, C. (1992) *The Role of Forensic Science Evidence in Criminal Proceedings*, RCCJ Research Study No. 11, HMSO) found that reports written on behalf of the prosecution could be highly selective documents in which the uncertainties and limitations of forensic science evidence are not always revealed. Selectivity was also encouraged by a belief that it is for the defence to draw out the limitations of prosecution evidence – an example of the way in which scientists adopt an adversarial approach. There were instances where the prosecution scientist simply stated his/her findings without any attempt to highlight their deficiencies or draw appropriate inferences from them. A report may, as a result, have been misinterpreted as providing much stronger evidence of the defendant's involvement than it actually did. Since then, increased disclosure to the defence has reduced the likelihood of this happening.

The reason for the low level of defence forensic activity may be the perception that the prosecution case may be difficult to challenge:

- the defence may lack financial resources;
- the availability of forensic science evidence to the defence is dependent on their being able to afford to have the necessary work expertly carried out within the time frame of the court proceedings. The defence do not have

the collective financial resources or muscle of the police and the prosecution, and are at a disadvantage within the adversarial system, which assumes a level playing field, as a result;

- the conduct of, and the reasoning behind, the crime scene investigation and selection of materials for forensic examination may not be apparent and available for scrutiny;
- the defence may be limited to checking the prosecution scientist's work. A scientist working for the defence seldom examines items which are in the same condition as they were when they were examined by the prosecution scientist (who is likely to have seen the item in its original condition). Steventon reported that estimates from the Forensic Science Service (FSS) suggested that this would occur in 65 per cent to 70 per cent of cases after the prosecution have carried out DNA profiling on a sample. The defence will often need to work from information and results provide by the prosecution scientist. The defence scientist's focus is on assessing the way in which the initial examination took place and involves a detailed scrutiny of the procedures followed. The conclusions which the defence scientist can draw are limited to that extent.

The difficulties which the defence solicitor faces when the prosecution discloses the existence of DNA evidence are similar to the problems which occur in relation to much forensic evidence. They were summarised in Steventon's research:

- lack of pre-trial notice of the existence of DNA evidence;
- it may take a considerable time for the defence to locate a suitable expert – DNA profiling is a highly specialised technique and there are relatively few experts outside the FSS who are experienced in this field;
- work is delayed whilst the defence apply for legal aid prior authority to instruct the expert;
- the number of experts is small and their workloads high; it may be several weeks before the defence expert is able to visit the prosecution laboratory to examine the results;
- there may be insufficient crime stain remaining for the defence expert to conduct an independent laboratory analysis.

Roberts and Wilmore's research (1992) for the RCCJ predicted that defence solicitors would find their choice of defence expert becoming even more limited. The experience of many defence lawyers is that this has happened.

9.2 QUESTIONING EVIDENCE

What is the defence looking for?

9.2.1 Potential contamination of evidence

Contamination is the addition, changing, relocation, removal, obscuring or obliteration of evidence or evidence patterns, or the relative position of items of evidence. Physical evidence may have been altered prior to or during its collection and examination. It may have been inadvertently transferred between objects or people subsequent to the original exchange and not associated with the circumstances that produced the original exchange. Where this is exposed it may lead to an alternative interpretation of the evidence.

Possible agents are:

- the actions of the victim before or after the crime: which may add, transfer or obliterate evidence, for example by clearing/cleaning up;
- witnesses present at the scene: who may steal or move things or try to help the victim;
- the weather: which may obliterate evidence;
- decomposition: which can obscure or obliterate evidence of injury;
- insect activity: which can remove or destroy transfer evidence or obliterate an injury;
- animal activity: which can move evidence and obliterate patterns;
- fire: which can destroy evidence;
- fire fighting and medical emergencies: which can move evidence, obliterate patterns and transfer evidence;
- firefighters and emergency medical personnel, police officers, forensic scientists and scene examiners: who can move evidence, obliterate patterns and transfer evidence.

Possible contamination scenarios

- The first officer attending (FOA) at the crime scene who picks up material from there and uses the same police car to transport the suspect to the police station: possible contamination car/officer to suspect.
- The FOA who visits the crime scene has other contact with the suspect at the police station when the suspect is searched or examined: possible contamination officer to suspect.
- The crime scene examiner who also examines the suspect at the police station: possible contamination crime scene examiner to suspect.
- The investigating officer (IO) who visits the crime scene and then has contact with the suspect before the suspect is searched or examined: possible contamination officer to suspect.
- The investigating officer who visits the crime scene after having had contact with the suspect but before all the evidence has been removed from the crime scene: possible contamination suspect to officer to crime scene.

Some further examples are given from their own files by W. Jerry Chisum and Brent E. Turvey in an article 'Evidence dynamics: Locard's Exchange Principle and Crime Reconstruction' in the *Journal of Behavioural Profiling*, vol. 1, no. 1 (**www.profiling.org/journal/vol1_no1/jbp_ed_january2000_1-1**).

Example 3: Secondary transfer and scene technicians

The body of an adolescent female was found on a couch in her home. Cause of death was manual strangulation. The DNA of one of her mother's lovers was found on her perineum in the form of sperm.

The suspect and the victim's mother had sexual relations in the mother's bed, where the victim had been playing previously with her brother. There were also reports that the suspect and the victim's mother may have had sexual relations on the couch, where the victim would have been sitting. A review of the crime scene video showed several evidence technicians moving evidence around on the couch and other locations and then touching the victim's body in multiple locations, examining her body as it is being photographed, with and without gloves.

Given the circumstances and the victim's history, the following are potential evidence transfers:

(1) from the suspect to the victim during a forced sexual assault;
(2) from the suspect to the victim during a consensual (but unlawful) sexual encounter;
(3) from the couch to the victim's perineum;
(4) from the mother's bed to the victim's perineum;
(5) from the scene technician's fingers to the victim's perineum.

[...]

Example [...]: [secondary transfer by a witness at the scene]

An offender wearing a wool sweater kills a female in her home. The offender leaves a number of wool fibres behind on the victim's body. The victim's neighbour hears the struggle and discovers the body. While attempting to revive the victim, several of the wool fibres transfer onto his clothing. When the clothing of the victim and the neighbour are examined in the laboratory, wool fibres foreign to the location are found on both their clothing, causing investigators to suspect him of the crime.

[...]

Example 6: victim activities

A woman had sexual relations with her boyfriend in his vehicle. He dropped her off at her home. When she entered the bedroom she surprised a burglar. In the struggle, her clothes were torn before the burglar strangled her and fled. The boyfriend's DNA was found in her vagina and he was suspected of having raped and murdered her. Fortunately he had a cast iron alibi.

9.2.2 Other areas of enquiry

These are:

- potential forensic evidence which the police have not obtained;
- potential forensic evidence which the police have chosen not to send for analysis;
- a prosecution scientist whose procedures are questionable, whose analysis is incorrect, or whose opinion is mistaken;
- a different interpretation of the significance of the evidence (or lack of it) such as the commoness or rarity of certain types of CTM;

  The defence may be able to counter the prosecution case by proposing an alternative explanation. The area that a defence forensic scientist is likely to make most ground in is the interpretation of the evidence in the context of the facts of the case rather than faulting the identification of the sample or its comparison with another exhibit.

  The prosecution scientist works from information supplied by the police; the defence scientist also has the defendant's instructions, which may put the prosecution scientist's findings in a different light.

- absence of forensic evidence which would be expected to be present shortly after the offence may also be of significance; a careful scene search that uncovers no trace evidence linking the defendant to the scene could be exculpatory evidence.

  Dr Angela Gallop of Forensic Alliance provides an instance of this. A woman alleged that she had been raped by a taxi driver. He admitted getting into the back of the taxi cab with her and kissing her, but denied assaulting her. There were no semen traces and she said that he had not ejaculated. The defence forensic scientist was able to satisfy the court that it was inconceivable that he could have behaved as she alleged without fibres being transferred from her woolly skirt to his underclothes (but see further about transfer and persistence of fibres in **Chapter 16**).

- evidence presented in isolation: if all the forensic evidence obtained was presented together a different interpretation could be placed on it;
- a selective prosecution scientist's report;
- it will not always be obvious from the prosecution forensic scientist's written statement what the strengths and weaknesses of the evidence are. There is a danger that if the prosecution forensic scientist gives oral evidence he or she will strengthen the evidence contained in the witness statement by commenting on the significance of the findings. FSS scientists will have looked at very many scenes of crimes and exhibits and acquired a 'feel' for what they would expect to see following any given crime. A forensic scientist instructed by the defence should be able to warn of any such risk in advance, and how to counter it in cross-examination.

9.3 PUBLIC FUNDING

A defence investigation must be focused: the defence should know what the purpose of it is.

There should be a reasonable chance of the defence investigation succeeding, i.e. it should be more likely than not that the defence investigation will produce something of significance for the defence in the case. The defence have to justify to the Legal Services Commission (LSC) the logic of their investigation.

The defence must keep full records. At the time when the defence make the decision to carry out the further investigation, they should record:

- the information available to them at the time;
- the reason why they consider that the investigation should be carried out.

In hindsight, the defence should be judged by the reasonableness of their decision to undertake the investigation at the time when they made that decision:

> Reasonableness of undertaking work – solicitor's knowledge at the time 'When considering whether or not an item in a bill is reasonable, the correct approach is to consider whether it was reasonable for the solicitor, in the light of his knowledge at the time when the work was done, to undertake the work.': Legal Aid Board ref. CRIMLA 38.

9.3.1 Obtaining prior authority

EXTENSION OF ORDER

If an expert's report is required the defence should consider applying to the LSC for prior authority on Form CDS4 for the magistrates' court and for the Crown Court by way of extension of the Representation Order. Applications are processed by the LSC in accordance with contract specification Part B, r.5.2 which states:

(1) Where you consider it necessary for the proper conduct of criminal proceedings for costs to be incurred under a Representation Order by taking any of the following steps.

    (a) obtaining a written report or opinion of one or more experts;

    (b) employing a person to provide a written report or opinion (otherwise than as an expert);

    (c) obtaining transcripts of tape recordings of any proceedings, including police questioning of suspects;

    (d) where a legal aid order provides for the service of solicitor and counsel, instructing a Queen's Counsel alone without a junior counsel; or

(e)   performing an act which is either unusual in its nature or involves unusually large expenditure;

you may apply to the Regional Director before the expenditure is incurred.

(2)   An appeal lies to the costs committee.

If authority is granted, the defence can then instruct the expert in the knowledge that the expert's fees will be publicly funded providing that the terms of the authority are not exceeded.

EXCEPTION TO 'NO TOP-UP' RULE

If prior authority is not granted, the defence can arrange for their client to pay privately for the preparation of an expert's report. It is one of the exceptions to the restriction on private payment provided for by Part C, r.1.20 of the General Criminal Contract Specification:

In respect of any expenses or fees incurred in:

(i)   preparing obtaining or considering any report, opinion or further evidence whether provided by an expert witness or otherwise; or
(ii)   obtaining or preparing transcripts of shorthand notes or tape recordings of any criminal investigation or proceedings, including police questioning;

where an application under Part B rule 5.2 for authority to incur such expenses or fees has been refused.

Authority will be granted if the area committee is satisfied that the steps are necessary for the proper conduct of the proceedings and are reasonable in the circumstances. Applications must be made in good time and with sufficient information to allow the area office to make the decision.

The information which is required directly from the defence is:

- a brief summary of the prosecution case;
- the likely plea;
- a summary of the defence or mitigation;
- the name and address of the expert;
- whether there are other defendants, with whom there is no conflict of interest, who would benefit from the expenditure;
- whether alternative quotes have been obtained and, if so, the amounts quoted. The absence of alternative quotes will not, in itself, lead to refusal.

If the final fee is difficult to predict, an initial sum may be authorised to establish the benefit and costs involved in undertaking further work. There is no right of appeal against a refusal of authority, but the area director must give reasons for any refusal and the application can be renewed.

Authority is not needed if the solicitor is prepared to take his or her chance of being allowed the costs on assessment or taxation. Only in exceptional cases should a solicitor take such a risk. If an authority is obtained, then no question as to the propriety of the step taken or the amount authorised will be raised on the eventual determination of costs, unless the solicitor knew or ought reasonably to have known, before incurring the costs, that the purpose of the authority had failed or become unnecessary or irrelevant.

If authority is not obtained, or is applied for but refused, or the maximum amount allowed is exceeded, the solicitor is able to make a claim for the costs which still may be paid on determination. Alternatively, if authority is refused, the solicitor can pay for an expert's fees out of private funds.

PAYMENT OF A DISBURSEMENT ON ACCOUNT

In Crown Court cases, where authority is granted for individual (rather than aggregated) expenditure of £100 or more and actual expenditure of £100 or more is incurred, the solicitor may apply to the National Taxing Team (NTT) for a payment on account of the disbursement.

9.4 INSTRUCTING AN EXPERT

The information which is required on CDS4 and needs to be obtained from the expert is:

- the type of expertise and qualifications;
- for medical reports, whether the expert is a consultant;
- the details of the charging rates (excluding value added tax (VAT)) per hour for preparation;
- the details of the charging rates (excluding VAT) per hour for travel time.

The authority will usually specify a maximum rate as well as a maximum amount.

When calculating a fee, the expert should take into account that where an area committee gives prior authority, it will authorise the maximum fee to be paid for any report, opinion, expert advice or transcript. This means that the expert should consider carefully how much time he or she is likely to spend on the case, which may include: reading documents, listening to tapes, watching videos and making any necessary transcriptions and analyses from them, examining the client, examining prosecution exhibits, research and preparing a report.

The expert should be told that court attendance fees of witnesses cannot be authorised. These are payable by the court out of central funds under the Costs in Criminal Cases (General) Regulations 1986 (SI 1986/1335) regs.

16(1) and 20. A witness is defined in reg. 15 as: 'A person properly attending to give evidence, whether or not he or she gives evidence or is called at the insistence of one of the parties or of the court.' The solicitor should find out the court attendance fee which is likely to be allowed and tell the expert.

The defence should explain to the expert whom they consider instructing, in the fullest terms:

- what they want the expert to establish;
- the significance of this in the context of the prosecution and defence case;
- deadline dates – there may be other investigations which the defence need to carry out, depending upon the expert's findings;
- date of pre-trial review (in the magistrates' court) or plea and directions hearing (PDH) (in the Crown Court); trial date, if known.

The defence should ask the expert to specify the material that he or she will need to see in order to carry out a full examination. Items which the defence should always send to the expert at this early stage include:

- the charge sheet or indictment;
- the victim's statement;
- any prosecution witness statements which are relevant to the area of enquiry by the expert;
- copies of prosecution photographs (not colour photocopies);
- the defendant's proof of evidence;
- client's letter of authority for medical report;
- statements of any defence witnesses which are relevant to the area of enquiry by the expert;
- any legal advice on expert evidence;
- any prosecution exhibits which the expert may need to examine.

The expert should be asked to give a detailed breakdown of the tasks which he or she proposes to fulfil, such as:

- the amount and type of material to be processed;
- what the processing involves;
- the number, type, duration and location of interviews;
- the number, type, duration and location of assessments, analyses or other activities to be conducted;
- the use of support staff.

On the basis of this work specification, the expert must provide an estimate of:

- total hours for services at a specified rate;
- total hours' travelling time at a specified rate;
- travel costs;
- the report size.

The expert may be able to give a preliminary view on how the report can assist the defence case. This information and the expert's full curriculum vitae (CV) can be attached to the application.

If there is a refusal of authority, the area director must give reasons. These can be reported back to the expert and the application renewed with further information from the expert dealing with the points raised by the area director.

The defence expert may have to examine an exhibit held by the prosecution. The prosecution will not (normally) release exhibits to the expert: the expert must go to them at whichever laboratory dealt with the case.

The Joint Operational Instructions for the Disclosure of Unused Material (JOPI), guides the CPS, police practitioners, and forensic science providers (FSPs) on their disclosure duties and responsibilities. The revised JOPI 2003 was placed on the CPS website **www.cps.gov.uk** in June 2003. Annex I deals with the disclosure of forensic science material and Annex H with scientific support material: fingermarks and photographs.

Detailed arrangements for the defence to have access to material retained by the FSP are set out in JOPI 2003. The prosecutor will have provided the defence with an endorsed copy of the index and the schedule of non-sensitive unused material (form MG6C) (see **Chapter 12** for a fuller explanation of these documents). Where the prosecutor has indicated with a 'D' or an 'I' that an item of unused material in the possession of the FSP should be disclosed, the disclosure officer will send a copy of the index, MG6C, and any letter at secondary stage to the forensic scientist (JOPI 2003, Annex H14.4).

The FSP should grant the defence access to that material, on the production of the MG6C schedule, or index, or covering letter (H14.5). As best practice, the investigator or disclosure officer should be present when the defence examine any forensic material (H14.6).

The FSP will (H14.3):

- notify the police of any requests by the defence for access and any arrangements made;
- advise the police where the defence seek to carry out further tests which may alter, damage or destroy the material;
- make arrangements for ensuring that the integrity of exhibits is maintained, and a continuity record is made where these are subject to defence examination;
- keep a record of any defence examination, including the nature and extent of the examination and any views expressed;
- notify the police if the forensic scientist's views are likely to change as a result of the defence examination.

Any requests received by the CPS for disclosure of unused material which has not been revealed by the FSP should be the subject of consultation between the prosecutor and the disclosure officer (H13.1). Consideration should be given to the prosecutor advising the police to seek access to the material (H13.2). If the prosecutor decides not to seek access to the material, the defence should be asked to refer their request directly to the FSP who will decide whether to volunteer access (H13.3)

REFERENCES

Chisum, W. & Turvey, B. (2000) 'Evidence dynamics: Locard's exchange principle and crime reconstruction', *Journal of Behavioural Profiling*, 1, no. 1.

Ede, R. & Edwards, A. (2002) *Criminal Defence*, 2nd edition, Law Society Publishing.

Ede, R. & Shepherd, E. (2000) *Active Defence*, 2nd edition, Law Society Publishing.

Roberts, P. & Wilmore, C. (1992) *The Role of Forensic Science Evidence in Criminal Proceedings*, RCCJ Research Study No. 11, HMSO.

Steventon, B. (1992) *The Ability to Challenge DNA Evidence*, RCCJ Research Study No. 9, HMSO.

Zander, M. & Henderson, P. (1992) *The Crown Court Study*, RCCJ Research Study No. 19, HMSO.

CHAPTER 10

Finding a defence forensic expert

The defence will need to satisfy themselves about the competence and ability of a particular 'expert' to undertake work in an individual case. To remedy the lack of a system of independent accreditation, the Council for the Registration of Forensic Practitioners (CRFP) has been established with support from the Home Office.

10.1 PARTICULAR PROBLEMS WITH FINDING FORENSIC SCIENTISTS

Where can the defence go in order to test out or get an alternative interpretation of the evidence that a prosecution scientist would give the court, or to show how the defence case is supported by the presence or absence of other forensic evidence which may not have been touched upon by the prosecution?

Not everyone appreciates that different areas of forensic expertise require different training and skills. Furthermore, apart from one or two notable exceptions, the Forensic Science Service (FSS), which now includes the former Metropolitan Police Forensic Science Laboratory, is the repository of practical experience and expertise in the use of forensic science. There are relatively few other properly trained, experienced, competent forensic scientists, from whom the defence can seek advice.

The number of independent forensic scientists who are prepared to work for the defence when the defendant is legally aided is limited because of the low fees paid and the delays before payment. Forensic scientists are tempted to concentrate more on prosecution and civil, than on criminal defence, work because of the cash flow problems that legal aid work brings.

Delays in serving prosecution forensic evidence on the defence, due to limited personnel and financial resources at the FSS, coupled with other delays in the system – the request by the police in the first place; the report being sent to the police and then on to the Crown Prosecution Service (CPS); the report having to be shown to prosecuting counsel before it can be served on the defence – result in the defence expert sometimes being instructed at very short notice, making it difficult for the defence to find someone suitably qualified who is prepared and able to do the work. This was the conclusion of Roberts and Wilmore, the Royal Commission on Criminal Justice 1993 (RCCJ) researchers who predicted that defence solicitors could find their choice of independent expert becoming even more limited.

If the defence find a forensic scientist willing to take instructions they must find out:

- on what basis they feel qualified to advise in that particular case;
- their recognised scientific qualifications;
- what practical experience they have:
  - in investigating the sort of case which involves that client;
  - in applying scientific techniques to assess the evidence at issue.

10.2 ORGANISATIONS AND PUBLICATIONS WHICH THOSE SEEKING AN EXPERT MAY FIND HELPFUL

10.2.1 The Council for the Registration of Forensic Practitioners

Tavistock House, Tavistock Square, London WC1H 9HX. Tel. 020 7383 2200; fax 020 7383 0888; www.crfp.org.uk.

The CRFP has established the first and only register of currently competent forensic practitioners in the UK which relies upon peer review. The CRFP publishes the register, ensures through periodic revalidation that forensic practitioners keep up to date and maintain competence, and deals with registered practitioners who fail to meet the necessary standards. CRFP has a code of conduct which defines the essential standards and values that apply to every forensic practitioner (see **Appendix 3**).

The register had opened by 2003 to forensic scientists, scene examiners, volume crime scene examiners (vehicle crime and burglary), fingerprint examiners, fingerprint development officers (enhancement and assessment), forensic odontologists, forensic anthropologists (including osteology and facial reconstruction) and forensic archaeologists. Over the next couple of years it will be open to other mainstream groups in forensic practice, such as forensic physicians (police surgeons), child protection paediatricians, road transport investigators, information technology specialists, fire examiners, and others. Police forces actively encourage scientific support staff to register.

The register is published on the CRFP website for anyone to consult, and is kept up to date daily (see **Appendix 3** for details of how to search (**www.crfp. org.uk/register.asp**)). Applicants for registration have their current competence individually assessed by an external assessor from their own speciality. The assessor looks at the quality of the applicant's work. CRFP is a regulatory council, not a professional association. By August 2003 over 900 practitioners were registered. Its focus is the public interest rather than representing the interests of forensic practitioners. It was started with funds from the Home Office, but will become self financing through registration fees. The Law Society is represented on its governing council and executive board.

The register lists the forensic practitioners who have been assessed as fit to practise a forensic speciality. For the individual forensic practitioner, the register is a clear statement that they are part of a coherent professional group, and subscribe to explicit standards and values against which they are prepared to be judged, if a question arises about their practice. Practitioners registered with CRFP are entitled to use the letters RFP (registered forensic practitioner) after their name. They also have their name, speciality and contact details included in the database on the CRFP website which may be accessed free of charge by anyone who wants to commission forensic work. A sealed certificate confirms a practitioner's registration, when it is granted, but enquirers need to check the register itself for the up-to-date position.

The register includes a document 'The Forensic Specialities' which briefly describes the scope of each of the specialities to which the register is open.

Users of forensic services will appreciate the reassurance that an RFP's competence has been independently verified. An important advantage for the solicitor is that the Legal Services Commission (LSC) has in mind working with the CRFP so that RFPs who agree to carry out work on terms approved by the LSC are identified on the CRFP register. The LSC would then allow solicitors funded by the LSC to instruct those RFPs without having to get any prior authority from the LSC and (subject to safeguards) the amount of their fees would not be questioned on assessment. The 'terms approved by the Commission' would include obligations on the solicitor regarding their instructions to the RFP, and an obligation on the RFP's part to turn around work within a reasonable period and to charge a reasonable fee. The LSC would issue guidance on what it considered to be reasonable fees. This would not prevent a solicitor from either instructing an RFP who had not agreed to work on the LSC-approved terms or from instructing a practitioner who was not registered. However, in those circumstances, the payment assurances would not apply and, in the latter case, the LSC would be likely to want justification as to why a non-registered practitioner was being instructed.

10.2.2 The Directory of Expert Witnesses

The directory and CD is published annually by Sweet & Maxwell and is available from the Law Society shop (tel. 020 7320 5640; fax 020 7320 5643) **www.lawsociety.org.uk**.

There is a supporting helpline, tel. 020 7393 7780.

10.2.3 The Academy of Experts

2 South Square, Gray's Inn, London WC1R 5HT. Tel: 020 7637 0333; email: admin@academy-experts.org; **www.academy-experts.org**.

The Academy provides the names and addresses of suitable members from their directory for a small charge. The Academy has some 2,000 members.

10.2.4 The British Academy of Forensic Sciences

Enquiries to: The Secretary, BAFS, Anaesthetics Unit, The Royal London Hospital Medical College, Turner Street, London E1 2AO. Tel. 020 7377 9201 (Dr P.J. Flynn, Secretary of the Academy). A body to 'encourage the study, improve the practice and advance the knowledge of legal, medical and forensic science'. It keeps a list of experts, including forensic pathologists.

10.2.5 The Expert Witness Institute

Africa House, 64–78 Kingsway, London WC2B 6BD. Tel. 020 7405 5854; fax 020 7405 5850; **www.ewi.org.uk**. Services and supports experts and lawyers who use the service of experts.

10.2.6 Forensic Access

Forensic Access, Building F4, Culham Science Centre, Abingdon, Oxfordshire OX14 3ED. Tel. 01865 408150; fax 01865 408170; email Science@forensic-access.co.uk; **www.forensic-access.co.uk**. Consists of former FSS or Metropolitan Police forensic scientists, specialising in defence work and in training new forensic scientists.

10.2.7 Forensic Alliance

Building F5, Culham Science Centre, Abingdon, Oxfordshire OX14 3ED. Tel. 01235 551800; fax 01865 407431; email forensic_alliance@aeat.co.uk; **www.aeat.com/forensic-alliance/contact**

They provide the same sort of comprehensive forensic science services as the FSS. It also has a unique forensic ecology department containing, e.g. forensic entomologists, botanical profilers, palynologists, etc. It has laboratories in Oxfordshire and Risley, Cheshire and they are open to both the prosecution and the defence.

10.2.8 The Forensic Science Service

Trident Court, 2920 Solihull Parkway, Birmingham Business Park, Birmingham B37 7YN. Tel. 0121 329 5200; fax 0121 788 3470; **www.forensic.gov.uk** (see **para 7.3.1** for more details).

Open to prosecution and defence alike. It has a marketing division in Birmingham which solicitors can telephone to find out about the facilities they offer and their charges. Where work is conducted by the FSS for the prosecution and the defence in the same case, the work is carried out in different laboratories which do not disclose confidential information to each other.

10.2.9 The Forensic Science Society

Clarke House, 18a Mount Parade, Harrogate, North Yorkshire HG1 1BX. Tel. 01423 506 068; fax 01423 566391; **www.forensic-science-society.org.uk**.

An international body whose object is to advance the study of forensic science. It runs a directory of independent consultants.

10.2.10 LGC Ltd

Formerly the Laboratory of the Government Chemist, LGC is a large private provider of chemical analysis and diagnostic services. Its range of services, provided by laboratories in Teddington, London and Runcorn, Cheshire, include DNA profiling, toxicology, illicit drugs analysis, and questioned documents analysis.

10.3 THE SCOPE OF FORENSIC EXPERTISE

The type of expert will necessarily be dictated by the nature of the offence with which your client is charged and the nature of the evidence in question.

The defence scientist is charged with investigating the soundness of the prosecution's scientific findings and the scope, if any, for some alternative innocent explanation for them. The scientist does this by:

- checking the analytical results emerging from the police and external scientist's work, and undertaking any such further tests as may be warranted;
- clarifying the nature of the police and external scientist's findings and the interpretation of them;
- assessing, and advising on, the significance of the scientific evidence overall in the light of the circumstances.

When selecting an expert, the defence need to be aware of the different areas of forensic expertise. These are explained in detail in the chapters which follow.

REFERENCES

Ede, R. & Edwards, A. (2002) *Criminal Defence*, 2nd edition, Law Society Publishing.

Ede, R. & Shepherd, E. (2000) *Active Defence*, 2nd edition, Law Society Publishing.

Roberts, P. & Wilmore, C. (1992) *The Role of Forensic Science Evidence in Criminal Proceedings*, RCCJ Research Study No. 11, HMSO.

CHAPTER 11

Defence investigation of the crime scene

The defence will need to consider how the crime scene investigation was conducted: who was involved? What resources were used? What records were generated? Is a further investigation of the crime scene by the defence likely to be of assistance? A lack of knowledge in forensic science matters; a lack of awareness about the proper use of scientific support; financial constraints; a failure to take and submit samples for the purpose of checking the reliability of the prosecution case; or the lack of a visit to the crime scene by a forensic scientist or scenes of crime officer (SOCO) are all possible reasons for a failure in the initial forensic investigation.

Questions which need to be asked include:

- Who should have been involved in the forensic investigation?
- Who was involved?
- What are these personnel trained to do?
- What should these personnel have been able to do?
- What was the strategic approach taken to the incident investigation?
- What was the scene examination strategy?
- How may their involvement (or lack of involvement) have influenced the nature/plan/outcome of the investigation?
- What records were or should have been kept/generated?
- What records should have been disclosed?
- What other resources should have been employed in the forensic investigation?
- What other resources were employed?
- How should these resources have been used?
- How were they or how were they likely to have been used?
- How may their use (or lack of use) have influenced the direction/outcome of the investigation?

By reference to **Chapters 2**, **3** and **4**, the defence should be able to analyse and understand the rationale of the forensic investigation, how the prosecution forensic case was put together and discover what evidence which may help the defence may be missing, overlooked or avoided. They describe how the forensic investigation should have been conducted (including the available resources) and the processes involved.

Chapter 2 listed the different personnel who may at some stage or other have been involved in the forensic investigation:

- the force control room;
- the divisional control room;
- uniform relief or shift;
- crime desk of the basic command unit (BCU);
- uniform beat crime officer;
- volume crime scene examiner;
- crime scene attender;
- crime scene analyst;
- case investigation team;
- duty Criminal Investigation Department (CID) operational officer;
- area CID team;
- SOCO;
- forensic physicians;
- fingerprint bureau;
- crime management department (CMD);
- major crimes unit (MCU);
- senior investigating officer (SIO);
- exhibits officer;
- police search adviser (POLSA) officers;
- specialist photographers;
- technical support unit (TSU);
- specialist advisers;
- crime scene coordinator;
- scientific support manager (SSM);
- crime scene manager (CSM);
- national crime and operations faculty (NCOF) liaison officer;
- pathologist;
- forensic scientist.

The documentation described in **Chapter 5** of both the investigation of the crime scene and the removal of and submission of material for examination may assist in the task of examining the forensic investigation:

- incident report book (IRB) or pocket book;
- the crime report;
- scene examinations form;
- narrative report;
- the crime file;
- photographs of scene;
- videotape;

- photographic log;
- diagram/sketch;
- latent print lift log;
- evidence recovery log;
- form MG FSS (Manual of Guidance for the Preparation, Processing and Submission of Files; Forensic Science Service);
- entry/exit documentation;
- the crime scene log;
- scene release documentation;
- the actions log;
- scene manager's notes;
- scientific support coordinator's notes;
- post-mortem examination notes;
- administrative worksheet.

The defence should also investigate the actions of the forensic physician, as set out in **Chapter 4**:

- examining the suspect/victim;
- communicating with the SOCO;
- forensic physicians;
- what the forensic physician does;
- medical examination of the victim;
- taking samples from the suspect and submission for analysis.

11.1   VISITING THE CRIME SCENE

The defence should consider visiting the scene of the crime in an attempt to understand and record the scene, examine and test the logic of the forensic investigation and the reasonableness of its findings in the context of the scene and obtain material which may support the accused and/or undermine the prosecution case. Photographs often do not do justice to the scene and a true 'feel' for it can only be obtained by visiting it.

Often it is very useful for the scientist instructed by the defence to visit the scene. Even long after the incident they can assess what would be expected to have been found and compare with what was actually found.

The defence investigation should be conducted utilising and modifying, as necessary, the information contained particularly in **Chapters 1** and **4**, to understand the potential for obtaining forensic evidence:

- the availability of physical evidence;
- the importance of physical evidence;
- uses of physical evidence;

- types of physical evidence;
- initial crime scene processing and analysis;
- Locard's principle of exchange at the scene;
- material commonly collected in volume crimes.

The methods and techniques described in **Chapter 4**, modified as necessary, will also help the defence to conduct their own investigation:

- the search;
- search/examination list;
- searching by SOCOs;
- videotaping the crime scene;
- photographing the crime scene;
- sketching the crime scene;
- types of samples.

11.1.1 Preparations

The defence should make use of the relevant case material, including:

- descriptions contained within statements and other documents disclosed by the prosecutor and the accused (wherever possible converting the verbal description into a visual representation);
- drawings, sketches, photographs, annotated plans and maps;
- video recordings of the scene and other key locations.

The defence will need at least:

- an Ordnance Survey plan;
- measuring materials – a surveyor's tape is particularly useful;
- materials to enable them to draw diagrams and sketches;
- a tape recorder – to record observations and commentary upon the comparison between what is contained in case material and the actual scene;
- a camera with flash.

11.2 AT THE SCENE

By going to the crime scene the defence will be able to 'reality' test:

- people's accounts of where they were positioned;
- what was (or was not) observed, heard, or found, in terms of entry and exit routes, the vicinity of the scene, and the scene.

1. The defence should review the evidence from witnesses and CCTV surveillance indicating that:

   - the offender was at the actual crime scene;
   - the offender was the accused;
   - the offender entered or left the crime scene by a particular route;
   - the offender who entered or left by that route was the accused.

2. The defence should look for possible alternative, entry/exit routes. They should review and check out:

   - Which routes were (or were likely to have been) taken?
   - What obstacles were there on an entry/exit route?
   - How obstacles were allegedly negotiated?
   - Is it possible to negotiate an obstacle?
   - How could an obstacle be negotiated?

3. The defence should look for forms of observation of entry/exit routes. They should review and check out:

   - Was the entry/exit route covered by security surveillance closed circuit television (CCTV)?
   - Did the system have all-weather (infrared) recording capability?
   - What were the manning and monitoring arrangements of the system?
   - Were the cameras, and recording, automatically (intruder/time) activated or were they manually operated?
   - If the camera rotated to scan a larger area, what arc did it traverse?
   - What was the height of the camera above ground? (A likely source of distortion of images.)
   - What is distance from the camera to the nearest point on the entry/exit route? (A likely source of poor resolution of images.)

     - Have the police taken possession of, and examined, the video recording?
     - Was the video recording retained by the police? If not, is it still retained by the third party?

4. The defence should consider the forensic evidence derived from the entry/exit route and the scene. They should use common sense, experience from other cases, and knowledge of the present case, to review and to check the entry/exit route and scene to assess the significance of each type of forensic evidence, e.g. what contact trace material (CTM) was found, and where, which links:

   - the offender with entering and exiting by that route;
   - the route with the offender;
   - the accused with the route;
   - the route with the accused;

113

- the accused with the scene;
- the scene with the offender;
- the scene with the accused.

11.3   RECONSTRUCTING THE CRIME

The defence is attempting to reconstruct the past. The reconstruction may show that something could not have happened in the way described. A reconstruction is also able to reveal what witness and other evidence should be available (but may not be because of inadequate police investigation).

11.4   PROSECUTION OBJECT EVIDENCE

If, in the course of making investigations into the accused's defence, evidence is found which is clearly material to the prosecution case, some common-sense rules must be observed:

- it should not be interfered with in any way;
- a record should be made of its being found;
- it should be left as it was found;
- a written record or sketch, sketch plan, photograph, or video recording of it should be made.

The defence is under no obligation to report the discovery of the evidence to the police.

REFERENCE

Ede, R. & Shepherd, E. (2000) *Active Defence*, 2nd edition, Law Society Publishing.

CHAPTER 12

Forensic evidence: pre-trial

12.1 POLICE AND CRIMINAL EVIDENCE ACT 1984 (PACE) AND CODE OF PRACTICE D

PACE Code D covers identification, including identification by fingerprints, body samples and impressions. The revised Code, which came into force in 2003, has effect in relation to any identification procedure carried out after midnight on 31 March 2003.

Fingerprints may be taken without consent (and reasonable force used if necessary) in the following circumstances (extracted from Code D):

4.3 PACE, section 61, provides powers to take fingerprints without consent from any person over the age of ten years:

(a) under section 61(3)(a), from a detainee at a police station if authorised by an officer of at least inspector rank who has reasonable grounds for suspecting that person is involved in a criminal offence and for believing their fingerprints will tend to confirm or disprove involvement, or assist in establishing their identity (including showing that they are not a particular person), or both. However, authority may not be given solely to establish the person's identity unless they have refused to identify themselves or the authorising officer has reasonable grounds to suspect the person is not who they claim to be;

(b) under section 61(3)(b), from a detainee at a police station who has been charged with a recordable offence, see *Note 4A*, or informed they will be reported for such an offence if, in the course of the investigation of that offence:

(i) they have not had their fingerprints taken; or
(ii) the fingerprints taken do not constitute a complete set of their fingerprints or some, or all, of the fingerprints are not of sufficient quality to allow satisfactory analysis, comparison or matching;

(c) under section 61(4A), from a person who has been bailed to appear at a court or police station if the person:

> (i)   has answered to bail for a person whose fingerprints were taken previously and there are reasonable grounds for believing they are not the same person; or
>
> (ii)   who has answered to bail claims to be a different person from a person whose fingerprints were previously taken;
>
> and in either case, the court or an officer of inspector rank or above, authorises the fingerprints to be taken at the court or police station;

(d)   under section 61(6), from a person who has been:

> (i)   convicted of a recordable offence;
>
> (ii)   given a caution in respect of a recordable offence which, at the time of the caution, the person admitted; or
>
> (iii)   warned or reprimanded under the Crime and Disorder Act 1998, section 65, for a recordable offence.

[. . .]

4.7   Before any fingerprints are taken with, or without, consent as above, the person must be informed:

(a)   of the reason their fingerprints are to be taken;

(b)   of the grounds on which the relevant authority has been given if the powers mentioned in *paragraph 4.3(a)* or *(c)* apply;

(c)   that their fingerprints may be retained and may be subject of a speculative search against other fingerprints, see *Note 4B*, unless destruction of the fingerprints is required in accordance with *Annex F, Part (a)*; and

(d)   that if their fingerprints are required to be destroyed, they may witness their destruction as provided for in *Annex F, Part (a)*.

A non-intimate body sample may be taken without their consent from a person in the following circumstances (extracted from Code D):

6.6   A non-intimate sample may be taken from a person without consent in accordance with PACE. The principal circumstances provided for are as follows:

(a)   under section 63(3), from a person in police detention, or police custody on the authority of a court, if a police officer of inspector rank or above has reasonable grounds to believe the sample will tend to confirm or disprove the suspect's involvement in a recordable offence, see *Note 4A*, and gives authorisation for a sample to be taken. However, the officer may not give authorisation to take a non-intimate sample consisting of a skin impression if a skin impression of the same part of the body has already been taken from that person in the course of the investigation of the offence and the impression previously taken is not one that has proved insufficient;

(b) under section 63(3A), from a person charged with a recordable offence or informed they will be reported for such an offence: and

    (i) that person has not had a non-intimate sample taken from them in the course of the investigation; or

    (ii) if they have had a sample taken, it proved unsuitable or insufficient for the same form of analysis, see *Note 6B*; or

(c) under section 63(3B), from a person convicted of a recordable offence after the date on which that provision came into effect. PACE, section 63A, describes the circumstances in which a police officer may require a person convicted of a recordable offence to attend a police station for a non-intimate sample to be taken.

6.7 Reasonable force may be used, if necessary, to take a non-intimate sample from a person without their consent under the powers mentioned in *paragraph 6.6*.

6.8 Before any intimate sample is taken with consent or non-intimate sample is taken with, or without, consent, the person must be informed:

(a) of the reason for taking the sample;

(b) of the grounds on which the relevant authority has been given, including, if appropriate, the nature of the suspected offence;

(c) that the sample or information derived from the sample may be retained and subject of a speculative search, see *Note 6E*, unless their destruction is required as in *Annex F*, Part A.

6.9 When clothing needs to be removed in circumstances likely to cause embarrassment to the person, no person of the opposite sex who is not a registered medical practitioner or registered health care professional shall be present, (unless in the case of a juvenile, mentally disordered or mentally vulnerable person, that person specifically requests the presence of an appropriate adult of the opposite sex who is readily available) nor shall anyone whose presence is unnecessary. However, in the case of a juvenile, this is subject to the overriding proviso that such a removal of clothing may take place in the absence of the appropriate adult only if the juvenile signifies, in their presence, that they prefer the adult's absence and they agree.

A 'non-intimate sample' means:

- a sample of hair (other than pubic hair) which includes hair plucked from the root;
- a sample taken from a nail or under a nail;
- a swab taken from any part of the person's body including the mouth but not any other body orifice;
- saliva;

- a skin impression (other than a fingerprint) which is a record of the skin pattern and other physical characteristics or features of the whole or any part of their foot or any other part of their body.

An intimate sample may only be taken from a person in police detention with the suspect's written consent and in the following circumstances (extracted from Code D):

6.2 PACE, section 62, provides that intimate samples may be taken under:

    (a) section 62(1), from a person in police detention only:

        (i) if a police officer of inspector rank or above has reasonable grounds to believe such an impression or sample will tend to confirm or disprove the suspect's involvement in a recordable offence, see *Note 4A*, and gives authorisation for a sample to be taken; and

        (ii) with the suspect's written consent;

    (b) section 62(1A), from a person not in police detention but from whom two or more non-intimate samples have been taken in the course of an investigation of an offence and the samples, though suitable, have proved insufficient if:

        (i) a police officer of inspector rank or above authorises it to be taken; and

        (ii) the person concerned gives their written consent. See *Notes 6B and 6C*.

6.3 Before a suspect is asked to provide an intimate sample, they must be warned that if they refuse without good cause their refusal may harm their case if it comes to trial, see *Note 6D*. If the suspect is in police detention and not legally represented, they must also be reminded of their entitlement to have free legal advice, see Code C, *paragraph 6.5*, and the reminder noted in the custody record. If *paragraph 6.2(b)* applies and the person is attending a station voluntarily, their entitlement to free legal advice as in Code C, *paragraph 3.21* shall be explained to them.

6.4 Dental impressions may only be taken by a registered dentist. Other intimate samples, except for samples of urine, may only be taken by a registered medical practitioner or registered health care professional.

References to an 'intimate sample' mean a dental impression or a sample of blood, semen or any other tissue fluid, urine, or pubic hair, or a swab taken from a person's body orifice other than the mouth.

Fingerprints or a DNA sample taken from a person who has been arrested on suspicion of being involved in a recordable offence or has been charged with such an offence or has been informed that they will be reported for such an offence may be subject of a speculative search. This means that the fingerprints or DNA may be checked against other fingerprints and DNA records held by or on behalf of the police and other law enforcement authorities in the UK. Fingerprints and DNA samples taken from any other person may be subject to a speculative search only if they give their consent to this in writing.

Annex F of Code D gives further details of destruction and speculative searches of fingerprints and samples.

1. When fingerprints or DNA samples are taken from a person in connection with an investigation and the person is not suspected of having committed the offence, see *Note F1*, they must be destroyed as soon as they have fulfilled the purpose for which they were taken unless:

   (a) they were taken for the purposes of an investigation of an offence for which a person has been convicted; and

   (b) fingerprints or samples were also taken from the convicted person for the purposes of that investigation.

   However, subject to *paragraph 2*, the fingerprints and samples, and the information derived from samples, may not be used in the investigation of any offence or in evidence against the person who is, or would be, entitled to the destruction of the fingerprints and samples, see *Note F2*.

2. The requirement to destroy fingerprints and DNA samples, and information derived from samples, and restrictions on their retention and use in *paragraph 1* do not apply if the person gives their written consent for their fingerprints or sample to be retained and used after they have fulfilled the purpose for which they were taken, see *Note F1*.

3. When a person's fingerprints or sample are to be destroyed:

   (a) any copies of the fingerprints must also be destroyed;

   (b) the person may witness the destruction of their fingerprints or copies if they ask to do so within five days of being informed destruction is required;

   (c) access to relevant computer fingerprint data shall be made impossible as soon as it is practicable to do so and the person shall be given a certificate to this effect within three months of asking; and

   (d) neither the fingerprints, the sample, or any information derived from the sample, may be used in the investigation of any offence or in evidence against the person who is, or would be, entitled to its destruction.

4. Fingerprints or samples, and the information derived from samples, taken in connection with the investigation of an offence which are not required to be destroyed, may be retained after they have fulfilled the purposes for which they were taken but may be used only for purposes related to the prevention or detection of crime, the investigation of an offence or the conduct of a prosecution in, as well as outside, the UK and may also be subject to a speculative search. This

includes checking them against other fingerprints and DNA records held by, or on behalf of, the police and other law enforcement authorities in, as well as outside, the UK.

[. . .]

F1   *Fingerprints and samples given voluntarily for the purposes of elimination play an important part in many police investigations. It is, therefore, important to make sure innocent volunteers are not deterred from participating and their consent to their fingerprints and DNA being used for the purposes of a specific investigation is fully informed and voluntary. If the police or volunteer seek to have the sample or fingerprints retained for use after the specific investigation ends, it is important the volunteer's consent to this is also fully informed and voluntary.*

F2   *The provisions for the retention of fingerprints and samples in paragraph 1 allow for all fingerprints and samples in a case to be available for any subsequent miscarriage of justice investigation.*

12.2   PRE-TRIAL DISCLOSURE

12.2.1   Disclosure by the scientific support department (SSD) to the disclosure officer

The Code of Practice under the Criminal Procedure and Investigations Act (CPIA) 1996 requires the recording and retention of all relevant material and information obtained in a criminal investigation.

Joint operational instructions (JOPI) 2003, Annex H (see **Appendix 5**) requires SSDs to keep accurate and full records of all scene examinations, including details of any items retained as potential exhibits and where they are submitted for further examination. The records of SSDs in relation to a criminal investigation should be made available to the disclosure officer. This will ensure that the disclosure officer can carry out the task of scheduling unused material for the prosecutor. If necessary, scientific support staff should help the disclosure officer identify material which might undermine the prosecution case or which might assist the defence.

12.3   DISCLOSURE TO THE POLICE BY THE FORENSIC SCIENCE PROVIDER (FSP)

JOPI 2003, Annex I sets out the detailed procedure to be followed by the FSP to disclose material to the police. The FSP should provide the police with an index in the form of a list describing all material in their possession, as it will not be known at that stage whether it is likely to be used or unused material (I8.1). The material should be individually listed with clear and accurate descriptions. Any single item which is known to be of particular significance should be listed separately (I8.4) 'Intelligence information'.

The index is prepared by the scientific reporting officer and submitted to the police investigating officer (IO) when the report or statement is supplied (I8.2). Where material is generated or fresh material received after the initial preparation and submission of the index, a supplementary index should be supplied to the IO. Any material that it is thought might undermine the prosecution case or assist the defence should be mentioned in the report or statement or indicated in a covering letter. If not so mentioned, such material should be indicated on the index. Wherever possible, copies of the material should be sent to the disclosure officer with the index (I8.5)

JOPI 2003, Annex I goes on to set out the detailed procedure to be followed by the IO when the index has been received. The IO must retain the index, together with any other report, statement or document supplied by the FSP. Any relevant oral information received by the IO or the disclosure officer relating to the material held by the FSP should be recorded and retained (I9.1).

12.4 DISCLOSURE BY THE POLICE TO THE PROSECUTOR

On submission of a full file to the Crown Prosecution Service (CPS), the disclosure officer should list the index on the MG6C. The index may be described generically, e.g. 'Forensic Science Service Index – compiled (date) – list of all non-sensitive material in possession of FSS' (I9.2). Where the disclosure officer believes that any of the material appearing on the index might undermine the prosecution case or assist the defence, the item should be drawn to the disclosure officer's attention by being listed on Form MG6E (I9.3). The schedules should then be sent to the CPS with the full file. The index and any undermining or assisting material should be sent to the CPS with the full file (I9.4). Where the prosecutor indicates that unused material in the possession of the FSP requires disclosure, the disclosure officer should send a copy of the index endorsed with the prosecutor's decision to the forensic scientist.

If the schedule of unused material fails to describe the contents of documents adequately, they should be closely examined by the CPS and appropriate action taken. The CPIA Code requires that the description of each item should make clear the nature of the item and should contain sufficient detail to enable the prosecutor to decide whether he needs to inspect the material before deciding whether or not it should be disclosed.

12.5 DISCLOSURE BY THE PROSECUTOR TO THE DEFENCE

A full account of the disclosure provisions of CPIA 1996 is given in the main body of JOPI 2003.

Under CPIA, on the defendant pleading not guilty in the magistrates' court or being committed to the Crown Court for trial, the prosecutor is required to disclose to the accused previously undisclosed material which in the opinion of the prosecutor might undermine the prosecution case, or else to give the accused a written statement that there is no such material (s.3(1)). The government explained in parliament that this was intended to mean: 'material which, generally speaking, has an adverse effect on the strength of the prosecution case'.

Paragraphs 36–8 of the Attorney General's 'Guidelines on Disclosure of Information in Criminal Proceedings' (2000) define material for primary disclosure as follows.

36. Generally, material can be considered to potentially undermine the prosecution case if it has an adverse effect on the strength of the prosecution case. This will include anything that tends to show a fact inconsistent with the elements of the case that must be proved by the prosecution. Material can have an adverse effect on the strength of the prosecution case:

   (a) by the use made of it in cross-examination; and
   (b) by its capacity to suggest any potential submissions that could lead to:

      (i)   the exclusion of evidence;
      (ii) a stay of proceedings;
      (iii) a court or tribunal finding that any public authority had acted incompatibly with the defendant's rights under ECHR.

37. In deciding what material might undermine the prosecution case, the prosecution should pay particular attention to material that has potential to weaken the prosecution case or is inconsistent with it. Examples are:

   i.   Any material casting doubt upon the accuracy of any prosecution evidence.
   ii.   Any material which may point to another person, whether charged or not (including a co-accused) having involvement in the commission of the offence.
   iii. Any material which may cast doubt upon the reliability of a confession.
   iv.   Any material that might go to the credibility of a prosecution witness.
   v.   Any material that might support a defence that is either raised by the defence or apparent from the prosecution papers. If the material might undermine the prosecution case it should be disclosed at this stage even though it suggests a defence inconsistent with or alternative to one already advanced by the accused or his solicitor.
   vi.   Any material which may have a bearing on the admissibility of any prosecution evidence.

38. Experience suggests that any item which relates to the defendant's mental or physical health, his intellectual capacity, or any ill-treatment which the

defendant may have suffered when in the investigator's custody is likely to have the potential for casting doubt on the reliability of an accused's purported confession, and prosecutors should pay particular attention to any such item in the possession of the prosecution.

The Criminal Justice Bill considered by Parliament during the 2002–3 legislative session amends the definition of primary disclosure by substituting 'might reasonably be considered capable of undermining' for 'in the prosecutor's opinion might undermine' and adding 'or of assisting the case for the accused'.

Defence practitioners must carefully consider such primary disclosure as is made by the Crown. They may wish to bring further lines of enquiry to the attention of the prosecution (for example the existence of undisclosed medical evidence at the police station).

The schedule of non-sensitive material MG6C and the index will be provided to the defence at the same time as primary disclosure. The prosecutor will record disclosure decisions on the schedule and on the index itself (I10.2). The defence should examine the schedule and index with care and consider which other items should appear on the list and be prepared to challenge their absence. The defence should identify the true nature of each item listed and consider how it might assist the defence, and be ready to give reasons for its disclosure in a specific request to the prosecution, and ensure that the reasons are supported by the defence statement.

Examples of unused material which lawyers report has not been disclosed under CPIA include a forensic report showing the detection of fingerprints which were not the defendant's.

Secondary disclosure is limited to prosecution material which has not been previously disclosed; which might reasonably be expected to assist the accused's defence as disclosed by the defence statement: s.7(2). JOPI 2003, Annex I sets out the detailed procedure to be followed by the police investigator and the CPS when a defence statement has been received.

When a defence statement is received or information comes to light which might affect any evidence supplied by a forensic expert, the disclosure officer will consult with the investigator and the CPS to decide whether further enquiries need to be made (I11.2). The disclosure officer should send the defence statement to the FSP together with instructions as to any further report or work required. If the disclosure office is not clear whether the defence statement has any impact upon forensic material, the FSP should be contacted for advice on whether it may be desirable to review the material in the light of the defence statement (I11.4). In certain circumstances, a consultation may be arranged between the police investigators, the CPS and the forensic scientist to decide upon a suitable course of action (I11.5).

JOPI gives examples of situations where further enquiries by the FSP may be appropriate (I11.3):

- where forensic evidence is challenged directly;
- where issues raised in the defence statement may have an impact on the interpretation of scientific evidence;
- where the scenario put forward by the defence statement differs significantly from that upon which expert evidence is based;
- whenever it is necessary to ask the forensic science service (FSS) to review the forensic material or to conduct further tests in order to clarify the issues raised by the defence statement;
- where any issue is raised that might have an impact on forensic material, either used or unused;
- where a new line of enquiry is indicated and the officer in the case considers that it should be pursued.

Types of unused material which you may wish to request from the prosecution include:

- CCTV film;

from the forensic scientist scenes of crime officer (SOCO):

- SOCO's report;
- list of items and contact trace material (CTM) collected/removed;
- list of items and CTM submitted for testing;
- fingerprints lifted/identified;
- photographs/video recordings/sketches;
- reports of work carried out by forensic scientists;

from the forensic physician/police officer:

- samples taken;
- samples submitted for testing;
- samples not submitted for testing.

They will need to be likely to support the defence set out in the defence statement. However, most prosecution advocates would allow the defence access to non-sensitive material, even if it fell outside the statutory criteria. Find out if the prosecutor has inspected the item concerned.

The Attorney General's 'Guidelines on Disclosure of Information in Criminal Proceedings' (2000) list in para. 40 the material which might reasonably be expected to be disclosed to the defence where it relates to the defence being put forward.

The material is:

i.   Those recorded scientific or scenes of crime findings retained by the investigator which relate to the defendant; and are linked to the point at issue; and have not been previously disclosed.

ii.   Where identification is or may be in issue, all previous descriptions of suspects, however recorded, together with all records of identification procedures in respect of the offence(s) and photographs of the accused taken by the investigator around the time of his arrest.

iii.   Information that any prosecution witness has received, has been promised or has requested any payment or reward in connection with the case.

iv.   Plans of crime scenes or video recordings made by investigators of crime scenes.

v.   Names, within the knowledge of investigators, of individuals who may have relevant information and whom investigators do not intend to interview.

vi.   Records which the investigator has made of information which may be relevant, provided by any individual (such information would include, but not be limited to, records of conversation and interviews with any such person).

The defence should be prepared to make an application to the court for further prosecution disclosure (s.8(1)). The Magistrates' Court (Criminal Procedure and Investigations Act 1996) (Disclosure) Rules 1997 (SI 1997/703) and the Crown Court (Criminal Procedure and Investigations Act 1996) (Disclosure) Rules 1997 (SI 1997/698), require the application to be made by notice, in writing, to the appropriate office of the court and to specify: the material to which the application relates; that the material has not been disclosed to the accused; the reason why the material might be expected to assist the applicant's defence as disclosed by the defence statement given under s.5; and the date of service of a copy of the notice on the prosecutor. The defence should consider what further evidence may be in the hands of people other than the investigators.

12.6   DUTY OF DISCLOSURE BY MEMBERS OF THE 'PROSECUTION TEAM'

The disclosure duties set out in the CPIA and the Code of Practice apply to prosecutors, police officers and others charged with the duty of conducting an investigation, and replace the common law rules relating to disclosure by them. The duty to reveal material to the prosecutor, in accordance with the Code of Practice under the Act, does not extend to expert witnesses who are instructed by the police. Duties under the Act and the Code are limited to material that the expert has communicated to the investigator and the prosecutor. The investigator is under a duty to retain, and the prosecutor to disclose in accordance with the provisions of the Act, communications between the police and experts, reports of work carried out by experts, and schedules of scientific material prepared by the expert for the investigator: Code of Practice, para. 5.4

The common law duty of the prosecution to disclose has been extended by the courts to cover material produced by anyone who has been instructed by the prosecutor or the investigator to offer an expert opinion, such as psychiatrists, forensic scientists and forensic physicians (police surgeons). They have all been regarded as members of the 'prosecution team' and under a duty to disclose material to the prosecutor which may assist the defence. In *R.* v. *Bolton Magistrates Court ex p. Scally* [1991] 2 All ER 619; [1991] 1 QB 537, Glidewell LJ said:

> While the prosecuting authority as such may not have failed in its duty, the total apparatus of prosecution has failed to carry out its duty to bring before the court all the material evidence.

In *R.* v. *Maguire* [1992] 2 All ER 433, CA, the court held that that the duty of disclosure is not confined to prosecution counsel but includes forensic scientists retained by the prosecution and accordingly failure by a forensic scientist to disclose material may be a substantial irregularity in the course of the trial providing grounds for an appeal against conviction to be allowed. Stuart-Smith LJ, giving the judgment, said:

> We are of the opinion that a forensic scientist who is an adviser to the prosecuting authority is under a duty to disclose material of which he knows and which may have some bearing on the offence charged and the surrounding circumstances of the case. The disclosure will be to the authority which retains him and which must in turn (subject to sensitivity) disclose the information to the defence.
>
> We can see no cause to distinguish between members of the prosecuting authority and those advising it in the capacity of a forensic scientist. Such a distinction could involve difficult and contested inquiries as to where knowledge stopped but, most importantly, would be entirely counter to the desirability of ameliorating the disparity of scientific resources as between the Crown and the subject.

An expert acting for the prosecution is under an obligation to inform the prosecution of tests or experiments that disprove or cast doubt upon the opinions reached. In *R.* v. *Ward* [1993] 1 WLR 619 the court added that:

> An expert witness who has carried out or knows of experiments or tests which tend to cast doubt upon the opinion he is expressing is under a clear obligation to bring records of those tests to the attention of the solicitor instructing him.

Writing about the prosecution disclosure of unused material, Sir David Calvert Smith QC, the then Director of Public Prosecutions (2003), said:

> One only has to look at the recent case of *R.* v. *Sally Clark* to know that third party disclosure creates particular challenges both for the interests of justice generally and the prosecution in particular. In this case, as is by now well known, the late discovery of the significance of microbiological pathology results from the second child's post mortem meant that the defence had been denied the opportunity at trial to argue that death might have been caused by accidental biological infection. However, I understand that these microbiological results were only known to the prosecution pathologist and, as the court found, neither police officers nor prosecutors nor the defence were made aware of their significance.

This highlights some of the difficulties for police officers and prosecutors who are dependent upon the good faith, competence and professionalism of experts whom they instruct but over whom they have little or no control should they depart from accepted standards.

12.7 CONTINUOUS REVIEW

Prosecutors are under a duty continuously to review what amounts to primary and secondary disclosure. The defence should be ready to remind prosecutors of their duty as new issues arise.

12.8 SENSITIVE MATERIAL

The prosecutor must obtain the court's permission to withhold relevant but sensitive material. This will take place by a procedure established by the Court of Appeal. If a PII application to withhold sensitive forensic material in the possession of any member of the prosecution team is to be made to the court, the CPS must first consult the police and the FSS. The decision to allow non-disclosure must be kept under review. The defence should be ready to bring to the court's attention any change of circumstance.

12.9 MATERIAL IN THE HANDS OF A THIRD PARTY

Any unused material or information not given to the police but retained by a forensic science organisation and not volunteered can only be acquired by the defence by their obtaining a witness summons (Criminal Procedure (Attendance of Witnesses) Act 1965, s.2 or Magistrates' Courts Act 1980, s.97). For these purposes the forensic science organisation is a third party.

12.10 CUSTODY TIME LIMITS

A failure by the prosecution to comply with the timetable for forensic disclosure to the defence, so that the defence's ability to be ready for trial is affected, may constitute a failure to act with all due diligence and expedition in the progress of the case so that the court refuses an extension of the custody time limit. In the case of *R. (on the appln of Holland)* v. *Leeds Crown Court* [2003] Crim LR 272 the court had set 17 January 2002 as the date by which the forensic evidence (on which the case largely relied) had to be served on the defence. Despite that, the officer in charge of the case and the person in charge of the forensic investigation agreed that the forensic enquiries had to be completed and evidence received by the police by the end of March at the latest. The FSS coordinator was not aware of the 17 January date for disclosure. The court was not told this by the prosecution at any of the pre-trial hearings which took place, and no application was made to extend the date for service of the evidence. The forensic material was served on the defence on 10 April 2002, 12 days before the trial, and the defence were unable to obtain an independent expert's opinion on it, causing a new trial date to be set. The Divisional Court quashed the judge's decision to extend the custody time limit.

If the fault is entirely that of the FSS, it is not treated as a lack of due diligence and expedition on the part of the prosecution for the purpose of custody time limit hearings: *R. v. Central Criminal Court, ex p. Johnson* (1999) 2 Cr App R 51.

REFERENCES

Ede, R. & Shepherd, E. (2000) *Active Defence*, 2nd edition, Law Society Publishing.

Ede, R. & Edwards, A. (2002) *Criminal Defence*, 2nd edition, Law Society Publishing.

CHAPTER 13

Forensic evidence in court

13.1 ADMISSIBILITY

The general rule is that evidence of opinion is not admissible, as inferences from facts should be drawn by the court. However, there is an exception for expert witnesses.

The opinion of an expert is admissible on those matters where the subject is one in which competency to form an opinion can only be acquired by a course of special study or experience. The expert witness provides the court with information which is outside the experience and knowledge of a judge or jury. In each case it must be for the judge to decide whether the issue is one on which the jury could be assisted by expert evidence. If a judge or jury can form their own conclusion without help, the opinion of the expert is unnecessary: *R.* v. *Turner* [1975] QB 834.

Expert witnesses, as well as giving opinions, also give evidence of facts which would be recognised only by someone possessed of special knowledge or experience.

An expert must have appropriate qualifications: *R.* v. *Silverlock* (1894) 2 QB 766. Expert opinion may be excluded if the expert lacks expertise on a topic on which he/she is giving evidence: *R.* v. *Silverlock* (1894) 2 QB 766; *R.* v. *Inch* (1990) 91 Cr App R 51. This will only apply if the court is aware that the expert is acting outside their area of competence. The central plank of the Council for the Registration of Forensic Practitioners' (CRFP) registration scheme is that forensic practitioners are registered as competent within a specific speciality only and the Council for CRFP Code of Conduct (see **Appendix 3**) reminds registered practitioners to provide expert advice and evidence only within the limits of their professional competence.

The Police and Criminal Evidence Act 1984 (PACE), s.78 may be used to exclude unreliable prosecution expert evidence.

Experts can rely upon hearsay evidence in justifying their opinions, for example by reference to authoritative works written by others. If it is not a recognised field of specialised knowledge, it can be excluded, e.g. expert evidence based on novel scientific techniques that are not generally accepted by the scientific community. Although the Criminal Justice Bill considered by

Parliament during the 2002–3 legislation session abolishes the common law rules governing the admissibility of hearsay evidence in criminal proceedings, it specifically preserves the rule of law under which in criminal proceedings an expert witness may draw on the body of expertise relevant to their field.

In court, the first stage of the expert's testimony is to establish their qualifications. This is necessary before the expert's evidence can be admitted and lays the foundation for the court's acceptance of the opinions to be given.

As the CRFP register becomes established (see **Chapter 10**), registration will increasingly be seen as a benchmark. Expert and professional witnesses can expect to be asked before, and during court proceedings, whether they are registered. Although the courts will remain free to admit evidence from any witness they choose, conclusions may well be drawn from an individual's answer to such a question.

The prosecutor can ask the expert a number of questions about relevant aspects of his/her educational background, training and professional standing (where educated; what degrees; special training; continuing education and specific courses undertaken; articles and publications authored; membership of scientific societies and other professional organisations; how many times he/she has given expert testimony). The expert is also asked about his/her work experience (current position; duties and responsibilities; laboratory accreditation).

The defence advocate may later cross-examine the prosecution expert on his/her qualifications and ability to give an opinion in the field of science concerned, trying to undermine his/her credibility with the court. It may be suggested that the expert is not adequately qualified or does not have sufficient working experience of the type of case being tried to give an informed opinion.

Although an expert witness can give evidence of experiments conducted by others in order to support an inference, and can interpret factual evidence given by another witness in the light of scientific findings and knowledge, factual evidence in relation to the case being conducted must be given by the person who carried out the work which led to the facts being found. The scientist can give evidence of work carried out under his/her direct supervision, but where laboratory work was carried out by an assistant hearsay evidence cannot be given about that, but the prosecution or defence should seek to prove it by agreed statements or formal admissions under the Criminal Justice Act 1967 (CJA), ss.9 and 10.

The Criminal Justice Bill considered by parliament during the 2002–3 legislative session makes special provision for admitting statements, as an exception to the hearsay rule, prepared by witnesses who conducted preparatory work on which an expert will base an opinion or inference. The court can order that this provision does not apply if it is not in the interests of justice (an example of this would be that relevant evidence could be given by that person which could not be given by the expert).

Where scientific examinations are relied upon, the methods used should be based on established principles, validated, and preferably published, so that they can be scrutinised by the scientific community at large. Where scientific findings require interpretation, the basis of the interpretation should be available to the scientific community.

An expert's report may be admitted, either in addition to the expert's testimony (CJA, s.30(1)) or instead of it if the court grants leave (s.30(2)). In deciding whether or not to grant leave s.30(3) requires the court to have regard to what the report says, the reasons for not calling the expert, and the risk of unfairness to the defendant that might result (such as the inability to cross-examine).

13.2 ADVANCE NOTICE OF EXPERT EVIDENCE

In the magistrates' court, expert evidence (except in relation to sentence) may not be given unless advance notice of the evidence is provided to the other parties: the Magistrates' Courts (Advance Notice of Expert Evidence) Rules 1997, SI 1997/705, rr.2, 3. The party seeking to admit the evidence must provide other parties with a written statement of the findings or opinions to be relied upon. On request, the party must provide an opportunity for the other party to examine the material on which the finding or opinion is based.

The position is the same in the Crown Court: Crown Court (Advance Notice of Expert Evidence) (Amendment) Rules 1987, SI 1987/716. Disclosure must take place as soon as reasonably practicable after committal or transfer to the Crown Court.

A party who fails to disclose expert evidence must obtain leave of the court to adduce it. The court will balance the interests of both parties in reaching a decision. The purpose of the rule is to give the other party the opportunity to evaluate any expert evidence before trial.

13.3 PRIVILEGED INFORMATION

If the defence instruct a forensic practitioner but decide not call the expert to give evidence, the information obtained by the defence from the expert is privileged. The expert's opinion, which is based on that privileged information, is also privileged and the defendant is entitled to assume that any communication the defendant has with the expert is protected in the same way as any communication the defendant has with his solicitor: *R. v. Davies* [2002] EWCA Crim 85.

The Criminal Justice Bill considered by parliament during the 2002–3 legislative session requires the defence to notify the court and the prosecutor of the name and address of any person whom the defence instruct with a view to that person providing an expert opinion for possible use as evidence at the trial. There is not a similar duty on the prosecutor.

Bruce Houlder, QC and Rob Brown, solicitor, told the 'Justice for All' conference that this could range from a scientist whom the defence solicitor telephones to sound him/her out and obtain some advice, but who never provides an opinion, to an expert who provides a report to the defence which the defence decides not to use.

Although this would allow the prosecution to interview an unused expert, the expert would consider himself/ herself bound to keep confidential any information relating to or following from the defence instructions and if required to appear in court, could rely upon legal professional privilege.

The prosecution would be able to comment at trial on the fact that the scientist was instructed but was not called to give evidence – the inference being that the unused expert would not have given evidence favourable to the defence, whereas the reason for not using the expert may be something quite different: the expert's opinion was unhelpful in peripheral matters; the report was poorly prepared or formulated on a wrong basis; or a report was subsequently obtained from a scientist who would carry much more weight in court.

During the Second Reading debate in the House of Lords on 16 June 2003, Lord Woolf referred to a document which he had placed in the Lords' library setting out what the judiciary regarded as the problem areas in the Criminal Justice Bill. Professor Michael Zander (2003) gave extracts from the document. Referring to the requirement on the defence to disclose the identity of any witness who had been instructed, it said:

> It is not clear what legitimate use can be made of the information about 'unused' experts . . . this procedure must not be used as a backdoor way of obtaining privileged information . . . . The question arises as to what use is to be made of the names of experts instructed by the defendants. Is it intended that they should be interviewed by the police? If so, this could be highly undesirable because in order to instruct an expert, it is often the case that privileged information has to be given to the expert. Are questions to be asked at the hearing by the prosecution about experts instructed by the defence who are not called? If so, should not the defence be in the position to ask similar questions about the prosecution's experts . . .

13.4 HOW INFORMATION IS PRESENTED BY THE SCIENTIST TO THE FACT FINDER

The second stage of the expert's testimony deals with the scientific concepts and technologies used in the case.

The expert must keep in mind that courts and advocates may know little of, and be intimidated by, the science involved. The lawyer needs to ensure that what his/her own expert says makes sense and addresses the issues which need to be addressed. The lawyer also needs to ensure that the other party's expert evidence is challenged effectively. To achieve this, the lawyer has to have some understanding of the forensic expertise involved.

The prosecutor will ask questions which will enable the expert to give short, direct and simple statements. The expert will give an explanation of the field of science involved (keeping it as simple and jargon free as possible), any testing carried out, the results found, expert opinion interpreting and drawing conclusions from those results, and their likely significance and meaning in the context of the particular case and the basis for that opinion.

The defence advocate may later cross-examine the prosecution expert, challenging the test results and expert opinions and conclusions. The laboratory procedures may be questioned and the possibility of contamination of the evidence raised.

The defence advocate may ask the prosecution expert to agree that contamination can occur, and if it does that it may affect the test results and conclusions drawn. But the court should be concerned with evidence based upon facts, not hypothetical situations. The prosecution expert may also be asked if it is possible to draw an alternative conclusion from the scientific facts presented. An alternative may be possible, but so unlikely as to be capable of being discounted.

In an article 'How to Succeed as an Expert Witness' by Lisa Kahn and Daniel Feldstern, Los Angeles County District Attorney's Office in Profiles in DNA, vol 2 no. 2 (www.promega.com/profiles/202/202_09), some sample questions to an expert giving DNA testimony are suggested:

Establishing the expert's qualifications

Where are you employed?
Is your laboratory accredited for DNA testing?
What is your job title?
What are your duties?
What education do you have that qualifies you to perform these duties?
Have you taken any specific courses or workshops related to your duties?
Does your laboratory conduct any type of training?
Are you a member of any professional organisations?
Do you attend professional meetings?
Do you read the scientific literature that is relevant to your job?
Have you ever testified before?
Approximately how many times?

Questions about the technology used

What is DNA?

Is DNA the same in every cell of the body?

With the exception of identical twins, is a person's DNA unique?

Are there tests available to detect an individual's genetic type?

What test was used in the present case?

Can you explain briefly how this test is conducted?

Are controls performed to ensure that a reliable and accurate result is obtained?

Can you describe the safeguards and controls used to ensure the integrity of the test?

Questions about the particular case

Did you conduct a DNA test on the crime scene and reference samples in this case?

What were the results of the test?

What is the chance that this same genetic profile would be found in a random member of the population?

Are there samples remaining to retest, should someone wish to dispute the accuracy of the result?

13.5 PROBABILITY

Science does not deal in certainty. Samples may never match perfectly, yet within certain limits they are regarded as a 'match'. These limits will be drawn at a negotiable point.

Graham Cooke, a barrister, told the 'Justice for All' conference that lawyers dealt with statistics either 'badly' or 'very badly'. He recommended that a lawyer addressing a tribunal should take the same pains to present the information in an understandable way as he/she would when addressing a jury. He also advised against using words such as 'significant' which also have a special statistical meaning.

A statistician may say, for example, that 'A is significantly higher than B'. In advance of conducting tests, a 'significance level' may have been set, such as five per cent. A is significantly higher than B then means that in repeat sampling, in 19 out of 20 samples (95 per cent) A and B were not the same and A was higher than B.

On the other hand, probabalistic statements such as 'likely', 'very likely', 'highly likely', 'probably', 'very probably' have no special meaning, are just vague quantifiers and are to be avoided. If two people who used the term 'highly likely' were asked how many times out of 100 an event would have to happen before they would describe its happening as 'highly likely', they would both give different answers. These terms and others used in Likert scales are ordinal in that they imply a rank ordering of response, but no more. 'Very likely' equates to greater certainty than 'likely' but it is not known from the use of those words how much more certain (Renis Likert invented a measurement method used in attitude surveys which allowed answers from 'strongly agree' to 'strongly disagree').

Another word to be avoided because of its ability to mislead, is 'consistent'. A scientific finding will often prove that a fact was likely rather than certain because a scientific finding may be consistent with more than one fact. For example, if a person is found after a fight with blood on his shoes (finding A) that does not prove that he was the assailant (fact B) but it may be consistent with fact B. Finding A may also be consistent with fact C (that he was merely present when the fight took place), or D (that he went to give first aid to the victim).

The court will have to decide, with the aid of the other evidence, whether the truth is B, C or D.

With DNA evidence, there are three propositions to consider:

1. What is the probability that the crime profile would match the defendant if he had in fact left it? If the DNA profiling is correctly carried out, then there is an almost certain probability that they will match.
2. What is the probability that the crime profile would match the defendant, if some unknown person had in fact left it? This is termed the 'match probability' (or by courts the 'random occurrence ratio'). The answer to this will typically be one in a billion.
3. What is the probability that the defendant is innocent given that his DNA profile matches the crime sample? If the prior odds (the likelihood depending upon the other available evidence) are not taken into account, a court may conclude that the odds of the defendant being innocent are a billion to one.

The match probability is the domain of the experts. The guilt probability is the question which is of direct relevance to the court, and which requires an assessment of all the evidence. It is, therefore, in the domain of the court and not the expert. An expert should never calculate the probability of the defendant's guilt as the DNA evidence must be looked at in the context of the other evidence.

The Court of Appeal in *R. v. Doheny and Adams* [1997] 1 Cr App R 369 gave guidance that the judge should explain to the jury the relevance of the 'random occurrence ratio' and draw attention to the extraneous evidence which provides the context which gives the ratio its significance. The judge should also draw attention to the evidence which conflicts with the conclusion that the defendant is responsible for the crime stain. The judge may direct the jury to decide if they are sure that it was the defendant who left the stain, or whether it is possible that it was one of the small group of men who share the same DNA characteristics.

Bayes' Theorem is a mathematical statistical method for calculating the weight to be given to such scientific evidence taking the prior odds into account. However, the Court of Appeal has expressly disallowed an account of the Bayesian approach being given to the jury, since the court took the view that it was the jury's task instead to evaluate the relationship between one piece of evidence and another, and feared that the court and the jury would be confused by exposure to the mathematics involved. Lord Bingham CJ said that it would be 'a recipe for confusion, misunderstanding and mis-judgement, possibly among counsel, probably among judges and certainly among jurors' (*R.* v. *Adams* (1998) 1 Cr App R 377).

The Royal Statistical Society (RSS) criticised the evidence of Professor Sir Roy Meadow, a paediatrician in the Sally Clark case, for telling the jury that in his opinion the probability of two children dying from a cot death in the same family was one in 73 million. In the *RSS News*, December 2001, the Society said that this 'is one example of a medical expert witness making a serious sta-tistical error, one which may have had a profound effect on the outcome of the case'. This figure had been obtained simply by squaring the figure for the prob-ability of one cot death. Professor Meadow had failed to take account of family background or the reasons why a second death is actually more likely in a family which has already suffered a death and other experts, taking pre-disposing factors into account, reduced the probability of it happening a second time in the same family to a figure in the region of one in 60.

According to Dr Colin Aitken (2003) of the School of Mathematics and Joseph Bell Centre for Forensic Statistics and Legal Reasoning, University of Edinburgh, due regard must be paid to the reference group when probability is calculated. He gave as one example a Scottish case in which an accused was charged with murdering three of her children at birth. The alternative prop-osition was that they had died of natural causes. 'It is not sufficient', Dr Aitken wrote, 'to consider the relative frequency of one neo-natal death and then take the cube of this.' He went on to explain that in the Scottish case the deaths had occurred in a private flat in which no medical support was avail-able. 'The probability of three neo-natal deaths in such an environment will almost certainly be different than that in a hospital and there are no formal records from which a valid estimate of that probability may be made. It is not the role of a statistician, who may testify to the relative frequencies in the hospital environment . . . to testify to the nature of such a difference.' He gave a second example, an American case, in which an accused was convicted of arson of four of his properties. 'The probability of four fires was calculated as the fourth power of the probability of one fire . . . the figure had been produced without due regard to . . . residences comparable to those of the defendant.'

The RSS says 'although many scientists have some familiarity with statistical methods, statistics remain a specialised area. The Society urges courts to ensure that the statistical evidence is presented only by appropriately qualified experts, as would be the case for any other form of expert evidence.' Statisticians do not have a section in the CRFP register and, because of the very small size of the speciality, are unlikely to in the near future. There is a professional qualification C.Stat. and courts, when establishing an expert's qualifications could ask whether the expert had received any specific training in statistics or probability

REFERENCES

Aitken, C. (2003) 'Conviction by probability?', *New Law Journal – Expert Witness supplement*, 25 July.

Hodgkinson, T. (1990) *Expert Evidence: Law and Practice*, Sweet and Maxwell.

Kahn, L. & Feldstern, D. 'How to succeed as an expert witness', *Profiles in DNA*, vol. 2, no. 2.

Redmayne, M. (2001) *Expert Evidence and Criminal Justice*, Oxford University Press.

Royal Statistical Society (2001) *RSS News*, December.

SECTION B

Understanding Areas of Forensic Speciality

CHAPTER 14

Drugs, toxicology, and related areas of expertise

14.1 SCENE ASSESSMENT IN DRUGS/DRUG DRIVING CASES

In cases involving drugs/drug driving a search of the subject and the scene (including vehicle) will be conducted for the purpose of locating either drugs or associated drug paraphernalia.

In suspected drug driving cases visual observation of drugs/drug paraphernalia at the scene is considered to be an initial indication that a suspect is a drug user or may be drug impaired. Such observation will also be used by a suitably qualified drug recognition officer (DRO) as an initial basis for considering whether to carry out a field impairment test upon a subject (see 'drug search plan', Form MG/DD/F). An 'aide memoire' may be used by some officers who were originally trained in these techniques. However the second generation of training encourages officers to use only form MG/DD/F as their original note.

Any physical evidence of drugs, including powders, tablets, other substances, and any drug paraphernalia (e.g. syringes, needles, glass pipes, plastic bags, lighters, foil, containers) which may contain drug traces and be susceptible to testing will be removed and taken for laboratory analysis. Drugs/drug paraphernalia removed from the crime scene should be packaged and labelled prior to transportation to the laboratory.

In order to ensure the preservation of the condition of any drugs, certain specialised packaging techniques should be used. This will vary depending on the nature of the drug. Generally, each drug sample or specimen should be placed in a paper container and sealed (this technique is used for drugs in tablet form, and loose material such as herbal cannabis and marijuana). Certain drugs susceptible to deterioration (e.g. PCP (Phenylcyclohexylpiperidine/ketamine (angel dust)) should be packaged in heat-sealed bags.

The Forensic Science Service (FSS) Safescene Unit recommends the use of small or large evidence bags for the packaging of drugs. These bags are tamper-proof, uniquely labelled, and have a printed exhibit label.

Medicinal or 'legal' preparations found at a scene should be left in any prescription containers in order to assist in the identification process. The prescription containers should also be packaged, sealed and labelled.

All items should be transported to the laboratory in separate sealed packages in order to prevent cross-contamination between specimens. The chain of custody should always be checked in relation to drug specimens removed from a crime scene (including the type of packaging used to package the drug prior to transportation), particularly in cases where the origin of multiple specimens (e.g. wraps of heroin) is at issue and the possibility of cross-contamination needs to be carefully investigated.

14.2 DRIVING WHILST UNFIT THROUGH DRINK OR DRUGS

14.2.1 Drink/drug driving statistics

Studies by the Department of the Environment, Transport and the Regions (DETR) (now the Department for Transport (DfT)) indicate that 18 per cent of all drivers and 21 per cent of passengers involved in road death have an illegal substance present in their bodies. Notably, an additional four per cent of drivers will have taken a prescribed or 'over the counter' medication that may impair their fitness to drive.

Multiple or 'poly-drug use' (a term used to indicate the simultaneous use of multiple drugs – whether legal, illegal, or 'over the counter') is also becoming increasingly common. A 1995 study conducted by the FSS indicated that 67 per cent of blood specimens submitted for suspected Road Traffic Act 1988 (RTA), s.4 offences (being unfit to drive through drink or drugs) were found to contain two or more drugs.

Drink driving, unlike drug driving, has been highlighted as a serious social problem for many years. Since 1976, the DETR has initiated extensive annual television, radio and media campaigns to heighten awareness about the dangers of drink driving. Market research indicates that drink driving is now generally viewed as socially unacceptable and that the anti-drink-driving campaigns have been one of the most successful of their kind. Drink driving fatalities have fallen by over two-thirds since 1976. Conversely, instances of drug driving are rising and the full extent of the problem is not fully appreciated by the general public. While no official statistics have yet been made available in relation to drug-impaired driving, a 1997 DETR survey indicated that there was a fourfold increase in illicit drug consumption (with an increasing amount of poly-drug use) between 1995 and 1997. This figure continues to increase along with, it can be assumed, the level of drug-impaired driving. There is also evidence that many people are not aware that driving whilst under the influence of drugs is a criminal offence.

14.3 ROADSIDE TESTING TO DETERMINE WHETHER SUSPECT IS UNFIT TO DRIVE THROUGH ALCOHOL OR DRUGS/DRIVING WITH EXCESS ALCOHOL

Evidence of impairment through drink or drugs can be shown by adducing evidence of:

- the manner of driving;
- a driver's physical condition;
- a toxicological specimen.

Drink or drug driving potentially involves the opinions of the following investigators or experts: first officer attending (FOA) or arresting officer (AO); DRO (if available); forensic medical examiner (FME), drug analyst, and toxicologist.

14.4 ALCOHOL

An assessment of unfitness to drive through alcohol (RTA 1988, s.4) is often initially based on the visual recognition of one or more notorious physical signs of alcohol impairment (erratic driving; suspect's physical condition, e.g. drowsiness, frequently falling asleep, inability to stand, mental confusion) coupled with evidence that this condition is due to alcohol (e.g. smell of alcohol on subject's breath, clothing, alcohol containers present in vehicle).

In cases of doubt, it should always be considered whether a suspect's physical condition, which may at first appear to be due to alcohol, is in fact symptomatic of some other pre-existing physical condition (such as illness, diabetic hypoglycaemic reaction, etc.). A suspect's medical history should also be investigated (including any medications taken, whether prescribed, purchased 'over the counter', or otherwise, which may have caused or contributed to the apparent impairment).

Absence of alcohol in the system can also be proved by a blood or urine test (evidenced by a certificate of a drug analyst or toxicologist) which will be taken into account by a court when considering a charge of unfitness.

14.4.1 Preliminary breathalysers

A roadside screening device for testing blood/alcohol levels, the well-known screening or preliminary breathalyser, has been in use in the UK since 1967. Preliminary breath testing is extensively used by all police forces. In 1999–2000, some 715,000 screening breath tests were administered in the UK, 13 per cent of which proved either positive or were refused (Crime and Criminal Justice Unit (Research, Development and Statistics) Home Office Statistics, 30 November 2001). If the preliminary breath test is positive, a subject will be asked to take an 'evidential' breath test.

The following devices are currently approved by the Home Secretary for the purpose of administering preliminary breath tests:

- Lion Alcolmeter S-L2A (manufacturer, Lion Laboratories plc);
- Lion Alcolmeter SL-400 (manufacturer, Lion Laboratories plc);
- Lion Alcolmeter SL-400A (indicating display form) (manufacturer, Lion Laboratories plc);
- Lion Alcolmeter SL-400A (software version 3.31) (manufacturer, Lion Laboratories plc);
- Alert (manufacturer, Draeger);
- Alcotest 7410 (manufacturer, Draeger);
- Alcotest 80 (manufacturer, Draeger) (crystal tubes – not used by many forces now);
- Alcotest 80A (manufacturer, Draeger) (crystal tubes);
- Alcosensor IV UK (manufacturer, Intoximeters UK Ltd).

Further information on preliminary breathalysers is available online via **www.homeoffice.gov.uk/ppd/oppu/orders.htm**.

If there is any doubt or suspicion of operational error, it should be ascertained whether a device has been operated in accordance with the manufacturer's operating instructions. For operating instructions for the devices listed above see Wilkinson (2001) vol. 1, ss. 4.90–4.100.

In cases in which a suspect has been charged with failure to supply a specimen of breath (RTA 1988, s.11(3)), the suspect's medical history should be investigated in order to ascertain whether any mental or physical condition is in existence which may have rendered the subject unable to provide a breath specimen (in *R. v. Lennard* [1973] RTR 252 the Court of Appeal held that the defence of reasonable excuse must arise out of a physical or mental inability to provide a specimen or a substantial risk in its provision).

It is possible that people who suffer from bronchitis, asthma, or medical conditions resulting in loss of lung capacity may be unable to blow into a bag in one continuous breath, or with sufficient force, to operate either the Alert, Alcometer, or Alcosensor devices. The Alcosensor IV will analyse any amount of breath it takes in, which the manufacturers say will be sufficient for a preliminary test.

14.4.2 Evidential breathalysers

Evidential breath testing was first introduced in 1983 as an alternative to taking blood samples. In 1998 (pursuant to the Criminal Procedure and Investigations Act 1996 (CPIA), s.63) the so-called 'second generation' evidential breathalysers were introduced in police stations. The following evidential devices are currently approved by the Home Secretary:

- Camic Datamaster (manufacturer, Camic (Car and Medical Instrument Company) Ltd);
- Lion Intoxilyzer 6000UK (and software version 2.34) (manufacturer Lion Laboratories plc);
- Intoximeter EC/IR (and software version EC/IR-UK5.23) (manufacturer, Intoximeters Inc of St Louis, Missouri).

For further details and operational instructions of the above devices see Wilkinson (2001) vol. 1, ss.4.239–4.245 and Appendix 1. Lion Laboratories provide a training course for police, supervisors and instructors in the operation of the Intoxilyzer. The course provides guidance on the proper maintenance of records and logs, monitoring, and operating of the device (note that a recent case on the operation of a device from the Lion Intoxilyzer 6000UK series and final calibration checks indicated that considerations relevant to the operation of first generation breathalysers did not automatically apply to second generation devices, see *Mercer v. DPP* [2002] All ER (D) 13 (Feb)).

The Lion Intoxilyzer has built-in error messages which indicates that either the device or the breath specimen has become unreliable. If an 'error message' appears all breath measurements obtained during that cycle should be invalidated. Mechanical error may also occur if the device is physically damaged. Both Camic and Intoximeter machines do the same. The Intoxilyzer is designed to incorporate a self-cleaning mouthpiece to prevent cross-contamination of specimens between subjects.

For further information on Lion Laboratory devices see **www.lion-breath.com**.

All evidential breathalysers provide printouts. The police retain a copy and the suspect is provided with another copy. For information on the breathalyser procedure and sample printouts, see Wilkinson (2001) vol. 1, Appendix 1, A1.07 and A1.12.

In cases in which the lower of the two evidential breath specimens is less than 50mg alcohol per 100 ml breath the suspect may elect that the specimens be replaced by a specimen of blood or urine (see Wilkinson (2001) vol. 1, s.4.145 et seq). The subject is entitled to retain a portion of the specimen taken in order to have it independently tested. It is important that this sample is properly handled (see **para 14.12**).

In order to comply with statutory requirements a suspect must be asked whether there are any special reasons why a specimen of blood cannot be taken (*Ogburn v. DPP* [1994] RTR 241). The suspect must be appropriately informed of this option and any refusal to provide a specimen must be equivocal (see *Dhillon v. DPP* (1993) 157 JP 707 where the Divisional Court held that a defendant's claim that 'I can't stand the sight of blood' was not capable of interpretation as a refusal and that the AO should have made further enquiries in order to obtain a clear answer about whether or not the defendant was willing to exercise his statutory option).

A suspect should be given the option of providing a sample of urine if they may have a medical reason for not providing a blood sample (*Johnson* v. *West Yorkshire Metropolitan Police* [1986] Crim LR 64). Improper pressure must not be put upon a suspect to exercise the option of providing a laboratory sample for analysis (*Green* v. *Lockhart* (1986) SLT 11).

14.5 DRUGS

A 'drug' for the purposes of road traffic legislation has been widely defined to include all medicaments or medicines (see RTA 1988, s.11; *Armstrong* v. *Clark* [1957] 1 All ER 433, and *Bradford* v. *Wilson* [1984] RTR 116. Note that the definition is not restricted to 'illegal' drugs and necessarily includes all prescribed drugs and medicines purchased 'over the counter'). For the purpose of drug recognition techniques, DROs will refer to the more generic definition provided by the World Health Organisation (WHO) as 'any substance taken into a human body which may modify one or more of its functions'.

The Misuse of Drugs Act 1971 relates to prohibited drugs. The Medicines Act 1968 governs the manufacture and supply of medicinal products and divides drugs into prescription only medicines which must be prescribed by a doctor, a dentist (or, in certain circumstances, another health professional) and pharmacy medicines sold under the supervision of a pharmacist from a pharmacy, and general sale list medicines which can be sold from any premises without supervision. In this regard, see also the provisions of the Pharmacy Act 1933.

A charge of 'driving whilst unfit through drugs' (RTA 1988, s.4) can solely result from a subject having consumed prescribed drugs or 'over the counter' medicines (or having mixed such drugs with an amount of alcohol that would not normally, by itself, have resulted in any impairment of the suspect's ability to drive or in the suspect having a blood/alcohol level in excess of the legal limit for driving).

Many individuals continue to drive without realising that certain prescribed or 'over the counter' drugs and medicines can cause drowsiness or in some other way affect their ability to drive. This is often due to a failure to read the instructions on the packaging (typical warnings which indicate that certain drugs are liable to cause impairment include 'may cause drowsiness' or 'not to be used when operating heavy machinery or driving').

Police Research Group (PRG) studies have indicated that there is a general lack of information supplied with prescribed and 'over the counter' medications warning about possible dangers associated with driving after having consumed a particular drug. When advising a suspect faced with a charge of unfitness under RTA 1988, s.4, enquiries should be made about any underlying medical conditions and any prescriptive or other medications that may have been consumed. It is possible that the suspect may not be aware of the potential effect of the medications on the ability to drive.

Note that in *R. v. Cooksley, R. v. Stride, R. v. Cook, A.-G.'s Ref. (No. 152 of 2002)* [2003] All ER (D) 58 (Apr), in which the Court of Appeal issued sentencing guidelines for offences of causing death by dangerous driving and causing death by careless driving when under the influence of drink or drugs, the consumption of drugs including legal medication known to cause drowsiness was identified as a high level aggravating factor for sentencing purposes.

Injections of insulin can, if administered contrary to medical advice so that a hypoglycaemic attack is induced, be an effective cause of unfitness to drive (see *R. v. Ealing Magistrates' Court, ex p. Woodman* [1994] RTR 189 and Wilkinson, vol. 1, s.4.128).

Inhaled substances such as toluene (inhaled during glue sniffing) can cause impairment and are also considered to be 'drugs' for the purposes of RTA, s.4 (see *Bradford v. Wilson* [1984] RTR 116).

At present no roadside screening device is available to detect the presence of drugs in a suspect (devices are currently undergoing trials but will not be introduced for police use until 2005 at the earliest). Section 107 and Schedule 7 of the Railways and Transport Safety Act 2003 has amended RTA 1988, s.6 to make express provision for preliminary impairment and drugs tests using sweat or saliva. Roadside recognition of drug impairment or unfitness to drive through drugs is confined to visual observation. Due to the subjective nature of each individual interpretation of these terms and the signs of impairment, visual observation has some limitations and shortcomings and has caused major problems for police officers at the roadside and forensic physicians conducting subsequent examinations of suspects.

Fleming and Stewart (1998) found that:

- 84.5 per cent of traffic officers and 41 per cent of forensic medical examiners (FMEs) (see **para. 22.1**) had not received any formal training in the identification of the signs and symptoms of drug use amongst drivers;
- police officers and FMEs had wide ranging interpretations of the term 'unfit to drive', varying from the smell of alcohol on a person's breath to a complete incapacity to move;
- traffic officers stated that they occasionally disagreed with FMEs on whether or not drug impairment was evident and had expressed concerns about the success of their working relationships with FMEs.

In *MacNeill v. Fletcher* 1966 SC (J) 18 an accused was found to have four times the permitted blood/alcohol level, was unsteady on his feet, and had glazed eyes. It was held that an FME was entitled to refuse to certify that a driver was unfit to drive in the circumstances (although it is now notorious that a high blood alcohol level will result in substantial impairment of a suspect's ability to drive properly, see Wilkinson, para. 4.122)).

14.6 DRUG RECOGNITION: GENERAL TRAINING OF POLICE OFFICERS

All police officers may receive comprehensive training in relation to applicable legislation and associated procedures to be adopted in relation to suspects suspected of committing a drug or drug related offence.

The general training currently offered to police officers in relation to the recognition of the signs and symptoms of impairment through drug consumption, other than the fact that the evidence required will be similar to drunkenness, is generally rudimentary and non-specific. Officers are advised to some degree to be aware of certain signs and symptoms, including manner of walking, demeanour, condition of clothing, slurred speech, and glazed eyes.

While most police forces are now sending officers to be trained and certified in drug recognition, to date only a small proportion of police officers will have received specific drug recognition training (DRT). The opinion of a non-trained officer in relation to drug impairment can thus be more readily challenged than the opinion of a certified DRO.

14.6.1 DRT for police officers and the role of DROs

In response to concerns regarding the ability of police officers to properly identify drug impairment and anecdotal evidence from officers regarding the difficulties encountered at the roadside in identifying whether a suspect was unfit through drugs, research was undertaken by the PRG. Following the publication of the research findings (Fleming and Stewart (1998)), five police forces took part in an eight-week trial in 1999 to identify a system of field impairment tests (FIT), and to determine whether drug influence recognition (DIR) could assist officers in identifying impairment through drugs. This trial being deemed successful, the National Drug Recognition Training Scheme was accepted as best practice by the Association of Chief Police officers (ACPO). In August 2000 the national training of DRT for all forces was launched by the ACPO (Road Policing) Committee at Bramshill, where this training is now available to all forces.

Northamptonshire Police force was involved in the piloting of the training scheme and is now the only force in England and Wales that can offer DRT to both practitioners and instructors. Two of the force's officers have attended a drug recognition expert (DRE) training course in the USA and are currently the only certified DREs in Europe.

Additionally, the Northamptonshire Police force has 250 certified DROs in all units.

Each police force has a different policy in relation to the number of officers that will be trained in drug recognition. Some forces have restricted the training to their traffic officers, while others have trained specific officers on general shifts.

In future it is the aim of police forces that all or a high proportion of officers should receive standard training in drug recognition.

14.6.2 Training and experience of DROs

In order to become a certified DRO, a police officer must successfully complete a national FIT and DIR course. The standard course consists of a minimum of two days of instruction followed by an examination. Thereafter certified DROs will be expected to gain experience in the field in DIR and the carrying out of FITs. These tests were derived from standard field sobriety tests (SFST) that have been used by the majority of police forces in the USA since 1979.

Officers trained in drug recognition should also be able to identify the category of drug taken through observation of known side effects.

For the purposes of DIR, drugs are divided into seven main groups:

- cannabis;
- opiates (heroin, opium, morphine, codeine, and methadone);
- central nervous system (CNS) stimulants (including cocaine, amphetamine, and ecstasy (MDMA – which has visible effects similar to stimulants));
- CNS depressants (including alcohol, barbiturates, tranquillisers, anti-depressants);
- dissociative anaesthetics (including ketamine and PCP, commonly known as angel dust);
- hallucinogens (including lysergic acid diethylamide (LSD), magic mushrooms, and ecstasy);
- inhalants (petrol, glue, solvents, aerosols, and paint).

An additional category is concerned with the effects of poly-drug use.

The DRT course advocates three stages of detection in drug driving cases:

(i) initial observations, including manner of driving (the following ways in which a vehicle is driven have been shown to correlate with impairment: wide turn, straddling centre lane/line; weaving; sudden swerving; slow speed (less than 10 m.p.h. below limit); stopping without cause in carriageway; driving too close to the vehicle in front; drifting; braking erratically; driving onto opposite carriageway; signalling inconsistent with driving conditions; slow response to traffic signals; turning sharply/illegally; accelerating/decelerating sharply; headlights off), and condition of subject;
(ii) subject interview (DIR);
(iii) suspect evaluation (FIT).

14.6.3 FITs

The FIT has five steps:

1. Pupillary examination (examination to detect any reading outside the normal range of pupil size on a 'pupilometer').
2. Romberg test (requires subject to tilt head backwards and estimate the passage of 30 seconds).
3. One leg stand test (subject is asked to stand on one leg with foot raised six to eight inches off the ground, for a period of 30 seconds whilst counting out loud. This is repeated for both legs).
4. Walk and turn test (walking in a line heel to toe for nine steps out and nine steps back and turning correctly as demonstrated).
5. Finger to nose test (subject is asked to close eyes and touch their nose with index finger, using the hand instructed by the officer).

The FIT is not an interview for the purposes Code C of the Codes of Practice to PACE and so does not require a caution. It is, however, the general practice of DROs to administer an additional warning to a subject before carrying out the FIT test. The pre-FIT warning should take the following form:

*   that the driver is not under arrest and is not obliged to remain with the officer (unless impairment was so obvious that the driver was immediately arrested and then asked to participate in the test);
*   that the purpose of the test is to enable the officer to ascertain whether there are grounds to suspect that the driver's ability to drive is impaired by drugs;
*   that the driver is not obliged to participate in the tests, and that if the driver does participate, the results may be given in evidence.

Failure to so warn may be ground for excluding the results and findings of the FIT (see *Procurator Fiscal (Glasgow) (McDivett)* v. *McKeuan* (Glasgow Sheriff Court, 12 May 2000, unreported) in which the FIT findings were excluded as evidence because the defendant had not been given a warning).

Despite its standardisation, the FIT is necessarily based on the subjective opinion of an officer and this can cause inconsistency. For this reason DROs are instructed to bear in mind that there are great differences among individual human beings and their reaction to drugs. For example, with regard to the pupillary examination, even a small amount of drugs can affect the functioning of the eye and there is no guarantee as to how the pupils will react in any given individual. The steps in the FIT may also be affected by pre-existing medical conditions, injuries, or balance/coordination difficulties. It is for this reason that the forensic physician maintains an important role in the determination of unfitness to drive.

The National Drug Recognition Training Manual suggests the following contents of a DRO's statement of evidence:

1. Officer's experience and training: (a) detail dates and place of FIT/DIR training; (b) detail experience in FIT assessments since training; (c) (instructors only) detail National Validation undertaken.
2. Date, time and location of incident: (a) found by officer; (b) called to assist.
3. Details of manner of driving seen (if seen by officer).
4. Initial observations of state of driver.
5. Other officers present during assessment.
6. Results of breath test.
7. Details of request to perform FIT (as per the preamble on card (meaning Form MG/DD 'Aide Memoire')).
8. Results of pupillary examination (stating the standard against which the pupils of both eyes were checked, e.g. Form MG/DD/F), the size of the pupils measured in millimetres, and any other observations, such as eyes bloodshot or watery).
9. Detail results of psychophysical tests: (a) Romberg test; (b) walk and turn (including any specific observations such as loss of balance, stepping off line, and failure to turn correctly); (c) one leg stand (including observations regarding swaying or loss of balance); (d) finger to nose (including any observations of subject missing tip of nose, and number of times missed).
10. Significant statements made during tests or after.
11. Opinion of officer/assessor (including the specific category of drug under the influence of which the subject is, and that the subject is unable to operate a motor vehicle safely).
12. Any other relevant information.

In addition to the above, some officers may simply exhibit Form MG/DD/F as their original notes, making a passing reference to it in their statement. Whilst this practice is not incorrect, it is not advised by DREs.

14.7   POLICE NATIONAL DRINK/DRUGS DRIVE PRO FORMA

The following national pro forma are now used by all forces in England and Wales for drink/driving offences. The DRO training course provides specific guidance upon the completion of these forms (in particular forms MG/DD/E and MG/DD/F):

Available online via **www.homeoffice.gov.uk/ppd/oppu/ orders.htm** are the pro forma:

- MG/DD/A drink/drugs station procedure;
- MG/DD/B drink/drugs station procedure – specimens/impairment for use with MG/DD/A;
- MG/DD/C drink/drugs hospital procedure;
- MG/DD/D alcohol technical defence form;
- MG/DD/E drug sample information form;
- MG/DD/F and MG/DD/F/a impairment assessment forms. (These forms are for use by police forces participating in the National Drug Driving Programme launched by the Police College, Bramshill in August 2000 and recommended by the ACPO (Roads Policing) as best practice. The forms should only be used by officers, who have been trained in the recognised drug recognition and FIT techniques. Form MG/DD/F is complete in itself. Form MG/DD/F may only be used in company with a card printed with the identical questions as in form MG/DD/F.);
- MG/DD 'Aide Memoire'.

Forensic physicians now have their own assessment form available on the website of the Association of Forensic Physicians (AFP) for download and has taken the form MG/DD/F as a template. The FIT tests within that form are exactly the same as those described on Form F. See **www.afpweb.org.uk**.

14.8 TREATMENT OF DRUG USERS IN CUSTODY

Some 61 per cent of all subjects in custody have taken an illegal drug and one in five have recently consumed multiple drugs, including alcohol (these figures were considered to be an underestimate because of restrictions that prevented the testing of certain detainees, see Bennett, T. (1998).

The Royal College of Physicians (2001) has published guidance for forensic physicians in relation to the treatment of substance misuse detainees in custody. It is recommended that in the case of a drug user detainee, a forensic physician should liaise with the custody officer and obtain any known details, including the circumstances of the arrest. The forensic physician should obtain the following information: type(s) of substances misused, duration of use, quantity of daily use, route of administration, time of last dose. It has been found, however, that frankness on the part of a user in custody with regard to the history of drug use may be inconsistent in an attempt to acquire some perceived secondary gain.

A physical examination should be undertaken in order to ascertain any signs of intoxication, withdrawal, or overdose. The effects of nicotine withdrawal on a subject should also be assessed. A craving for nicotine can result in mood swings, threats of self-harm, and may affect fitness to interview. The Education and Research Committee of the AFP advise that nicotine gum (as a form of nicotine replacement therapy – NRT) be used by the subject, who will take personal responsibility for its use. The AFP considers that asking forensic physicians to authorise the use of NRT – which means that the physician takes over any risk in relation to its use – is an inappropriate use of professional skills (see Dr Margaret Stark (January 2003); online via **www.afpweb.org.uk**).

A suspect's mental health should also be examined because prolonged drug or alcohol abuse may give rise to psychotic states that have implications in relation to fitness for interview. The overriding concern of the forensic physician is the clinical safety and wellbeing of the suspect, but the forensic physician will also be required to make assessments of the suspect's fitness to be detained and fitness for interview.

In cases in which a suspect is thought to be a 'body packer' or a drug swallower immediate transfer to hospital should be considered. If an intimate search of a subject for drugs is considered to be required it must be authorised by a police officer of the rank of superintendent or above. The search should be carried out in a hospital or other medical facility, not at a police station (see Association of Police Surgeons and British Medical Association *Guidelines for Intimate Body Searches* (1999)).

For further information and considerations relating to the searching of body packers or 'mules' see Dr Margaret Stark and Dr Guy Norfolk 'Substance Misuse' in W.D.S. McLay (1996), and on consent in relation to intimate searches and generally, see Dr Michael A. Knight 'The Practitioner's Obligations' in W.D.S. McLay (1996).

14.9 ROLE OF THE FORENSIC PHYSICIAN IN ASSESSING UNFITNESS TO DRIVE THROUGH DRINK OR DRUGS

An opinion of a police officer in relation to a subject's unfitness will be subject to consideration by a forensic physician. The opinions of a police officer/DRO and the forensic physician regarding impairment may differ. It must be noted that the role of the forensic physician in these cases is not pivotal. The forensic physician, under RTA 1988, s.7(3)(c) (as amended) only has to determine that the suspect may have a condition due to some drug. The forensic physician *does not* have to determine that the suspect is impaired at the time of the examination.

Fleming and Stewart (1998) reported that 32 per cent of traffic officers had indicated that there had been occasions when they had arrested a person for driving whilst impaired through drugs and the forensic physician had disagreed with that opinion. The officers indicated that the reasons for this difference of opinion included:

- effects of drugs had worn off before the medical examination;
- lack of interest of the forensic physician;

- lack of knowledge of the forensic physician;
- lack of knowledge of the police officer;
- lack of communication.

The ability of a forensic physician to properly assess the suspect's unfitness at the time of driving may be affected by any delay between arrest and examining the suspect.

Different drugs produce visible effects at different times and the length of time for the side effects to wear off/the length of time that the drug remains in the system varies between categories of drugs. Side effects/length of time drugs remain in the system can also be different if a number of different drugs have been mixed.

If there is a delay between arrest and examination by a forensic physician it is possible that the effects of the drugs on the suspect may have worn off. If the effects of a particular drug have dissipated by the time a blood test is administered, a court is entitled to look at all the evidence including the opinion of the AO and any observations made by the officers at the time of arrest (see *Leetham* v. *DPP* [1999] RTR 29 where a defendant was convicted under RTA, s.4 after a blood test failed to establish conclusively that cannabis was present in the system).

14.10 TRAINING AND EXPERIENCE OF FORENSIC PHYSICIANS IN DRUG RECOGNITION

The National Training Centre for the Scientific Support to Crime Investigation (NTCSSCI) national training course for forensic physicians does not currently provide specific training in drug impairment testing or drug symptom recognition.

In a questionnaire completed by 24.4 per cent of the members of the AFP, 41 per cent stated that they had not received any formal training in the identification of the signs and symptoms of drug usage amongst drivers. Eighty-seven per cent indicated that they would benefit from specific training in this area (Fleming and Stewart (1998)).

The Chairman of the Police Complaints Authority has stated that he was unsure as to whether forensic physicians were properly trained to assist in the identification of drug usage. The Honorary Secretary of the AFP has commented that there are different levels of competency amongst forensic physicians in identifying the signs and symptoms of drug use (D. Adams 'Custody Review' (1997) pp. 16–17).

It is incumbent upon each individual force to ensure that their forensic physicians receive training. It is now recommended that all forensic physicians attend Day One of the standard DRT course, with an option to attend Day Two. The difficulty is that most want to be paid for their attendance, or see no reason for attending, or plead lack of time and other work commitments. It has been suggested that forces make such training compulsory (the Northamptonshire Police force has made DRT a mandatory part of forensic physician training in the contract of employment).

14.11 THE ROLE OF THE LEGAL ADVISER IN RECOGNISING DRUG/ALCOHOL IMPAIRMENT

Considering the shortcomings of current police training and general lack of awareness of symptoms of drug impairment, a legal adviser attending the police station should always consider whether drug impairment in a suspect is evident.

In cases of doubt, the suspect should be asked whether they have taken any drugs, what kind of drugs, and when they were taken. It will also be helpful to have some awareness of the symptoms of the main drug groups.

14.11.1 Symptoms of main drug groups

The visible symptoms of the main drug categories and the average length of time that the drugs remain in the system are listed below:

Cannabis: detectable by smell, poor coordination, loss of balance, disorientation, reddening of eyes, body and eyelid tremors. Cannabis causes user to have impaired perception of time and distance, poor attention span, lack of inhibitions, paranoia, confusion, short-term memory loss. Symptoms are visible within 10 seconds of inhaling; peak effect is within 10–15 minutes, and continues for two–three hours with impairment remaining for up to 24 hours.

Opiates: constricted pupils; sleepy appearance, slow reflexes and speech, facial itching, cold skin and nausea; causes nervousness, irritability, inability to concentrate or think clearly; there is extreme fatigue as the drug wears off. As these drugs can be injected, check for the presence of needle puncture marks. Tolerant users may exhibit little psychomotor impairment, except in withdrawal. The effects of injected drugs are visible within seconds; visible effects continue for four–six hours; incorrect doses of methadone may cause impairment which can last for up to 24 hours.

CNS depressants (alcohol, barbiturates, tranquillisers, anti-depressants): watery eyes, drowsiness, slurred speech, uncoordination, disinhibition, impaired judgment and concentration, impaired vision, wide emotional effects, rancid breath. Effects last anything between one and 16 hours.

CNS stimulants (cocaine, amphetamine): dilated pupils, eyelid tremors, anxiety, euphoria, easily irritated, foul or rancid odour, nervous movements, burnt lips or fingers. Cocaine, if smoked, has immediate effects and lasts five–ten minutes; if injected, effects are immediate and last for 45–90 minutes; if snorted effects occur within 30 seconds, and last 30–90 minutes; by mouth, effects occur in three–five minutes, and last 15–30 minutes longer than if snorted/injected. The onset of amphetamine effects is within seconds, and lasts for four–eight hours.

Dissociative anaesthetics (Ketamine, PCP): dilated pupils, horizontal gaze nystagmus, flushed and sweaty appearance, sudden bursts of violence, anaesthesia (no response to pain stimulus), slurred speech, hallucinations, bizarre behaviour, blank stare, depersonalisation. When smoked/injected effects occur in one–two minutes, peak at 15 minutes, last for four–six hours, and return to normal in up to 48 hours.

Hallucinogens (LSD, ecstasy, magic mushrooms): normal or dilated pupils, dazed appearance, uncoordinated, poor balance, distorted time and distance perception, sweating, goose bumps, paranoia, nausea, hallucinations, flash-backs. The effects of LSD occur within 20–30 minutes and last for up to 12 hours; ecstasy takes effect within 20–30 minutes, lasting four–six hours; magic mushrooms take effect within 60–90 minutes, lasting two–three hours.

Inhalants (solvents, petrol): substance residue around mouth, substance odour, nausea, slurred speech, disorientation, confusion, drowsiness, blood-shot watery eyes, loss of muscle control, flushed face, non-communicative, intense headache. Solvents take immediate effect, and last between six and eight hours.

Poly-drug users: note that multiple drug use or mixing of different drugs is increasingly common. Users will exhibit a combination of symptoms depending upon the kind of drugs mixed. Observation is difficult and specialised. The DRT student manual instructs that there are four possible effects of combining drugs: a null or no effect; an overlapping action; an additive effect (where one drug reinforces the particular effect of another); and an antagonistic effect (unpredictable).

For further information on the symptoms and effects on individuals of particular drugs and issues in relation to withdrawal, overdose and conceal-ment see Dr Margaret Stark and Dr Guy Norfolk 'Substance Misuse' in W.D.S. McLay (1996).

Further information on the symptoms of illicit drugs, prices of drugs at street level, and other general information is contained on the following websites:

- **www.drugscope.org.uk** (homepage of the website of a UK drug charity containing information on effects of drug and up to date guidance as to prices of drugs at street level);
- **www.erowid.com** (general information in relation to illegal drugs);
- **www.release.co.uk** (general information in relation to illegal drugs).

14.11.2 Determining fitness for interview when suspect is under influence of drink/drugs

Research for the Royal Commission on Criminal Justice (Study No. 12, 1993) has found that while the police are able to identify juveniles and people with serious mental disorders or disabilities, they were less able to assess minor disorders or handicaps, including drug impairment. The study also found that 35 per cent of the subjects were not in a normal mental state, due either to extreme distress, mental disorder, or being under the influence of drugs.

Under general procedure, a custody officer must immediately call a forensic physician if a person fails to respond normally to questions or conversation (see Police and Criminal Evidence Act 1984 (PACE), Code C, para. 9.2). No person who is unfit through drink or drugs to the extent that he is unable to appreciate the significance of questions put to him and his answers, may be questioned about the alleged offence in this condition, other than in exceptional circumstances (PACE, Code C, para. 12.3).

An initial assessment of the suspect should be made, including manner of speech and behaviour. Ask if the suspect is taking medication. If the suspect is incapable of understanding the significance of any questions put or answers thereto, the custody officer should be informed. This does not constitute a breach of confidentiality. If such assessment is as a result of being familiar with the suspect's history, the suspect's consent to disclose this information should be obtained (see **para. 22.2.1**).

The stress of being in custody may also produce physical effects that mirror drug or alcohol impairment because a suspect is rendered vulnerable to some degree by the atmosphere of a custody suite which can be intimidating. Lack of sensory stimulation in the police cell can also dull a suspect's mental reflexes.

For the role of the forensic physician in assessing the fitness to be detained and to be interviewed see Stephen P. Robinson 'Care of Detainees' in W.D.S. McLay (1996) pp. 104–7.

Note that suspects who are on remand may still be using drugs notwithstanding the introduction of mandatory drug testing in prison. A Home Office research study in relation to mandatory drug testing in prisons noted that:

> 'A majority of all the prisoners interviewed (57 per cent) and a sizeable minority of staff (40 per cent) believed that the drug-testing programme was likely to cause harm by encouraging prisoners to change from cannabis to heroin because the latter is less easily detectable by tests.'

The study noted, however, that very few prisoners began to use heroin as a consequence of mandatory drug testing. The implications of mandatory drug testing and the inclination to use drugs that are more difficult to detect should also be considered in relation to drug dependent suspects who are subject to drug treatment and testing orders. See K. Edgar and I. O'Donnell (1998).

14.12 TAKING AND STORAGE OF BLOOD AND URINE SPECIMENS FROM SUSPECTS

Blood specimens must be taken from a suspect by an approved forensic physician at a police station in a private appropriate room. The suspect is entitled to be accompanied by another individual (e.g. lawyer, appropriate adult, legal friend) for observation purposes.

The suspect must consent to the taking of blood by the forensic physician and should not be unduly pressurised into providing a blood sample. The Education and Research Committee of the AFP has produced a sample consent form for the use of forensic physicians which should be signed by the suspect and any witness in order to indicate that the suspect consents to examination (including the taking of specimens), and understands that a report based on that examination may be revealed in court.

The forensic physician must be satisfied that the subject is capable of making an informed choice to consent (see *Friel* v. *Dickson* [1992] RTR 366 and *Re C* [1994] 1 WLR 290).

For further information about the obligations of a forensic physician in relation to obtaining consent from subjects to take intimate samples see Michael A. Knight 'The Practitioner's Obligations' in W.D.S. McLay (1996).

Generally, blood is preferred to urine because it enables testing within a more accurate timeframe. The FSS, AFP and ACPO recommend the taking of blood and urine samples in every case where analysis is to be performed to test for the presence of alcohol, drugs and volatiles. Where the incident has occurred more than four days prior to the examination, however, only a urine specimen is recommended to be taken.

If an AO requests that a blood specimen be taken, the suspect (absent medical reasons) cannot elect to provide a specimen of urine. A whole blood specimen should immediately be placed in an appropriate airtight container to avoid contamination or deterioration.

The Forensic Science Service Safescene Unit manufactures the following standard kits for the collection of blood and urine specimens:

- *Alcohol/Blood Module.* Includes a blood container with preservative and anti-coagulant and an outer plastic security container;
- *Alcohol/Drug/Urine Module.* Includes urine container with preservative tablet and outer plastic security container;
- *Blood/Alcohol and Urine/Alcohol (RTA kits).* The standard kit used in England and Wales for the collection of blood or urine specimens from a suspect in connection with an offence of driving whilst under the influence of drink and/or drugs.

It is recommended that 10 ml of venous blood be taken and that an anticoagulate (potassium oxalate) and a preservative (sodium fluoride) be added (this will not affect the concentration of the blood for analytical purposes).

It is recommended that a urine specimen of 20 ml be collected and preserved by the addition of sodium fluoride (see FSS, APS [now known as AFP] and ACPO *Guidelines for the Collection of Specimens* (2000)).

Blood should be refrigerated immediately (ideally at between four to six degrees centigrade). Refrigeration during transportation is not generally required. A suspect should be advised to refrigerate any portion of a specimen that they are provided with as soon as possible and not to open or tamper with the container.

Each specimen should be appropriately labelled. It is good practice for the FME to record the following: the time blood is taken; the volume taken; the origin of the blood (e.g. specify left/right arm and vein). This record commences the chain of custody of the specimen and should be confirmed in cases where there are issues in relation to contamination or deterioration.

It is good practice for police forces to submit duplicate specimens to two different laboratories for analysis. If this has not been done automatically a subject should be advised that a second analysis should be carried out.

Improper storage of specimens by the police or laboratory which results in the specimen being unusable for testing purposes can, in certain circumstances, result in a subject being acquitted of a charge of driving with excess alcohol (see *Archbold* v. *Jones* [1986] RTR 178 in which a Divisional Court overturned a conviction for driving with excess alcohol because the specimen provided by the defendant later proved unusable through no fault of his own).

The loss of specimens or drug samples following analysis on behalf of the prosecution (thus depriving the defendant of seeking an opinion from his own expert) will not necessarily be a ground, absent any bad faith on the part of the prosecutor or significant prejudice to the defendant, for staying proceedings as an abuse of process (see *R.* v. *Elliott and another* [2002] All ER (D) 129 (May), CA).

14.12.1 Taking blood specimens from incapacitated drivers

Under the Police Reform Act 2002, blood specimens may be taken from subjects who are unable to give consent following involvement in road traffic accidents. The Medical Ethics Department of the British Medical Association (BMA) and APS recommend that a specimen can be obtained for future testing for alcohol and drugs from a non-consenting person who has been involved in a traffic accident where:

- the person's capacity has been assessed by a police officer and the person has been found to be incapable of giving valid consent due to medical reasons;
- the FME taking the specimen is satisfied that the person is not able to give valid consent; and

- the person does not object to the specimen being taken; and
- in the view of the doctor in immediate charge of the person's care, taking the specimen would not be prejudicial to the proper care and treatment of the patient.

The specimen should not be tested until the person is competent and gives valid consent for it to be tested (for more detail see **para. 22.2.1**).

14.13 TAKING AND STORAGE OF SPECIMENS FOR ANALYSIS FROM AUTOPSY SUBJECT

In cases of suspicious deaths, or those suspected of having been caused by poisons, drugs, or alcohol overdoses, a blood or urine specimen will usually be taken by the examining coroner or pathologist and sent directly to a laboratory for testing.

In addition to blood and urine, the following body fluids, tissues, and organs are susceptible to toxicological screening:

- hair;
- nail clippings;
- saliva;
- stomach contents;
- optical fluid;
- liver;
- bile;
- vitreous humour;
- cerebrospinal fluid;
- brain;
- lung.

The following techniques are recommended for obtaining autopsy samples:

Blood: Intravascular blood should be obtained if possible. Ideally this should be obtained before any dissection or disturbance of the organs. Blood should never be obtained from bodily cavities after evisceration as it will probably be contaminated with other body substances.

Urine: Can be obtained prior to autopsy by catheter or suprapubic puncture with syringe and long needle. At autopsy, a sample can be obtained by puncturing the fundus with syringe and needle.

Cerebrospinal fluid: The body is placed on its side and a needle on a syringe should be passed between two lumbar or lower thoracic spines and stopped as soon as any penetration of the theca is felt. This fluid is rarely required for toxicological analysis, but it may be needed for microbiological and virological studies (see **Chapter 24**).

Vitreous humour: A puncture should be made through the sclera at the outer canthus with a fine gauge needle.

Stomach contents: Should be collected directly into a wide-mouth glass or plastic pot of at least 250 ml volume. To collect, the exterior of the stomach should be washed clean of blood or other contamination and pulled with attached organs to the edge of the dissecting board or sink.

Intestinal contents: Not routinely required for analysis unless gastro-intestinal poisoning is suspected (e.g. with a heavy metal). If the toxicologist requires a sample, both ends of the small gut should be ligated by string sutures at duodenum and ileum. The intestine should be cut through and the intact gut sent for laboratory analysis in a container.

Vomit: Rarely collected at autopsy unless large quantities found in air passages. However, if poisoning is suspected, any vomit collected by ambulance crews or police should be collected and transported in a clean container for laboratory analysis.

Analysis for volatile substances: In cases involving solvent abuse and deaths from gaseous or volatile substances, it may be possible to isolate the toxic material from a whole lung. The lung should be removed upon opening of the thorax, the main bronchus tied off with string ligature, and the lung placed in a nylon bag. Blood samples for testing for volatile substances should be collected using suitable tubes only (glass with aluminium foil-lined cap or Teflon liner). Collection in any other type of tube may result in a significant decrease in concentration of compounds such as toluene or other solvents after a few days in storage.

Body tissues: Liver is the most usual because it concentrates many substances and their metabolites which may be recoverable after blood and urine levels have declined. The whole organ should be saved or a 20–40g aliquot should be collected. If brain and kidney are being collected, the same quantity is required. The total original weight of each organ should be recorded and notified to the toxicologist. If a toxic substance has been injected into subcutaneous tissue or muscle, the tissues should be excised and submitted for analysis.

See further 'The site of sampling for toxicological analysis' in Bernard Knight (1991) pp. 483–497.

If a corpse has decomposed and blood and urine specimens can no longer be obtained, certain other tissues and organs may still be available for analysis. A sample of the vitreous humour may be obtained in bodies with considerably post-mortem decomposition because the fluid in the eye resists putrefaction longer than any other body liquids.

It should be noted that post-mortem levels of many substances are unreliable because of post-mortem diffusion of blood and body fluids which makes the interpretation of physiological and other components unreliable. See further D.J. Pounder and G.R. Jones (1990).

The concentration of toxic compounds may also vary considerably depending on the sampling site. Hence a note should always be made of the body site from where any sample was taken and it may be necessary to ascertain whether this sample is representative of general levels of toxicity throughout the body.

Where liquid blood is available it should be stored (as with blood from a living subject) in either a 'stoppered vacutainer' or (other appropriate container) and be sealed and labelled (both the container and the lid should be labelled because mixing of lids between specimens can cause cross-contamination and thus, if contamination is an issue in a case, the integrity of the specimen, container and lid should be investigated). If containers are not properly sealed certain volatile substances, such as alcohol, are liable to evaporate.

When the specimen is received by the laboratory it will be assigned a case number and a record will be opened which will include all the relevant details in relation to the deceased.

During the entire laboratory testing process container storage jars should remain closed and opening should be kept to a minimum in order to prevent evaporation. Specimens should remain refrigerated throughout at a constant temperature of between four and six degrees centigrade. If the specimen is to be tested for the presence of alcohol, testing should ideally be carried out within 24 hours of receipt. The laboratory records should reflect the storage and handling procedure and should be checked in cases of doubt about the integrity of a specimen.

In addition to the analysis of bodily fluids, tissues and organs, analytical tests can be carried out on any unidentified tablets and drug paraphernalia.

14.14 FSS POLICY ON BLOOD AND URINE ANALYSIS

In an attempt to increase the effectiveness of the way the police service deals with drug drivers, the FSS has developed a dedicated unit to provide a quicker and more cost-effective service for the analysis of blood and urine specimens. These new arrangements are based on the observation that a very high proportion of drug driving is caused by a limited number of drugs of abuse. These drugs, collectively classified as the 'standard panel', are heroin, cocaine, amphetamine, methadone, cannabis, the 'ecstasy' group and two benzodiazepine drugs, diazepam and temazepam.

- In cases of suspected poly drug use, officers are advised to specifically note this on the supporting information to the submission form.
- Unless force protocol dictates otherwise, the general FSS procedure for drug screening of blood or urine will follow a two step process:

  1. All samples will be submitted to a battery of screening tests for the 'standard panel' of drugs.

2. One drug will be selected for confirmation testing according to the measurement and results of the screening tests, taking into account the proportions of the drugs present and any information provided about the condition of the motorist.

If more than one drug is detected at the screening stage, a view will generally be reached, depending on the quantities present, of which drug is more likely to have caused the impairment. Results from screening and confirmation steps should be noted as of course in the analyst's statement. Other interpretations, further information or comment, should be mentioned in the analyst's statement if the case so requires.

Forensic Alliance and LGC Ltd have also adopted a 'standard panel' for drug testing.

14.15 IDENTIFICATION AND MEASUREMENT OF DRUGS, ALCOHOL, AND POISONS IN THE HUMAN BODY

Traditionally, toxicology has been concerned with the effect of poisons on living organisms and their origins and properties.

14.16 THE ROLE OF THE TOXICOLOGIST

In the context of a medico-legal inquiry toxicology is concerned with the study of the effects of drugs and poisons on human beings and the investigation of fatal intoxications (e.g. deaths caused by suicidal or accidental overdoses of drugs, or occurring due to accidents when the subject was under influence of drugs) and, occasionally, homicidal poisonings (e.g. cyanide, carbon monoxide, insulin, or pesticide poisonings).

Toxicologists can be instructed for the following purposes:

*   analysing blood or urine specimens in relation to road traffic offences;
*   screening for standard and illicit drugs; identification and analysis of unknown powders and tablets; opinions on drug actions; drug toxicity;
*   interactions of different drugs/alcohol, influence of particular drugs on behaviour of subject under examination;
*   drug abuse screening of clients of drug abuse clinics or subjects of drug treatment and testing orders;
*   investigation of fatal intoxications.

14.16.1 The investigation of fatal intoxications

A toxicologist will work in close collaboration with the forensic pathologist but will not, in general, be required to attend the crime scene or autopsy. Any bodily specimens for analysis will be delivered to the toxicology laboratory for analysis.

14.16.2 Procedures for testing bodily fluids for the presence of drugs and alcohol

A technique known as gas chromatography is most widely used for determining alcohol levels in blood.

Drugs are analysed in accordance with guidelines provided by the United Nations Drug Control Programme (UNDCP) (see online via **www.undcp. org**). Identification of drugs involves a two-stage approach:

(i) a screening test (e.g. thin layer chromatography (TLC), gas chromatography (GC), and immunoassay),

(ii) a confirmation test (e.g. gas chromatography-mass spectrometry (GC-MS).

Separate portions (aliquots) of the specimen should be used for each test. The unknown specimen should be compared during the course of testing with a known control (calibrator) of a similar matrix (e.g. blood with blood). Laboratory records should always state the origin of the calibrator blood (which should be obtained from an approved government blood bank), confirm that the blood was initially drug and alcohol free, and that the blood was screened by the laboratory and verified as being 'blank' for analytical purposes.

In addition to the 'blank' calibrators, a further quantity of calibrators will be 'spiked' with the drug of interest (these calibrators will provide positive and negative controls for testing purposes). The reactions of each set of calibrators will be compared with the unknown blood specimen.

In cases of doubt, confirmation should be obtained that positive controls were used; how these were made, and how they were stored during the course of testing.

Screening is available for a number of standard drugs (e.g. paracetamol, benzodiazepines) and illicit drugs (e.g. amphetamines, ecstasy, cannabinoids, cocaine, opiates, and methadone).

All steps of the testing process should be recorded by the laboratory. This record will form part of the chain of custody of the specimen.

14.16.3 The toxicologist's report

The toxicologist's report should list all drugs tested for and all drugs found or not found (and any possible significance of the latter finding in relation to the particular case, if any). It should also explain the significance of the level of the drugs found (e.g. lethal, fatal, therapeutic, recreational).

A toxicologist will generally be expected to obtain information on quantitation of drug levels from one or more of the following texts:

- Moffatt, Tony, Osselton, David and Widdop, Brian (2002);
- Baselt, Randall C. (1982);
- Levine, Barry (1999);
- Winek, Charles L. and others (2001).

In more complex cases, a toxicologist will be forced to work 'blind' with only cursory background information about the subject's medical history, symptoms, circumstances of death (such as that certain drugs, containers, or paraphernalia were found at the scene). Without specific information, the toxicologist has no option but to use general screening procedures in the hope of narrowing the possibilities. The findings of the toxicologist are directly dependent upon the input received from the attending physician, forensic physician, coroner (and, if relevant, the scenes of crime officer (SOCO) or FOA). When instructing a toxicologist, it is advisable to supply as much relevant medical information about the suspect as possible.

The provision of specific instructions is of particular importance in view of the strict budgetary constraints imposed by the cost guidelines for publicly funded cases. Note also that the findings of a toxicologist are limited by the following considerations:

1. There is very little information published on the toxic levels of most drugs.
2. Effects of drugs vary between individuals.
3. Even if data on levels of toxicity are available, its interpretation must be predicated on the assumption that the victim's physiological behaviour [in cases of fatal intoxications] is in agreement with that experienced by the subjects in previous studies. In some cases, such an assumption may not be entirely valid without knowing the subject's case history. It has also been observed that no experienced toxicologist would be surprised to find an individual walking around with a toxic level of a drug that would have killed most others (see Richard Saferstein (1998) p. 312).
4. In cases of doubt a second opinion should be obtained. In serious cases, most GLP (good laboratory practice) compliant laboratories will automatically submit specimens to another laboratory.

14.16.4 Qualifications and experience of toxicologists

Before specialisation, toxicologists commonly hold a degree in an analytical science (e.g. chemistry, biology) or a related discipline. An analytical toxicologist with the following academic qualifications and experience is suitably qualified to give opinions in court:

1. A graduate degree and seven years' specialist toxicology experience.
2. A master's degree and five years' specialist toxicology experience.
3. A doctorate and three years' specialist toxicology experience.

Practising toxicologists will generally also undertake research projects, publish papers, attend conferences, and maintain membership of professional societies (e.g. the International Association of Forensic Toxicologists (TIAFT), Society of Forensic Toxicologists (both special membership); Royal Society of Chemistry (RSC) (general membership); Forensic Science Society, and American Academy of Forensic Science (Toxicology Section).

The Council for the Registration of Forensic Practitioners (CRFP) will be opening a register for forensic toxicologists. Additionally, if the toxicologist is based in an NHS laboratory, it should be confirmed that is a GLP compliant facility. GLP facilities are certified by the Department of Health (DOH). Facilities holding certification are subject to periodic inspections by DOH officials and any complaints made against the facility will be investigated by the DOH. A GLP compliant facility must meet certain minimum standards in its general practice and a minimum standard is assured in relation to the procedures for storage, handling and testing of specimens, and maintenance of laboratory records (including computerised data and any written notes).

For further information on GLP compliant facilities and forensic toxicology see: **www.doh.gov.uk/practice/htm** and **www.londontox.org**

14.17   THE ROLE OF THE DRUG ANALYST

Drug analysts are concerned with the identification and quantification of the drugs of abuse (generally the controlled drugs listed in the Misuse of Drugs Act 1971, Sched.2, Parts I–II).

14.17.1   Identification of the drugs abuse

Identification of drugs involves a number of initial steps:

1. *Visual identification* – while this is not conclusive, it may give an initial indication of the nature of a specimen or be used to eliminate certain drug classes. The nature of any associated drug paraphernalia (e.g. measuring scales, cutting knives, syringes, spoons, and pipes) and debris from drug use (e.g. residues from heating drugs, smoke) can also give an indication of the nature of the drug.
2. *Dosage form* – drugs of abuse tend to have distinct dosage forms that can assist with identification. Examples include: heroin (powder form); cannabis (leaf, resin, or oil); cocaine (powder); amphetamines (powder, capsules, tablets); ecstasy (MDMA) (tablets often with distinct logos). See Michael Cole 'Drugs of Abuse' in Peter White (1998), and Ian Hogg and Brian W.J. Rankin and Ian Shaw 'The Scene of Crime and Trace Evidence' in W.D.S. McLay *Clinical Forensic Medicine* (1996), pp. 263–270.

3. *Sampling and quantification* – the analytical techniques will vary depending on whether trace or bulk samples are available. For trace samples non-instrumental methods of analysis are used. Bulk samples will be subject to presumptive tests for elimination purposes (note that presumptive tests are relatively rudimentary, can record reactions to other non-controlled substances present in a specimen and, as such, are designed to give only an indication of the class of drug) and further scientific tests (e.g. TLC).

14.17.2   The drug analyst's report

The report of the drug analyst should generally state the findings in relation to the identity of a particular drug, including physical description and any associated paraphernalia recovered. It should also confirm whether the form (dosage) of the drug is typical of the dosage and quantity of that drug normally in street use (in relation to certain drugs, the Misuse of Drugs Act 1971 requires quantification of the amount of a drug in a specimen as it may be relevant for sentencing purposes; quantification may also be relevant to link batches of drugs). In accordance with good practice, the notes of a drug analyst should be maintained and be made available in cases of query. In accordance with quality assurance practices (e.g. BS (British Standard) 5750 and ISO (International Organisation for Standardisation) 9000) it is recommended that a number of precautions be taken in relation to records and also to prevent contamination (e.g. protective gloves should be changed between testing samples and a note should be made of this). There may be variations between laboratories in the type of techniques used but minimum levels of quality assurance (carrying out drug analysis) should be maintained.

14.17.3   Qualifications of drug analysts

Drug analysts will usually hold a qualification in an analytical science or related discipline before specialisation.

14.18   DRUG DATABASES

A number of visual drug identification databases are now maintained which cover medicines, illicit drugs, vitamins, food supplements, herbal remedies, and products (e.g. confectionery) that might be mistaken for drugs.

See **www.tictac.org** which is a subscriber database used widely by police forces and other law enforcement agencies. It contains, in addition to a visual drugs database (including video footage), a summary of known drug side effects, an index of pictorial monograms on illicit drugs (e.g. markings on

167

ecstasy tablets), and a thesaurus of slang terms for drugs. For further information contact the Toxicology Unit, St George's Hospital Medical School, Cranmer Terrace, London SW17 0RE.

REFERENCES

Adams, D. (1997) 'Custody review' *Police Review*, 5 December, pp. 16–17.

Anderson, R. 'Forensic Toxicology' in White, P. (ed.) (1998) *Crime Scene to Court*, The Royal Society of Chemistry, pp. 232–62.

Association of Police Surgeons and British Medical Association (1999) *Guidelines for Intimate Body Searches.*

Baselt, Randall C. (2002) *Deposition of Toxic Drugs and Chemicals in Man* (3rd edn).

Bennett, T. (1998) *Drugs and Crime: The Results of Research on Drug Testing and Interviewing Arrestees* (Home Office Research Study 183).

British Medical Association (Medical Ethics Department) and Association of Police Surgeons (2002) *Taking Specimens from Incapacitated Drivers.*

Cole, Michael, 'Drugs of Abuse' in White, P. (ed.) (1998) *Crime Scene to Court*, The Royal Society of Chemistry, p. 220, Table 9.2.

Collier, S. (2003) *An aide memoire for use in Field Impairment Testing and Drug Influence Recognition for police officers, lawyers and magistrates*, National Drug Recognition Training (copies available from the author – see acknowledgements).

Department of Health (2002) *Taking blood specimens from those involved in road traffic accidents to test for levels of alcohol or drugs*; online via **www.doh.uk/consent/praguidance**.

Department of Transport (2002) *Taking Blood Specimens from unconscious drivers at hospital.*

Edgar, K. & O'Donnell, I. (1998) *Mandatory drug testing in prisons: The relationship between MDT and the level and nature of drug misuse*, Home Office Research Study 189, Home Office Research and Statistics Directorate Report.

Fleming, P. & Stewart, D. (1998), 'Drugs and Driving: Training and Implications for Police Officers and Police Surgeons', a survey compiled from responses to questionnaires circulated to traffic officers and FMEs.

Forensic Science Service, Association of Police Surgeons and Association of Chief Police Officers (1999) *Guidelines for the Collection of Specimens.*

Hogg, I., Rankin, B.W.J. & Shaw, I. 'The Scene of Crime and Trace Evidence' in W.D.S. McLay (1996) *Clinical Forensic Medicine*, Greenwich Medical Media, pp. 263–70.

Knight, B. (1991) 'The Site for Sampling for Toxicological Analysis' in *Forensic Toxicology*, Arnold, pp. 493–7.

Knight, Dr M.A., 'The Practitioner's Obligations' in W.D.S. McLay (1996) *Clinical Forensic Medicine*, Greenwich Medical Media, pp. 39–56; 43–50; 104–7; 166–172.

Levine, B. (1999) *Principles of Forensic Toxicology,* American Association for Clinical Chemistry.

McLay, W.D.S. (1996) *Clinical Forensic Medicine*, Greenwich Medical Media, pp. 172, 263–70.

Moffatt, T., Osselton, D. & Widdop, B. (eds) (2002) *Clarke's Isolation and Identification of Drugs* (3rd edn), Pharmaceutical Press.

Pounder, D.J. & Jones, G.R. (1990) 'Post-mortem drug redistribution – a toxicological nightmare', *Forensic Sci Int,* (45) 253–63.

Ramskill, A. (2000) *'Blood, sweat and beers': The law and procedure relating to hospital breath tests*, Home Office.

Robinson, S.P. 'Care of Detainees', in W.D.S. McLay (1996) *Clinical Forensic Medicine*, Greenwich Medical Media.

Royal College of Physicians (2001) *Substance Misuse Detainees in Custody*.

Saferstein, R. 'Drugs' and 'Forensic Toxicology' in Saferstein, R. (1998) *Criminalistics: An Introduction to Forensic Science* (6th edn), Prentice Hall.

Stark, Dr M. (2003) 'Nicotine Dependent Prisoners, APS view', Education and Research Committee of the APS.

Stark, Dr M. & Norfolk, Dr G. 'Substance Misuse', in W.D.S. McLay (1996) *Clinical Forensic Medicine*, Greenwich Medical Media, p. 172.

Wallis, P., McCormick, K. and Niekirk, P. (eds) (2001) *Wilkinson's Road Traffic Offences,* Sweet and Maxwell (20th edn) Vol. 1, ss.4.90–4.100, 4.239–4.245, Appendix A1, Appendix 1, A1.07 and A1.12.

White, P. (1998) *Crime Scene to Court*, The Royal Society of Chemistry.

Winek, C. et al. (2001) 'Drug and Chemical Blood-Level Data 2001', *Forensic Science International* 122 (2–3) 107–23.

CHAPTER 15

Footwear impressions and instrument marks

15.1 MARKS AND IMPRESSIONS

'Mark evidence' is a term used in conjunction with both impressions and prints.

Impression evidence arises when there is an indentation (three dimensional) in a material, which has retained characteristics related to the shape or movement of part of the object that was pressed against the material. Examples are a heel mark in soil, a bite mark in a discarded apple, a jemmied gouge in a door frame, and an impression of handwriting on an underlying page of a notepad.

Prints, or simply marks, are created when material is transferred to, or removed from, a surface in a way that reflects the form and condition of the object. Prints are normally two dimensional in character. Examples would be a footwear mark or a fingerprint on a rigid surface and a fabric mark left on a vehicle in a hit and run accident.

Mark evidence of each type is likely to be based on inherent features – manufactured or naturally occurring – in the object responsible and possibly also damage features. In either case the association between mark and object may in favourable circumstances be unique. Footwear impressions, toolmarks and tyremarks are often examples of damage based evidence. Fingerprints generally provide non-damage based evidence.

15.2 FOOTWEAR IMPRESSIONS

There is anecdotal evidence that footwear impression evidence has been neglected in many cases because of a perception that the evidence will have been lost as a result of the movement of emergency services and other authorised personnel through the crime scene prior to the arrival of the investigation teams. It may, however, often be possible to obtain partial footwear impressions made by the subject even if the impression has been tracked over.

Searches of a scene may also be incomplete because of the difficulty in determining the points of entry/exit.

Given that a subject will have to walk in and out of a crime scene, footwear impression evidence is likely to be present and should not be neglected. One expert in the field notes that while not all of the impressions will be visible or detectable, the chances are 'excellent' that some will be (see William J. Bodziak (1990), p. 3).

15.3 SECURING, PRESERVING, AND SEARCHING THE CRIME SCENE

The scene should be sealed and the number of personnel walking through the scene limited. The use of 'stepping stones' at scenes helps to minimise disturbance to footwear marks. Footwear impressions discovered outdoors should be protected against the elements until photographs and impressions can be taken. Searching parameters should be defined (and, if necessary, certain areas protected by taping) if details of the crime are known.

Impressions should not be covered with tape for preservation purposes as this can obliterate the impression and preclude chemical enhancement. Examples of areas and objects commonly searched for impression evidence include: point of occurrence (e.g. in a homicide case, a search for footwear impressions should be made underneath and around the body); points of entry/exit (good sources include window sills, tabletops, panels of doors that have been kicked in, soil or flowerbeds); any known route of passage through the crime scene; certain materials at the crime scene which the suspect may have stepped on (e.g. paper, card, broken glass, and glossy tiled floors).

15.4 EVIDENCE COLLECTION TECHNIQUES

Footwear impressions can be two dimensional if made by a transfer of materials or residue between the footwear and the surface (e.g. floors, paper, etc.) or three dimensional if made on soft surfaces that cause the undersole to sink (e.g. soil, earth, snow or sand). Like fingerprints, footwear impressions can be visible (if a contaminant is present) or latent.

15.4.1 Detection and development of latent footwear impressions

Impressions can be detected by searching surfaces with oblique lighting. Latent impressions are developed using either powders or chemical enhancement techniques (if contaminants such as blood, oil, or grease, are present). Luminol is becoming increasingly popular for searching for footwear marks in blood.

15.4.2 Likelihood of detectable footwear impressions occurring on different two dimensional shoe/surface combinations

Whether an impression will be made on a particular surface of contact will be determined by the condition of the shoe and the nature of the surface. The table below gives an indication of when footwear impressions will be detectable on a range of surfaces:

SURFACE	Damp or wet shoes	Shoe with blood, grease, oil, etc.	Dry shoes with dust or residue	Clean dry shoes (no dust or residue)
CARPET	Unlikely	Very likely	Likely	Unlikely
DIRTY FLOOR with accumulation of dust, dirt and residue	Likely	Very likely	Unlikely	Unlikely
RELATIVELY CLEAN, but unwaxed floor	Likely	Very likely	Very likely	Unlikely
CLEAN WAXED tile or wood floor	Likely	Very likely	Very likely	Likely
WAXED bank counter, desk top, etc.	Likely	Very likely	Very likely	Likely
GLASS	Very likely	Very likely	Very likely	Likely
KICKED IN DOOR	Very likely	Very likely	Very likely	Likely
PAPER, CARDBOARD, etc.	Very likely	Very likely	Very likely	Likely

Table reproduced from William J. Bodziak (1990), p. 18.

15.4.3 Photographing of footwear impressions in situ prior to lifting

Impressions should be photographed with a scale prior to any attempt to lift. Photographs should be of a quality sufficient for examination purposes because the impressions may have to be examined exclusively from the photograph if lifting is not possible or if the impression should become damaged.

Notes should be made in relation to the exact position of any impressions discovered at the crime scene.

15.4.4 Techniques for recovering footwear impressions

The following techniques are available for lifting two-dimensional impressions:

(i) lifting with adhesive film/gel (used mainly for impressions made on smooth surfaces);
(ii) electrostatic lifting device (impressions made in dust). An example of a portable electrostatic device is Pathfinder (manufactured by Kinderprint Co, PO Box 16, Martinez, California 94553, see **www.kinderprint.com**). Pathfinder can also be used to reveal latent impressions;
(iii) adhesive backed fingerprint lifting material, after dusting the mark with suitable powder.

For three-dimensional impressions: Class I dental stone (a hard form of plaster).

Portable objects bearing impressions should be removed from the scene for development and examination in a laboratory.

15.5 INFORMATION PROVIDED BY FOOTWEAR IMPRESSIONS

The following information may, in certain circumstances, be ascertained from footwear impressions:

- type, make, and description of footwear that made impression;
- approximate or precise size of footwear;
- degree and position of wear present (wear will be influenced by many factors, including design and manufacture, characteristics of wearer's foot, and habits and activities of the wearer. There will generally be differences between the degree and positioning of wear on the left and right shoes);
- random damage pattern;
- reconstruction of crime by reference to location of footwear impressions at the scene;
- determination of the number of suspects present at the crime scene and the nature of their involvement in the crime (in all cases the possibility of legitimate access to the crime scene should be considered);
- corroborating/refuting evidence of witnesses;
- while there have been some claims that walking gait measurements can be ascertained by reference to the features of an impression (e.g. the angle of each foot), it is generally not possible to measure gait from footwear impressions with any certainty due to the difficulty in determining whether the impressions were made as a result of normal walking or whether the subject was running or otherwise altering his gait at the time that the impressions were made.

15.6 PREPARING A TEST IMPRESSION, AND COMPARING AN IMPRESSION WITH KNOWN SHOES OF SUSPECT

In order to compare the characteristics of a questioned footwear impression with the footwear of a suspect, the suspect's actual shoes must be seized because examinations conducted by reference only to photographs can be severely limited.

Both shoes should be seized because it may not initially be possible to attribute a partial impression to either a right or left foot. If the seizure takes place some time after the crime, it is good practice to seize multiple pairs of the suspect's shoes because individuals may own more than one pair of shoes of a similar design. Consideration should also be given to the possibility that more than one suspect may have been wearing shoes of similar design at the crime scene.

When making a test impression an examiner should generally try to reproduce as accurately as possible the mechanism used to make the questioned impression. Slight variations between the test impression and the questioned impression will almost inevitably occur due to the unavoidable variables.

Examination of the shoe for other trace evidence (e.g. hair, fibres, glass and blood) will generally take place before examination by a footwear examiner in order to maintain the integrity of the trace evidence.

15.7 DATABASES

A number of databases exist whereby an examiner can compare crime scene impressions with reference databases to determine what type of shoe caused the imprint, e.g. SICAR (shoeprint image capture and retrieval) (manufacturer Foster & Freeman, see **www.fosterfreeman.co.uk**). SICAR allows shoeprints to be searched against a crime database, suspect database, and a shoe sole pattern reference collection (SOLEMATE). This reference collection contains over 4,000 different sole patterns from over 200 brands and has collections for sportswear, work wear, and casual wear.

Some manufacturers (e.g. W.H. Griggs who produce Dr Martens boots) maintain records of their moulds.

Imported shoes are problematic because it is difficult to trace the manufacturer.

The use of databases will be useful for elimination purposes if no suspect has been apprehended.

15.8 MAKING A POSITIVE IDENTIFICATION

It is possible to positively identify footwear impressions as having been made by a particular shoe. This identification is based on random characteristics that the shoe has acquired (size, design, and mould characteristics will not generally, on their own, be sufficient to positively identify impressions with a specific shoe because shoes are often mass produced).

15.8.1 Wear

While wear alone is not accepted as a means of positive identification it can be used to determine or rule out an identification.

15.8.2 Degree of wear

The wearing down of the shoe is a continuous process which will constantly change as the shoe is worn. A positive identification based on specific degree of wear is more likely if the suspect's shoe is seized soon after the crime and has not sustained further wear. However, obtaining the shoes some time after the crime or after they have been subjected to further wear will not necessarily preclude the possibility of an identification.

If the degree of wear apparent on the shoe is more advanced than on the impression, caution must be used when reaching any conclusions due to the possible variable factors. For instance, during any lapse of time between the commission of the crime and the seizure of the shoes, the shoes may not necessarily have been worn and it is also difficult to estimate how quickly a particular suspect will wear down a pair of shoes.

If the degree of wear on the suspect's shoes is less than that apparent on the questioned impression, caution should be used before concluding that the shoe could not have made the impression because variables can occur in the impression-making process which could account for misrepresented wear.

15.8.3 Position of wear

The positioning of wear will be relevant to positive identification if it corresponds with that in the questioned impression.

15.8.4 Number of characteristics required for identification

The features used to identify a footwear impression are not the same as those used to identify a fingerprint.

Both the features and areas of an impression will be taken into account when making an identification. One random characteristic may be enough to make a positive identification if that characteristic is confirmed, has sufficient

175

definition, clarity, features, and is in the same location and orientation on the outsole, and could not be due to coincidence or contamination.

The criteria for establishing the uniqueness of footwear impressions is summarised by William J. Bodziak (1990) as follows. Footwear impressions:

(i) represent only one of many thousands of possible designs, each of which is available in a wide variety of possible sizes;

(ii) can have manufacturing variables and characteristics within that size and design;

(iii) can have wear characteristics, which relate to both the degree of wear and the position of wear and which are changing throughout the life of the shoe;

(iv) can have randomly acquired characteristics which, based on the presence, location, shape, and size, can make that shoe outsole unique.

Where the issue of ownership of shoes arise it can be resolved by comparing DNA or footmarks inside the questioned shoe with those inside a shoe belonging to the suspected owner.

15.9 INSTRUMENT MARKS

Instrument or tool marks generally occur as indented impressions into a softer surface, or abrasion or striation marks caused by the instrument cutting or sliding against another object. These marks most often occur in cases of burglaries or in crimes involving forced entries into buildings or objects (e.g. a safe or bank vault). Characteristics of the unique surface of an instrument can be transferred to any surface into which it comes into contact. This can permit an examiner to match an impression to a particular tool. It is possible to make a positive match between a mark and a particular instrument even if only a small area of the mark is available.

While no comprehensive instrument database exists, the type of instruments normally used for the commission of crimes fall into two categories: cutting instruments (e.g. bolt croppers, drills and knives) and instruments used to act as levers (e.g. jemmies, screwdrivers and chisels).

The unique mark that is left by an instrument occurs as a result of damage that the instrument has acquired either during the manufacturing process or through use. An instrument will continue to acquire damage throughout the lifetime of its use. This possibility should be borne in mind if there is a long lapse of time between the commission of the crime and the seizure of the instrument.

Instrument marks can also be important in identifying the source, or common source, of manufactured items, e.g. polythene bags used for drug deals. Fine scratch marks can show up on the surface of bags caused by specific build up of polythene on the dye from which they have been made.

15.10   SECURING, PRESERVING, AND SEARCHING CRIME SCENE

Instrument marks may be found at points of entry (e.g. jemmy or screwdriver impressions on doors, window frames; impressions of cutting instruments on damaged padlocks, chains or cables).

The scene should be protected from further damage and no repairs to damage or redecoration should be undertaken until the scene has been processed. No attempt should be made to introduce any tool into the mark or impression in order to see if it fits as this will compromise the impression.

15.11   EVIDENCE COLLECTION TECHNIQUES

If possible, the mark or impression should be removed in its entirety and sent for laboratory analysis; otherwise the mark should be cast with a moulding material. Materials developed for reproducing detail in dentistry are particularly suitable.

Examination from a photograph is problematic, but may be considered if there is no other option.

Special care should be taken when packaging and handling any evidence in order to preserve any contact trace evidence that may be present (e.g. paint chippings).

Comprehensive notes should be made in relation to the position of the impression at the crime scene and entirety photographs should also be taken whereby the positioning of the impression can be ascertained in relation to the overall crime scene. The impression should also be photographed in close up at a perpendicular angle with a scale.

15.12   COMPARISON OF TEST MARKS WITH SCENE MARKS

It is difficult to produce a control impression from a submitted instrument under laboratory conditions, particularly from levering instruments as the test impressions must be produced in a way that mimics the mechanism by which the impression was left at the scene. This will require knowledge of, amongst other things, the angle at which the instrument was held and the amount of force used. Assistance will be gained by the carrying out of a careful examination of the questioned impression preferably under laboratory conditions.

15.12.1   Cutting instruments

A test cutting will be produced from the submitted instrument. This will be compared with the mark recovered from the scene.

When producing a test cutting, which will typically be made in a soft material, it is important to be sure that the instrument in question (for example a pair of bolt croppers) is also capable of cutting the material of the crime related object (perhaps a hardened steel hasp). In this context the construction and dimensions of the tool, its blades and handles, are important factors. Hard materials often fracture after shallow indentation by the jaws of a cutting tool and this will be confirmed by microscopic examination.

15.12.2 Levering instruments

The comparison will be carried out in a similar way as for cutting instruments.

15.12.3 Trace evidence

The presence of trace evidence will greatly enhance the evidential value of the instrument and its mark (e.g. flecks of paint from the crime scene present on the instrument, paint from the instrument transferred onto the impression, or a two-way transfer, i.e. transfer of trace material from the crime scene onto the instrument and vice versa). Trace evidence (e.g. fingerprints, DNA present on the instrument) may also be available to demonstrate that a particular individual had been in possession of, or had handled, a particular instrument if this is denied).

15.13 QUALIFICATIONS OF EXPERT

The qualifications of an expert reporting on impression evidence will generally be the same as for experts reporting on other physical evidence. See qualifications of expert in **Chapter 16**.

REFERENCES

Barnett, K. 'Marks and impressions' in White, P. (1998) *Crime Scene to Court*, The Royal Society of Chemistry, pp. 73–104.

Bodziak, W. (1990) *Footwear Impression Evidence*, CRC Press, pp. 3, 18, 353.

Gaule, M. (2002) *The Basic Guide to Forensic Awareness*, New Police Bookshop.

CHAPTER 16

Contact trace and other particulates: fibres, glass, and paint

16.1 THE OCCURRENCE OF CONTACT TRACE EVIDENCE

Contact trace evidence is the result of the transfer of material between two surfaces (a donor surface and a recipient surface) that have come into contact. More precisely, contact trace evidence is established when an examination of trace materials indicates that contact has occurred, or may have occurred, between two surfaces. A given surface may be both a donor and a recipient of traces. Where a two-way transfer of material is indicated, this is of particular evidential significance. There may also be transfers of trace evidence without the donor and recipient surfaces coming into contact (e.g. glass transfer onto clothing from a shattered window)

There are two general types of trace evidence produced by contact – pattern evidence and transferred material. The transferred material itself will become evidence in cases in which the comparison of the transferred material with its suspected source is used as evidence of association/common origin between the transferred material and the donor surface. In other cases it is the comparison of the pattern of the transferred matter on the recipient surface with the pattern of matter removed from the donor surface that it is of evidential importance.

Examples of trace evidence include hair (human and animal), DNA, bloodstains and other body fluids, fibres, glass, paint, firearms residues, oils, greases, waxes, vegetation, soil, etc.

Fibres, glass and paint trace evidence are considered in this chapter because they are examples of some of the most common types of such evidence encountered in criminal cases. DNA and hair are considered in **Chapter 17**. Some of the same general considerations will apply to different types of trace evidence, e.g. principles in relation to the gathering of the evidence, standards applied in order to avoid contaminating the evidence, and the general assessment and interpretation of the evidence.

16.2   FIBRES

16.2.1   Assessment of the crime scene and searching considerations

In certain cases fibres will be visible to the naked eye (e.g. tufts of fibre caught in a wire or on a knife, or unusually coloured fibres against a background of numerous assorted fibres). However, the presence of fibre evidence at a scene will not usually immediately be apparent without the use of light sources.

Whilst not necessarily in routine use, a number of automated systems for fibre searching are also now marketed, including:

- Fibre finder and Maxcan (manufacturer Cox Analytical Systems AB);
- Fx5 Forensic Fibre Finder (manufacturer Foster and Freeman);
- Q550fifi (manufacturer Leica Vertrieb GmbH);
- Lucia Fibre Finder (manufacturer Laboratory Imaging s r o).

Given that most individuals committing a crime will be wearing clothes, there is a possibility that fibre transfer will occur in most types of crime.

Searching for fibre and other trace evidence is time consuming and labour intensive. For that reason, save in perhaps very serious cases, a scenes of crime officer (SOCO) will generally only search within defined parameters.

Examples of areas commonly searched for fibres include:

- clothing – in cases where clothing to clothing contact has occurred (note that SOCOs do not generally search (i.e. take tapings from) clothing – the investigating officer (IO) will decide what items of clothing are to be examined and these will be searched by forensic scientists under controlled conditions at the laboratory);
- skin (in sexual assault or unlawful killing cases);
- bedding, car seats;
- points of entry and exit of premises (e.g. in burglary cases).

In order to ensure optimal search results the following types of information should be elicited by the SOCO:

- what clothing was worn by the suspect/victim at the time of the alleged crime/and in what order (i.e. what was on the outer surface) (to avoid unnecessary searching of garments not worn during the incident)?
- are there any descriptions of the clothing worn by the suspect?
- were any items of clothing removed during the incident?
- what crime is alleged to have taken place, who was involved, and how?
- is it possible to reconstruct evidence for the purpose of defining area(s)/object(s) to be searched? (E.g. if a suspect climbed through a window, fibres may have been transferred onto the window sill; in a rape case fibres from the suspect's clothing may have been transferred onto the victim's pubic hair or underwear.);
- in sexual assault cases – where did the assault take place (e.g. floor, bed)?

Were bed clothes present on the bed? Were they removed? Was underwear put back on afterwards, or new underwear worn? – In which case, which pair is which?

- who had legitimate access to the crime scene?
- when did the incident take place and was there any delay before the scene was examined?
- what did the suspect pick up from the scene (e.g. fibres from victim's bedding, carpet, clothing)?

While fibre evidence may prove a suspect's presence at a particular place, it will not necessarily prove involvement in any crime.

The circumstances, including the timing, of any subject's presence at a crime scene should be ascertained and all possible innocent explanations explored and accounted for.

16.2.2 Securing and processing the crime scene

The following steps should be taken in order to promote the proper collection and preservation of fibre evidence:

- the perimeters of the crime scene should be secured;
- individuals entering or passing through the scene should be kept to a minimum;
- the order of collection of evidence should be considered.

Generally a crime scene should not be fingerprinted until all trace evidence has been secured. Tape lifting on some surfaces may destroy potential fingerprint evidence so, if necessary, a compromise will be reached depending on the circumstances of the case.

16.2.3 Evidence collection techniques

Wherever practicable, it is best to preserve the article itself and allow the forensic scientist to recover any fibres under optimum conditions of lighting, cleanliness, etc. This might apply, e.g. to weapons and other easily transportable items, or splintered wood from the point of entry on which fibres might have been caught.

METHODS FOR RETRIEVING FIBRES

There is no single preferred technique for the recovery of fibre trace material. The most common evidence collection techniques are as follows:

1. Hand retrieval: Used in cases where fibres are visible to the naked eye. The fibres should be photographed while *in situ* before being removed using clean tweezers or forceps and placed in a folded sheet of clean

paper. Loose fibres should be packaged and stored in rigid glass containers. Items of clothing that may contain fibres should be seized and securely packaged in individual evidence bags (no two items of clothing should ever be packaged together).

2. Tape retrieval: The most common method of retrieving fibres from a crime scene is taping. The aim of this method is to recover transfers without altering their distribution and it is thus the best way of preserving all the information that can be ascertained from the fibres.

   An adhesive tape (e.g. clear household tape, fingerprint tape or a commercially manufactured adhesive lifting sheet) is touched repeatedly and systematically to the surface of interest and immediately placed, adhesive side down, on a clean transparent acetate sheet. It is recommended that adhesive tape lifts are placed in a heat-sealable or ziplock clear polythene bag (tapes should never be stuck onto paper or cardboard).

   Low reliance will be placed on fibres either at the edge of a tape or protruding under it. This is because possible contamination or that the fibre attached post crime scene cannot be ruled out with absolute certainty. The best practice therefore is for tape edges to be immediately protected by covering with a further strip of adhesive tape.

   Taping is also used to retrieve fibres from the skin of a corpse. Fibre retrieval from a corpse should ideally be undertaken at the crime scene before the body is removed to the mortuary in order to preserve as much evidence as possible and to minimise the potential for contamination (see further **Chapter 24**).

3. Combing or brushing: This method is used to remove fibre trace evidence from hair. The comb or brush used to comb the hair and any trace evidence should be wrapped in paper and secured in a tamper proof evidence bag.

4. Vacuum sweeping: Surfaces upon which tape lifts cannot be performed (e.g. dirty or damp surfaces) can be vacuumed using a vacuum cleaner equipped with a special forensic trap and filtration system. The nozzle of the cleaner should be thoroughly cleaned between uses to avoid contamination. However, vacuuming should be avoided if at all possible because of potential difficulties that may be encountered later in demonstrating that the nozzle was clean.

5. Scrapings: This method is used to collect fibre, flaking material, and other trace evidence from the clothing of buried or decomposed bodies. The scrapings should be placed in Beecham's style paper packets or Petri dishes for examination by stereo microscopy.

For further information see Springer, Faye, 'Collection of Fibre Evidence from Crime Scenes' in J. Robertson and M. Grieve (1999) p. 101 et seq.

All collected or seized items should be appropriately labelled. Information on the label should include a description of the item; the item number and case number; the time and date collected, and the name of the person who collected/seized each item. It is important to establish the chain of custody in fibre cases due to the high risk of contamination or secondary transfer of fibres by individuals present at the crime scene.

16.2.4 Taking known fibre samples and preparation of reference samples for comparison purposes

A control sample of the surface from which unknown fibres have been removed should be taken if the whole surface area cannot be sent to the laboratory for examination (e.g. carpets, sofas). Any control should include the full range of the fibres present on the item (e.g. in the case of a patterned carpet a number of control samples should be taken from different areas in order to be representative).

16.2.5 Contamination

Due to the volatile nature of contact trace evidence, it is imperative that steps are taken from the outset to avoid accidental primary (direct) or secondary (indirect) transfer of evidential trace material between one item and another.

In cases where there is a risk that an accidental transfer may have occurred, the examining expert should be informed so that this consideration is taken into account when formulating any conclusions in relation to the evidence.

A certain level of contamination will be caused to the scene by everyone who enters it. Trace materials may be unwittingly added or taken away. While in reality, such contamination will not necessarily be detrimental to the identification of suspect materials, an expert may, in certain cases, consider that it is inappropriate to carry out an examination if he or she considers that the evidence has been compromised.

In cases of doubt a second opinion should be obtained or the expert should be asked to state the reasons for considering why the evidence has been compromised.

Procedures to ensure the integrity, continuity and non-contamination of trace evidence should be stringent.

The following steps have been be recognised as necessary measures in order to minimise the potential for contamination of trace evidence:

1. Witnesses, victims, and suspects should be separated until trace evidence and/or clothing has been secured.
2. Whenever possible, different people and vehicles should deal with the suspect and scene, or suspect and victim.
3. Anyone taking part in the examination of a scene or of a deceased should not take part in the examination of a suspect.

4. Different personnel should be involved in the removal of the victim's clothing and the collection of the suspect's clothing.
5. Protective clothing, including disposable gloves and outer clothing, should be worn by crime scene personnel, scientific staff, and by medical doctors/pathologists engaged in searching the scene.
6. Any tools and other supplies used for collecting trace evidence should be kept free from any possible cross-contamination between suspect and victim. Separate fibre collection kits should be used for suspect and victim items and these duplicate kits should be labelled 'victim' and 'suspect'.
7. Ideally, all items should be packaged at the scene in clean tamper proof bags in order to preclude any possibility of post-scene contamination.
8. All items and clothing garments should be packaged in separate bags in order to eliminate the potential for the redistribution of fibres between garments or items while in the packaging.
9. Packaged items should not be opened or tampered with except for the purposes of examination in controlled laboratory conditions.
10. Items should be examined under laboratory conditions in a purpose-designed room with suitable air filtration.
11. Different rooms in the laboratory should be used to search items from different sources, scenes, or people. These rooms should be located some physical distance from each other.
12. Ideally, different examiners should examine items from the victim and items from the suspect. Where this is not possible there must be confirmation of a clear time gap and evidence of decontamination between examinations.
13. Laboratory examiners must wear suitable protective clothing.
14. Benches used for searching must be cleaned prior to any examination and the bench should be covered with clean paper.
15. Any packaging and repackaging of victim and suspect items in the same room of a laboratory should be avoided.
16. If the victim and suspect clothing is wet, care should be taken to dry the items in separate areas. The items should not be dried upon surfaces which could cross-contaminate the garments.

Where the integrity of the evidence is at issue, the precise nature of the anti-contamination measures taken at the crime scene and thereafter should be carefully ascertained and considered.

16.2.6 Transfer and persistence of fibres

The presence or absence of fibre evidence at a crime scene will depend upon a number of factors, including:

• whether there was any contact between a suspect and surfaces;

- the nature and area of the surfaces in contact, and the force or pressure and duration of contact;
- the nature of the donor and recipient garments (e.g. textiles with smooth surfaces such as nylon jackets are poor recipients and far fewer polyester fibres will generally be transferred than cotton, acrylic and wool fibres; longer fibres will be lost more quickly from a recipient garment than shorter fibres);
- the passage of time between the commission of the crime/presence of the suspect at the scene, and the search.

Research has shown that there is a rapid loss of transferred fibres (about 80 per cent after four hours and a further loss of between five and 10 per cent over the remaining 24 hours). It follows that in all cases it should be ascertained when (and how long after the commission of the alleged offence) the search of the crime scene took place and the victim's and the suspect's clothing was collected. Additionally the following considerations may be material:

- whether there was continued wearing of the recipient garment;
- how active the wearer might have been;
- whether other garments were worn on top of or over the recipient garment;
- whether the recipient garment was washed;
- whether the transferred fibres were situated on an area of the recipient garment more prone to contact with other surfaces;
- whether the pressure of the original contact was low.

In assessing the significance of a fibre transfer, or absence thereof, the following considerations should always be taken into account:

1. Unless a suspect is apprehended fairly quickly, failure to find fibres matching the complainant's clothing on the suspect's clothing does not necessarily imply lack of contact.
2. As the time of wear of a garment increases, any remaining transferred fibres will be persistent and hence difficult to remove. In such cases, particularly efficient recovery methods have to be used.
3. Evidence of contact/association found through comparison of transferred fibres will generally involve recent transfer.
4. Because fibres are readily lost and retransferred, undue significance should not be placed on the exact distribution of a small number of fibres. A small number of fibres transferred onto underclothing may not be as damaging as it appears at first glance.

Redistribution of fibres between garments may have been caused by a failure to package items properly.

The possibility that the fibre has been transferred as a result of a secondary transfer should always be considered and discounted. For instance, fibres may be transferred from a jumper onto a car seat (the primary transfer) and later a second person sits on the car seat and the fibres from the jumper are transferred onto the clothing worn by the second person (the secondary transfer). The number of fibres found will be of critical importance in assessments here.

Other examples of secondary transfers include transfers of carpet fibres onto third surfaces via clothing fabrics or shoe soles, and transfer of clothing fibres from garment A onto garment B via a seat belt.

Tertiary and quaternary transfers (and so on) are also possible, but these are rare and the number of fibres transferred will be small (usually in single figures).

16.2.7   Evaluation and interpretation of fibre evidence

In order to evaluate and interpret fibre evidence in any given case, an expert should consider the following questions:

WHAT IS THE FIBRE?

It is generally accepted that an expert should not attempt to identify a fibre merely by appearance and with reference to previous experience. A fibre should be systematically identified by using appropriate microscopical, chemical and physical tests, and if necessary compared with a properly maintained fibre reference collection.

HOW COMMON IS THE FIBRE?

Generally, in assessing the significance of fibres that match, the more common the fibre, the less the value of the evidence (an example of a common fibre is the cotton used in blue denim). However, the opposite may be true in the case of very rare fibres, even if they are present in very low numbers. Note however that the smaller the numbers the greater is the attention that must be given to possibilities for contamination.

As with many areas of forensic science it will not usually be possible to give a precise meaning to 'commonness'. Meaningful, comprehensive data relating to fibre production, pigmentation, usage, and distribution are not available. Textile fashions change rapidly and fibres of different types and colours are not spread evenly throughout all sections of the population. A very general indication of frequency of occurrence may only be possible. This is ascertained by reference to information contained in a number of databases compiled from the findings of various garment population studies. Databases contain information such as the frequency of usage of fibre types in different textiles, frequency of fibre combinations in different textiles, and the frequency of uncommon fibre types in the general fibre population.

The commonness of the fibre is generally dictated by its physical and chemical properties and those of the dyes, pigments and delustrants that are present. These properties can be studied under a microscope using a variety of light sources, by infrared spectrophotometry, by microspectrophotometry (MSP) and by thin layer chromatography tests (TLC).

In serious cases (e.g. terrorism, robbery, murder, and rape) industrial enquiries may be carried out from a network of contacts within the textile trade and rope industry in order to determine the manufacturer of a particular fibre (in the past industrial enquiries have been used to trace the origins of rope, twine, bank security bags, labels, jackets, overcoats, and carpets). Such enquiries are expensive and time consuming and not all textile material and garments will necessarily lend themselves to such enquiries. See Wiggins and Cook (1992).

The modern mass production of garments has limited the value of fibre evidence. Richard Saferstein notes:

> Regardless of where and under what conditions fibres are recovered, their ultimate value as forensic evidence will depend on the criminalist's ability to narrow their origin to a limited number of sources or even to a single source. Unfortunately, the mass production of our garments and fabrics has served to limit the value of fibre evidence in this respect, and it is only under the most unusual circumstances that the recovery of fibres at a crime scene will provide individual identification to a high degree of certainty.

(See Richard Saferstein (1998) p. 222.)

Certain international standards in respect of the terminology of man-made fibres and the methods used for testing those fibres have been established by the International Bureau for the Standardisation of Man-Made Fibres (BISFA). However, these standards apply only to those manufacturers who are members of the association.

The objectives of BISFA are to establish a standard terminology in relation to manmade fibres for the continuous improvement of inter-company, customer and consumer communications. BISFA aims to establish technical rules for fibres and yarns for delivery conditions which have to be applied for each type of man-made fibre and which are mandatory for all members of the association. Therefore BISFA establishes internationally agreed procedures and test methods for different categories of man-made fibres and may be a useful enquiry source. For further information see **www.bisfa.org**.

IS THE FIBRE THERE BY CHANCE?

Research has shown that coincidental matches where the fibres originate from a source other than the putative one are unlikely to occur in the majority of cases. The exceptions, where alternative sources may be responsible, are with low numbers of matching fibres (five or less) or when certain common fibres are involved (see Martin Salter and Kenneth G. Wiggins 'Aids to Interpretation' in J. Robertson and M. Grieve (1999) p. 367.

If a control sample matches a crime scene fibre, it should be considered how often such a fibre would be encountered in everyday life, e.g. how many individuals in a particular room at any given time would be likely to be wearing a garment that would contain such a fibre. Regard should be taken of any special factors that apply – for example clothing in current fashion worn by people in a particular category, e.g. younger people.

In relation to the finding of only one matching fibre see *R.* v. *George* [2002] All ER (D) 441 (Jul); [2002] EWCA Crim 1923 (especially at para. 109).

16.2.8 Other interpretative issues

In order to support inference of contact and to verify (i) that the crime scene is not a possible source of fibres that are thought to have originated from the suspect or (ii) that the suspect's environment is not a source of fibres supposedly coming from the crime scene, an expert must compare samples of the questioned fibres with a control sample of fibres from a known source. In forming a conclusion, a number of considerations should be taken into account, including the following influential factors:

CIRCUMSTANCES OF THE CASE:

- consider the possibility of legitimate access or of the transfer having taken place during legitimate contact (this is possible between total strangers if they come into contact, for instance, on public transport or in a pub);
- consider other possibilities, such as accidental transfer as a result of victim and suspect having been transported in same car;
- the length of time between incident and collection of evidence (the more minimal the delay generally the greater the value of the evidence);
- whether the fibre is classified as common or is unusual in some way;
- whether there is a possible/plausible alternative source;
- whether the fibres found are present in large numbers.
  Note (i) that very common fibres can assume increased evidential importance if present in particularly large numbers in circumstances in which they would not normally be expected to be found; (ii) the finding of only a few fibres may indicate that the transfer has been secondary or tertiary, etc. as opposed to primary;
- whether there is any possibility of contamination.

16.2.9 Quality assurance

A laboratory should use appropriate and generally accepted, documented technical procedures for collection of fibre evidence and analysis, including keeping of a written record of all procedures and instruments used. Any opinions of an expert should be supported by appropriate scientific data.

It is also recommended that any infrared spectra fibre reference collections are produced in house using appropriate standards obtained from manufacturers.

Notes of all examination results should be maintained for inspection (for instance by an expert instructed by the defence) and verification of results and cross-checking of reports by qualified peers should be demonstrated.

See Michael Grieve 'Interpretation of Fibres Evidence' in J. Robertson and M. Grieve (1999) p. 364.

16.2.10   Contents of expert's report

A survey carried out by the European Fibres Group considered that it is best practice to include the following information in any report:

- the techniques used to carry out any examination;
- objectives of the examination (e.g. to look for any evidence of fibre transfer between items X and Y);
- a summary offering possible interpretations of the findings;
- the number of matching fibres found;
- specification of the type of target fibres that were being sought (because not all fibre types involved will be suitable as targets);
- list of items which were not examined and an explanation of why not;
- whether, under known circumstances, legitimate contact could have occurred in the given case;
- whether there could have been a possibility of contamination/why an examination was considered possible in such circumstances/possible effects of contamination on findings;
- whether certain fibre types are considered as common and reasons for this;
- the possibility of secondary transfer;
- the donor capacity ('sheddability') of various garments.

See Michael Grieve 'A survey on the evidential value of fibres and on the interpretation of findings in fibre transfer cases' (1998) *Proceedings of the 6th European Fibres Group Meeting*, Dundee.

16.2.11   Expression of conclusions

CLASSICAL AND BAYESIAN STATISTICAL APPROACHES

There are currently two schools of thought about assessing the value of fibre evidence – the classical approach which expresses the results in terms of statistical odds and the Bayesian statistical approach. The latter approach considers a ratio of the likelihood of the results obtained having been caused by two competing possibilities, those of the evidence being present if the suspect did, or did not, commit the crime. In the field of fibre transfer evidence the likelihood ratio will be assessed with reference to a number of parameters including the relevance of the traces (which depend on the circumstances of the case; time between offence and recovery; location of the traces); number of the matching fibres recovered; number of fibre types involved; relative frequency of these types of fibres; extent of the analytical information obtained, and presence of cross-transfer. In this case it is important to be aware that the opinion expressed is of the degree of support (or otherwise) that the fibre evidence provides to whatever other evidence there may be in favour of a proposition, for example that A's sweater came into contact with B's underwear. The fibre findings are not evaluated in isolation.

See Christophe Champod and Franco Taroni 'The Bayesian Approach' in J. Robertson and M. Grieve (1999) p. 379. See also **para. 13.4**.

16.3   GLASS

16.3.1   Introduction

Broken glass can be used to link a suspect to a particular scene. Glass recovered from a crime scene or suspect may be indicative of forced entry (e.g. from a broken window pane) or a struggle or an assault involving a broken bottle/drinking glass.

Glass at the crime scene may provide other information such as sequence of gunshots, whether a petroleum accelerant was used in an arson case, and broken automobile window or light glass can be useful evidence to link a vehicle to a hit and run case.

16.3.2   Assessment of the crime scene and searching

Glass will be visually searched for by the scenes of crime officer (SOCO) at the scene. Non-conspicuous glass either at the scene or in the clothing of individuals will be searched for with the use of a microscope, normally by a forensic scientist.

16.3.3   Evidence collection techniques

Visible particles of glass found outdoors should be picked up using forceps – or if the pieces are large enough they can be picked up by hand, provided that care is taken not to compromise the surfaces (which may also contain footwear impressions or fingerprint evidence). Pieces of glass – large or small – should be carefully packaged and enclosed in leak-proof rigid containers within appropriate evidence bags.

Any clothing from suspect/victim which may contain glass should be seized as soon as possible and suitably packaged. If the clothing is still being worn, the suspect/victim should be asked to stand on top of a paper sheet when removing the clothing so that none of the fragments are lost (the glass and paper sheet will then be packaged separately).

Any combing of the hair for glass should take place before clothing is removed. Hair should be combed over a large sheet of paper using a clean comb. The comb should be packaged with the hair combings separately from the paper before being sent for laboratory testing.

16.3.4 Taking control samples of glass

The overriding consideration is that any control sample is a representative of the material transferred.

If a window has been broken at a scene, a control sample of the glass from the window should be taken (including samples from each pane where more than one pane has been broken – samples from all around the pane should be taken as there may be a variation of the refractive index (RI) of the glass in different areas). A broken window pane may be reconstructed if all the broken pieces are recovered. The side from which the window has been broken may also be determined in such circumstances and this may be of particular relevance in the given case.

Properties of glass bottles will differ, e.g. the neck will be different from the base. Therefore a number of control samples from different areas of a bottle should be taken.

16.3.5 Transfer and persistence

Any glass transferred onto clothing or hair will be lost very rapidly. Studies have shown that most fragments of glass disappear from clothing within half an hour of breaking. Larger fragments will disappear before smaller fragments.

In assault cases, the number of fragments recovered will be determined by the number of strikes; the distance between the glass and the person breaking the glass; the size of the fragments; the composition of the weave of the fabric of the clothing, and the time interval between the breaking of the glass and the subsequent recovery of the glass from the clothing.

Glass fragments may remain in pockets or other 'traps' for long periods of time. Fragments can be transferred into pockets via the hands. Studies have shown that glass fragments may still remain in clothing following dry cleaning (most of the particles were found in cuffs and pockets). Certain fabrics, such as wool, capture more particles than other fabrics, e.g. denim.

See E. Pearson, R. May and M. Dabbs (1971).

16.3.6 Contamination

Control samples taken from the scene must be stored separately from any glass recovered from clothing or hair in order to avoid cross-contamination.

16.3.7 General interpretative issues

EVIDENCE OF COMMONALITY AND PHYSICAL MATCHES OF BROKEN GLASS

Occasionally it will be possible to demonstrate a physical or mechanical fit between two pieces of glass, e.g. glass at a scene from a broken vehicle headlight. This will be conclusive evidence of commonality.

In most cases the evidence of a match comes from measurements of RI and composition, whether or not the glass is toughened, the nature of any original surface present (flat or curved), and possibly the overall thickness. When there is agreement in these properties between fragments (suspect and reference, or 'test' and 'control') it indicates that they could be from the same source. It does not by itself rule out a chance match. Reference to databases assembled in forensic science laboratories will however indicate how often glass of the given type has been encountered – whether commonly or rarely. The information is used to assess the likelihood of chance replication. Precise figures cannot be given.

16.3.8 Interpretive issues in relation to glass fragments found in clothing

The following issues should be considered:

- possibility of innocent presence of glass particles on clothing – a suspect's occupation/version of events may offer an explanation for the presence of glass on clothing;
- generally the more particles found the higher the evidential value (except if the glass is particularly unusual);
- glass found in hair or on clothing is generally of greater evidential value than that found on the soles of shoes;
- glass fragments with sharp edges are likely to have been formed more recently than those with blunt edges, generally speaking;
- studies have confirmed that fragments of glass can be present in the clothing of persons not suspected of having committed a crime.

Research conducted using a large number of random samples of clothing found that 29 per cent of trousers, 42 per cent of jackets, and 44 per cent of pullovers had glass particles present. The largest number of fragments found on a single garment was 57 from 27 different glass sources. Glass fragments were generally found in low numbers (usually one or two fragments).

In a study conducted on glass fragments recovered from the clothing of persons suspected of involvement in crime (and the clothing was suspected of harbouring evidential glass due to the nature of the crimes), 12 per cent of persons had no glass on their clothing, 45 per cent had between one and 10 fragments, 20 per cent had 11 to 20 fragments, and nine per cent had more than 50 fragments. Glass was found to be most prevalent in shoes, followed by trousers, jackets, knitwear, and shirts. See J. McQuillan and K. Edgar (1992).

A study has found that the following factors influence the final numbers of fragments of glass observed in clothing:

- the degree of fragmentation;
- the type and thickness of glass;
- how many times the window was struck; the position of the person relative to the window that was struck; the size of the window (some of these considerations will also apply in relation to broken bottles);
- the type of clothing worn by the person breaking the window;
- the activities of the person between the time of the commission and the time of apprehension;
- the time between apprehension and confiscation of clothing;
- the efficiency of the laboratory searching process;
- whether or not the person gained entry to the premises;
- the mode of clothing confiscations, e.g. whether force was required or not;
- the weather at the time of the incident.

16.4 PAINT

16.4.1 Searching the crime scene and evidence collection techniques

Whenever possible the item or part of the item bearing the paint should be preserved in its entirety for laboratory examination. Otherwise, a representative area of paint should be cut from close to any damaged area.

If the paint is flaking, samples of loose flakes close to the damaged area should be lifted. If any instrument marks are visible, these marks should be recovered (where possible) or photographed before any control sample is removed.

Paint may transfer onto instruments used to effect entry. Any instrument suspected of being so used should be seized and packaged in a manner that protects any tipped or bladed area. The item should be secured in a rigid box and sealed in a polythene or paper bag.

Any instrument used, e.g. to effect entry, at the scene may also leave traces of paint. Any alien paint should also be cut out (or scrapings taken) before any control sample is removed.

It is also possible to recover traces of paint from a suspect's hair/clothing. In such cases the procedures followed for combing of the hair and the removal of the clothes should follow the same procedure as for glass (see above). Any clothing or combings should be stored away from control samples in order to avoid any suggestion of contamination.

16.4.2 Taking of control samples for comparison purposes

Control samples should be taken within close proximity to any area of paint that appears to have been damaged or from any areas where paint appears to be flaking or damaged (a number of control samples should be taken from different areas if damage is extensive). Control samples must be of full thickness so as to include all paint layers.

16.4.3 Securing and processing the crime scene

Any areas where damage is apparent on painted surfaces or areas where there may be evidence of paint transfer (e.g. point of entry or exit in burglary cases) should be protected from the elements. Redecoration or repair of any damage should be delayed until the scene has been processed.

16.4.4 Transfer and persistence

Transfer may occur in a number of ways:

1. A transfer of wet paint can occur when a person or object rubs against the painted surface, or by splashing or dripping.
2. A transfer of dry paint is most often caused by the flaking of paint from the surface.
3. Dry paint may also be forced from a surface by a tool (e.g. screwdriver, case-opener, or jemmy bars used to open doors or windows in burglary cases). In such cases there may also be a transfer of paint onto the surface from the tool itself and tool-mark impressions may have been left.
4. Vehicular paint is commonly transferred onto other surfaces and objects as a result of impacts during traffic accidents (e.g. a transfer of paint between two colliding vehicles; flakes or smears of paint from a vehicle may be left at the scene of the accident or on a victim's hair or clothing) (see **Chapter 19**).
5. Paint fragments in hair and clothing will be lost very rapidly after the commission of an offence.
6. The general persistence of paint fragments is thought to be similar to that of glass (see above).
7. The issue of a secondary transfer of smeared or impressed paint between, say a jemmy and an attacked surface, generally does not arise. However, when an isolated loose paint flake is found on the surface of

clothing the possibility that it got there by secondary transfer, i.e. via an intermediate surface, may have to be addressed.

16.4.5   Interpretation of paint evidence

The most common types of paint encountered in criminal cases are household paint and vehicular paint. For the purposes of assessment and matching, vehicular paint is different form household paint.

HOUSEHOLD PAINT

Household paint can provide evidence of association. The level of significance of any match depends on the volume of the type of paint produced. This information is not generally available.

The properties of paint flakes that lead to individualisation are colour, layer structure, bulk, and surface texture, appearance in different conditions of illumination under the microscope, and the chemical composition of pigments, resins and fillers determined by instrumental techniques. Paint flakes may be distinguished by characteristics produced by ageing, i.e. significantly different conditions of weathering and degradation will enable paints from the same original batch to be distinguished.

The significance of a matching also depends on the commonness of the paint in question – white and black are the most common colours for paint (although there can be a considerable degree of difference even among white paints). Multiple layers of paint can provide strong evidence of association.

VEHICULAR PAINT

The evidential value of vehicular paint has been assessed in a number of studies over the years. It has been ascertained that the evidential value of this paint depends on factors such as the type of paint, unusual pigments, and the probability of another car of the same colour/model being at the scene at the same time as the suspect vehicle. See I.G. Holden (1962) 'The evaluation of scientific evidence in relation to road accidents', *Medicine, Science and the Law*, (3) 541–5.

GENERAL CONSIDERATIONS

The strength of the evidence will be affected by:

- the number and size of paint flakes recovered;
- whether edging of suspect flakes match edging of any paint removed from the scene;

- whether there has been a two-way transfer of paint between surface and tool/instrument.

16.5 QUALIFICATIONS OF EXPERT

Experts should have a degree qualification of at least graduate level in an analytical science (e.g. chemistry or physical and biological sciences). Experts may then undergo 'apprenticeship' type training in a laboratory, shadowing an experienced expert in the given field for a specified time before reporting on their own cases. Attendance on expert witness courses is also part of the training. The Council for the Registration of Forensic Practitioners (CRFP) register includes forensic practitioners specialising in and reporting on particulates and other contact trace evidence. Additionally, experts may belong to other professional bodies, such as the Royal Society of Chemistry (RSC).

REFERENCES

Fibres

Champod, C. & Taroni, F. 'The Bayesian Approach' in Robertson, J. & Grieve, M. (eds) (1999) *Forensic Examination of Fibres* (2nd edn), Taylor and Francis, p. 379.

Kidd, C. & Robertson, J. (1982) 'The transfer of textile fibres during simulated contacts', *J Forens Sci Soc* (22) 301–8.

Lowrie, C. & Jackson, G. (1991) 'Recovery of transferred fibres', *J Forens Sci Soc* (50) 111–19.

Lowrie, C. & Jackson, G. (1994) 'Secondary transfer of fibres', *Forens Sci Int* (64) 73–82.

Moore, J., Jackson, G. & Firth, M. (1986) 'Movement of fibres between working areas as a result of routine examination of garments', *J Forens Sci Soc* (26) 433–40.

Pounds, C. & Smalldon, K. (1975) 'The transfer of fibres between clothing materials during simulated contacts and their persistence during wear: part 1 – fibre transference and part 2 – fibre persistence', *J Forens Sci Soc* (15) 17–27 and 29–37.

Robertson, J. & Grieve, M. (eds) (1999) *Forensic Examination of Fibres* (2nd edn), Taylor and Francis, pp. 101 et seq, 364, 367.

Robertson, J. & Lloyd, A. (1984) 'Redistribution of textile fibres following transfer during simulated contacts', *J Forens Sci Soc* (24) 3–7.

Robertson, J. & Olaniyan, D. (1986) 'Effect of garment cleaning on the recovery and redistribution of transferred fibres', *J Forens Sci* (31) 73–8.

Saferstein, R. 'Hairs, Fibres and Paint' in Saferstein, R. (1998) *Criminalists: An Introduction to Forensic Science* (6th edn), Prentice-Hall, p. 222.

Salter, M., Cook, R. & Jackson, A. (1995) 'Transfer of fibres to head hair, their persistence and retrieval', *Forens Sci Int* (81) 211–21.

Wiggins, K. & Cook, R. (1992) 'The Value of industrial inquiries in cases involving textile fibres', *J. Forens Sci Soc* (32) 159–67.

Glass and Paint

Caddy, B. (ed.) (2001) *Forensic Examination of Glass and Paint: Analysis and Interpretation,* Taylor and Francis.

Holden, I. (1962) 'The evaluation of scientific evident in relation to road accidents', *Medicine, Science and the Law* (3) 541–5.

McQuillan, J. & Edgar, K. 'A survey of distribution of glass on clothing', *J Forens Sci Soc* (32) 333–8.

Pearson, E., May, R. & Dabbs, M. (1971) 'Glass and paint fragments found in men's outer clothing. Report of a survey', *J. Forens Sci* (16) 283–300.

Thornton, J. 'Interpretation of physical aspects of glass evidence', in Caddy, B. (2001) *Forensic Examination of Glass and Paint: Analysis and Interpretation*, Taylor and Francis, pp. 97–120.

Willis, S., McCullough, J. & McDermott, S. 'The Interpretation of Paint Evidence', in Caddy, B. (ed) (2001) *Forensic Examination of Glass and Paint: Analysis and Interpretation*, Taylor and Francis.

CHAPTER 17

DNA, blood and hair

17.1 INTRODUCTION

It is frequently said that the application of DNA profiling to criminal law enforcement is the biggest development in the field of human identification since the discovery of fingerprinting at the start of the 20th century. Furthermore, the sensitivity and discriminatory powers of DNA profiling, the range of biological material which can be subjected to DNA analysis, and the fact that minute pieces of material (possibly many years old) may be successfully analysed, has meant that since its introduction in the early 1990s, DNA analysis has virtually replaced all other methods of trace analysis involving biological fluids. Given this consideration, this chapter concentrates on DNA analysis, with blood grouping (which DNA analysis has basically replaced) and macroscopic/microscopic analysis of hair being considered only briefly. The chapter also makes a brief reference to bloodstain and blood spatter analysis.

17.2 WHAT IS DNA?

DNA is found in all living cells and it carries the information that makes every person individual. This code is inherited by children from their parents and can be used to prove family ties. DNA is made up of four base chemicals (abbreviated as A, T, C and G). The bases are arranged in pairs with A and T binding together and C and G binding together. DNA is composed of millions of such bases and it is their *particular combinations* that are unique to each person (identical twins share the same DNA). DNA is found in two places in the body of a cell – the mitochondria (mitochondrial DNA) and the nucleus (nuclear DNA). Mitochondrial DNA (mtDNA) is inherited only from the mother. Each cell has many mitochondria (as opposed to only one nucleus) and, therefore, mtDNA is useful when only a very small amount of trace evidence is available to test or if the nucleus is missing or has degraded.

17.3 DNA PROFILING IN THE UK

In simple terms, DNA profiling is a technique which enables a scientist to compare two biological samples and to determine the likelihood that these samples originated from the same individual.

So-called DNA profiling or typing (sometimes known by the misnomers 'DNA fingerprinting' or 'genetic fingerprinting') as now used in criminal investigations was first developed in 1984 as a result of research to detect the presence of genetic diseases by Professor Sir Alec Jeffreys at the University of Leicester.

A DNA profile is constructed by extracting a DNA sample from body tissue, body fluids (blood, semen, saliva, perspiration, etc.) or hair. DNA analysis involves the identification of gene types (alleles) at a particular locus on a chromosome. Identifying alleles at a number of different loci (regions) provides a DNA profile. The types and number of loci chosen depend on many factors including their discriminatory power and sensitivity. DNA is extracted from a sample and quantified, amplified, typed and loaded onto a database. Laboratories in the UK have used a number of analytical techniques over the years.

The first use of DNA analysis in a criminal investigation was by Leicestershire Police in 1986 (as a result of that investigation Colin Pitchfork pleaded guilty to two rape/murders at Leicester Crown Court on 22 January 1987). The first analytical techniques to be used were multilocus probes (MLP) and single locus probe (SLP). These tests were used until the early 1990s. Since then short tandem repeat (STR) analysis has been used and that remains the current method of analysis in criminal cases. STR analysis is different to previous systems because it involves the multiplying up (or amplification) of DNA for analysis which means that results can be obtained from smaller samples than previously. A further test involving the analysis of single nucleotide polymorphisms (SNPs or 'snips'), which requires less equipment and is less time consuming than STR analysis, is currently being developed and may be used for forensic analysis in the future. This has the potential to provide information about the physical characteristics of the person from whom the DNA comes. SNPs were used to identify badly degraded remains following the September 11th disaster. Service provider, Forensic Alliance is now using the technique for intelligence purposes, only in cases where STR has failed because DNA has degraded.

A DNA profile is a computerised alpha-numerical value obtained from a visualised output of the DNA analytical process. The profile is stored in a computer file to provide intelligence for crime investigation. A typical database contains three indices:

(i) profiles contained from forensic case work from material left at crime scenes (crime scene profiles);
(ii) profiles of suspected offenders;
(iii) profiles of persons or relatives of missing persons.

Whenever a new profile is loaded onto the system it may be searched against the other indices to determine if it is a 'match' to any other profile. Matches are sometimes referred to as 'hits'. The structure of the database enables searches to be conducted scene to scene, person to person, and person to scene. A database may have a facility for comparing unsolved crime profiles with DNA profiles from suspects to establish their innocence or to confirm their probable involvement.

When a DNA profile of an individual matches a crime scene profile the significance can be assessed only if the probability of that profile occurring in the relevant population is known. The frequency of a profile is calculated by multiplying the frequencies of the alleles at each locus using population databases of randomly selected and unrelated individuals. Statistical databases are maintained for this purpose.

In the UK, the National DNA Database (NDNAD) became operative on 10 April 1995. The Forensic Science Service (FSS) is:

(i) a supplier to NDNAD;

(ii) the custodian of the NDNAD (in which role it is responsible for ensuring and approving other suppliers of analytical services, a position currently under review); and

(iii) the manager of the NDNAD (in which role it carries out a matching and 'hit' notification service).

Different components of NDNAD have different owners. The hardware and technology is owned by the FSS. The data is the legal property of the relevant police force which submitted the sample. The FSS act as a police force's agent in passing information on to other police forces.

Operation of the database is subject to the Data Protection Act 1998 which determines who may have access to information and how it must be destroyed. Data is held on a password protected system and the security is layered so that data protection regulations are met.

For further information on the FSS and NDNAD see **www.forensic.gov.uk**.

17.4 THE CRIME SCENE SAMPLE

Under current testing methods, it is theoretically possible to produce a DNA profile from a single cell. It is therefore possible to obtain DNA profiles from saliva deposits left on drinks containers, cigarette ends, balaclavas, envelope flaps or stamps, and half eaten foodstuffs. A DNA profile may also be obtained from an item that has been touched because DNA material in skin cells will have been transferred onto the 'touched' item. It has even been suggested that DNA analysis will replace traditional fingerprinting in the future. In 1990 consultant geneticist, Wilson Wall, pioneered an experimental technique whereby DNA extracted and analysed from fingerprints found on sound, clear surfaces was used as a substrate for DNA profiling. Regardless of the kind of sample being used, it is generally accepted that the lower limit for forensic analysis should be the DNA mass present in approximately 1,000 cells (although many laboratories are now profiling on less than that).

17.5 CONSIDERATIONS IN RELATION TO SEARCHING, SECURING, AND PROCESSING THE CRIME SCENE

Due to the volatile nature of all contact trace evidence – biological or otherwise – particular care has to be taken in securing and processing the crime scene in order to ensure the integrity of the exhibit at all points up to, and until, its arrival at the laboratory.

The issues of contamination and secondary transfer of contact trace evidence are considered in detail in **Chapter 16**; see **16.2.2** and **16.2.5**. See also in this regard, *R.* v. *Hanratty* [2002] EWCA Crim 1141; [2002] 3 All ER 534 at paras.110–28, where issues in relation to contamination of biological traces submitted for DNA analysis many years after their original deposit are discussed.

17.6 COLLECTION AND PRESERVATION OF HUMAN CONTACT TRACE EVIDENCE

In relation to DNA and human contact traces generally, the prevailing view is that the best evidence is secured if a complete item can be seized and sent for laboratory testing (e.g. in sexual offences, where the assault has allegedly taken place on a bed, the entire bedding should be seized and submitted to the laboratory). In certain cases this will not be possible. The accepted methods of collecting biological traces from the scene involve swabbing, pipetting (if sufficient liquid is present), or scraping.

The following methods are suggested as best practice for the collection of blood, semen and hair deposits.

17.6.1 Bloodstains

Liquid blood should be collected by pipetting into a plastic tube. If the blood is to be taken directly to a laboratory for DNA profiling freezing is not necessary. However, wherever there is any delay, freezing or cooling should be carried out. DNA analysis can still be carried out on blood that has been frozen, but it should be noted that frozen blood may be useless for other forensic tests, such as blood grouping and other serological tests (which ideally require that blood be stored at 4 degrees centigrade).

Dried bloodstains on hard surfaces can be scraped off with a scalpel into a small plastic container. This should be kept as cool as possible to prevent degradation of DNA during transit. The surface can also be swabbed with a cotton wool swab moistened with water. The swab should be air dried without heat and frozen.

17.6.2 Seminal stains

Seminal stains on small items of fabric or any other small objects should be frozen or kept as cool as possible during transit. Bulk clothing cannot be frozen and should be kept cool. Clothing should be placed in new paper bags (not polythene as this can encourage mould formation) and transported to the laboratory without delay.

Alternatively, damp swabs may be taken of suspect stains, which are then dried and frozen. As with blood, suspect dried seminal stains on hard surfaces may be scraped off and transported to the laboratory in a suitable container.

17.6.3 Hair

It is possible to obtain a full DNA profile from a hair. At the crime scene, there is a good chance that hair that has been forcibly removed from a person during a struggle or hair caught on sharp edges at the point of entry/exit may have been plucked out at the root. A DNA profile can be obtained from plucked hairs because the nucleated root and follicle cells will be present. Any retrieved hair should be placed in a plastic bag and frozen if there is likely to be a delay in transit. The same considerations apply to pubic hair as apply to head hair.

Shafts of hairs which have been shed naturally, as in 'moulting', will generally contain little or no root material. This type of hair will contain only mtDNA and will be of limited evidential value in criminal cases (see **17.7.1**).

17.6.4 Autopsy samples

Various samples will be taken during an autopsy for the purpose of DNA profiling. This may serve to identify either the assailant or the deceased. In cases where it is suspected that the deceased has been sexually assaulted vaginal and anal swabs will be taken. Seminal stains on the skin will also be searched for by using ultraviolet light. Any areas where seminal staining is suspected to be present will be swabbed.

DNA profiling also plays an important part in the identification of unknown human remains. In cases of remains with minimal decomposition, a blood sample will be taken. It is recommended that a sample of between 1 ml and 5 ml is taken into an EDTA tube (which extracts metallic ions, prevents clotting, and inhibits enzymes in blood and microorganisms which may break down DNA during storage). Tissue samples can also be taken for DNA testing. Spleen is possibly the best organ for DNA recovery, although liver, muscle, kidney, and brain may also be used.

17.6.5 Samples from live victims/suspects of sexual assault

The finding of biological trace evidence (e.g. semen) is important in cases of sexual assault in order either to establish that sexual intercourse/assault has taken place or, in cases of an unknown assailant, for the purposes of identification.

The FSS, the Association of Forensic Physicians (AFP) and the Association of Chief Police Officers (ACPO) have issued guidelines for forensic physicians in the collection of specimens from victims/suspects in sexual assault cases. The nature of the alleged assault will dictate from where samples are taken. If skin swabs are taken (e.g. if either saliva or semen are suspected to be present), a control skin swab and unused swab should be provided to the testing laboratory.

Material which may yield a DNA profile may still be collected from the victim's body a number of days after the assault has taken place. Body fluids commonly submitted for DNA analysis include:

- saliva (10 ml of liquid), followed by mouth swab, and mouth washing (for detection of semen if oral penetration within two days);
- head hair (for detection of semen and other bodily fluids);
- pubic hair (for detection of semen and other bodily fluids);
- vulval swab (for detection of body fluids if vaginal intercourse has taken place within seven days or anal intercourse within three days, or ejaculation onto perineum); followed by low vaginal swab (for detection of body fluids if vaginal intercourse took place within three days); followed by high vaginal swab (for detection of body fluids if vaginal intercourse took place within seven days or if anal intercourse took place within three days); followed by endocervical swab (only in cases where intercourse occurred more than 48 hours previously);
- penile swab (for detection of body fluids if intercourse took place within two days);
- perianal swab (for detection of body fluids if anal intercourse occurred within three days); followed by rectal swab (for detection of body fluids if intercourse took place within three days); followed by anal canal swab (for detection of body fluids if anal intercourse occurred within three days);
- fingernails (for recovery of bodily fluids);
- condoms (for detection of bodily fluids (e.g. seminal fluid) if used during intercourse);
- sanitary towels/tampons (for detection of bodily (e.g. seminal fluid) if in situ or after vaginal intercourse).

It is recommended that all the above specimens are frozen and placed in tamper proof bags before being sent to the testing laboratory.

See the FSS, the APS (now known as AFP) and the ACPO *Guidelines for the Collection of Specimens* (2000).

The FSS produce a forensic medical examination kit which it designed in conjunction with AFP and ACPO for the use of forensic physicians in the recovery of evidence from either victims or suspects in cases of sexual assault. The kit contains a number of self-contained modules which, given proper use, are designed to comply with rigorous quality assurance standards providing evidence of continuity and a guarantee of the integrity of the particular exhibit.

17.6.6   Samples from suspects generally

The taking of intimate and non-intimate samples from a person in police detention is governed by the Police and Criminal Evidence Act 1984 (PACE), Code D, para.5. Head hair plucked at the root and mouth swabs (or buccal swabs, 'buccal' having come from the buccinator muscle located inside the cheek) may be taken by a police officer, but intimate samples (e.g. blood) may be taken only by a registered medical practitioner. For this reason, and because they are convenient and potentially less hazardous to take and handle than blood, buccal swab samples are usually the sample of choice in mass screening exercises (see National Crime Faculty 'Draft Operational Order for the obtaining of intelligence led buccal (mouth) swab sample' in ACPO Crime Committee (2000) *The Manual of Standard Operational Procedures for Scientific Support Personnel at Major Incident Scenes.*

17.7   ISSUES IN RELATION TO THE NATURE AND QUALITY OF DNA SAMPLES

'The greatest advantage of DNA analysis also contains its greatest risk of error – that is, the sensitivity of the test.' Wilson Wall (2002) p. 53.

As can be seen from the above, the nature of the sample will determine the type of analysis that can be carried out and the results (e.g. hair that does not contain root material will only contain mtDNA and any profile obtained will be less discriminating than a profile obtained from material containing nuclear DNA). Wilson Wall points out that, while it is possible to produce some sort of result from any sample, the interpretation of that result depends on several fundamental questions, namely:

- is this the right sample for the analysis?
- can the sample be analysed at all?
- is the fundamental science behind the analysis sufficiently understood for the results to be held valid?

- to what degree can errors in sample handling affect test results?
- What is an acceptable level of error for the analysis of the sample? (See Wilson Wall (2002), pp. 23–36.)

17.7.1 Degradation of a sample

DNA is an organic compound and it is therefore liable to degradation and recycling into the environment. The process of decay is speeded up by factors such as temperature, humidity and the presence of insects. If the DNA has degraded to such an extent that a DNA profile cannot be produced from the nucleus, it may still be possible to obtain a profile from mtDNA.

Given that mtDNA is maternally inherited, all the children (both male and female) of a particular mother will share the same mtDNA and all the descendants originating from the female line will share the same mtDNA. The discriminatory power of mtDNA is thus not the same as that of nuclear DNA. Therefore the possibility that the DNA could have originated from a sibling should be considered in cases involving mtDNA (the methods now used for analysing nuclear DNA are so discriminating that there is little difficulty in distinguishing between the DNA of even the closest relatives). The main uses of mtDNA in the forensic context tend to be associated with the identification of modern and ancient decomposed or skeletonised human remains (mtDNA present in the long bones, teeth and hair shafts can survive for thousands of years in appropriate conditions). In criminal investigations, mtDNA analysis may be used to eliminate a suspect, but it cannot be used to discriminate between individuals in the same way as nuclear DNA can.

For further information see Joseph A. Dizinno, Mark R. Wilson and Bruce Budowle, 'Typing of DNA Derived from Hairs' in James Robertson (1998), pp. 155–73.

17.7.2 Naturally occurring 'errors' in a sample

Examples of this sort of error include cases in which DNA from two different individuals is present in a sample originating from one individual. This frequently occurs in rape cases where epithelial cells and sperm cells are both present in a swab taken from the victim's vagina. The potential for this type of error is well known and separation techniques exist (e.g. centrifugation) whereby it is possible to produce DNA profiles which do not contain mixtures of DNA. New techniques, such as YSTRs are now coming into use which single out just male DNA in a male/female mixture. There may also be cases where a weapon used in an attack, such as a knife, has a number of possible sources of DNA on it, e.g. where the knife contained the blood of more than one human victim or, in the case of a kitchen knife, contained both animal and human blood. In the latter case a DNA profile should only be produced from the human material.

17.7.3 Accidental introduction of errors into a sample

This type of error generally takes the form of contamination of a sample with extraneous DNA. This can take place at the crime scene, examples include:

(i) sneezing or even breathing in close proximity to an area from where a swab is being taken which can result in the deposit of extraneous DNA; or

(ii) where two individuals have shared the crime scene sample, e.g. cigarette, drinking glass.

For this reason scenes of crime officers (SOCOs) and other investigators are advised to wear protective clothing, including gloves, mask, and hood when collecting biological evidence from a crime scene.

Accidental contamination is, however, most likely to take place within the laboratory and it is for this reason that accredited laboratories operate strict protocols. A number of American cases have turned on defence arguments that the procedures employed by a laboratory were inadequate or incorrectly used (see *People* v. *Castro* (1989) 545 NYS 2d 985).

If laboratory contamination of DNA samples is a likely issue in a case, the practices and procedures of the laboratory should be scrutinised. While most laboratories in the UK carrying out DNA analysis will be United Kingdom Accreditation Service (UKAS) accredited and subject to strict quality assurance procedures, examples of good practice that should be in place include:

- appropriate air filtration systems to prevent airborne contamination;
- the use of different suites of rooms for reception, processing, and results generation of samples;
- storage of all protective clothing in one particular area (in order to prevent potential contamination being moved from one part of the laboratory to another);
- washing and rinsing of all glassware in distilled water;
- sterilisation of all solutions to break down extraneous DNA;
- sterilisation of all plastic disposables before use and use of disposables only once;
- wearing of gloves and protective clothing by technicians involved in handling containers or reagent;
- solutions stored at a temperature which shows degradation;
- recording of reagents with batch numbers and dates received;
- labelling of all reagents with reagent name, use-by date, or date made up;
- suitable storage conditions being maintained for all reagents.

17.7.4   Deliberate introduction of errors into a sample

Examples of this include the artificial introduction of DNA material into the crime scene before samples are collected from the scene by crime scene investigators (CSIs) (e.g. the 'planting' of evidence such as a cigarette end that has been smoked by a person other than the perpetrator of the crime). In such cases, it should be remembered that, as a matter of interpretation, a person's DNA recovered from an item at the scene (e.g. where the sample originated from a cigarette end or a glass) does not necessarily, without more, prove either presence at the scene or involvement in any crime committed there.

A second example is that of an individual involved in a mass screening exercise persuading another individual to give a sample on their behalf using falsified identity documents (as occurred in the case of Colin Pitchfork).

The integrity and chain of custody of a sample taken from an individual whilst in custody, however, should usually be ensured as these solutions are placed in tamper proof evidence bags and passed to the testing laboratory where the integrity of the seal will be checked as a matter of course. For further information see Wilson Wall (2002), pp. 23–36.

Once the SOCO has taken a sample at the scene of crime, the Police National Computer (PNC) Bureau will be informed. The PNC Bureau is the custodian of the PNC where *police* records are kept of convictions, car registrations, and offences.

The PNC Bureau creates a record for the offence and allocates an Arrest Summons number (AS) which is given to the SOCO.

The SOCO records the AS on the DNA sample form (DNA1) which is part of the FSS kit. The AS becomes the unique *police* reference number for that sample. The FSS kit contains many copies of the same bar code which is attached to the samples and the DNA1 form. The bar code becomes the unique 'database' reference number for the sample and the DNA profile. The PNC Bureau create and note a DNA Taken flag (DT) on the PNC.

The SOCO submits the FSS kit to the FSS or another approved forensic analytical service provider (e.g. LGC Ltd or Forensic Alliance).

17.8   CURRENT METHODS OF DNA ANALYSIS

As already mentioned the current method of DNA analysis used for both intelligence and evidential purposes is STR analysis.

The main steps in the technical process involve:

- dissolving the crime stain or other sample;
- separating, cleaning and measuring the quantity and quality of DNA;
- targeting the specific pieces of interest within the DNA molecule;
- producing multiple copies of these pieces;
- sorting the pieces according to size;
- measuring the size of the pieces.

STRs are the basis of the differences between different people's DNA and, as the name implies, consist of short lengths, or sequences, of DNA which are repeated end to end. Different people will have a different number of repeat units and hence will have different lengths of DNA.

The DNA profiling system that has been used to set up and maintain the NDNAD is Second Generation Multiplex (SGM). The SGM is based on six loci (regions) of the DNA molecule and the sex determining region. Where there is a match between the DNA profile of a suspect and that of a trace of material associated with an incident, it is standard practice to calculate the probability that an unknown person, unrelated to the suspect, would have the same DNA as the suspect. Match probabilities for unrelated individuals profiled by the SGM have typically been in the range of one in 10 million to one in 100 million. In 1999, a new profiling system, SGM Plus (Perkin-Elmer Corporation (1999), User's manual for the AmpF/SRT Plus™ PCR amplification kit, PE Applied Biosystems, USA) based on 10 loci and the sex determining region on different chromosomes was introduced. The match probabilities in such cases would be in the range of one in 10 billion to one in 100 trillion (a billion is one thousand million; a trillion is one million million). However, such high probabilities cannot be evaluated by statistical experiment, given the size of current databases. The policy of the FSS is to report a general figure of one in one billion for all 10 loci match cases.

For further information see Evett, Ian W., Lindsey A. Foreman, Graham Jackson and James A. Lambert 'DNA profiling: A discussion of issues relating to the reporting of very small match probabilities' [2000] Crim LR 341.

17.9 THE NDNAD

Once profiled the DT marker on the PNC is updated to a DNA profiled marker (DP). If the sample fails then the marker on the PNC is updated to a DNA failure marker (DF). The successful profile is downloaded onto the DNA database by the approved analytical service provider.

The NDNAD in the UK (the equivalent national DNA databank in the USA is known as CODIS (the Combined DNA Index System)) contains:

- the DNA profile (from the crime scene samples and subject samples);
- the sample identification number (bar code);
- the PNC reference number;
- the full name, sex, date of birth and ethnic appearance of the subject ('identifying information');
- details of the police officer, offence for which the sample was taken and police force details.

The FSS as custodian of the database, challenges the database with all profiles of samples submitted and reports any 'presumptive matches' to the analytical suppliers involved. 'Presumptive matches' will not be notified to the relevant police force. Suppliers of analytical services are required to recheck the results and confirm their validity to the FSS. The checking procedures designed by the FSS must be used for confirmation of matches. For suspect samples this involves independent re-analysis. For scene of crime samples it involves checking the allele designations.

Once confirmed, the FSS releases all details of matching profiles (including identifying information) to the relevant police force.

Each police force has a dedicated DNA unit which receives, records, monitors and researches hit/match notifications from the FSS before submission to police officers for action (the DNA unit within the Directorate of Identification at New Scotland Yard is the nominated unit in the Metropolitan Police Service).

Once notified of a hit, the relevant police force DNA unit notifies its police officers who may arrest the suspect and conduct an interview. It is important to remember that the hit information is only treated as an investigative tool, not an evidential tool.

Depending on the outcome of the 'hit':

(i) the suspect is released (e.g. because of insufficient evidence or they have been eliminated from the inquiry),
(ii) the suspect is charged without further samples being obtained (e.g. there may be other sufficient evidence), or
(iii) a further sample is taken and the suspect is released on bail, pending case work submission.

This latter sample is treated as an 'evidential sample' or 'case work sample'. The results of the evidential sample are used in any court proceedings.

17.10 STORAGE OF DNA SAMPLES AND DATA DERIVED FROM SAMPLES

The local police force is responsible for notifying its own DNA unit and the PNC Bureau of the court/disposal result. The PNC Bureau updates the PNC record by charging it to a DNA confirmed marker (DC) if there is a conviction. The PNC Bureau notifies the FSS who amend the DNA database. In the case of a conviction, once a DC marker is contained no further samples need to be taken from the convicted person, although as a matter of practice some police forces still do. Under PACE, s.64 (as amended by s.82 of the Criminal Justice and Police Act 2001) it is no longer necessary for a DNA sample or data derived from it to be destroyed if the suspect is acquitted of the original offence or is not prosecuted for it. For a discussion of issues in relation to the usage of DNA samples and derived data see *A-G's Ref (No 3 of 1999)* [2001] 2 AC 91 and *R(S)* v. *Chief Constable of South Yorkshire and another, R(Marper)* v. *Same* [2002] EWCA Civ 1275, [2003] 1 Cr App R 16.

17.11   PRESENTATION OF DNA EVIDENCE IN COURT

It is apparent that the public tend to have a perception that DNA evidence is infallible. This factor, coupled with the consideration that juries tend to give considerable weight to the testimony of expert witnesses generally, means that there is a real danger that the jury may undervalue all the other evidence in the case in favour of an assumption that the match between the crime scene profile and that of the accused is probative of guilt. For this reason, it is important that any expert opinion should be entirely confined to objective issues in relation to the DNA evidence.

The judgment of the Court of Appeal in the case of *R.* v. *Doheny and Adams* [1997] 1 Cr App R 369 gave the following guidance on the proper procedure for introducing DNA evidence in trials:

> The scientist should adduce the evidence of the DNA comparisons together with his calculations of the random occurrence ratio.
>
> Once the scientist has found a match between the suspect and the profile of samples taken from a crime scene, a calculation will be made to estimate the rarity of that profile, a random occurrence ratio. This ratio is calculated by using information stored in a database of other DNA work done in the laboratory. The result is a statement:
>
> > *'it is estimated that the frequency with which the DNA characteristics in the profile is likely to be found in the population at large is one in . . .'*
>
> Whenever such evidence was to be adduced, the Crown should serve upon the defence details of how the calculations were carried out, which are sufficient for the defence to scrutinise the basis of the calculations.
>
> The FSS [or other supplier] should make available to a defence expert, if requested, the databases upon which the calculations were based.
>
> The scientist should not be asked his opinion on the likelihood that it was the defendant who left the crime stain, nor when giving evidence, should he use terminology which may lead the jury to believe that he is expressing such an opinion.

Statisticians would prefer the statement 'in the relevant population (the population at large) there would be an estimated (number of) people with the DNA characteristics'.

17.12   THE 'PROSECUTOR'S FALLACY'

If a match has been found between an individual and a crime stain, two questions will generally arise from the finding of that match:

1.   What is the probability that the defendant's DNA profile matches the crime sample, given that the defendant is innocent?

2. What is the probability that the defendant is innocent given that the DNA profile matches the profile from the crime scene sample?

The first question relates to the evidence given by the expert witness and assumes innocence. The second question assumes that the DNA matches and it requires assessment of all the evidence (which is subjective) and it therefore lies within the domain of the jury as the finder of fact. The answers to the two questions can be radically different and an expert can only give an accurate assessment in relation to the first question. This is not an opinion but a statement of fact based upon the assumption that the analysis has been carried out properly and that the comparison database is reliable.

The 'prosecutor's fallacy' or the 'error of the transposed conditional' occurs when the answer to the first question is given as the answer to the second question. This is why the case of *R. v. Doheny and Adams* pointed out that experts should confine themselves to expressing their conclusions in terms of either a 'match probability' or a 'likelihood ratio' as referred to above.

Even if the expert has given his evidence in appropriate terms, there remains a risk that the jury may fall into the 'prosecutor's fallacy' themselves. While this may be cured by a specific direction to the jury in summing up that the data as presented should be interpreted only in the way that it has been presented by the expert, there is also a danger that the drawing of the jury's attention to this issue will lead them to do precisely the opposite.

See further David J. Balding and Peter Donnelly 'The Prosecutor's Fallacy and DNA Evidence' [1994] Crim LR 771; Ian W. Evett, Lindsey A. Foreman, Graham Jackson and James A. Lambert 'DNA Profiling: A discussion of issues relating to the reporting of very small match probabilities' [2000] Crim LR 341, and *R. v. Dallagher* [2002] EWCA Crim 1903; [2002] All ER (D) 383 (Jul) (where the Court of Appeal considered how a jury should properly be directed in relation to expert evidence pertaining to human identification).

17.13 INTERPRETATIVE ISSUES IN RELATION TO DNA EVIDENCE

As has already been mentioned, the fact that a DNA match has been found between a crime scene sample and an individual does not necessarily prove that the individual was present at the scene, let alone that the individual committed the alleged crime. However, certain factors will affect the strength of the evidence. These include:

- amount of DNA present;
- condition of the DNA;
- location where the DNA was found;
- type of body fluid/material (e.g. in an allegation of sexual assault where the individual had legitimate access to the area where the assault is alleged

to have taken place, a semen sample recovered from the clothing of the victim will be of greater evidential value than saliva recovered from a drinking vessel – in all major cases DNA will be regarded as secondary to what blood/fluid/tissue have been found);

- the nature of the database used as a comparator (e.g. in cases where an individual comes from an unusual minority ethnic group there is a concern that the match probability figure derived from a national database in a country with a heterogeneous population will not be truly representative, see *R. v. Musa-Gbengba* [1998] Crim LR 478).

17.14 DEFENCE CHALLENGES TO DNA EVIDENCE AND INSTRUCTING A DEFENCE EXPERT

Difficulties encountered by defence lawyers in relation to the ability to challenge DNA evidence were considered in a 1991 study by the Royal Commission on Criminal Justice. The difficulties were summarised as follows:

(i) lack of pre-trial notice of the existence of DNA evidence;

(ii) it may take a considerable time for the defence to locate a suitable expert – DNA profiling is highly specialised and there are relatively few experts outside the FSS who have experience in this field (since this study was conducted Forensic Alliance now have approximately 90 scientists engaged in DNA profiling, of these, about 30 report to court. LGC Ltd also have scientists reporting to court and Forensic Access have five). (Since the FSS adopted agency status in 1991 it has carried out DNA work for the defence in a number of cases. That the experience of the FSS is recognised as available to the defence is very important. However, where the FSS have carried out the DNA work for the prosecution, the defence may be reluctant to employ them);

(iii) work is delayed while the defence apply for legal aid prior authority to instruct an expert;

(iv) the number of experts is small and their workloads high; it may be several weeks before the defence expert is able to visit the prosecution laboratory to examine the results;

(v) there may be insufficient crime stain remaining for the defence expert to conduct an independent laboratory analysis.

However, the value of the defence forensic work is illustrated by the fact that, in the study 38 per cent of defence lawyers who obtained an independent analysis of the evidence stated that their conclusions differed from those of the prosecution's expert.

17.15 OTHER METHODS OF BIOLOGICAL CONTACT TRACE ANALYSIS

17.15.1 Presumptive tests

Prior to any analysis of human contact traces for purposes relating to human identification, a number of presumptive tests for blood and other biological material are commonly deployed at the crime scene. Generally, before steps are taken to collect what is thought to be dried blood, it first must be established that the stain is blood and that it is human blood. Presumptive testing for blood is usually carried out using either the Kastle-Meyer colour test or the luminol test. The species from which the blood originated is determined using a test known as the precipitin test (although this test will not be used at scenes). Additionally, the acid phosphatase colour test is used at crime scenes to locate seminal staining (this test is usually employed by a scientist as opposed to a SOCO).

17.15.2 Blood grouping

In 1901 research published by Karl Landsteiner confirmed that not all humans share the same blood group. The blood classification system known as the A-B-O system came out of this work. Since then, additional characteristics which further differentiate blood have been discovered, including the Rhesus (Rh) factor and MN blood grouping. Blood groupings can also be further distinguished by the identification of select antigens, enzymes, and proteins. In all, 100 different blood groups have been shown to be in existence. Furthermore, the antigens of the A-B-O system are not confined to red blood cells. Around 80 per cent of the population are 'secretors', which means that they have blood type antigens present in high concentrations in most body fluids (e.g. saliva, semen, vaginal secretions and gastric juices – in certain cases A-B-O typing has also been carried out on muscle, skin and solid tissue). The implications for criminal investigations are obvious. Whilst blood grouping was used as a basis for systems of personal identification for many years it is now viewed as somewhat otiose since the advent of DNA analysis. There are a number of reasons for this. First, the discriminatory power of blood grouping cannot, in practice, equal that of DNA analysis. If a crime scene sample and a suspect's blood group do not match, blood grouping can clearly eliminate that suspect. However, if there is a match, the converse is not true. The range of possibilities is relatively small so even unusual blood groups are well represented in the population. Secondly, most crime scene bloodstains are dry and the drying process will have destroyed some of the characteristic blood factors making even A-B-O testing difficult to carry out. Thirdly, whilst blood grouping as a preliminary screen has been used in mass screenings in the past, DNA technology has advanced and is so widely available that it is now both cheaper and quicker to carry out DNA profiling directly. The cost of manpower and equipment needed to obtain liquid blood from individuals in a mass screening exercise is also prohibitive when compared to that needed to obtain buccal swabs or plucked head hair for equivalent DNA testing.

17.15.3 Macroscopic and microscopic analysis of human hair

While macroscopic and microscopic forensic hair comparison provides good evidence, its evidential value cannot meet that of DNA analysis. While experts in the field recognise that this could mean that traditional methods of hair analysis will cease to be routinely practised, in the short to medium term it is thought that a gulf will remain between the potential of DNA analysis as a hair comparison method and the practical realisation of this potential. The reason for this is that only a small percentage of hairs encountered in case work will contain root material. Therefore any DNA testing that can be carried out on such hairs will have limited value in criminal cases. It has also been suggested that, in certain situations, DNA results may be integrated with the macroscopic and microscopic comparison result to provide a common statement of evidential value (see Barry D. Gaudette 'Evidential Value of Hair Examination' in James Robertson (1998) pp. 243–259).

Forensic scientist, Angela Gallop, points out that, in summary:

(i) microscopic examination of hair is a valuable screening tool; and
(ii) increasingly improved STR results are being achieved from hair shafts with no root material attached.

17.16 BLOODSTAIN AND BLOOD SPATTER PATTERN ANALYSIS (BPA)

Analysis of bloodstain and blood spatter patterns (BPA) is an area of forensic expertise in its own right and should only be undertaken by an expert with training and experience in making such determinations. It is important that those involved in crime scene investigation and in the criminal justice system are aware that the appearance of bloodstains and spatters may be of use for interpreting and reconstructing events that have occurred in order to produce the bleeding. The interpretation of bloodstain and blood spatter requires carefully controlled experiments utilising surface materials comparable to those found at the crime scene. In analysing bloodstain or spatter patterns, a number of issues should be considered, including:

1. *Surface texture.* In general the harder and less porous the surface, the less spatter results. Correlations between standards and unknowns are valid only if identical surfaces are used.

2. *Trajectory.* The direction and travel of blood striking an object can be discerned by the stain's shape. The pointed end of the bloodstain faces its direction of travel.

3. *Impact angle.* The impact angle on a flat surface can be determined by measuring the degree of circular distortion of the stain.

4. *Origin.* The origin of blood spatter in a two-dimensional configuration can be established by drawing two straight lines through the long axis of several individual bloodstains. The intersection or point of convergence of the lines represents the point from which the blood emanated.

For further information see Herbert L. MacDonnell (1993), and Richard Saferstein (1998) pp. 379–385.

Critically, blood stain analysis is central in indicating to the scientist which particular samples to send for DNA profiling. DNA profiling is a very expensive process (currently between £400–£500 in major crime cases) so it is important that scientists be as selective as possible. For example, looking for 'foreign' blood from the perpetrator of a repeated assault where the vast majority of the blood will inevitably be from the victim.

Angela Gallop considers that BPA is definitely undervalued and concludes that DNA will tell you from whom the blood is likely to have come, whereas BPA will tell you how it most probably got there. She also notes that, in reality, scientists employ BPA and DNA analysis in every case involving bloodstains, no matter how trivial.

17.17 QUALIFICATIONS OF EXPERT REPORTING ON CASES INVOLVING HUMAN BIOLOGICAL CONTACT TRACE EVIDENCE

Experts reporting on human trace evidence will generally have at least a graduate level background in an area such as biological science. Before reporting they should have received extensive in-house training and should be able to demonstrate their experience by reference to casework undertaken. In all accredited UK laboratories (currently FSS, Forensic Alliance and LGC Ltd), expert opinion will be subject to stringent peer review. The Council for the Registration of Forensic Practitioners (CRFP) has opened up a register for experts reporting on biological contact trace evidence.

REFERENCES

ACPO Crime Committee (2000) *The Manual of Standard Operational Procedures for Scientific Support Personnel at Major Incident Scenes*, 1st edn.

Balding, D. & Donnelly, P. 'The Prosecutor's Fallacy and DNA Evidence' [1994] Crim LR 711.

Evett, I., Foreman, L., Jackson, G. & Lambert, J. 'DNA profiling; A discussion of issues relating to the reporting of very small match probabilities' [2000] Crim LR 341.

Forensic Science Service, *The Lawyers' Guide to DNA* (version 1).

Foster, C. 'Plunge in the deep end of the gene pool', *The Times*, 19 November 2002.

Gaudette, Barry D. 'Evidential Value of Hair Examination' in Robertson, J. (ed.) (1998) *Forensic Examination of Hair*, Taylor and Francis, pp. 243–59.

Gaule, M. (2002) *The Basic Guide To Forensic Awareness*, New Police Bookshop.

MacDonnell, H. (1993) *Bloodstain Patterns*, Laboratory of Forensic Science.

Mahendra, B. (2002) 'The Lawyer's Guide to DNA evidence in criminal cases', 152:7041 *NLJ* 1110 (19 July).

Robertson, J. (ed.) (1998) *Forensic Examination of Hair*, Taylor and Francis, pp. 243–59.

Saferstein, R. (1998) *Criminalistics: An Introduction to Forensic Science* (6th edn), Prentice Hall, pp. 379–85.

Stevenson, B. (1992) *The Ability to Challenge DNA Evidence, RCCJ Research Study No 9*, London, HMSO.

Wall, W. (2002) *Genetics and DNA Technology: Legal Aspects,* Cavendish Publishing, p. 53.

Western Australia Legislative Council (1999) *Report of the Legislative Committee In Relation To Forensic Procedures and DNA Profiling: The Committee's Investigations in Western Australia, Victoria, South Australia, The United Kingdom, Germany and The United States of America* (Report 48).

CHAPTER 18

Firearms

18.1 PROCEDURES AT THE SCENE INVOLVING FIREARMS

The initial overriding concern is to save life and to facilitate the attendance of medical aid for any wounded.

The immediate area of the scene should be cordoned off (possibly by firearms officers). Scientific support personnel and a firearms/ballistics expert may also attend the scene.

An initial examination under controlled conditions will usually by made by a firearms expert to ensure the safety of other officers and investigative personnel attending.

The scene should be photographed and videoed to include the position of any spent ammunition or fired components of ammunition (e.g. cartridges, shotgun cartridges/wads) and the state of any weapons (e.g. whether loaded/unloaded, safety catch applied, etc.).

If an offender has been shot at the scene, any weapon that the offender was carrying should be examined by a suitably qualified officer, who will record, for evidential purposes, the positions of safety catches, hammers, rounds, etc. before making the weapon safe. No unqualified person should interfere with the offender's weapon as it may be in a dangerous state.

A plan should be drawn of the scene, including the positioning of cartridges, wads, bullet marks, etc.

Once made safe, weapons should be handed to a Scenes of Crime Officer (SOCO) and packaged in an appropriate manner (see below). In certain circumstances (for instance, where it is uncertain which particular weapon was fired) the inside of spent cartridges should be swabbed in order to match propellants to a particular weapon.

Fingerprints, and in certain cases DNA, may be obtained from spent cartridges. All packaging must be protected in order to prevent contamination of this evidence.

See Association of Chief Police Officers (ACPO) (Crime Committee) *Manual of Standard Operating Procedures for Scientific Support Personnel at Major Incident Scenes* (1st edn, 2000).

18.2 PARTICULAR SEARCHING CONSIDERATIONS

Personnel involved in searching a scene where a firearm has been discharged should ascertain whether there has been any bullet or ricochet damage to buildings, furniture or other items. Damaged items should be removed for laboratory analysis if possible. Other damage should be photographed (with a scale) and carefully documented.

18.3 THE ROLE OF THE EXPERT AT THE SCENE

An expert may assist in assessing certain aspects of the scene that may not be immediately apparent to a SOCO, e.g. the presence of ricochet marks or locating firearms paraphernalia (e.g. damaged bullets can resemble pieces of scrap metal which may not be apparent to non-experts).

18.4 THE ATTENDANCE OF THE EXPERT AT A POST MORTEM EXAMINATION

A firearms expert will attend if requested to do so, otherwise the expert will work with reference to photographs (which should be scaled and sequential in cases involving firearms injuries) of the deceased's body and the patho-logist's report. An expert will consider the external injuries (although in some cases the expert may be able to offer an interpretation of internal injuries, e.g. in relation to the direction or course taken by a bullet).

In certain cases it may be desirable for the expert to examine bodily wounds *in situ*, e.g. in order to aid an estimation in relation to firing distance. In other cases the expert will carry out an examination of wounds that have been excised from the body.

The expert will also examine any clothing worn by a victim which may contain bullet or shotgun pellet holes.

For further information on forensic examination of gunshot wounds see Vincent A.J. Di Maio (1999) *Gunshot Wounds: Practical Aspects of Firearms, Ballistics and Forensic Techniques* (2nd edn).

See further **Chapter 24**.

18.5 PACKAGING AND HANDLING OF FIREARMS AND AMMUNITION

The most important consideration when handling a firearm is safety. Precautions should be taken in order to prevent the accidental discharge of the weapon while in transit. If the weapon is loaded, it is necessary to unload the weapon prior to transit. A record should be made of the weapon's hammer and safety position and whether or not it was loaded when discovered.

Caution should be used when removing any bullets lodged in surfaces or objects in order to avoid compromising any striation marks present. Care must also be taken when handling bullets in order to preserve any contact trace materials (CTM), such as fibres and paint that may be adhering to any particular bullet.

Firearms should be packaged in sealed tamper-proof packages and appropriately labelled before submission for laboratory testing. Bullets, cartridges, or shotgun wads should be packaged separately. Further specialised packaging and safety considerations will apply depending on the exact nature of the weapon.

If the weapon is rusted, jammed, corroded or in a condition that it cannot be rendered in a safe condition, it can be transported in a specially constructed container. For further information on packaging firearms see Mike Byrd 'Packaging Firearms' online via **www.crime-scene-investigator.net/ packagingfirearms.html**

18.6 LABORATORY EXAMINATIONS

If the firearm, victim's clothing, ammunition, or other items are to be submitted for testing for firearms discharge residues (FDRs), DNA, or fingerprints, these tests should be carried out by different scientists in a separate area of the laboratory *before* any firearm is fully examined by a firearms expert (note that the expert will probably have conducted an initial examination of the weapon at the scene for safety purposes). This is to avoid any suggestion of contamination.

18.7 CLASSIFICATION OF FIREARMS AND AMMUNITION

An expert will identify whether a particular weapon or ammunition is prohibited under the legislation controlling the use and possession of firearms. They will also have expertise in the identification of imitation firearms and weapons. Air guns present problems in relation to their classification. Currently low-powered air guns (with a muzzle energy of six ft/lbs, or less for pistols, and 12 ft/lbs or less for guns) are not subject to licensing under the Firearms Act 1968 and do not require a firearms certificate. Therefore air guns will require test firing in order to measure the velocity of the pellets and calculate their energies.

For further information on the difficulties presented by air guns see (2003) *Police Review* (vol 111, no. 5710, 7 February).

18.8 IDENTIFICATION OF FIREARM FROM AMMUNITION RECOVERED AT CRIME SCENE

The act of firing a weapon and the passage of the bullet through the barrel simultaneously pushes back the cartridge case and impresses various marks on the surface of the ammunition which can be reproduced in test-fired ammunition to provide distinctive points of comparison for individualising spent ammunition to a particular weapon. Spent bullets, cartridges, pellets (from air guns) and some wads (from shotguns) will all have striation markings which can all be successfully compared in this manner.

The fact that the ammunition has been damaged does not necessarily preclude a comparison being made. When making comparisons of striation marks on bullets and cartridges in order to show, e.g. that the bullets were fired from a particular weapon, the expert will rely upon:

(i) visual observations and experience;
(ii) automated firearm search systems (a computerised imaging system which stores bullet and cartridge surface characteristics).

18.9 ESTIMATION OF DISTANCE OF FIRING

The accuracy with which an estimation of firing distance can be made during test firing is dependent on the use of the same type of ammunition as that used in the offence, and the quality of the ammunition. If ammunition is old or of poor quality, firing distances may be more difficult to predict.

18.10 DATING – LAST TIME GUN FIRED

It is generally not possible to state when a particular gun was last fired.

18.11 ACCIDENTAL DISCHARGE OF FIREARM

Tests will be carried out in order to ascertain whether the weapon could have been discharged without the trigger having been pulled, e.g. by carrying out drop tests.

The internal safety mechanisms of the weapon will be tested.

The number of shots and their locations may be indicative of whether the discharge was accidental, whether there has been a suicide, or whether a third party was involved. However, it is possible for a gun to discharge accidentally more than once, e.g. if a particular defect in a self-loading pistol has caused the gun to fire once, it may cause it to fire a number of times.

The characteristics of the weapon, including the length of the barrel and the positioning of the trigger may be indicative of whether or not it was possible for the deceased to manually pull the trigger in order to commit suicide. Other factors that can be taken into account when assessing if gunshot wounds were self-inflicted include the presence and location of any FDRs on the body and hands and the presence of the DNA or fingerprints of the deceased on the weapon (see e.g. *R.* v. *Bamber* [2002] EWCA Crim 2912; [2002] All ER (D) 165 (Dec)).

18.12   FDRs

FDRs should be searched for, processed, and examined by different personnel in a different part of the laboratory from the firearm in order to avoid any suggestion of contamination. Testing of firearms or other items for residue should be completed before the firearm (and other relevant items) are examined by the firearms expert. Firearms residue is collected by swabbing.

For further information on FDRs see A.J. Schoweble and David L. Exline (2000).

18.13   THE ROLE OF THE DEFENCE EXPERT

An expert should be instructed for the defence if:

- no expert opinion has been sought by the prosecution;
- if the prosecution expert's statement is unclear or does not address certain issues that may be relevant to the defence case;
- if there are any discrepancies between the labelling of exhibits referred to in the statement and the labelling of the actual exhibits.

At present, experts instructed for the defence may use the FSS facilities for testing firearms (the FSS will also carry out work on behalf of the defence).

18.14   THE EXPERT'S REPORT

In reaching an opinion, the expert will consider any available scene notes and photographs, report of the pathologist (if applicable), eye witness statements, and the results of any scientific tests.

The statement and disclosure schedule will detail the type of scientific tests carried out by the expert and details of the results obtained. These will be made available and can be checked by a defence expert if necessary.

18.15 QUALITY ASSURANCE PROCEDURES

All laboratory procedures will be fully documented and peer reviewed in order to accord with NAMAS (National Accreditation of Measurement and Sampling) standards.

18.16 QUALIFICATIONS OF THE EXPERT

Experts may have a background in the military or in the firearms trade. Most experts, however, will have a graduate education in an analytical science and have received in-house training in a firearms laboratory. For example, the FSS provides in-house training for graduate entrants in all aspects of firearms investigation, including the relevant statutory framework and the identification of ammunition and cartridges.

REFERENCES

Association of Chief Police Officers (Crime Committee) (2000) *Manual of Standard Operating Procedures for Scientific Support Personnel at Major Incident Scenes* (1st edn).

Beavis, V. & Wallace, J. 'Firearms' in White, P. (ed.) (1998) *Crime Scene to Court*, The Royal Society of Chemistry.

Byrd, M. 'Packaging Firearms' online via **www.crime-scene-investigator.net/ packagingfirearms.html**.

Di Maio, V.A.J. (1999) *Gunshot Wounds: Practical Aspects of Firearms, Ballistics and Forensic Techniques* (2nd edn).

Heard, B. (1996) *Handbook of Firearms and Ballistics*, Chancery Wiley Law Publishers.

Schoweble, A.J. & Exline, D.L. (2000) *Current Methods in Forensic Gunshot Residue Analysis*, CRC Press.

Warlow, T. (1996) *Firearms, The Law and Forensic Ballistics*, Taylor and Francis.

CHAPTER 19

Traffic accident investigators

19.1 ROAD ACCIDENT STATISTICS

The motor car is over a century old and in that time it has changed the world, the way we live, where we live, and transformed the face of our towns and countryside. It has been a wonderful liberating invention but has also brought untold grief. Since 13 February 1898, when the first fatal road collision involving a motor car occurred, 25 million people worldwide have died and the number is rising.

Yearly, 3,500 people are killed on the roads in the UK with a further 320,000 injured, of which 38,000 are serious. The economic costs to the community are in excess of £12 billion per year; however, the human and emotional costs can not be quantified.

19.2 DUTY TO INVESTIGATE ROAD ACCIDENTS

In most dictionaries 'accident' is defined as 'an event happening by chance'. It is estimated that 95 per cent of traffic accidents are due to driver error therefore the term 'accident' may be a misnomer. Police forces are now using the term 'crash or collision' which is probably a more accurate description. There is a large school of thought that society treats traffic accidents lightly because of the name we give them. The title suggests no blame or 'are they just one of those things?'.

Article 13 of the European Convention on Human Rights (ECHR) suggests that 'when an individual dies in suspicious circumstances' there is a requirement that a 'thorough and effective investigation capable of leading to the identification and punishment of those responsible and including effective access for the relatives to the investigatory procedure' (see *Kurt* v. *Turkey* (*Application 24276/94*) (1998) 27 EHRR 373).

19.3   INVESTIGATORY METHODS

Thorough investigations of fatal and serious injury traffic collisions now take place but until 1974 the only method of assessing a vehicle's speed was by measuring the length of skid marks it left which was referenced against the *Highway Code* braking distances, e.g. if a car travelling at 30 mph needs 14 metres (45 feet) to brake and the car in the 'accident' has left 55 metres (180 feet) of skid marks, then it must follow that the 'accident' car must have been going *very* fast!

This, not very scientific, method of speed assessment was used for many years in this country, until 12 November 1974, when a case before Liverpool Crown Court changed the course of events.

In this particular case, *R.* v. *Chadwick* [1975] Crim LR 105, the accused was being tried on a charge of causing death by dangerous driving. His vehicle had left skid marks of 67.9 metres (223 feet), which according to the *Highway Code* was equivalent to a speed of about 68 mph. However, it was held that while the 'typical stopping distances' diagram accompanying rule 105 of *The Highway Code* may be used in cross-examination to prove a breach of the code, it is otherwise inadmissible by itself to prove speed as it is hearsay.

As a result of this ruling, the only way that a vehicle's speed can now be admitted in evidence in this country is by proving it mathematically by using Newton's *Laws of Motion*. Following this case procedures were put in place to train traffic police officers the skills required to calculate vehicle speeds from skid marks.

So, perhaps accident investigation, can best be described as a science of dynamics based on Newton's three *Laws of Motion* together with the laws of friction and reliant on evidence left at the scene of the accident and witnesses accounts. Much of this investigation is dependent upon the amount and quality of the information that can be gathered from the scene itself.

By far the most common example is when a vehicle leaves skid marks at the scene. From these marks it is a relatively simple matter to determine, very accurately, the minimum speed for the vehicle immediately prior to the wheels locking.

Similarly, speeds can be calculated for a motor cycle that falls onto its side and leaves scrape marks as it slides along the road surface. The same applies to a car that overturns and slides along on its roof.

Certain objects that are thrown or 'launched' from a vehicle on impact may also assist in calculating a speed of launch and therefore the speed of the vehicle.

In a similar manner, if the point of impact and the distance that a pedestrian is thrown are known, then the likely impact speed of the vehicle can be determined.

19.4 TRAINING AND EXPERIENCE OF TRAFFIC ACCIDENT INVESTIGATORS

Currently within the UK there are only two training courses that have been designed especially for the 'accident' investigator, the City & Guilds Police Forensic Collision Investigation and Edexcel BTEC Forensic Accident Investigation.

The City & Guilds course is a copyright of ACPO (Association of Chief Police Officers) and is held at their nominated training centres thereby limiting the course only to 'police personnel'.

The Edexcel BTEC course is a distance learning programme run via De Montfort University (Leicester) by AiTS Training Ltd. It attracts students from all parts of the UK as well as overseas.

Both courses are of equal standard and ACPO approved, and provide the basic academic knowledge requirement for the investigator. The more conscientious investigator would treat these qualifications as being the first steps to becoming more competent within the field of accident investigation. They should then further their expertise and knowledge and obtain training in ancillary topics, e.g. tachograph analysis, vehicle dynamics, vehicle examination, electronic surveying, damage analysis, etc. This would then enable them to combine these additional qualifications and apply for City & Guilds Licentiateships in 'Traffic Accident Investigation' and 'Motor Vehicle Inspection'. From the 1 October 2003, the CRFP register is open to road transport investigators, in the two sub-specialities of collision investigation and vehicle examination.

19.5 POLICE TRAFFIC ACCIDENT INVESTIGATORS

ACPO has recognised that a thorough investigation of the circumstances surrounding death and serious injury on the roads is one of the most important activities within the field of traffic policing. They also appreciate that in order to achieve this the role of the accident investigator is crucial to this process.

Every police force within England, Wales and Scotland has accident investigators trained to various levels. All English and Welsh police forces have signed up to ACPO (Road Policing) Collision Investigation Protocol 2002. Its purpose is to safeguard expertise and credibility by providing a common standard for the conduct of the accident investigator within the police service. It states that all investigators should receive adequate training, be provided with sufficient equipment, and have the opportunity to practise their skills. Importantly, it also states that effective procedures should exist for the validation of their evidence.

19.6 THE PROTOCOL FOR COLLISION INVESTIGATION

The Protocol advises that the investigators should seek to become members of a suitable institute that covers their area of expertise. The only such institute currently in existence within the UK is the Institute of Traffic Accident Investigators (ITAI) who have two levels of membership, affiliate and full member.

19.7 THE ROLE OF THE ITAI AND INSTRUCTING A TRAFFIC ACCIDENT INVESTIGATOR

Affiliate membership of ITAI cannot be used as a qualification as its purpose is to welcome members who have an interest in the subject but may not have the expertise to obtain full membership. Those who want to achieve full membership can use their affiliate period to gain experience and commence their continued development portfolios.

Both ACPO and ITAI insist that accident investigators must keep up to date with current developments and further expand their knowledge. They acknowledge that learning is a lifetime experience and a record should be kept of their achievements in a continuing professional development (CPD) portfolio.

As a requisite to full membership, members of ITAI must keep up to date with developments and be able to provide evidence by means of their CPD portfolios. ITAI keeps a yearly updated record of those members who submit their CPD portfolios for assessment. This can be found on the ITAI web page. It is advisable to consult this website when seeking a suitable investigator (see **www.itai.org**).

ITAI is currently considering the introduction of the Fellow grade of member which will be based on the competency framework used by the Council for the Registration of Forensic Practitioners (CRFP).

19.8 PROTOCOL FOR THE INVESTIGATION OF ROAD DEATH

In 2001 the National Operations Faculty of ACPO produced the *Road Death Investigation Manual* which recognises that the investigation of a road death is equivalent in complexity to that of a homicide. The manual was written to complement the already existing ACPO *Murder Investigation Manual* and its intention was that it should form a suite with it.

The *Road Death Manual* states that the aims of all investigations are to:

- investigate fatal and serious collisions to the highest possible standards;
- ensure that families of victims are provided with the highest level of

support from trained officers dedicated towards the provision of family liaison;

- provide a documented investigation plan during every incident, ensuring each investigation is:

  - managed effectively by trained officers;
  - adequately resourced;
  - thoroughly and impartially investigated;
  - monitored to ensure effectivenes;

- provide the necessary support to all personnel involved in an investigation.

The manual provides a definitive document to all involved in the investigation and is amended as and when necessary. The manual is available as a download from **www.acpo.police.uk/policies/ba_road_death_manual.pdf**.

19.9   THE ROLE OF THE TRAFFIC ACCIDENT INVESTIGATOR AT THE SCENE

In general there are two classes of accident investigator, those who attend the scene immediately after the collision (primarily police officers) and those who receive instruction (private consultants)

As per the *Road Death Manual*, police officers should attend the scene of all fatal collisions and collisions where the injuries are known to be life threatening. There may be other circumstances in which a police force would want their investigators to investigate a collision, such as police vehicle collisions or instances that may attract a large amount of media attention.

The police investigators, on their attendance, should identify the full extent of the scene and ensure it is secured to prevent the loss of evidence. An audit trail should be commenced with evaluation of the available evidence ensuring that the scene is adequately recorded by plans, photographic and/or video means.

Throughout the enquiry the investigators should recognise the limits of their own expertise and of the equipment available to perform the necessary tests and should be prepared to call on specialist help before they get out of their depth.

19.10   TESTING AND EXAMINATION OF CRASH VEHICLES

Investigators will conduct or arrange for a thorough examination of the vehicle(s) involved in order to establish roadworthiness. This examination will also be used to confirm if any defects were contributory to the collision or not. To avoid any complications as found in the case *R. v. Beckford* [1995] RTR 253 (driving offence; destruction of vehicle before charge), consideration should be made regarding the retention of the vehicles.

Items seized for further examination such as light bulbs, tyres, airbags, tachograph charts, etc. that may be outside the investigator's area of expertise should be packaged and sent for laboratory examination. Places that such items would be sent would include Forensic Science Services (FSS), Transport Research Laboratory (TRL) and Motor Industries Research Agency (MIRA).

The investigator should be competent in considering the whole environment surrounding the collision scene and be able to identify marks, debris and damage to vehicles, property, pedestrians or vehicle occupants.

They should accurately gather details of the circumstances of an incident from the available sources and record them using all available means such as scale plans and photographs.

19.11   FINDINGS OF THE TRAFFIC ACCIDENT INVESTIGATOR

Once the evidence has been gathered they should be able to form opinions, based on established criteria, which are balanced and realistic in the context of the investigation. At an early stage they, wherever appropriate, should discuss the interpretation of the results and their meaning with others involved in the investigation. Should additional evidence or witness statements become available they must be ready to review their findings.

When preparing a file or report the investigator should document their findings and interpretation concisely and clearly. Any conclusions and opinions they express must be within their area of expertise and soundly based on the available evidence.

No matter how knowledgeable the investigator is they must be able to present their findings and results orally and in writing, clearly and accurately to others in the investigation and, where necessary, the court. In order to do so they should have an adequate knowledge and understanding of court procedures and the rules of evidence.

REFERENCES

Association of Chief Police Officers *Murder Investigation Manual*.

Association of Chief Police Officers (National Operations Faculty) (2001) *Road Death Investigation Manual* online via **www.acpo.police.uk/ policies/ba_road_death_manual.pdf**.

Association of Chief Police Officers (Road Policing) (2002) *Collision Investigation Protocol*.

CHAPTER 20

Questioned document examiners

20.1 SCENE EXAMINATION

20.1.1 When should a questioned document examiner visit the crime scene?

In certain circumstances (e.g. where graffiti is present) it is preferable for an examiner to visit the crime scene. Materials at the scene that have been found to contain written messages include boards, walls, and bodies. Live viewing of such writings provides optimal examination conditions.

Examiners should also visit the scene to examine any office equipment which is suspected of having been used in the production of any document, e.g. printed, photocopied or typewritten documents (while it is usually preferable to take equipment to a laboratory for examination, note that switching off of some equipment may cause loss of memory). A visual examination of this equipment may also reveal any physical properties that may have been transposed onto documents (e.g. 'trashmarks ' caused by faults in a printer or photocopier mechanism).

Any paper or electronically stored documents should be removed from the scene for laboratory examination.

20.1.2 Items removed from the scene

If paper, ink identification, or a particular kind of writing instrument is an issue, any material of that kind should be removed from the scene as it may assist with the examination, e.g. by providing evidence of frequent use of certain types of materials or placing questioned material within a particular timeframe.

Other materials upon which no writing is apparently visible should also be removed for testing purposes (e.g. notebooks, chequebooks, blotters, carbon paper from typewriters). Apparently 'blank' material may contain indented impressions from writing on other documents or latent writing which is only visible under certain light sources.

Other than when an at-the-scene examination is required, documents should ideally be examined in laboratory conditions with appropriate lighting. For this reason, a request should always be made for the original documents to be released to the custody of the examiner. Examinations of documents in designated locations, e.g. in police stations, provide less than ideal conditions.

20.2 GENERAL AND SPECIALISED AREAS OF QUESTIONED DOCUMENT EXAMINATION

A forensic scientist who specialises in questioned document examination will have knowledge of all or a variety of the following:

- examination of handwriting and printed documents (including strict comparisons of questioned handwriting with a handwriting sample; comparisons of typewriting/output from modern office equipment (including printers, faxes and photocopiers); ascertaining whether or not physical alterations have been made; study of indented impressions (including knowledge of imaging techniques, such as electrostatic detection of impressions and infrared imaging);
- comparison of signatures;
- ink comparisons;
- pulp and paper examination (including mechanical fits and document reconstruction from torn or shredded material);
- determination of whether envelopes have been opened/resealed;
- historic office printing processes (e.g. typewriters) and commercial printing processes (these areas require specialist knowledge).

Forensic documents examiners should not be referred to as 'handwriting experts' because their expertise is not confined to the examination of handwriting. Some forensic practitioners will specialise in handwriting analysis and the CRFP has included this as a sub-speciality in its register.

A distinction should also be made between questioned document examiners and graphologists. Graphology is a pseudo-science which purports to determine personality from handwriting and it has no role in handwriting comparison.

20.3 IDENTIFICATION OF INDIVIDUALS FROM HANDWRITING

Two initial issues should be considered:

- whether there is an innocent explanation for apparent differences/similarities in the writing;
- the nature and extent of the material with which the questioned writing is to be compared.

20.3.1 Accidental variation in handwriting

The possibility of accidental variation has to be considered in all cases of questioned writing. While every individual's writing will be subject to constant natural variation, certain conditions can lead to alteration of writing above and beyond that which can readily be discounted as natural variation from the usual writing range.

The following conditions have been found to so alter an individual's handwriting:

1. Age: the style of an individual's writing varies throughout their lifetime. Childhood and adolescent writing will be very different from the writing style adopted by an adult. The style of writing will also vary as the writer ages or becomes infirm.
2. Health: mental/physical illness, local injury, and visual impairment can significantly alter an individual's style of writing.
3. Drugs/alcohol: the influence of these substances can temporarily or permanently (depending on the type of usage) alter writing style.
4. Writing instrument/surface/writing at speed/jolting of pen/control difficulties at extremities of a page: can cause significant alterations to the writer's normal range of style.
5. Stress: has been found to cause alterations to writing style

20.3.2 Constant natural variation to writing style

Writing is subject to constant natural variation. Examples of this variation include:

1. Certain writing styles have been found to contain significant variations in single letters; short frequency words such as 'of' or 'to' being written in a way which is different to their component letters found elsewhere in the text.
2. Use of more than one separate form of letter (e.g. use of both capital and cursive forms within words).

Examiners can generally account for such variations because they tend to occur within a definable range from which the writer can otherwise be identified.

20.3.3 Can deliberate modification/disguising of writing be detected?

ANY INNOCENT EXPLANATION HAS FIRST TO BE DISCOUNTED

The writing of two different individuals can naturally share a common overall appearance. When two writings are somewhat similar, they can be mistakenly believed to have been written by the same person. Scientific examination can generally ascertain that the writings have two different authors as the likelihood that the writings of two people will be identical in every way is negligible.

In deciding whether writings have been written by the same person, an examiner will access not only overall form, construction, and proportion but also frequent spelling mistakes and text analysis (which can also permit the comparison of handwriting with typewriting; this technique is specialised and controversial and the amount of writing required for such an analysis will be greater than in other situations).

DELIBERATE DISGUISE OR SIMULATION OF WRITING

Handwriting that has been deliberately varied (unnatural writing) falls into two categories:

(i) writing that has be disguised to make it appear that it was not written by the person who wrote it; and

(ii) the simulation of the writing of another person.

DISGUISED WRITING

It is difficult to disguise writing because the natural writing style which is ingrained in the subconscious has to be suppressed. For this reason aspects of the writing style of the writer may appear in the disguised writing. Before a finding is made that the writing is disguised all other possible explanations for any variants in the writing (e.g. accidental variations above) have to be considered and discounted.

SIMULATED WRITING

Classic indications of simulated writing include difficulty in construction, lack of fluency, poor line quality, indentations, remains of pencil or carbon lines which have been traced onto the paper. As with disguised writing, a finding that writing has been simulated should not be made until all other explanations for the variants (e.g. accidental variations and, in particular, old age, ill health or impaired vision of writer) have been considered and discounted.

20.4 COMPARISON MATERIAL/KNOWN WRITINGS

The nature and extent of the comparison (or known) material is of extreme importance and care should be taken to ascertain the nature of any comparison material that has been made available to the examiner.

One examiner, Dr Audrey Giles, has commented that 'the choice of comparison handwritings may well determine the scope of the final analysis'. The comparison material should therefore be as representative as possible of the writer's natural handwriting.

When considering the adequacy of the comparison material, the following questions should be considered.

20.4.1 How has the comparison material/known sample been obtained?

Verified 'course of business' or day-to-day writing is considered to be preferable to writing that has been produced specifically for comparison purposes (because the latter may be 'unnatural' as a result of the stress on the writer and the unfavourable conditions).

If, in the event, no course of business writing is available and a sample of an individual's writing has to be requested, it has been suggested that the following steps be taken to minimise any conscious writing effort:

1. The writer should be sitting comfortably at a desk without any distractions.
2. The writer should not be shown the questioned document or be provided with any instructions in relation to the construction of the document, including punctuation and spelling.
3. The writer should be supplied with a pen and paper similar to those used in the questioned document (it is the practice of some police forces to provide a document which resembles the questioned document, e.g. a cheque).
4. The text should be dictated to the writer. It should either be the same as the contents of the questioned document or should contain some of the same words, phrases, and letter combinations found in the document. Depending on the nature of the writing in the questioned document, the writer should be instructed to use either upper case or lower case lettering as appropriate (if the questioned document contains figures, then numeric samples should also be obtained). The sample obtained should be at least one A4 page in length.
5. Dictation of the text should take place at least three times. If the writer is making a deliberate effort to disguise the writing, noticeable variations should appear among the repetitions. If this is discovered, a continued repetitive dictation of the text must be insisted upon. If it is possible to leave a time gap between the different sittings this is preferable.
6. It has been found that signature exemplars can best be obtained when other writings are combined with the signature (e.g. instead of being asked to compile a set of signatures alone, the writer may be asked to fill out completely 20 or 30 separate cheques or receipts, each of which includes a signature).

7. Before requested exemplars are taken from a writer, it is a good idea to consult a document examiner for advice in relation to the kind of samples which are required in order to best resemble the writing in the questioned document.

20.4.2 Has like been compared with like?

Block capitals cannot be compared with cursive writing and vice versa. Figures should not be compared with alphabetical letters.

Writings have also been found to vary depending on the layout and in relation to certain guiding marks which may appear on the page (e.g. cheques, bank forms). In cases involving cheques or other financial pro forma documents it is desirable to obtain samples of handwriting on special forms which simulate the layout of the questioned financial document. This is in order to show other components in addition to the writing itself, e.g. a practice of writing well above or partly below a line on a cheque, etc. This practice is adopted by many police forces.

20.4.3 Has adequate comparison material been obtained?

It is essential to obtain as many samples of a person's writing as possible in order to ascertain the full range of the style of writing and to enable certain extrinsic factors to be discounted, e.g. natural variations which may appear at first to be significant.

If insufficient handwritings are available, no firm conclusion should be drawn as to authorship.

20.4.4 Is the comparison material/known writing contemporary with the writing in the questioned document?

Given that writing and signatures will vary with age and can vary as a result of medical conditions, use of drugs, etc. a writing sample as contemporary to the writing in the questioned document as possible should be obtained.

The writings of a person as a child should not be compared with that person's adult writings. Similar considerations apply if the person has aged or had a significant change of health since the time that the questioned document was written.

EXAMINATION OF COPIES OF DOCUMENTS WHEN ORIGINAL DOCUMENT NOT AVAILABLE

Certain fine details of handwriting and signatures are lost during the copying process.

Any conclusions that are drawn from the examination of copies should be restricted, e.g. only a qualified conclusion as to authorship can usually be drawn from the examination of handwriting images transmitted by fax.

An examiner should always be provided with original documents if they are available. Avoid the use of carbon copies, photocopies or faxed documents.

20.5 SIGNATURES

While the basis of signature identification is similar to that of handwriting, certain special considerations apply to the identification of signatures because of:

(i)   the small amount of comparable material;
(ii) the natural variation that occurs in all signatures; and
(iii) the stylisation of the writing in signatures.

It is therefore imperative that original signatures (as opposed to photocopies) are available for examination because photocopies compromise a number of features essential for detection purposes, e.g. pen lifts, striations, determination of pen movement.

The following possibilities will be considered in relation to signatures that at first appear to be similar:

(i)   pure chance;
(ii) tracing involved;
(iii) copying involved; or
(iv) written by the same person.

20.5.1 Special considerations

A signature is usually the most common piece of writing performed by an individual. It will therefore have a higher degree of fluency than other writings.

Like other writings, a signature is susceptible to constant natural variation – no person will ever reproduce the exact same signature. Signatures should only be compared with signatures written in the same name; however, some stylised signatures may be ascribed to more than one name but could still be compared.

Consideration should be given to the fact that signatures are made in a variety of different places often under conditions that are less than ideal for writing (e.g. unfavourable writing surface, no writing surface available, writer has cold hands, or is rushed, or under stress). This can explain why some considerable variations in signatures occur.

Signatures, like other writing, should be compared with contemporaneously written samples (as with general writing, verified course of business signature samples are preferred).

The fluency of a signature may sometimes give the impression that a piece of writing and the signature following it are in different hands. This may not necessarily be the case. When comparing a signature with other writing care is needed because the writer may have adopted a special method of writing their signature or may be more skilful at writing it.

DETECTION OF SIMULATED SIGNATURES

Freehand simulation is detectable by unusual hesitations, pen lifts and reversions to the simulator's natural handwriting.

It is not usually possible to identify the author of a simulated signature by comparing it with a writer's natural handwriting because the simulator has suppressed their own characteristics and adopted those of the person whose signature is being forged.

DETECTION OF TRACED SIGNATURES

Tracing is a widely adopted method of simulating signatures. Common 'tracing' methods include the use of carbon paper, tracing heavily along the original document so that indented impressions (which are later inked in) are made on the document below; use of a light box; writing in pencil and then inking over.

Traced signatures, unlike freehand simulations, will be virtually free of inaccuracies caused by imperfect observations and powers of reproduction. However, certain features of the writing will not be noticed by the copier and will be omitted in the tracing.

Any indented impressions and guidelines caused by tracing can be detected with the use of oblique light sources and an electrostatic detection apparatus (ESDA).

Any attempts to erase pencil markings may cause either smearing to the signature or damage to the document.

Possible explanations for the presence of the signature other than forgery should also be considered, e.g. could an individual have been tricked into signing a document without realising the nature of that document? Does the individual possess any characteristics that may inhibit their ability to see or understand a particular document (e.g. the person is elderly or has impaired vision)?

20.5.2 Assisted or guided hand signatures

The elderly or shortsighted are particularly at risk of being tricked into signing a document by this method. Such a signature can be detected because it may contain a mixture of the characteristics of the person signing and the person assisting.

20.5.3 Vulnerable signatures

Some signatures are particularly vulnerable to forgery in that it is more difficult to detect the presence of forgery because any lack of fluency will be attributed to the natural signature. Examples of vulnerable signatures include short simple signatures which contain a number of pen lifts (these are easier to simulate because they require a lower level of fluency than more complex signatures), signatures of an elderly or infirm persons which show a lack of pen control, and other variations.

20.6 EXAMINATION OF NON-ROMAN SCRIPTS

Some UK document examiners will also have a particular expertise in the examination of writings in other than Roman scripts (e.g. Arabic, Chinese). Most trained document examiners will be able to detect significant differences between handwritings in other languages or scripts. However, they should be cautious in attributing significance to any particular differences because the examination will have been limited to the extent that the examiner will not be familiar with the expected range of variation for aspects of the writing.

20.7 EXPRESSIONS OF CONCLUSIONS IN RELATION TO AUTHORSHIP OF HANDWRITING

Most commonly, conclusions are expressed with reference to a nine-point scale of certainty from 'definitely the same' – followed by three other degrees of conclusion down to 'inconclusive' – followed by three other degrees of conclusion down to 'definitely different'.

Note that these conclusions do not necessarily accord with statistical probabilities expressed in other areas of forensic science. The expressions of conclusions may also vary between document examiners because there is no agreed form or standardisation.

20.8 DATING OF DOCUMENTS

Generally it is not possible to 'date' a document with any degree of accuracy by examining it. It may be possible to place a document within a particular timeframe or sequence as a result of extrinsic factors, e.g. by considering alterations/obliterations/indented impressions, a time pattern in relation to the creation of the document may emerge.

20.9 INK

On rare occasions it may be possible to date a document by reference to the ink or paper (e.g. high quality notepaper may bear a watermark that can be dated within a particular time period by the manufacturer).

Certain tests of a destructive nature may be carried out on documents in order to ascertain the relative age of ink (e.g. the relative aging of ink from a ball point pen is possible by testing the solubility of the ink – which will vary depending on the length of time that the ink has been present on the paper (this technique is not yet universally employed); other procedures may be carried out to separate inks in order to determine whether more than one pen has been used on a document, e.g. thin layer chromatography (TLC), high performance chromatography, and other sensitive analytical procedures).

In the USA, the Laboratory of the Federal Bureau of Alcohol, Tobacco and Firearms operated an ink-tagging programme for a number of years. This is, however, limited to a restricted number of manufacturers in the USA and has now been discontinued. Very few laboratories will be able to reliably date inks.

20.10 DETECTION AND ANALYSIS OF INDENTED IMPRESSIONS

When writing is made on a piece of paper resting on others it will leave an indented impression on the lower page(s). A variety of information can be obtained from indented impressions, e.g. indented impressions on pages next to those torn out of a diary or other document can reveal what has been removed; origins and timeframe of a document may be determined as a result of impressions made by writing on other documents with which it has come into contact; the order of which writings on different pages were made can be established (showing, e.g. that the writings were not all made in the expected order or the relative alignment of indentations of certain particulars can show whether or not the different parts of the document were written at one time).

Electrostatic detection apparatus (ESDA) testing has been a crucial factor in a number of high profile appeal cases. It has been used to establish that notes of interviews made by police in their notebooks were not contemporaneous with the actual interviews and that alterations were made to notes post interview (see, e.g. *R*. v. *Edwards* [1991] 2 All ER 266; *R*. v. *McIlkenny and others* [1992] 2 All ER 417; *R*. v. *Malik* (unreported, CA, 4 October 1999); and *R*. v. *Hakala* [2002] All ER (D) 277 (Mar)).

Two common methods for detecting indented impressions are oblique lighting (the most common technique involving the examination of documents under a low angled light) and electrostatic detection.

ESDA is the apparatus designed for the purposes of electrostatic detection of impressions (manufacturer: Foster & Freeman Ltd, 25 Swan Lane, Evesham, Worcestershire, WR11 4PE).

The ESDA technique was developed in 1979 by the Royal College of Printing and the Metropolitan Police Forensic Science Laboratory in London. The ESDA technique has been routinely used ever since but the process is not yet fully understood and the ESDA response can be variable.

ESDA does not damage a document and can be used to detect faint impressions because the process causes a black toner to adhere to the surface of a film (which has been placed on top of the document) which corresponds with any impressions. This film constitutes the original ESDA 'lift'. It may be photographed. The original lift should be retained and it is also disclosable upon the request of the defence.

The ESDA technique is not always successful and will not work on documents that have been chemically treated (e.g. with fingerprint reagents) or on some types of paper (e.g. heavily loaded or super calendered). Therefore the sequence in which the document has to be subjected to scientific tests is important because potential evidence may be destroyed as a result of any destructive testing.

Particular care should be taken in the handling and storage of documents which are to be subjected to ESDA testing in order not to compromise the impressions. The presence of 'secondary impressions' caused by the storage of two documents together has been reported – these can obscure primary impressions.

20.11 DETECTION OF ALTERATIONS, OBLITERATIONS, AND ERASURES

Most documents, whatever the medium, will be damaged as a result of physical or chemical alteration. Any damage (and also the use of different inks to make inserts or alterations) is detectable by the use of ultraviolet (UV) spectrum or infrared light sources. This technique is non-destructive and hence may be verified, e.g. by an examiner instructed for the defence.

20.12 SEQUENTIAL TESTING OF DOCUMENTS

Paper documents are susceptible to testing for fingerprints, drug traces, Deoxyribonucleic acid (DNA), fibres, and hair. Given the potentially destructive nature of this kind of testing, the sequence in which examination of the document and chemical testing is carried out is of importance if the full potential of the evidential value of the document is to be maintained.

20.12.1 Testing for fingerprints

The presence of fingerprints may be revealed by an ESDA test. This will prove that a certain individual has handled a document, but not that that individual has written or created the document.

Chemical testing (mostly of a destructive nature) is also available. The most common method is by immersing the document in a solution of ninhydrin. This generally causes little damage to handwriting but will preclude ESDA testing.

20.12.2 DNA testing

Saliva used to seal envelopes can be tested for blood groups and DNA in order to identify or exclude a particular suspect. This testing should be done before the document is examined in order to avoid contamination. The testing procedure is difficult because the saliva has dried and been mixed with envelope glue. Even if DNA testing is destructive it does not usually preclude an examination of the document because of the limited area usually available for testing (e.g. stamp or gummed portion of envelope).

20.13 OFFICE AND PRINTING EQUIPMENT

20.13.1 General

If attempting to confirm the origin of photocopies or any printed matter – any comparison made with known material should be with contemporaneous like matter because particularly distinctive features (such as visible faults or marks) will disappear gradually or change over time.

20.13.2 Photocopiers/photocopies

In certain circumstances, it is possible to link a photocopy to a particular photocopier by means of certain unique marks which may be made as a result of dust or dirt on the screen. It is crucial to have known photocopies made by the same machine at a time contemporaneous to the questioned photocopies because any unique markings on the copies will usually be transient (unless the result of a particular long term local fault).

20.13.3 Faxes

The same considerations as for photocopies apply.

20.13.4 Modern office printers and typewriters

It is generally not possible to identify a particular make or model of an item of modern office equipment from its output because a number of different machines may produce identical output.

If faults are apparent it may be possible to link a particular document to a known machine if that machine is found to output similar faults. Certain faults created during the manufacturing process may be common to a large number of machines. Certain machines may also be predisposed to a particular type of damage which can lead to similar faults developing in the long term (e.g. contamination of the moulding process of certain typewriter characters).

Generally, if a large number of similar faults are present in two documents it will probably be concluded that the documents were the output of the same piece of equipment.

20.14 COMMERCIALLY PRINTED DOCUMENTS

This area usually requires specialist knowledge.

If attempting to link documents to the same printing source, one should consider where this source may be because input into a printed document tends to emanate from multiple sources (and perhaps geographical locations).

20.15 INK IDENTIFICATION AND THE EXAMINATION OF PAPER

A number of destructive and non-destructive tests are available to ascertain the properties of an ink and to separate one or more inks that may have been blended together. This requires specialist laboratory equipment and the area is a fast developing one.

Numerous tests may be carried out on paper in order to ascertain certain information, e.g. country of origin.

Certain 'relative' dating can also be carried out (e.g. documents that were purported to be antique have been exposed as forgeries based on information in relation to historical paper manufacturing techniques and chemical testing).

20.16   PACKAGING, HANDLING, AND STORAGE OF DOCUMENTS

While documents are usually self-identifying, certain steps should be taken and recorded to ensure the integrity of the document during any examination process.

Original documents or documents of a known origin should be labelled upon receipt (but they should not be written on or have labels stuck onto their surfaces) and any further steps taken in relation to the document should be appropriately recorded.

Details and results of any laboratory examinations or testing (including the details of any controls or standards employed) should be recorded in the laboratory notes.

It is increasingly common to package and store questioned documents in evidence bags because other storage mediums (e.g. polythene folders) have been found to cause chemical alterations to certain types of paper. For long term storage, documents should always be stored in contact with plain card or paper. Storage in plastic or in a medium that may cause indents in the document risk precluding ESDA testing in future.

20.17   QUALIFICATIONS AND TRAINING OF QUESTIONED DOCUMENT
EXAMINERS

Most examiners will have a background in an applied or analytical science (of at least graduate level): There is no formal academic training programme and all training is currently provided by way of 'apprenticeship' whereby a trainee examiner shadows an experienced examiner for a period of time.

Before reporting on their own cases, examiners are now expected to provide a portfolio of work undertaken during the supervision period. This will be assessed prior to any unsupervised reporting of cases.

The work of a document examiner will be checked and some form of quality assurance procedure in relation to the examiner's findings should be in place.

20.18   QUESTIONED DOCUMENT EXAMINER'S REPORT

The report should contain the following information:

- qualifications and experience of examiner;

- details in relation to continuity of any exhibits examined by the examiner (ideally including a list/description of items seized);
- details and results of any scientific tests carried out and any controls employed;
- conclusions in relation to the questioned documents, writing, etc.;
- details of any quality assurance measures employed (although this information will generally be included in the disclosure schedule).

20.19 MAIN SUPPLIERS OF QUESTIONED DOCUMENT EXAMINATION SERVICES IN THE UK

Forensic document examiners may be privately employed or attached to a laboratory.

The Forensic Science Service (FSS) currently has three forensic document units attached to its laboratories in London, Huntingdon, and Weatherby.

Document examination is also provided by private companies, including Document Evidence Ltd, Birmingham, and LGC Ltd.

A number of smaller companies and private individuals also provide document examination services.

Most examiners currently reporting in the UK will have been trained by one of the large laboratory providers, e.g. FSS (training is also provided by laboratories in Scotland and Ireland and the Federal Bureau of Investigation (FBI) runs a training course in document examination).

All laboratories providing examination services should be UKAS accredited and individual document examiners may apply for entry on the CRFP register.

Questioned document examiners may be members of the Forensic Society but there is no specialist corporate body for document examiners in the UK.

REFERENCES

Ellen, D. (1997) *The Scientific Examination of Documents: Methods and Techniques* (2nd edn), Taylor and Francis.

Giles, A. 'The Forensic Examination of Documents' in White, P. (ed.) (1998) *Crime Scene to Court*, The Royal Society of Chemistry, pp. 105–32.

Saferstein, R. 'Document and Voice Recognition' in Saferstein, R. (1998) *Criminalistics: An Introduction to Forensic Science* (6th edn), Prentice Hall, pp. 502–26.

CHAPTER 21

Fingerprints

21.1 THE FINGERPRINT SYSTEM

This is more accurately described as the friction ridge system found on the inner surface of the hand.

21.1.1 The ridge system on the hands (fingers, thumbs and palms)

The skin surface on the inner side of the fingers, thumbs and palm of the hand has developed and formed from the early stages of pregnancy as ridges (the dark lines in Figure 21.1) and furrows (the white interspaces). The ridges are referred to as 'friction ridges'.

Figure 21.1 Example of impression of ridge system on end joint of a finger ('fingerprint')

All finger, thumb, and palm impressions (prints and crime scene marks) can be identified because every impression consists of a unique configuration of friction ridges and ridge features. It is the type and position of these features relative to one another which determine identification.

By a basically simple, but accurate, process of correlating and cross matching friction ridge features the fingerprint examiner can decide whether (or not) two impressions have been made by the same area of friction ridge surface. This process is described in more detail below.

Note: The skin surface on the toes and sole of the foot also consists of a unique configuration of friction ridges and ridge features. These are known as plantar impressions but they are of limited relevance in crime scene examination but may be relevant, for example, in respect of sexual offences.

In the UK the following terms are used and therefore adopted in this chapter:

(i)   impressions of ridge detail taken from the person are referred to as 'prints' or 'impressions';

(ii)   impressions of ridge detail left at, developed at and retrieved from crime scenes and exhibits are referred to as 'marks'.

21.1.2   The crime scene mark

The ridge system on the hand is also distinguished by the presence of sweat pores on the ridges (see Figure 21.2). These discharge globules of sweat. When a hand touches a surface the sweat spreads and an impression of the ridge system is left on the surface which is touched (Locard's *Principle of Exchange*). These impressions are not normally visible and are referred to as 'latent' crime scene marks.

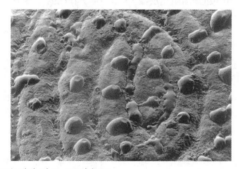

Figure 21.2   Sweat globules on ridges

If the hand is covered with a contaminant such as blood or paint, etc., a visible mark will be left on the surface touched. Similarly, a visible impression of the ridges may be left in a soft substance such as putty.

The development and recording of crime scene marks is discussed in detail below.

21.2   THE ROLE OF THE SCENE EXAMINER – SCENES OF CRIME OFFICER (SOCO)

21.2.1   Role and training

In many forces, SOCOs are civilian employees. They will have attended formal training courses either at the National Training Centre for Scientific

Support to Crime Investigation (NTCSSCI), Durham, or at the Metropolitan Police Service Scientific Support College, Hendon. The fingerprint element of the course will cover basic fingerprint theory (uniqueness and persistence of the ridge system), pattern recognition, identification principles, techniques to develop marks left at crime scenes and on exhibits, basic photography of marks at scenes and taking fingerprints (arrest, elimination and cadavers). After their formal training period they will have 'shadowed' and been supervised by an experienced SOCO before working independently. They are also required to attend continuing development and refresher training courses which will include relevant updates on fingerprint matters.

21.2.2 Assessment of the crime scene – extent of examination

Before undertaking an assessment and examination of the scene, the SOCO will generally be briefed by the person reporting the crime or the attending/ investigating police officer (IO) – either at the scene or in the details of the request to attend and examine the scene. Advice and assistance may also be sought from other sources, e.g. a fingerprint bureau, laboratory scientists and specialist photographers.

The search for finger/palm marks will be carried out on the basis of the above information and advice as well as the SOCO's own survey and assessment of the scene. The extent of the search will be determined by the circumstances of the case. In a typical burglary case, for example, the point of entry/exit and any known route followed by the intruder will be examined. Objects, or anything suspected of being handled or touched by the intruder, such as items considered to have been disturbed or items which are foreign to the scene, will be examined and, if necessary, exhibited, packaged and removed for examination in a laboratory. The extent of scene examination in serious crime cases will be determined by the type of crime, type of scene, and relevant exhibits.

21.2.3 Developing and retrieving marks at the scene

Latent marks can be developed and made visible for retrieval and recorded by either lifting or photography.

In general terms, marks left on non-porous surfaces can be developed by the application of a suitable powder which adheres to the sweat impression making it visible. The result can then be photographed or 'lifted' with low tack adhesive tape and mounted on an acetate sheet

Figure 21.3 Latent marks developed using powder

which will be labelled with the SOCO's exhibit number, date of the offence and address of venue, or vehicle registration number, etc. This 'lift' will be used as a 'negative' to produce photographs for later search and comparison in a fingerprint bureau.

It is also retained for production in court and/or for examination by an expert acting on behalf of the defendant if required. In some UK forces the mark(s) may be photographed rather than 'lifted'.

If the hand is covered with a contaminant such as blood or paint, etc., a visible mark will be left on the surface touched. This can be recorded using photography initially but may be further developed and enhanced by treatment with chemical and physical reagents or specialist lighting in a laboratory.

Similarly, a visible impression of the ridges may be left in a soft substance such as putty. This will be recorded by specialist photography either at the scene or in a laboratory as may be necessary.

Any marks found may be photographed by the SOCO if appropriate and if he/she is camera competent, or by a trained photographer or submitted for specialist photography. The appropriate course of action will be determined by the SOCO.

When a mark or marks are photographed either at a scene or in the laboratory, it/they will have a label placed adjacent to it/them showing the relevant exhibit number and/or description of the article, the relevant date and a mark(s) identifier.

On porous surfaces the main constituent of sweat – water – will be absorbed into the surface. However sweat contains not only water but also a variety of acids, greases and other chemical substances which are part of the residue left when a surface is touched. By the careful application of chemical or physical reagents, or the use of specialist lighting, any marks left can be made visible for recording by photography. As such treatments are not practical at crime scenes, the SOCO will submit exhibits of this type to the fingerprint laboratory for examination, development and photography.

21.2.4 Recording crime scene marks

The SOCO must keep a record of the scene examination and, in particular, this record should identify the exact location of any finger/palm marks found. Where necessary the written record may be supplemented by a diagram or plan. The SOCO's record (variously referred to as an 'examination' report, 'scenes of crime report' or a 'job sheet') contains the notes of the finger/palm mark examination and other forensic examinations carried out at the scene. It is the document from which the SOCO will compile any statement of evidence required and it will also prove useful to staff in a fingerprint bureau in determining the value of the marks submitted and the most appropriate search parameters to be applied. It is disclosable to solicitors acting for defendants or to experts instructed by them.

Details of any exhibits (location, etc.) submitted for treatment and examination in the laboratory will also be recorded.

The SOCO will also record any examination where the result of the search was negative. This may be significant in any subsequent trial – there are reasons why no marks may have been found. Unless specifically requested, the negative examination result is not usually the subject of a statement.

At all times the SOCO will exercise discretion, based on information received, local intelligence, knowledge, training and experience as to what should be examined, as to which marks, if any found, are useful for submission to a fingerprint bureau and which items found are relevant to the investigation and should be submitted to a laboratory for treatment if examination at the scene is not practicable.

Once marks have been 'lifted' or photographed victims are advised that the relevant areas may be cleaned and therefore the powder residue of any marks developed and lifted or photographed may no longer be available to defence experts. However it may be possible to check the location from which marks were lifted or on which they were photographed by examining the background from which they came or 'background noise' such as indentations or graining on the item/surface examined as revealed in lifts and photographs produced as evidence. Occasionally entirety photographs of the scene showing the location and position of marks may be taken. If available, these can be used to cross check the location and position of marks recorded in the SOCO's notes.

Lifted marks are sent to the fingerprint bureau for processing as are any marks photographed at the scene.

Articles submitted to laboratories for treatment and on which marks may or may not have been found will often be retained for the duration of the investigation, or longer, and are therefore available for inspection by defence experts prior to trial.

21.2.5 Submission of exhibits to a laboratory

Where items are not suitable for examination at a scene or where enhancement of visible marks on movable items may be possible, they will be submitted to a laboratory by the SOCO. They will be given exhibit numbers for continuity purposes and submission will be recorded both on the SOCO's report and on a separate laboratory submission form.

Exhibits will be placed in appropriate packaging to prevent any damage to visible or possible potential marks and placed in self-sealing exhibit bags with unique reference numbers for continuity purposes for dispatch to a fingerprint laboratory. Large or bulky exhibits will be transported directly to the laboratory with the appropriate documentation to preserve continuity.

21.2.6 Elimination finger and palm prints

Marks found may have been left by persons, e.g. householders, who have legitimate access to items and surfaces on which they have been found. SOCOs are advised to establish if there are any marks found or persons in this category and, where necessary, obtain and submit finger and palm prints for comparison against any marks found to avoid the necessity for fingerprint bureaux to compare or search marks which will prove to be of no evidential value. The finger and palm prints of police officers are retained in fingerprint bureaux for this purpose.

21.3 THE ROLE OF THE FINGERPRINT LABORATORY TECHNICIAN

Articles which cannot be examined at the crime scene are submitted to fingerprint laboratories for treatment to develop marks. Exhibits bearing visible marks will also be submitted for initial photography and then for consideration as to treatments to possibly enhance the quality of the marks.

The use of chemical and physical reagents to develop and/or enhance crime scene marks is the function of the fingerprint laboratory technician, who may or may not be a fingerprint examiner in his or her own right. Using the guidance published periodically by the Home Office Police Scientific Development Branch, the fingerprint laboratory technician will use the most appropriate technique to develop or enhance marks on exhibits submitted. A record will be kept on a standard force document which will record the receipt of the exhibit, the type of treatment(s) to which it has been subjected, and the result. It will also record the exhibit number, or any variations to it, and the name of any technician involved in the process of development or enhancement. Once marks have been developed, or at each stage of enhancement, they will be photographed and this will be recorded.

Advanced mark development techniques enable the development and enhancement of marks on a wide variety of surfaces such as paper, cardboard, plastics, vinyl, rubber, leather, metals, raw wood, waxed surfaces and fabric.

21.3.1 Examples of surface and suitable treatments

The table below is extracted from Kent, T. (1998).

For example, ninhydrin, a biological reagent, reacts with the amino acid content of the sweat to produce a visible mark. Silver nitrate will react with the salt content of sweat to produce a visible mark. Iodine will react with the grease content of the sweat – but requires the application of starch to fix the mark for photography.

Surface	Suggested Development Techniques (dictated by surface and availability)
Smooth non-porous (e.g. glass, paint)	powder, superglue, vacuum metal deposition, fluorescence examination
Rough non-porous (e.g. grained surfaces)	fluorescence examination, superglue
Paper and cardboard	ninhydrin, physical developer, powder, fluorescence examination
Plastics and polythene (e.g. bags)	fluorescence examination, vacuum metal deposition
Vinyl, rubber, leather	fluorescence examination, vacuum metal deposition, superglue
Untreated metal	fluorescence examination, vacuum metal deposition, superglue
Raw wood (untreated)	fluorescence examination, ninhydrin

However it is important to bear in mind that irrespective of the techniques used either at scenes or in laboratories to retrieve marks, the resultant quality of the marks, or if in fact any will develop, will depend upon the amount of sweat exuded by the handler, the time elapsed since the surface was touched, contaminants or other cover (e.g. gloves) on the hand, the amount of secretions in the sweat, which can vary from person to person or from time to time, and other similar factors which means that although an item/surface has been touched, it is not to be taken for granted that latent impressions of fingers or palms will always be left.

The nature of the surface will determine which development method or methods will be used to produce the best result or further enhance developed marks. If more than one method is used these will be applied in a particular sequence according to published guidelines – some treatments can be destructive if used in the wrong order. Where sequential treatments are used, particularly in serious cases, e.g. murder, terrorism, etc. then any marks developed or enhanced will be photographed on the completion of each stage before the next treatment is used. Appropriate records will be kept of each stage of the process.

The appropriate treatment or treatments to be used will be at the technician's discretion based on the nature of the surface to be examined, knowledge, guidance, experience and possible budgetary constraints.

For health and safety reasons, certain advanced techniques can only be undertaken by qualified scientists either at the scene, when items cannot be removed for transfer to a laboratory, or later in the laboratory.

Developed and/or enhanced marks will then be sent to the fingerprint bureau for processing.

Comparisons for identification purposes may also be made in respect of bare footprint or lip impressions. These will be on a one-to-one basis as there are no such database records held. Comparison of impressions of the ears is also possible on an individual basis and has been used successfully in courts both in the UK and elsewhere, particularly in the Netherlands.

21.4   THE FUNCTIONS OF THE FINGERPRINT BUREAU

Each police force in England and Wales has its own fingerprint bureau. The main functions of force fingerprint bureaux are:

- to establish whether a person charged with an offence has an existing criminal record or is wanted either locally or elsewhere for an offence;
- to compare marks found at crime scenes against the finger or palm prints of persons having legitimate access to scenes or articles;
- to compare marks found against the finger or palm prints of persons nominated as suspects by investigating officers;
- to search marks found at crime scenes against local, regional or national fingerprint databases;
- to provide evidence of the identification of crime scene marks in court;
- to provide evidence relating to the identity and/or previous convictions of defendants in court if they are denied;
- to assist in the identification of deceased persons where other means of identification may be lacking or not sufficiently positive;
- to transmit crime scene marks to other bureaux in the UK or abroad for search and comparison as necessary.

21.5   OUTLINE OF PRACTICE AND PROCEDURE IN A FINGERPRINT BUREAU

21.5.1   Fingerprints from arrested persons

The powers of police officers and other law enforcement agency personnel (e.g. HM Customs and Excise, Benefits Investigation Agency, Royal Military Police, etc.) to take or have fingerprints taken from detained persons are governed by the Police and Criminal Evidence Act 1984 (PACE) and subsequent amendments to that legislation (e.g. the Criminal Justice and Police Act 2001).

On receipt in the fingerprint bureau the fingerprint impressions will be scanned onto the National Automated Fingerprint Identification System (NAFIS). NAFIS is a computerised fingerprint database which holds the images of fingerprint records which constitute the National Fingerprint Collection. The system holds a database of unidentified crime scene marks and therefore can be used to search prints against prints, prints against marks, and marks against prints. In many forces fingerprint impressions are now recorded using the 'Livescan' system and electronically transmitted direct to NAFIS from police station terminals for processing by fingerprint bureau staff.

If the person is believed to have an existing criminal record then a direct comparison can be made against fingerprints which are held on the database as part of that record.

If the first fingerprint examiner (who may or may not be a registered fingerprint expert) is satisfied that they relate to the same person, a second officer who must be an expert will confirm the decision. The record will be updated and the arresting officer will be informed of the result.

If the fingerprints do not relate to the same person or in cases where it is not suggested that a record already exists, once scanned a search against the complete database will take place. The system will produce a list and the images of likely respondents. A comparison will be made between the enquiry prints and each respondent by the fingerprint examiner. If identified, the process will be repeated by an expert, and the record will be updated, etc.

If no match is found, then a new fingerprint database record will be created and retained subject to pertinent legislation.

21.5.2 Crime scene marks

On receipt of the marks, the case will be allocated to staff for processing.

It will be determined whether or not the marks are in such a position that they should be compared with the finger or palm prints of persons who might have had legitimate access to the surfaces on which they were found. If so, these comparisons will be carried out.

If the investigating officer has suggested possible suspects then the marks will be compared against the prints of the relevant persons.

When marks have not been identified for persons having access or who are considered to be suspects, their suitability for search will be considered. Not all marks are suitable for search – it will depend on the quality of the mark(s), the area of the hand disclosed in the mark(s) – for example a programme to facilitate searching palm marks against palm prints is still in the course of development.

Once a mark is deemed suitable for search, the officer will scan the mark onto the NAFIS database. A decision will then be made as to the extent of the search, local, regional or national – and the search will be set accordingly.

The system will produce a list of possible print matches which must then be compared against the mark by fingerprint staff. The system only suggests possible matches but does not make the identification – that is the role of fingerprint staff. No system has a 100 per cent hit rate, therefore potential matches do not always appear in numerically predetermined optimum respondent lists.

Marks which have not been identified but are relevant to the investigation of the crime are retained in the bureau. They form the database of marks against which the fingerprints of the person arrested are subjected to speculative search, to determine if they have been involved in crimes other than those for which they have been arrested. It is also possible that new or further suspects may come to notice some time after the date of the original crime.

21.5.3 Identification of marks and prints

Identification is a process of analysis, comparison and evaluation and is the same for print to print, mark to print, print to mark and mark to mark comparisons.

If the friction ridges from the enquiry impression (mark or print) form a pattern then the first step taken by the fingerprint examiner is to look for similar patterns on the respondent impressions (prints or marks) for comparison.

If no patterns are disclosed, the ridge flow of the enquiry and respondent impressions will be compared to find similarity of ridge flow. If the patterns or ridge flow are similar then the examiner will look at the friction ridge features, in particular, the ridge characteristics, that is, the natural deviations in the flow of the ridges.

The examiner will then determine:

- if the friction ridge features are of a compatible type in each;
- if they are in the same relative position to each other;
- if they are in the same sequence in each;
- if there is sufficient quantitative and qualitative detail present to arrive at a positive decision;
- that there is nothing in disagreement.

Figure 21.4   Example of fingerprint comparison

All these criteria must be satisfied before an officer will decide that both have been made by the same area of the hand and therefore the same person.

Crime scene mark identifications will be subjected to two further checks, which must be carried out by fingerprint experts, before an investigating officer (IO) is notified of the result. This checking and quality control procedure is mandatory in all UK fingerprint bureaux and has always been the practice before crime scene marks are produced as evidence in court.

21.6   THE 'STANDARD' REQUIRED FOR IDENTIFICATION

In 1953 following a meeting with representatives of the larger fingerprint bureaux and the Director of Public Prosecutions (DPP), the Home Office recommended that before a single mark identification was presented as evidence there should be a minimum of 16 ridge characteristics in agreement between mark and impression. It was intended to be applied to a mark used in evidence but did not set that as the requirement for an identification for 'police purposes'. It was an administrative recommendation which had no basis in either science or law.

From 1983, as a result of pressure from courts and prosecutors, it was agreed that under certain conditions and in serious cases, marks with fewer than 16 characteristics in agreement could be presented as evidence. Although there were many instances where judges ruled that such evidence was admissible, and accepted it in a wider range of offences, not all were of the same opinion.

The issue has arisen on four occasions in the Court of Appeal (Criminal Division):

1. *R. v. Pewter* (10 November 1988, unreported): the court ordered the production in evidence of a mark with 12 characteristics.

2. *R. v. Charles* (17 December 1999, unreported): the court rejected fingerprint/mark identification evidence based on statistics – it was the knowledge, experience and expertise of the fingerprint expert which gave the evidence its admissibility and reliability.

3. *R. v. McNamee* (17 December 1998, Court of Appeal, unreported): the court stated that:

    > We note that in the current 1998 edition of *Archbold* at paragraph 14–97 it is said that between 10 and 15 matching characteristics on a single fingerprint is regarded as a partial identification and might be forwarded to the investigating authorities but would not be adduced in court. If that statement is intended to be a statement of law we do not think it is accurate. Evidence of fewer than 16 characteristics is not inadmissible as evidence of identification.

4. *R. v. Buckley* (1999) 163 JP 561; [1999] All ER (D) 1521: in the circumstances the trial judge was correct in exercising his discretion to admit evidence of a mark with nine characteristics in agreement.

See also *R. v. Buisson and another* [1991] LRC (Crim) 302 (NZ CA), and *R. v. Reid* (unreported, QBD, 26 March 1996).

In 1994, the Crown Prosecution Service (CPS) raised a number of issues in relation to the Home Office recommendation and the 1983 amendment to it. There was inconsistency of practice between experts from different bureaux when requested to or when presenting evidence in cases where marks had fewer than 16 characteristics in agreement. It was felt that this undermined the arguments in favour of adhering to the 1953 recommendation. It also asked if the argument for the retention of the recommended 'standard' had any scientific basis. The CPS also pointed out that developments in the rules of disclosure meant that lawyers were now aware of partial identifications and that it was the function of the CPS, and not that of the fingerprint expert, to determine whether or not such evidence was sufficiently cogent to make a contribution to the prosecution case. It also asked for a comparison with practices in other countries – particularly Australia which had a similar legal system.

As a result the Association of Chief Police Officers (ACPO) set up a working party to review practice in relation to fingerprint evidence in England and Wales. The working party recommended that the principle of no predetermined or set numerical 'standard' should be adopted. This recommendation was accepted and ratified by ACPO in April 1996. The decision was implemented in June 2001 therefore allowing time for consultation with the Home Office and the CPS, as well as informing and seeking comment from other bodies such as the Lord Chancellor's Department, the Law Society, the Criminal Bar Association, the Criminal Cases Review Commission, etc., none of whom raised any objection to the change. The UK (England and Wales) is in line with other jurisdictions such as the USA, Canada and certain Australian states where a no set numerical 'standard' applies.

See Christopher J. Coombes (2000) and Donald Campbell 'Fingerprints: A Review' [1995] Crim LR 195.

21.7 THE ROLE OF THE FINGERPRINT EXAMINER (EXPERT)

No previous experience or necessary specific academic qualifications, other than a reasonable standard of education are required from a person who wishes to become a fingerprint expert in the UK. Once an individual has been accepted for employment in a fingerprint bureau the status of expert is gained by attending a series of formal courses or undertaking formal courses of study within the bureau, continuous monitoring, and assessment of work performance by trainers and managers. Formal courses are undertaken either at the NTCSSCI or at the Metropolitan Police Service Scientific Support College, Hendon. The culmination of training and formal courses will be an assessment at an advanced fingerprint course at either of the above institutions during which the suitability of the officer to appear in court as a fingerprint expert will be assessed. If successful, and with the approval of the head of the fingerprint bureau, who will take into account work performance and related issues, the officer will be entered on the National Register of Fingerprint Experts (NRFE) which is maintained on behalf of ACPO by NTCSSCI (superceded by the CRFP register). Courts accept individuals who have successfully completed this process as expert witnesses. A previous time-based criterion which needed to be satisfied has now been deemed untenable under sex discrimination, equal opportunities and European Union (EU) legislation. In future the FSS plans to train fingerprint experts in-house. There is no reason why fingerprint experts trained in Europe and elsewhere should not give evidence in court.

Officers may also seek membership of other bodies such as the Fingerprint Society, the International Association for Identification (USA), the Academy of Expert Witnesses, etc., as a personal choice. Membership does not necessarily prove qualification and expertise.

At the instigation of the Home Office a new organisation has come into being – the Council for the Registration of Forensic Practitioners (CRFP). Registration is not mandatory – it cannot be seen to interfere with a court's discretion to hear evidence from whom it might decide is a competent witness. However ACPO has agreed that all fingerprint experts should seek registration. The CRFP register will be open to those employed in the police service as well as those employed or working independently in the private sector. Specific criteria to be satisfied in seeking registration include:

- that the applicant has acquired recognised qualifications in fingerprint practice;
- has demonstrated an ability to apply that knowledge and experience practically in the workplace and in courts.

All applications for registration are ratified by the Incident Investigative Sector Assessment Panel which is comprised of members from the police service and private practice who ensure that any person placed on the register meets the specified criteria.

Persons on the register must undergo a process of reassessment and reregistration every four years.

Registration with the CRFP is also open to other categories of staff employed in fingerprint related roles such as crime scene examiners, fingerprint laboratory technicians, etc.

21.8 CATEGORIES OF FINGERPRINT IDENTIFICATION EVIDENCE

21.8.1 Positive

1. Expert opinion evidence which links the defendant to the crime or crime scene by the identification of marks either found at the scene or on exhibits submitted to a fingerprint laboratory for treatment.
2. Expert opinion evidence that one or more sets of fingerprints have come from the same person: proof of identity, proof of previous convictions, provision of Coroner's Certificates as formal identification of deceased persons.

21.8.2 Negative

1. No marks found at the crime scene or on exhibits submitted for treatment and the general reasons why marks may not always be left by the person touching the surface or handling the article.
2. Marks not identified for nominated suspect(s).
3. Marks not identified for persons having legitimate access.
4. Marks not identified after search on fingerprint databases.
5. Lack of ridge detail in marks or prints: expert unable to reach a positive conclusion.

21.9 THE PRESENTATION OF THE EXPERT'S EVIDENCE

Generally police fingerprint experts' evidence will be in statement form. Independent experts will do so by way of report which may or may not include the requisite 'witness declaration'.

In the statement the expert will state his/her qualifications (training, CRFP registration number) and experience (length of service, employing authority). He/she will then state which exhibits (finger/palm prints, crime scene marks) of which he/she has taken possession, including the date and venue where this happened and where subsequent comparisons were carried out. The fingerprint expert presenting evidence will again verify the identification of any marks which have been identified.

The statement will include the expert's conclusion and the reasons – what has been found in agreement between mark(s) and print(s) – which justify that conclusion. The detail of the identification comparison will normally be included. In serious cases where there may be multiple marks or multiple scenes and exhibits the expert will produce conclusions in a separate schedule for ease of reference.

21.10 THE ROLE OF THE INDEPENDENT FINGERPRINT EXPERT

An independent expert should be a qualified fingerprint expert who practices in the private sector either conducting investigations on behalf of private clients or providing a service to defence solicitors. Details of these persons can be obtained from the Directory of Expert Witnesses, the Academy of Expert Witnesses, or latterly the Council for the CRFP. It is extremely rare for police service experts to act on the instructions of a defendant's solicitor. They may of course be called as witnesses if legal advisers believe that any evidence they might present will be beneficial to the defendant's case.

In the context of criminal cases the main roles of a retained independent expert are:

- comparison of relevant marks and prints in accordance with instructions received;
- verification of the location of any marks or other exhibits found or submitted;
- verification of the location of marks on exhibits;
- review of scene examination and laboratory treatments used;
- examination and processing of untreated exhibits considered to be relevant by the defence;
- preparation of report for instructing solicitor;
- attendance in court as a witness.

21.11 CHALLENGES/DEFENCES TO FINGERPRINT IDENTIFICATION EVIDENCE

See per Rose LJ in *R*. v. *Buckley* (1999) 163 JP 561:

> In every case where fingerprint evidence is admitted, it will generally be necessary, as in relation to all expert evidence, for the judge to warn the jury that it is evidence of opinion only, that the expert's opinion is not conclusive and that it is for the jury determine whether guilt is proved in the light of all the evidence.

21.11.1 Erroneous identification(s)

A finger/palm mark is more likely to be attributed to an individual as a result of a database search or comparison against a specific suspect if there is no independent verification process in place. All UK police fingerprint bureaux operate a policy whereby all identifications are confirmed by two experts after the initial decision before informing an IO of the result. Evidence may be presented by another expert who has not been part of the process but who will also repeat the process of confirmation. There is always room for human error and, in cases of doubt, an independent expert should be instructed to review the police experts' findings.

For an example of an erroneous identification see '*HMA* v. *Shirley McKie*. The Fingerprint Bureau: Primary Inspection 2000' online via **www.scotland. gov.uk/hmic/docs/fppi-15.asp**.

21.11.2 Legitimate (innocent) access and the age of the marks found

The defendant may be able to offer an explanation as to why his/her marks were found at a scene or on an exhibit because he or she has had access to the premises, vehicle or property, for example an unwitting passenger in a stolen vehicle or a visitor/employee in a burgled premises.

It is generally accepted that a finger/palm mark cannot be aged reliably and it is therefore impossible to determine the time of its placement.

The *Scene of Crime Handbook of Fingerprint Development Techniques* (Home Office, Police Scientific Development Branch) (1998) states:

> Many fingerprint development techniques will sometimes show a change in the intensity or nature of reaction with older fingerprints compared with fresh fingerprints. It is however impossible to determine reliably the age of a fingerprint by preservation of its reaction within a fingerprint detection process.

A latent sweat mark begins to decompose soon after deposit. How long a mark will remain retrievable or capable of development (assuming it has not been removed, e.g. by cleaning, or deteriorated under adverse weather conditions) will depend on the original quality of the mark and the conditions it has been exposed to. It is possible for certain marks to 'survive' indefinitely if they have been contaminated by a stable substance, e.g. paint on the hands.

While it may be possible to get an indication of the possible age of the marks by studying the history of the contact surface (e.g. whether it was frequently cleaned), or by reference to the circumstances of the crime (e.g. marks on pieces of broken glass from a window which was intact prior to the committal of the burglary), or the location of the marks found (e.g. consistent with the actions of a person climbing through a window to gain access to premises), laboratory testing has shown that exposure to weather and other severe environmental factors (including water) may not significantly decrease the 'lifespan' of latent marks. A mark deposited on a document which is stored under optimum conditions may remain capable of development and retrieval for many years. Certain marks may also become integral to the surface on which they were deposited and therefore will remain indefinitely.

Experts will generally be unwilling to put a precise age on a mark because of the uncertainty involved. However they may be able to give an estimate or indication of the age of a mark taking into account the quality of the mark(s) retrieved, the location(s) from which the mark(s) have been recovered, the condition of the scene before and after the commission of an offence, etc.

See Charles R. Midkiff 'Fingerprints – Determination of time of placement. An age old problem' *Fingerprint Whorld* (October 1992) 125 and Charles R. Midkiff 'Lifetime of a latent – How long? Can you tell?' *Fingerprint Whorld* (October 1993) 85.

21.11.3 'Planting' or forgery of marks

The general view is that successfully 'transplanting' or forging latent finger/palm marks of an innocent person at a crime scene is extremely rare because of the difficulty in doing so, for example obtaining the fingerprint impressions or marks left on another surface by the person it is intended to incriminate.

It is possible to 'fabricate' a purported finger/palm mark identification and present it as evidence by introducing marks genuinely retrieved from a surface to which the person has had legitimate access but describing them as originating from another premises or surface to which that person did not have access. A cross check with any available photographs taken at the crime scene by the scene examiner, his or her notes and diagrams should be carried out by an independent expert retained by the defence where there is doubt as to the real location/surface from which the marks were 'lifted' or on which they were photographed.

Lifts may also be mislabelled and for that reason the examiner should always consider the 'background information' (if any) on the lift. Small background traces, which would have been expected had the mark been lifted from the particular surface claimed, may be missing from the lift. Conversely, background traces present on the lift may be inconsistent with the surface from which the lift was purportedly taken. This can also apply to marks which have been photographed in situ. The position of the retrieved mark, its orientation and the amount of pressure assumed from the quality of the mark should be consistent with the likely handling of the object or surface from which the mark or marks have been recovered. If the mislabelled lift exhibit is submitted with a number of other lift exhibits, the tape or powder or writing pen used may be inconsistent with those used in the other lift exhibits. Experts should also be aware of photographic fabrications which may include such telltale signs as suspicious artefacts, shadows and stray or unexplainable images.

Forged marks are those produced by an object, such as a cast of an individual's finger or fingers, used to produce a simulated mark on a surface. An expert should be familiar with and be prepared to discuss techniques available for fabrication and the methods available to detect such forgeries. Forgeries should be apparent to a trained eye. 'Lifts' fabricated from inked print impressions generally exhibit characteristics inconsistent with genuine latent mark lifts. These lifts will also have no background information. High power microscopic examination or chemical analysis may also disclose grain shape or type inconsistent with the normal latent mark development powder.

See Charles R. Midkiff 'Forger and fabricated prints: Their past and the future?' *Fingerprint Whorld* (July 1994) 83 and Pat A. Wertheim 'Detection of forged and fabricated latent prints. Historical Review and ethical implications of the falsification of latent fingerprint evidence' *Fingerprint Whorld* (July 1995) 87.

REFERENCES

Archbold (1998) para. 14–97.

Coombes, C. (2000) *Fingerprint Identification: Evidence Standards: The development of the standard in the UK and the National Fingerprint Evidence Standard* (Home Office Paper).

Council for the Registration of Forensic Practitioners Report of the Fingerprint Working Group (July 1999).

Kent, T. (1998) *Manual of Fingerprint Development Techniques: A Guide to the selection and use of processes for the development of latent fingerprints* (2nd edn) (Home Office (Police Scientific Development Branch)).

Midkiff, C. (1992) 'Fingerprints – Determination of time of placement: An age old problem', *Fingerprint Whorld* (October) 125.

Midkiff, C. (1993) 'Lifetime of a latent – How long? Can you tell?', *Fingerprint Whorld* (October) 85.

Midkiff, C. (1994) 'Forged and fabricated prints: Their past and the future?', *Fingerprint Whorld* (July) 83.

Scene of Crime Handbook of Fingerprint Development Techniques (abridged from Kent, T. (1998) *Manual of Fingerprint Development Techniques: A Guide to the selection and use of processes for the development of latent fingerprints* (2nd edn) (Home Office (Police Scientific Development Branch)).

Wertheim, Pat A. (1995) 'Detection of forged and fabricated latent prints: Historical Review and ethical implications of the falsification of latent fingerprint evidence', *Fingerprint Whorld* (July) 87.

CHAPTER 22

Forensic physicians

22.1 INTRODUCTION

Forensic physicians are self employed, independent, and contracted to provide their services to police authorities. They offer medical care and, when required, forensic assessment of:

(i) prisoners and suspects in police custody;
(ii) alleged victims (and alleged perpetrators) of crime;
(iii) police officers injured while on duty; and
(iv) attend scenes of death to pronounce life extinct.

Interpretations of any findings may, in due course, be presented to the police; the Crown Prosecution Service (CPS); the courts; the Criminal Injuries Compensation Board (CICB), or social services (e.g. in cases involving child abuse). Forensic physicians are also available to act on behalf of the defence, but are advised to avoid so acting in cases in their own locality due to potential conflicts of interest.

Forensic physicians are also known as police surgeons in the mainland UK (except in London where they are known as forensic medical examiners (FMEs)) and forensic medical officers in Northern Ireland.

22.2 THE DUTIES OF THE FORENSIC PHYSICIAN

The overriding duty of the attending forensic physician is the clinical safety and wellbeing of the detained person. Acceptance of this principle requires that physicians be alert to potential or actual abuse of detainees, and to ensure that appropriate representations are made in relation to the same. On the other hand, by virtue of being required by the police to attend to detainees in both a therapeutic and forensic capacity, the physician may be expected to make a report to the police. However, in relation to an examination for evidential purposes, the physician should only provide the police that information that he or she feels is material to the investigation.

22.2.1　Confidentiality

The Revised Interim Guidelines on Confidentiality for Police Surgeons in England, Wales and Northern Ireland (February 1998, the British Medical Association (BMA) and the Association of Police Surgeons (APS) [known as AFP from July 2003]) state that the duty of confidentiality owed to a patient by a forensic physician is the same as that owed by any other doctor. All forensic physicians are obliged to follow the guidance issued by the General Medical Council (GMC). Detained persons have the right to expect that forensic physicians will not disclose any personal information that they learn during the course of their professional duties, unless the detainee has given express permission to do so. This means that information collected during a forensic examination *not germane to the case* should only be disclosed with the permission of the detainee. Forensic physicians have a duty to keep this part of the examination confidential unless there are exceptional reasons to justify disclosure.

The presence of police officers during an examination creates difficulties in relation to issues of confidentiality. Under the Criminal Procedure and Investigations Act 1996 (CPIA), police officers (even when acting as a chaperone to the detainee where the detainee is of the opposite sex to the examining physician) have a duty to record events in cases in which they are involved. In relation to such situations, the Association of Forensic Physicians (AFP) advises that, where possible, forensic physicians carry out examinations of detainees with a police officer within earshot but out of close hearing.

22.2.2　Consent

The subject (whether this is an alleged perpetrator of a crime or an alleged victim) being examined must understand the role of the forensic physician and the difficulties that this presents for maintaining confidentiality.

Before any examination takes place, a forensic physician should ensure that the subject has consented to

(i)　the forensic examination;
(ii)　the provision of medical care; and
(iii)　the disclosure of forensic evidence and any other information likely to affect the outcome of the case.

A forensic physician will require specific written consent from the subject for the taking of intimate bodily samples (in those specific circumstances where the appropriate officer has so authorised that such samples may be taken). Intimate samples include dental impressions; blood; semen or any other tissue fluid; urine or pubic hair, or a swab taken from a body orifice other than the mouth. A non-intimate sample (i.e. a sample of hair other than pubic hair which includes hair plucked from the root, a sample taken from under a nail, a swab taken from any part of a person's body including the mouth but not any other body orifice, saliva, or a footprint or similar impression of any part of a person's body other than a part of his hand) may be taken by scenes of crime officers (SOCOs) or police officers in addition to forensic physicians, as can urine – an intimate sample. While reasonable force may used to take non-intimate samples, good practice indicates that the physician taking the sample does so with full, informed, and valid consent. For specific considerations in relation to intimate body searches for drugs see **Chapter 14**.

Special considerations in relation to consent arise in relation to juveniles and the mentally disordered. In short, it is good practice in such situations for the forensic physician to request the presence of a responsible adult at the examination. The APS issued guidelines in January 2002 in relation to consent from children and young people in police custody. At the age of 16, children who are competent (under the *Gillick* principle, see *Gillick v. West Norfolk and Wisbech Area Health Authority and another* [1986] AC 112) are entitled to consent to therapeutic examinations. In relation to forensic examinations (including the taking of forensic samples), it is good practice for the consent of a person under 17 to be overseen by a responsible adult, who may also act as the appropriate adult.

In certain situations forensic physicians may conduct forensic examinations (including the taking of intimate samples) upon subjects who are unable to give an informed consent. Examples of such situations include the taking of blood specimens from incapacitated drivers and cases in which a person who may have been sexually assaulted lacks the requisite capacity to consent (by virtue of intoxication, serious injury, mental disorder, or is a child). Such examinations may be required because any delay in obtaining the relevant forensic samples may lead to the loss of material which could have assisted with the identification and/or the apprehension of the assailant(s). These examinations can only be carried out where permitted by law and in accordance with specific guidelines (see BMA and APS *Taking Blood Specimens From Incapacitated Drivers* (guidance for doctors on the provisions of the Police Reform Act 2002) and the Education and Research Committee of the APS *Consent in Relation to Complainants of Sexual Assaults* (24 May 2001)).

22.2.3 Disclosure

Any notes made in police station records (e.g. Book 83 entries in the Metropolitan Police District or the custody record) should be relevant only to the care of the detainee and should only briefly describe the nature of the injuries in the case of a victim because these records are disclosable under the CPIA. Hence, in order to accord with the physician's duty of confidentiality, such entries should only contain a minimum amount of clinical information.

Any other notes (including drawings, photographs or recordings) are private and should not be disclosed without the consent of the subject. If the police or the CPS request further information about the medical examination which is not included in the report, the specific written consent of the subject should be obtained before disclosing this information. In the absence of such consent, disclosure can only be made under the terms of a court order and/or in accordance with any current GMC guidelines.

22.3 THE ROLE OF THE FORENSIC PHYSICIAN

The forensic physician has a wide role in all aspects and areas of clinical forensic medicine and recent European Council of Legal Medicine (ECLM) initiatives have resulted in a wider and more intensive syllabus being envisaged in relation to those training to specialise in forensic medicine (ECLM Syllabus of Postgraduate Specialisation in Legal Medicine, September and May 1999). For the purposes of this chapter, the broad areas in which a forensic physician may be required to have knowledge, and to give an opinion on, are as follows (each of these areas are, in turn, considered briefly):

- the care of detained persons in police custody (including assessment of fitness to be detained, released, charged, or interviewed);
- knowledge of mechanisms of intoxication and the medico-legal relevance of these (including assessment of alcohol and drug intoxication and withdrawal in detainees and assessment of a person's ability to drive a motor vehicle);
- familiarity with forensic aspects of mental health (including the requirement of the presence of an appropriate adult in cases of vulnerable or mentally disordered detainees);
- medical examination, detailed description, and assessment of injuries and their sequelae that would enable a full documentation and evaluation of such aspects of direct legal interest as their method of infliction, possible causation, consequences, and complications;
- examination of adult complainants and alleged perpetrators in sexual assault cases;
- examination of alleged child victims of neglect, or physical, or sexual abuse;
- knowledge of medico-legal criminalistics, in particular the detection, collection, and preservation of all trace evidential material;
- pronouncement of life extinct at the scene and to give an opinion as to whether there are any suspicious circumstances;
- familiarity with internal and external post mortem changes and issues in relation to the post mortem interval;
- knowledge of diagnostic clinical pathology required for elucidation of causes and the manner of death.

22.4 THE CARE OF DETAINED PERSONS IN POLICE CUSTODY

22.4.1 General obligations

Upon arrival of the detained person, a forensic physician should discuss with the custodian all the circumstances of the arrest and the proposed detention which may have a bearing upon the health and welfare needs of the detainee.

Physicians are advised to use common sense when assessing whether a detainee is fit to be kept in the cells. Certain specific conditions, while not necessarily precluding fitness to detain, may require specific treatment and prescription of medication (e.g. heart disease, epilepsy, diabetes, and asthma). The APS (now AFP) has issued guidelines in relation to the safety and security of administration of medication in police custody (APS (2002)).

22.4.2 Determination of fitness for interview

Assessment of fitness for interview is a forensic examination as opposed to a clinical one. As such, it requires appropriate consent. Dr Stephen Robinson indicates that, in assessing fitness for interview, the following issues should be considered:

(i)   the likely verbal rigour and its propensity for harm;
(ii) the interviewee's capacity to recall and recount the 'facts';
(iii) any undue suggestibility of the interviewee (it should be remembered that most people are suggestible to a certain extent).

(See Robinson, Stephen P. 'Care of Detainees' in W.D.S. McLay (1996).)

Any examination in relation to fitness for interview should be preceded by the taking of a full medical history and details of any medication or substance taken (legal, illegal and prescribed) either habitually or within the last 24 hours. Issues in relation to a detainee's health which may be relevant to fitness for interview include:

- certain physical illnesses (e.g. raised blood pressure, asthma or angina – which generally will require stabilisation before interview);
- particular psychiatric disorders (e.g. severe depression, bipolar disorder, schizophrenia and related disorders, and psychotic illness may preclude fitness for interview; for further information on the procedures for conducting interviews with persons suffering from mental disorder or mental handicap and the role of the appropriate adult, see *R.* v. *Aspinall* [1999] 2 Cr App R 115);
- intoxication as a result of alcohol and/or drugs (alcoholism per se does not necessarily bar the interview of a detainee, but alcohol intoxication will; certain consequences of drug addiction – e.g. severe withdrawal complex – may invalidate the recall of the detainee or result in distress sufficient to lead to false confessions, and the administration of the

dependency substance may have adversely affected the cognitive functions of the detainee);

- fatigue or drug withdrawal (if a detainee is suffering from withdrawal (e.g. opioid withdrawal) consideration may be given to the administration of certain drugs in order to expedite the interview. On the other hand, if the detainee is fatigued or has a degree of intoxication, the forensic physician may consider asking for the interview to be delayed until the detainee has had an appropriate period of rest. The physician should also, in certain circumstances, be prepared to offer symptomatic treatment for certain detainees in withdrawal).

Any declaration of fitness for interview will hold good only for three to four hours from the time of declaration (unless new symptoms develop within this time). Thereafter the fitness for interview should be reassessed.

For further information in relation to the role of the forensic physician in the assessment of fitness for interview in the case of detainees under the influence of alcohol and/or drugs; assessment of fitness to drive and impairment as a result of drink and/or drugs, see **Chapter 14**.

For information on the minimum standard for the assessment of drug- and alcohol-dependent individuals and treatment intervention see *Substance Misuse Detainees in Police Custody* (Royal College of Physicians, January 2001).

22.4.3 Mental health

An assessment of the mental condition of a detainee forms an integral part of the routine assessment of fitness to detain or fitness for interview. A forensic physician should also be alert to the unusual or less obvious presentation of mental disorder (e.g. senile dementia or depression). Any previously undiagnosed or suspected mental disorder should be brought to the attention of the custodian as soon as possible so that the position of the detainee can be considered. Assessment of suicide risk is also a crucial part of the forensic physician's task and it will be the duty of the physician to warn the custody staff of the need for extra vigilance or even the need for admission of the detainee to hospital in serious cases. Forensic physicians may also make recommendations for disposals under the Mental Health Act 1983, including compulsory admission for assessment or treatment in hospital, or compulsory admission to hospital for assessment in an emergency. Furthermore, those forensic physicians with special experience in the diagnosis or treatment of mental disorders may become approved physicians under Mental Health Act 1983, s.12.

22.5 ASSESSMENT AND DESCRIPTION OF INJURIES

Examination and description of injuries is one of the most important functions of the forensic physician and such examinations may be required in both cases of living victims and of deceased victims at the scene of death.

In all cases, the forensic physician should carefully document any marks or injuries which may be of medico-legal significance. Physicians should also be able to give an opinion as to how any injuries were caused. Examples of specific issues that should be considered when assessing the nature of injuries include

(i) whether the injuries could have been inflicted only as a result of a violent attack;

(ii) whether the injuries could have occurred due to self-mutilation (e.g. where an individual has deliberately inflicted injuries in order to support a concocted assault charge); and

(iii) whether the injuries could represent defence wounds that occurred as a result of the individual attempting to deflect an attacker.

22.6 EXAMINATION OF ADULT COMPLAINANTS AND ALLEGED PERPETRATORS IN SEXUAL ASSAULT CASES

Forensic physicians will be required to examine adult complainants of sexual assault and alleged perpetrators of such assaults and to give an interpretation of any medical findings resulting from such examinations.

In all cases, before undertaking such an examination, the forensic physician must consider the issue of the examinee's consent because the examination will usually have both therapeutic and forensic content. For further information see **22.2.2** above.

The AFP has produced a proforma aide memoire for forensic physicians conducting an assessment of adult complainants in sexual assault cases (Proforma for Post-Pubertal Female and Male Forensic Sexual Assault Examination, August 2002). Some of the procedures carried out during such examinations are summarised below.

A medical and sexual history of the subject should be obtained, including any behaviour or conditions which may cause the forensic physician to misinterpret any physical findings (e.g. a history of ano-genital surgery, whether menstrual bleeding is occurring, and the time of the last previous sexual intercourse in order to determine whether spermatozoa pertaining to that incident may still be present).

A history of the allegation should also be obtained in order to direct the medical examination and to identify the nature of any forensic samples that may be required (e.g. in cases where vaginal or anal intercourse are alleged, swabs should be taken from those areas; in cases where oral sex is alleged to have taken place, saliva or mouth swabs may be taken as spermatozoa can survive in the oral cavity for up to 36 hours, even after eating and drinking; in cases of unconscious subjects, the use of ultraviolet (UV) light may reveal possible saliva or semen staining thereby indicating the location from where swabs should be taken).

In addition to taking swabs and other samples, care should be taken to collect debris or other foreign matter located anywhere on the body (e.g. scrapings from underneath fingernails) as trace evidence may be present (such as the perpetrator's blood or fibres) which may be of evidential significance.

Guidelines for the collection of specimens in sexual assault cases have been issued (see the Forensic Science Service (FSS), the APS and the Association of Chief Police Officers (ACPO) *Guidelines for the Collection of Specimens* (2000)). The FSS manufactures a forensic examination kit for the use of forensic physicians in the collection of evidence recovered from either victims or suspects in cases of sexual assault. The kit is approved by the APS and the ACPO and complies with quality assurance standards providing evidence of continuity and a guarantee of the integrity of exhibits.

Forensic physicians should be aware of quality assurance procedures in relation to the detection, collection and preservation of trace evidential material in order to maximise the evidential value of this material and to negate any suggestion of contamination.

A general physical examination of the complainant should also be undertaken (e.g. a note of state of clothing should be made because torn clothing or clothing worn inside out can be indicative of a struggle). Furthermore, the complainant may not be aware that any physical injuries have been sustained and thus may not have reported them. Any injuries should be recorded precisely by reference to body charts and diagrams (noting in particular, for example, the position, shape, nature of the injury, the degree of healing, and the dominant hand (which will be pertinent if considering the possibility that the injuries were self inflicted)).

The absence of injuries does not necessarily negate an allegation of sexual assault. Therefore consideration should be given to various possibilities, including that the victim had submitted due to emotional manipulation; that the degree of force used was insufficient to produce injury; that lubricants were used or that the complainant is sexually experienced, and that any bruising sustained may not yet have become apparent (bruising can take up to 48 hours post assault to develop and/or may never become visible externally).

22.7 EXAMINATION OF CHILD VICTIMS OF NEGLECT, OR PHYSICAL OR SEXUAL ABUSE

Child abuse often goes unrecognised or it is either over-diagnosed or mis-diagnosed. In cases where non-accidental injury to a child is suspected, the police, social workers or a paediatrician may require that the child be examined by a forensic physician.

In such cases, a search of the whole body should be undertaken because the injuries may be hidden under clothing. In particular, careful observation of any bruising should be made because this type of injury frequently precedes more serious injury.

A diagnosis of child abuse should not rest on injury alone. The behaviour of the child will also be significant and should be noted.

Injuries which frequently occur in cases of child abuse include the following:

- slap marks;
- marks made by instruments;
- pinch marks;
- bite marks;
- torn fraenulum in babies (caused by forcing a feeding bottle into the mouth);
- friction burns caused by dragging;
- hair pulling and bald patches;
- marks around the mouth and face indicative of gagging;
- encircling marks around wrists or ankles where the child has been tied up; and
- burns or scalds (approximately 10 per cent of abuse cases involve burning (especially cigarette burns)).

Other indications that an injury is non-accidental include:

- whether the given history is consistent with the particular injury;
- multiple injuries of differing ages;
- discrepancies and varying or changing explanations;
- delay in reporting; and
- denial and collusion between both parents and the child (who, it should be appreciated, will only rarely implicate the parents).

A full skeletal survey should always be carried out because not all fractures are apparent upon clinical examination and some small children can have quite serious bone injuries old or new (e.g. skull, rib and long bone fractures in small babies) without showing any external sign. Skeletal surveys may also reveal old or healing injuries in a seemingly straightforward case.

A number of high profile cases over the years have highlighted the danger of misdiagnosing child abuse. The following conditions or injuries should be considered (if the particular case so requires) and ruled out when examining any case of suspected physical abuse:

- calcium deficiencies;
- rickets;
- scurvy;
- disorders of bone formation;
- pigment anomalies;
- birth marks;
- blood extravasations seeping or 'tracking' down tissues from a lesser injury simulating widespread bruising;
- alopecia areata mistaken for hair pulling;
- lesions of chickenpox mistaken for cigarette burns;
- accidental scalding from tipping pans or kettles producing secondary burns to main injury;
- accidental burns and scalds due to contact with hot radiators or child turning on hot taps in bath;
- accidental fractures or, in older children, self-inflicted injuries; and,
- in adolescents, striae running across the lumbar region have been mistaken for marks of beating.

(See Roberts, Raine 'Children' in McLay, W.D.S. (1996).)

Cases of child sexual abuse raise special issues in relation to consent to examine and also require extreme sensitivity. Any examinations or work carried out in this area should be undertaken by a physician with specialist training and experience. For further information see *Guidance on Paediatric Forensic Examination in Relation to Possible Child Sexual Abuse* (the Royal College of Paediatrics and Child Health and the APS, April 2001).

22.8   PROUNOUNCEMENT OF LIFE EXTINCT AT THE SCENE

In cases of suspicious death the forensic physician is often one of the first experts to attend the scene. His or her primary function at the scene is that of determining life extinct. The forensic physician should also ensure, as far as possible, that no further disturbance of the scene takes place until other investigators (in particular the forensic pathologist) attend. The physician should be directed by the instructions of the investigating officer (IO) who will have overall responsibility for the crime scene.

When examining a body for the purpose of pronouncing life extinct, disturbance should be kept to a minimum and clothing should not be unnecessarily dishevelled or removed, even if this may mean that some injuries (e.g. on the back of the body) are not observed. This care is necessary in order to prevent the removal or destruction of any trace evidence that might be present on, or in close proximity to, the body. In cases where the physician is required to take the body temperature of a deceased, the AFP recommends that the advice of the local Home Office pathologist should be sought (it should be noted, for instance, that the taking of rectal temperature can result in the contamination or loss of trace evidence in certain cases, e.g. if the deceased has been sexually assaulted, and should be avoided pre-collection of trace evidence in such cases).

The forensic physician should also be able to offer an opinion as to the possible nature (as opposed to cause) of death and to assist and supervise the removal of the body from the scene where necessary. Detailed contemporaneous notes (including diagrams) of any findings in relation to the deceased and the scene should be made. The Scene of Suspicious Death/Death in Custody proforma produced on behalf of the Education and Research Committee of the AFP recommends that a note be made of significant features of the scene, including such factors as the presence of medication, drug paraphernalia, alcohol, and bloodstains.

22.9   QUALIFICATIONS OF FORENSIC PHYSICIANS

In the UK, most forensic physicians are active general practitioners in the National Health Service (NHS). They will provide their services to the police on a rota basis and will be on duty for a number of hours to several days depending on the geographical area and nature of the workload. The specific post-graduate qualification for clinical forensic medicine offered by the Worshipful Society of Apothecaries is the Diploma in Medical Jurisprudence (DMJ). The examination is taken in two parts. The Primary Examination (Part I) is related to branches of medico-legal practice and does not carry a diploma. The Final Examination (Part II) is taken after three years' experience in clinical forensic medicine. The examination may be taken in either or both of two disciplines: DMJ (Clin) and DMJ (Path). Training for the diploma is offered in house by a number of police forces and by specific course providers, e.g. DMJ Study Club based at New Scotland Yard or Forensic Healthcare Ltd (a firm of course providers). A further qualification of Master of Medical Jurisprudence (MMJ) has recently been introduced by the Worshipful Society of Apothecaries. Most forensic physicians are members of the Association of Forensic Physicians (AFP) (formerly the APS which changed its name in 2003; any pre-2003 references to guidelines issued by the Association refer to the former name) which provides a social and academic forum for its members and represents their professional interests nationally (for further information see **www.afpweb.org.uk**).

Guidelines and advice in relation to clinical and forensic procedures issued by the APS to its members are available online via **www.afpweb.org.uk** by clicking on the 'Publications' section on the homepage (any guidelines or advice issued by the APS referred to in this chapter can be consulted on this website).

REFERENCES

BMA and APS (1998) *Revised Interim Guidelines on Confidentiality for Police Surgeons in England, Wales and Northern Ireland.*

BMA and APS (2002) *Taking Blood Specimens from Incapacitated Drivers.*

Education and Research Committee of the APS (2001) *Consent in Relation to Complainants of Sexual Assaults.*

ECLM (1999) *Syllabus of Postgraduate Specialisation in Legal Medicine.*

The Forensic Science Service, The Association of Police Surgeons and The Association of Chief Police Officers (2000) *Guidelines for the Collection of Specimens.*

Howitt, Dr J. & Stark, Dr M. (1999) *The Role of the Independent Forensic Physician* (revised September 1999 on behalf of the Education and Research Sub-Committee of The Association of Police Surgeons).

McLay, W.D.S. (1996) *Clinical Forensic Medicine,* Greenwich Medical Media, pp. 104, 118–19.

Roberts, R. 'Children' in McLay, W.D.S. (1996) *Clinical Forensic Medicine,* pp. 118–19.

Robinson, S.P. 'Care of Detainees' in McLay, W.D.S. (1996) *Clinical Forensic Medicine,* p. 104.

Royal College of Paediatrics and Child Health and the APS (2001) *Guidance on Forensic Examination in Relation to Possible Child Sexual Abuse.*

Royal College of Physicians (2001) *Substance Misuse Detainees in Police Custody.*

www.afpweb.org.uk (homepage of the website of The Association of Forensic Physicians).

CHAPTER 23

Forensic odontologists

23.1 BACKGROUND

Forensic odontology is a branch of forensic medicine and relates to the proper examination, handling, and presentation of dental evidence in court.

23.2 THE ROLE OF THE FORENSIC ODONTOLOGIST

An odontologist is qualified to offer an opinion on the following:

- identification of unknown human remains by dental examination;
- age estimation of living and deceased subjects (including neonatal remains);
- analysis of bite marks discovered on living and deceased victims;
- analysis of bite marks in other substances (e.g. foodstuffs);
- analysis of weapon marks using principles analogous to those of bite mark analysis (bite and weapon mark evidence is now often presented to the jury using a computer and projector which projects the marks of interest onto an eight-foot screen). Odontologists may also be able to give an opinion on the likely weapon used and the angle of the blow in cases involving facial injuries (e.g. fractured jaws).

23.3 IDENTIFICATION OF UNKNOWN HUMAN REMAINS

Most of the population will have received dental treatment and dental records should have been kept by the dental surgeon who carried out the treatment. Ante mortem dental records can play an important role in the identification of a deceased person whose identity is otherwise unknown. Due to the resistant nature of dental tissue, dental identification may be the only means of identifying decomposed or skeletonised remains and the victims of violent crimes, fires, explosions, drownings, and other accidents or disasters (including mass disasters) that may cause disfigurement making identification by fingerprints and visual identification either impossible or undesirable.

In most cases the forensic odontologist will first view a body after it has been transferred to the mortuary. On rare occasions, however, it may be beneficial for the odontologist to attend the crime scene, e.g. to advise on searching for missing dental fragments in cases of disarticulated remains.

Dental identification takes two main forms:

(i) the most frequently performed examination is a comparative identification that is used to establish (to a high degree of certainty) that the remains of a deceased person and a person represented by ante mortem dental records are the same individual;

(ii) in cases where ante mortem records are not available, and no clues to the possible identity exist, a post mortem dental profile is completed by the forensic odontologist suggesting characteristics of the individual likely to narrow the search for any ante mortem materials that may be available. Ante mortem records for comparison will then be assembled from persons on missing persons lists who share the same sex and age as the deceased. Any comparison should be systematic and value judgments should be made where the post mortem and ante mortem records are not an exact match.

When considering whether or not a positive match can be made, the following possibilities should be considered:

- inaccuracies or mistakes in the compilation of the ante mortem dental records/post mortem dental profiles;
- the possibility that the deceased may have had further dental treatment after the available ante mortem records were compiled.

In cases where conventional dental identifications cannot be made, it may be possible to compare DNA material from the teeth of an unknown individual with known ante mortem samples, where available, from a particular individual.

23.4   MAKING A POSITIVE IDENTIFICATION

In identification cases, the odontologist should produce a full report containing the following information:

- the dental and (where possible) oral status of the deceased;
- the dental and oral status of the ante mortem records;
- details of any similarities and dissimilarities between the ante and post mortem records;

- explanations for any dissimilarities or discrepancies between the two and whether these explanations are satisfactory for the purposes of making an identification;
- an opinion as to whether or not a positive identification can be made in the circumstances.

23.5 DETERMINATION OF AGE AT DEATH

The determination of the age of the deceased at death will simplify the identification procedure. A number of accepted techniques exist for estimating the age at death from the dentition. The age of neonatal remains can also be estimated because the teeth start to develop six weeks after conception. If the teeth of an individual are in the development stage (i.e. the period from foetal life until about the age of 23), it may be possible to determine age within a range of a few months to a couple of years. Whereas if the teeth are fully developed it may be possible to estimate the age at death (usually by reference to changes in the dentition) to within a period of seven years either way.

It may also be possible to determine the sex of an individual from dentition alone. While the accuracy of available techniques for so determining decrease after six months post mortem, DNA technology is being developed in this area.

23.6 BITE MARK ANALYSIS

While there is no database about the individuality (uniqueness) of the dentition during biting, in situations where sufficient detail is available, it may be possible to identify the biter to the exclusion of all others or to exclude suspects who did not leave the bite mark.

Bite marks are commonly found on the skin of victims in certain types of criminal cases, e.g. in cases of child abuse (non-accidental injuries) and in a variety of offences against the person, such as sexual and violent offences. Victims may also leave defensive bite marks on their attackers and may possibly make bite marks on themselves. For instance, there have been cases in which victims have bitten their own arms as a result of their attackers having forced the arm towards the mouth to prevent screaming (in such cases the orientation of the bite mark may be of relevance and can be a decisive factor in cases where, for instance, there are conflicting accounts in relation to the infliction of a mark). Bite marks may also be left by assailants in foodstuffs and other substances at scenes of crime.

Any circular or semicircular mark with indentations or discrete tooth-sized bruises should be considered as a possible bite mark. First, a forensic odontologist must be able to show that the mark is a bite and, if so, whether it is human or animal. If the mark is not a bite, the odontologist should give an opinion, where possible, as to what could have made the mark. Some other marks can mirror bite marks, such as those made by bicycle chains, fingernail scratches, fingernails pressed into the skin, parts of toys, saw-teeth marks, and shoe heels.

A bite mark is a crushing injury produced by pressure from teeth and other mouth parts and may include cutting from incisal edges of teeth and scrapes from the dragging of the teeth over soft tissue. An area of petechial haemorrhage may be seen in the central portion of the bitten area indicating that sucking took place. This is commonly referred to as a 'love bite' and occurs in sexual attacks, consensual situations, and in child abuse. Only human bites will contain suck marks.

The bite mark is made once the teeth have gripped the skin and held it in place while the bite is inflicted. With tooth and weapon marks, even where extreme force is exerted, the patterned bruise can be a precise match to the pattern of the weapon or teeth.

23.6.1 Evidence collection techniques

In cases of suspected bite marks, it is important that the mark is photo-graphically recorded (with a scale and in accordance with detailed technical procedures – one experienced forensic odontologist, Dr David Lewin, recom-mends that all injuries should be photographed in colour, in black and white with a green filter, and using ultraviolet (UV) photography) and that other biological evidence (e.g. blood and saliva) is collected promptly due to the rapid degeneration of this evidence and in order to minimise the potential for contamination.

Swabs should be taken from:

(i)   the bite mark area;
(ii) a control area adjacent to the bite mark; and
(iii) the victim's saliva (or a sample of the victim's saliva should be collected in a sterile container if the victim is still alive) for comparison with the sample from the bite mark.

The biological evidence will be subjected to DNA analysis. It is important that the victim's DNA profile is obtained in order to enable analysis of any mixtures found in the sample from the bite site that may involve contributions from both the depositor and the victim.

Bite marks on both live and deceased victims change over time (as the bruise comes out) and it is therefore good practice to re-examine the bite mark for up to five days because the bite may become clearer and can be re-photographed. For the purpose of examining bite marks, it is important to have live or dead victims warm as marks often fade if the victim cools down. Bite marks without bruising may have occurred at the time of death or after.

It is very rare to attempt to date bite marks by reference to bruising because susceptibility to bruising varies between people and is also dependent on the age, state of health, etc.

UV photography is now used in every bite or weapon mark case because it enhances skin detail. It can also reveal 'healed' injuries. The recommended method is used, in practice, between three and 12 months after the injury was inflicted. However, a result cannot be relied upon and, in the experience of one forensic odontologist, rarely reveals anything of interest.

An impression of the bite mark (using a dental impression material such as vinyl polysiloxane) may be made in order to reproduce the indentation and curvatures of the mark for comparison purposes (although this is rarely done).

23.6.2 Comparisons of known and questioned bite marks

In cases where there is a suspect, dental impressions should be taken. As the taking of dental impressions constitutes an intimate sample for the purposes of the Police and Criminal Evidence Act 1984 (PACE), authorisation from an appropriate officer and the suspect's written consent should first be obtained.

For comparison purposes, models of the suspect's dental impressions will be cast in dental stone. These should be signed and dated by the odontologist and the suspect's name should be written on the base of the casts in order to maintain the chain of custody.

The criteria used for comparing bite marks should not be confused with the 'points of correspondence' used for comparing fingerprints. One method of interpreting a bite mark is to build up a dental picture, from the injury mark of the perpetrator's teeth, before comparing the bite mark with a suspect's dentition. Another method of interpreting bite marks is to relate each part of the mark to a particular tooth or teeth of any possible suspect. Professor David Whittaker indicates that this is 'the ideal way to interpret bite marks since then a dental description of a possible assailant can be produced without bias and before a suspect is produced' (see Whittaker, D.K. 'Principles of Forensic Dentistry 2: Non-Accidental Injury, Bite Marks and Archaeology' *Dental Update*, November 1990: 386–90).

When comparing bite marks, note will be taken of any unusual features, including gaps due to missing teeth, lacerations due to sharp teeth or restorations, excessively small or excessively large arch widths, short teeth, displaced teeth, and malpositioned teeth. In some cases local malocclusions may be so severe that it is unlikely that the mark could be produced by anyone other than the suspect.

It should be noted, however, that bite marks rarely show the edges of every tooth and, in the case of a weapon, it is rare to see the whole of the pattern of the weapon. Often a partial mark is all that is left. Sometimes the upper teeth leave marks but there is no sign of lower tooth marks or vice versa.

Alternatively, the bite may be made with more force with one side of the mouth than the other. Therefore the tooth marks, say on the right side, may be more severe than those made by the left side teeth. Alternatively, the left side teeth may leave no marks at all (or vice versa).

Similarly marks made with weapons rarely show the whole of the pattern of the weapon – think of the rubber stamp 'paid with thanks' which, if not applied carefully, means that some of the lettering will not be stamped on the paper.

Specialist computer programs and digital imaging techniques pioneered and developed by Dr David Lewin are now also available for analysing bite marks.

23.6.3 Interpretative issues

When interpreting a bite mark, consideration should be given to the following issues:

- when a bite is in a position where the 'victim' could have made the mark it is necessary to exclude the possibility of self-biting. In cases involving children, the possibility that the mark has been made by a sibling or friend should also be excluded;
- the possibility that the bite mark was inflicted by a person other than the assailant (DNA profiling of saliva recovered from the site of the bite mark may also be relevant to this issue);
- whether the bite is of non-human origin. Dog bites are a common source of injury in both adults and children. Rodent bites may be found on the skin of deceased victims or in bones in cases of skeletonised remains. There have also been cases of infants and small children who have sustained extensive facial injuries as a result of being bitten repeatedly by rodents.

Forensic odontologists may also be able to give an opinion about the type and severity of a bite. For instance, by reference to teeth marks on the skin and the level of bruising or laceration, it can be ascertained that a bite was produced quickly. Bites of this kind will generally be considered to be of a particularly aggressive nature. Conversely, it may also be possible to ascertain that a bite mark represents a consensual bite by reference to the nature and type of bruising inflicted. This is of particular importance as such bites may, in certain circumstances, be designated as non-criminal.

23.7 BITE MARKS IN FOODSTUFFS AND OTHER MATERIALS

At a scene of crime, the investigative team should always consider the possibility that an assailant has left bite marks in foodstuffs (chocolate, cheese and apples are particularly receptive) or other materials (leather items and wooden items (e.g. pencils)), and cannabis resin (pieces are often bitten off for weighing prior to sale and the tooth marks in cannabis resin may often be as good as dental impressions) are examples of receptive materials. The act of biting into an item may also result in a deposit of saliva being left on the item from which a DNA profile may be obtained. As with bite marks in flesh, bite marks in other materials should be photographed with a scale in accordance with technical procedures to permit later examination.

These marks will be interpreted in the same way as bite marks in flesh.

It is usual to take impressions of the food or other item/surface in question and to make a stone model. A stone model of the perpetrator's teeth can then be placed in the marks in the model of the bitten item to show a physical fit (like a key in a lock).

23.8 QUALIFICATIONS OF FORENSIC ODONTOLOGISTS

Usually, forensic odontologists will have a background in general dental practice. Since 1984 there have been recognised postgraduate courses in odontology. Dentists who have completed these courses will have the letters 'Dip F Od' or 'DFO' after their names. These qualifications are likely to be replaced in future by the Diploma in Forensic Dentistry offered by the Royal Society of Apothecaries. This qualification is denoted by the letters DMJ (Odont).

There is now also a one-year taught MSc course in forensic odontology at the Biological Science Unit (Forensic Dentistry), University of Wales College of Medicine Dental School, Cardiff.

A current list of odontologists willing to undertake casework is maintained on the website of the British Association for Forensic Odontology (**www.bafo.org.uk**).

The Council for the Registration of Forensic Practitioners (CRFP) has also opened its register to forensic odontologists.

REFERENCES

Aboshi, H., Taylor, J., Takei, T. & Brown, K. (1994) 'Comparison of bite marks in foodstuffs by computer imaging: a case report', *J Forensic Odont* 12(2): 41–4.

Bowers, C. & Bell, G. (eds.) (1995) *Manual of Forensic Odontology*, Forensic Press.

Bowers, C. & Johansen, R. (2000) *Digital Analysis of Bitemark Evidence*, Forensic Imaging Institute.

Clark, D. 'Forensic Odontology' in McLay, W.D.S. (1996) *Clinical Forensic Medicine*, Greenwich Medical Media, pp. 287–395.

Clark, D. (ed.) (1992) *Practical Forensic Odontology*, Butterworth Heinemann.

Clement, J. & Ranson, D. (eds.) (1998) *Craniofacial Identification in Forensic Medicine*, Arnold.

International Journal of Forensic Dentistry (periodic publication) (ISSN 03069491).

Stimson, P. & Mertz, C. (eds.) (1997) *Forensic Dentistry*, CRC Press.

Whittaker, D.K. & MacDonald, D.G. (1989) *A Colour Atlas of Forensic Dentistry*, Mosby.

Whittaker, D.K. (1990) 'Principles of Forensic Dentistry 1: Identification Procedures', *Dental Update*, October, 17 (9); 315–321.

Whittaker, D.K. (1990) 'Principles of Forensic Dentistry 2: Non-Accidental Injury, Bite Marks and Archaeology', *Dental Update*, November, 386–390.

CHAPTER 24

Forensic pathologists

24.1 THE ROLE OF THE FORENSIC PATHOLOGIST AT THE SCENE

A pathologist will be called to a scene to examine a corpse found under obscure, suspicious, or criminal circumstances. In England and Wales, Home Office pathologists are 'on call' to attend scenes and this duty may be included in their contracts of employment.

At the scene a pathologist will make observations of the following factors which may be taken into account when determining cause of death:

- the environment of the scene;
- local circumstances;
- position of the body;
- condition of the body.

In some cases, the circumstances will be such that it may be possible to make an initial assessment as to whether there is an innocent explanation for the death (e.g. accident, suicide, or natural causes).

All necessary precautions should be taken by a pathologist, and indeed all other personnel present at the crime scene, to preserve the body and its immediate environment. The following initial steps should be taken:

1. The police should seal and cordon off the area around the body and thereafter limit access to that area.
2. All those visiting the scene should wear disposable protective clothing and overshoes in order to avoid accidental transfer of contact traces onto either the body or scene.
3. The body should be photographed in its original position.
4. The body should be approached only by a single pathway agreed with the officer in charge (OIC) or senior investiating officer (SIO).

The initial examination of the body will involve:

1. In appropriate cases, making an estimation of the post mortem interval by assessing (i) temperature by touching the hands and face, (ii) degree of rigor mortis by testing the limbs.

The taking of rectal temperature should be delayed until there has been collection of trace evidence, particularly in cases of a sexual nature. If temperature is to be assessed in this manner, care should be taken to avoid the introduction of any foreign material into the body. The nostril is a possible alterative site to take the temperature. Other sites, such as the mouth, will not give an accurate reading because of the level of exposure to air temperatures.

2. Examination of the eyes, neck, hands and, if necessary, throat or upper chest (moving clothing as little as possible).

3. Close-up photographs of any injuries, etc.

4. Scenes of crime officers (SOCOs) may wish to collect any contact traces from the body when it remains in its original position at the crime scene. Thereafter the body may be moved to check the sides and underneath. Further trace evidence will be collected. Consideration should also be given as to whether death occurred at the scene or whether the dead body was moved from elsewhere (e.g. evidence of such moving may include drag marks).

24.2 COLLECTION OF CONTACT TRACE EVIDENCE FROM THE SCENE

It is good practice to recover contact trace material (CTM) from the body at the scene because there is a risk that this material will be contaminated by the process of removal and transit to the mortuary.

The following order of examination for trace evidence has been suggested:

- visible traces (e.g. hairs, fibres) should be removed by hand using tweezers;
- tape lifts should be taken from the skin and surface of clothing. The body surface should be taped in a serial fashion in order to maintain information about the distribution of trace evidence. For instance, the distribution of fibres on the body may provide assistance in relation to reconstructing the crime;
- stains on skin surfaces should be examined for any embedded traces, such as fibres, prior to swabbing;
- any visible contact traces should be removed from head and pubic hair using tweezers, the hair should then be combed for further trace evidence;
- fingernails should be scraped or clipped;
- the mouth, genital, and nasal cavities should be inspected for trace evidence. In cases where a sexual offence is associated with the homicide, samples for DNA testing should be collected from the vagina, rectum, and mouth. Fluid samples should be collected either by pipette, or multiple swabs should be taken. Any swabs or fluid samples should be frozen if there is likely to be more that a few hours' delay before transit to the laboratory.

See Faye Springer 'Collection of Fibre Evidence from Crime Scenes' in James Robertson and Michael Grieve (1999).

24.2.1 Collection of trace evidence from decomposing bodies

Significant trace evidence may also be present on decomposing bodies.

Fibres and other trace evidence should be collected from the clothing of decomposing or buried bodies by scraping. The scrapings should be placed in Petri dishes for later laboratory examination by stereo microscopy.

Bodies that have become bloated should be processed for trace materials at the scene. This is because the body will become oily once placed in a body bag and the collection of trace evidence will be rendered extremely difficult.

Further specialist procedures will be applied in certain cases, e.g. deaths by shooting, drowning, or burning. Specialist advice will be sought.

The *Manual of Standard Operating Procedures for Scientific Support Personnel at Major Incident Scenes* of the Association of Chief Police Officers (ACPO) Crime Committee recommends that the following procedures are followed by SOCOs at the scene:

1. Photographing of the body in situ, including close-up photographs, of hands, feet, and face.
2. Notes to be made of:
   (i)   any visible marks or wounds on the body (e.g. scratches; drag, bite and ligature marks; gunshot wounds, etc.),
   (ii) blood distribution (droplets, smears and drainage),
   (iii) contaminants on body (grease, soil, vegetation, etc.),
   (iv) watches (a particular note of the time and the position of any other jewellery should be noted),
   (v)   tattoos (for identification purposes).

The following procedures should be carried out by a pathologist on the body:

- recovery of any loose items;
- swabbing of external surfaces (e.g. nipples, bite marks, gunshot wounds, etc.);
- tapings of exposed skin, areas of ligatures and binding, and recovery of loose items;
- bagging of head, hands, and feet;
- taking of body temperature;
- measuring of ambient temperature (recording at half-hourly intervals and attempting, if indoors, to keep doors and windows in original positions).

Consideration will also be given to the following:

- the removal of clothing if at risk from bleeding/bodily fluids during movement;
- taking control tapings and swabs from inside of body bag for control purposes;
- undertakers/removal;
- continuity of body;
- photographing area under body.

See the *Manual of Standard Operating Procedures for Scientific Support Personnel at Major Incident Scenes*, Pre-PM Scene Examination, s 3A.10.

24.3 THE AUTOPSY EXAMINATION

While the police may request the attendance of a forensic pathologist at a crime scene, the right to order an autopsy remains the sole prerogative of the coroner.

An autopsy has a number of objectives including:

- positive identification the body;
- assessment of size, physique, and nourishment;
- determination of mode of dying;
- determination of time of death, where possible;
- detection of any abnormalities or diseases;
- the obtaining of samples for microbiological, histological, and toxicological analysis;
- retention, where necessary, of any organs or tissues as evidence (e.g. retention of the brain (head injuries); neck organs (strangulations), and excising of wounds (firearms injuries);
- production of a written report of the autopsy findings to give an interpretation thereof.

In homicide cases where a suspect has been arrested, the defence solicitor may request that a second autopsy be performed by a pathologist instructed for the defence. A coroner may also request a second autopsy in cases where no suspect has been apprehended in order to obtain an independent opinion (although the value of the findings of a second autopsy is inevitably diminished as a result of the examinations and procedures carried out on the body during the first autopsy).

The coroner will only instruct the release of the body for burial once satisfied that all necessary examinations and tests have been carried out.

24.4   IDENTIFICATION OF THE BODY

There should be verbal confirmation of the identity of the body before the autopsy examination takes place.

The body should have been appropriately labelled upon arrival at the mortuary and the pathologist should be satisfied of the identity by making a comparison of the documents authorising the autopsy with the toe label or bracelet.

If the identity of a body is unknown an attempt will be made to establish identity by reference to the following characteristics:

- face;
- eyes;
- pigment;
- hair;
- tattoos;
- finger and palm prints;
- scars;
- stature;
- sex;
- age;
- race;
- DNA testing (the best material for this type of testing is the spleen);
- dental records, if available.

Identification of skeletal remains may also be possible.

24.5   EXTERNAL EXAMINATION

A careful evaluation of the external body surface is particularly important in criminal cases, particularly in cases involving trauma. In addition to standard procedures (such as identification, measurement of body length, weight (measurement or estimation), state of cleanliness, skin colour, congenital deformities, and acquired external marks), the following procedures are of particular importance:

(i)   checking of hands – for old/new injuries; defence wounds; bruised knuckles, or electric marks;

(ii)   presence of discharge – such as vomit, froth or blood in mouth or nostrils; vaginal discharge or bleeding; leakage of cerebrospinal fluid;

(iii)   assessment of degree of rigor mortis;

(iv)   examination and precise measurement (related to various anatomical points) of recent injuries – traumatic lesions should be differentiated into the following categories: (a) abrasions, (b) bruises, (c) lacerations, (d) incised wounds, (e) burns, etc. If the wound is a stab or firearm wound it is also useful to note the likely height of the wound above the ground – as this may become relevant if the stature of the victim/ assailant becomes an issue. In cases of head injuries, if the head is to be shaved, this should be carried out by the pathologist in order to avoid any artefactual cuts later being misinterpreted as part of the original wound;

(v) examination of the eyes – particularly to detect petechial haemorrhages on the outside of the eyelids, conjunctiva and sclera which will require explanation (and may, in some cases, be indicative of asphyxia);

(vi) examination of the mouth for foreign bodies, drugs, dried powders on lips, or corrosion of the mouth (which may be indicative of recent poisoning), damaged teeth, injured gums, and lips (especially rupture of the frenum in babies and children which can be indicative of child abuse);

(vii) examination of the genitals and anus. In sexual assault cases, observation for fresh mucosal tears should be made and swabs should be taken. Post mortem flaccidity of the sphincter may result in the anus opening considerably (this may occur in both children and adults). This factor alone, without further evidence, cannot be taken to be indicative that sexual assault has occurred.

24.6 INTERNAL EXAMINATION

The body is usually dissected by incision in a straight line from the laryngeal prominence to pubis (avoiding the umbilicus) to facilitate the internal examination.

24.7 COLLECTION OF BODY FLUID SAMPLES

In all cases with criminal connotations, samples of blood and other bodily fluids and tissues will be obtained for laboratory examination. The site from where the samples are taken will vary depending on the nature of the test that is to be carried out. The taking of blood samples from any sites which are likely to be contaminated by post mortem diffusion of the stomach and intestines should be avoided as this can give a false reading of the ante mortem blood level. For further information on taking bodily fluid and tissue samples from post mortem subjects see **Chapter 14**.

24.8 ANCILLARY INVESTIGATIONS

These investigations will vary depending on the nature of the death, but may include one or more of the following.

24.8.1 Microbiology

Occasionally in a forensic autopsy, culture samples for bacteriology, virology, and fungi will be needed. The advice of a microbiologist should be sought and cultures must be performed soon after death because contamination can occur as a result of organisms travelling through dead tissue.

24.8.2 Toxicology

In cases involving alcohol, drugs, or hazardous substances, samples of bodily fluids and tissue should be collected in appropriate, chemically clean containers in order to ensure the accuracy of the toxicological analysis.

The FSS Safescene Unit manufacture an autopsy specimen kit for this purpose. The kit contains:

- two 1 litre jars;
- two screw-cap universal containers;
- one large screw-cap container;
- three sterile syringes;
- three sterile needles;
- two large polythene bags;
- one 'return labels' envelope;
- six sticky labels;
- two glass septum vials;
- two small plastic security containers;
- two large plastic security containers;
- six cotton wool balls.

These items are contained within a watertight plastic tube to ensure sterility.

Samples/specimens submitted for toxicological analysis will be accompanied by a form which will indicate the type of analyses required, personal details of the deceased, a brief history of the case, and details of any suspected drugs/toxic substances (e.g. it may be noted that the subject was a known drug addict), and a statement in relation to whether the subject was known to be suffering from any infective condition.

24.8.3 Histology

Tests will be carried out on a range of tissues (e.g. liver, spleen, kidney, heart, lung, thyroid, adrenal, pancreas, muscle, and brain) in order to exclude the possibility of natural disease.

The *Manual of Standard Operating Procedures for Scientific Support Personnel at Major Incident Scenes* recommends the following checklist of good practice at the autopsy examination (see 'The Post Mortem Examination', s. 3A.13):

- retention of body bag and any bagging removed from head, hands and feet;
- photographing of body – in entirety, clothed and unclothed; close up of face (portrait/profile) and hands, and injuries, marks, distinguishing features, and tattoos;
- examination of injuries – Photographing with scale and taking precise measurements of injuries – making notes of nature and location;
- clothing – Photograph, note any damage or staining; search; consider submitting for examination for human and other contact traces;
- body identification – Recording any identifiable features including scars/tattoos, pathological abnormalities, clothing, jewellery (including any unique design, engraving, serial numbers/repair numbers);
- taking of autopsy samples:

  1. fingernail cuttings, all hair samples (including combings), orifice swabs, injury site swabs, extraneous material (vegetation, soil, grease, etc.);
  2. diatoms;
  3. toxicology (e.g. blood, urine);
  4. x-ray of corpse – particularly in cases of suspected child abuse (many paediatric pathologists will undertake a full skeletal survey and request radiology in all cases where a child did not die of an obvious disease) or gunshot wounds (in order to confirm the presence of bullet fragments which may not be visible to the naked eye);

- re-examination of the body:

  1. noting the developments of bruising, bitemarks, foot marks;
  2. consideration to be given to the use of ultraviolet (UV) and standard photography (certain injuries (including old bruising injuries) not visible to the naked eye can be revealed under UV light and the presence of certain contact traces, e.g. semen and saliva, can be detected).

24.9   KEEPING RECORDS AT THE SCENE AND AT THE AUTOPSY – PARTICULAR CONSIDERATIONS

Contemporaneous notes should be kept from the scene onwards in relation to the maintenance of the chain of custody, including what steps were taken to ensure that the body/contact trace evidence was not contaminated, who accompanied the body to the mortuary, etc.

At the scene, particular note should be made of the positioning of the body in relation to any surrounding objects; observations in relation to any identifying features, injuries, etc.

Photographs will also be taken and diagrams and body charts completed.

At the autopsy, a note should be made for evidential purposes of the time, date, and particulars of the person identifying the body.

Any negative findings should be specifically noted as these may be of significance.

Diagrams and body charts should also be used in relation to the noting of the positioning of recent injuries. All contemporaneous notes, diagrams, etc. should be retained and will be disclosable.

24.9.1   Special considerations in relation to the chain of custody of clothing

Pathologists should make a permanent request that bodies from road traffic accidents or other cases where trauma is suspected as a provisional cause of death be brought to the mortuary without clothing being removed.

Any blankets in which the body was wrapped whilst at hospital should also be retained.

In trauma deaths, the injuries on the body should be matched up with any damage to clothing. Tears, slashes, stab wounds, and especially firearms wounds, in clothes must be compared with the position of external lesions on the body making allowance for movement and displacement during life.

24.10   PHOTOGRAPHY AT THE SCENE, AND AT THE AUTOPSY

A pathologist may take his or her own photographs at the scene and at the autopsy, otherwise police or medical photographers may be used.

The ACPO Crime Committee *Manual of Standard Operating Procedures for Scientific Support Personnel at Major Incident Scenes* recommends that the following photographs be taken at the crime scene and at the autopsy.

1. At the crime scene, photographs should be taken of the body *in situ*.

2. Close-up photographs, as the particular circumstances of the case dictate, should be taken of the following:

   - hands, feet, and face;
   - tattoos (for identification purposes);
   - any visible marks or wounds on body, for instance scratches, drag, bite and ligature marks, gunshot wounds, etc.;
   - blood distribution (droplets, smears and drainage).

   In cases of violent assaults (such as stabbing), the pattern of blood spatter can provide an indication of the position of the assailant in relation to the victim at the time of the assault and, particularly if a weapon was used, the number of blows that were inflicted.

3. At the autopsy photographs should be taken of the following:

   (i)   the body in its entirety, both clothed and unclothed;
   (ii) close-up photographs of the following should be taken:

   - face (portrait/profile);
   - hands;
   - injuries, including marks, distinguishing features, and tattoos;
   - clothing should be photographed with a scale and measurements should be taken of all clothing.

24.11   THE AUTOPSY REPORT

During the autopsy, the pathologist will keep written notes, sketches, and body diagrams (which will be disclosable). The notes will form an aide memoire for the pathologist when compiling an autopsy report. The report provides a permanent record of the autopsy findings.

Professor Bernard Knight recommends that the history of the case should be taken into consideration when compiling the report. He notes:

> Some pathologists have in the past advocated that the autopsy should be performed 'blind', so that the history does not prejudice the opinion of the pathologist. This is patently impracticable, for every autopsy would then have to be totally comprehensive, including such techniques as the removal of the spinal cord in every case, and all possible ancillary investigations, such as toxicology, microbiology, virology, radiology, diatoms, histology and so on, as there would be no means of knowing what was necessary and what was irrelevant. Apart from the intolerable burden of work, the expense of such an approach would be prohibitive if applied to all autopsies.

(See Bernard Knight (1991) p. 9.)

Knight is also of the opinion that the report should be compiled as soon as possible after the autopsy. In criminal cases, in addition to time of death and cause of death, the report should discuss other relevant matters such as the possible type of weapon used, ranges (in gunshot wound cases), likely rapidity of death, and possible alternatives where the cause of death is obscure (see Bernard Knight (1991) pp. 31–3).

24.11.1 Finding of formal cause of death

Care should be taken not to confuse the mode of death (the abnormal physical state that existed at the time of death, e.g. cardiac arrest, pulmonary oedema) with the cause of death (the pathological condition).

A formal cause of death, in the format recommended by the World Heath Organisation (WHO), suitable for the completion of a death certificate, should be a bland statement, e.g. 'gunshot wound to the head' or 'knife wound to chest'.

The WHO format sometimes causes problems in cases where the cause of death is not clear cut or in cases of 'obscure autopsies'. Examples include sudden infant death syndrome (SIDS) or the sudden death of an asthma sufferer where the autopsy reveals no morphological cause for the death (for example, see *R. v. Clark* [2000] All ER (D) 1219 and [2003] All ER (D) 223 (Apr)). In such cases the pathologist should give the most likely reasoned cause of death.

24.11.2 Finding of time of death

The limitations on the accuracy of a precise finding of the time of death should be mentioned in the pathologist's report, particularly where it is of relevance in the given case (e.g. where a suspect is putting forward an alibi for a period of time).

The following post-mortem changes are of relevance to time of death:

RIGOR MORTIS

A spot check for the time of death by consideration of rigor mortis is as follows:

- if the body feels warm and is flaccid, it has been dead for less than three hours;
- if the body feels warm and is stiff, it has been dead from three to eight hours;
- if the body feels cold and is stiff, it has been dead from eight to 36 hours;
- if the body feels cold and is flaccid, it has been dead for more than 36 hours.

These timings provide a guide for use in average temperature conditions. The timing of rigor mortis will vary depending on the temperature and allowance should be made for this consideration if the body is found in either particularly hot or particularly cold conditions.

HYPOSTASIS AND THE DISTRIBUTION OF HYPOSTASIS

DECOMPOSITION

ABNORMAL SKIN COLOURATION

POST MORTEM SKIN COOLING

The human body will cool after death except where the ambient temperature remains at or above 37 degrees Celsius. The rate of post mortem cooling is not uniform and will vary depending on a number of factors, including:

- initial body temperature – this should not be assumed to be 37 degrees Celsius. Temperatures alter between different sites on the body, from person to person, and from time to time. Illness or trauma may result in a further variation;
- body dimensions – subcutaneous and abdominal fat will have insulating properties and will affect the body's cooling curve;
- posture – cooling will vary depending on the amount of body surface exposed to the air;
- clothing and coverings – these provide external insulation and will slow the cooling process. Heat can also be contributed to a body in this way, e.g. by an electric blanket (this can retard cooling and increase decomposition);
- ambient temperature – this is the major factor in cooling. Allowances should be made not only for climatic and seasonal changes, but also for local conditions which can distort the cooling process, e.g. heat from fires, electric blankets, warm water, and cold water;
- air movement and humidity – any air movement has a cooling effect. Damp air conducts heat more readily than dry;
- medium around the body – death in cold water (particularly if the water is moving) exacerbates the cooling process. Death in warm water reduces the cooling rate. If the water is very warm it may elevate the body's temperature. In such cases it is not possible to estimate the time of death with any accuracy;
- haemorrhage – it is sometimes thought that severe blood loss shortly before death will cause more rapid cooling. There is, however, little support for this opinion.

OTHER MEASURES OF TIME SINCE DEATH ARE:

- stomach emptying;
- alcohol back calculation.

These topics are controversial because a number of factors may frustrate the use of gastric emptying and alcohol absorption as measures of the post mortem interval.

POST MORTEM DAMAGE BY PREDATORS

This will vary depending on where the body was found. Depending on geographical considerations, bodies may be attacked and scattered over wide areas by large predators, such as dogs or foxes, or have flesh removed by rats or cats.

POST MORTEM PREDATORY DAMAGE CAN BE MISTAKEN FOR SUSPICIOUS INJURY

Predatory post mortem injuries can usually be distinguished from ante mortem or suspicious injuries by an absence of bleeding, shape and situation of the injury, and the presence of teeth marks around the areas of removed flesh.

ENTOMOLOGY

This is a specialist subject which can be of crucial importance to time of death because the maturation of certain colonising insects can be measured within certain cycles and this method can be used when other indicators have ceased to function. The process is subject to a number of variables and as such is an inexact science. The insect lifespan will also be affected by a number of geographical and climatic considerations (for instance members of the blowfly family will rarely fly in winter and will only lay eggs during daylight hours).

If there is evidence that the corpse has been colonised by sarcophagous insects, a pathologist is advised to enlist the aid of a consultant entomologist for an opinion and also for guidance in relation to the recovery of entomological evidence.

The most common insect to colonise fresh corpses is the blowfly group, which includes bluebottles, greenbottles, and the housefly. The egg-laying pattern and reaction of these flies to climatic conditions can provide information relevant to the time of death.

The *Manual of Standard Operating Procedures for Scientific Support Personnel at Major Incident Scenes* recommends the following procedure at the scene for the collection of entomological evidence (see 'Protocol for Collecting Entomological Evidence', Section 3, Appendix A (Part II)).

Direct observation

Care should be taken when approaching the corpse so as to ensure that any insects present are not disturbed. A note should be made of the appearance, colour, and location of the insects.

All batches of fly eggs and/or larvae should be noted (with approximate numbers) along with the presence of other insects, such as moths or beetles. Photographs, including close-ups, should be taken.

Collection of data and specimens for future use and identification

The ambient temperature of the scene should be measured at half-hourly intervals during the investigation. Temperature should be taken at different positions over the body surface, in all areas where maggots (fly larvae) have accumulated within the body, and (where applicable) the soil surface, and five to eight cm below the soil surface. The humidity and level of exposure to sunlight should also be recorded.

The blow fly cycle is as follows:

- eggs,
- larvae,
- pupae,
- adult.

Some of these specimens collected from the scene should be kept alive if possible. Adults should be caught in a net and placed in collecting tubes (no more than one or two adults should be stored in each tube). Eggs, larvae and pupae should also be stored in collecting tubes. Further specimens will be collected from the body. These specimens will be killed and preserved in ethyl alcohol. Further live insects will be collected from a radius of between three to four metres around the body, from the soil under the body, and from the body at the post mortem examination. Any live specimens should be examined by an entomologist within two days of collection.

For further information on entomology see: Byrd, Jason J. and Castner, James L. (1998); Erzinclioglu, Zakaria (2000); Goff, Madison L. (2000).

24.12   SUGGESTED CONTENTS OF AUTOPSY REPORT

Bernard Knight suggests that the following information should be included in all autopsy reports:

1. Full personal details of the deceased subject, unless unidentified (including name, sex, age, occupation, and address).
2. The place, date, and time of the autopsy.
3. The name, qualifications, and status of the pathologist.
4. Persons present at the examination.
5. The name/details of the authority commissioning the autopsy.
6. A record of who identified the body.
7. The name and address of the deceased subject's regular (or last) medical attendant.
8. The date and time of death, if known.
9. The history and circumstances of the death (this is useful for the purposes of justifying the finding in relation to cause of death, but may be omitted from the pathologist's statement made for the purposes of criminal proceedings because it offends the rule against hearsay).
10. External examination which should record the following details:

    (a) height, weight, and apparent state of nutrition;
    (b) the presence of natural disease such as oedema, abdominal swelling, cutaneous disease, and senile changes;
    (c) identifying features such as skin colour, tattoos, scars, deformities, dentures, eye colour, and hair colour. When identity is an issue, this section should be much more detailed;
    (d) the presence of rigor, hypostasis, decomposition, and abnormal skin colouration. Body and ambient temperature should be recorded where appropriate, with calculations concerning the estimated range of times since death (in criminal cases this aspect may well be deferred until the final summary and conclusions);
    (e) the condition of eyes, including petechiae, arcus senilis, pupil size, and the condition of iris and lens;
    (f) condition of mouth and lips, including injuries, teeth, and presence of foreign material;
    (g) condition of external genitals and anus;
    (h) listing and description of all external injuries, recent and old.

11. Internal examination which should record all abnormalities in a conventional sequence such as:

    (a) cardiovascular system: heart weight, any dilation, ventricular preponderance, the pericardium, epicardium, endocardium, valves, coronary arteries, myocardium, aorta, other great vessels, and peripheral vessels;

(b) respiratory system: external nares, glottis, larynx, trachea, bronchi, pleural cavities, pleura, lungs (including weight), and pulmonary arteries;

(c) gastrointestinal system: mouth, pharynx, oesophagus, peritoneal cavity, omentum, stomach, duodenum, small and large intestine, liver (weight), pancreas, gallbladder, and rectum;

(d) endocrine system: pituitary, thyroid, thymus, and adrenals;

(e) reticulo-endothelial system: spleen (weight), and lymph nodes;

(f) genitourinary system: kidneys (weight), ureters, bladder, prostate, uterus, ovaries, and testes;

(g) musculoskeletal system: skull, spine, remaining skeleton, and musculature where necessary;

(h) central nervous system: scalp, skull, meninges, cerebral vessels, brain (weight), middle ears, venous sinuses, and spinal cord (when examined).

12. A list of specimens and samples retained for further examination. Those handed to other agencies, such as the FSS laboratory, should be formally identified by means of serial numbers and the name of the person to whom they were handed.

13. The results of further examinations such as histology, microbiology, toxicology, and serology. When the main report is issued soon after the autopsy, these will not yet be available and a supplementary report will be necessary.

14. A summary of the lesions displayed by the autopsy (often coded for departmental computer retrieval).

15. Discussion of the findings, if necessary in the light of the known history.

16. An opinion as to the definite or most likely sequence of events leading to the death.

17. A formal cause of death, in the format recommended by the WHO, suitable for the completion of a death certificate.

18. The signature of the pathologist.

(See Bernard Knight (1991) pp. 31–2.)

24.13 QUALITY ASSURANCE

The pathologist's report and opinions will be subject to peer review and checking. The Court of Appeal considered good practice in relation to the contents of pathologist's reports in *R.* v. *Clark* [2003] All ER (D) 223 (Apr), see especially paragraphs 18–25.

24.14 CONSIDERATION OF PARTICULAR TYPES OF INJURIES

24.14.1 Stab wounds

By examination of the stab wound a pathologist may be able to offer an opinion upon:

- the dimensions of the weapon used;
- the type of weapon;
- the taper of the blade;
- the movement of the knife in the wound;
- the depth of the thrust;
- the direction of the thrust;
- the amount of force used.

24.14.2 Firearms wounds

The nature of the wound will be affected by the following:

- whether the weapon is smooth-bore or rifled;
- if rifled, the muzzle velocity of the weapon;
- the nature of the projectile(s);
- the nature of the propellant;
- the degree of choke, if any;
- the range of discharge;
- the angle of discharge.

A firearms examiner should be consulted. X-rays of the body may also be useful to indicate the path of the bullet.

24.14.3 Defence wounds, non-suicidal self-inflicted wounds and suicidal injuries

DEFENCE WOUNDS

Common in knife attacks or firearms attacks. They are important because they indicate that the victim was conscious and at least partially mobile at the time of attack. Common sites of defence wounds include the outer sides of forearms, backs of hands, wrists, and knuckles.

NON-SUICIDAL SELF-INFLICTED INJURIES

These usually occur in subjects with a history of mental illness. Such injuries have often been found to take the form of multiple, superficial, and parallel cuts.

SUICIDAL INJURIES

Common methods of committing suicide include poisoning, stabbing and cutting, firearms/explosives, jumping from a height, jumping into water, burning, asphyxia, hanging and strangulation, electrocution, and road/ railway injuries.

Telltale signs of suicidal injury include presence of a weapon, non-alignment of clothing damage with injuries, and site/nature of injuries.

OTHER INJURIES

Bodies that have been burnt in fires will often sustain heat fractures of limbs and heat contracture tearing. These fractures can sometimes be mistaken for ante mortem injuries.

24.15 WHEN THE INPUT OF OTHER FORENSIC EXPERTS IS REQUIRED

A pathologist may consult one or more of the following experts for specialist advice as the nature of the case dictates:

- forensic anthropologist;
- forensic archaeologist;
- blood spatter pattern analyst;
- entomologist;
- fingerprint expert;
- firearms examiner;
- microbiologist;
- odontologist;
- road traffic investigator;
- serologist;
- forensic toxicologist.

In addition, some pathologists may specialise in particular types of injuries, e.g. neuropathology (head injuries).

24.16 SPECIAL CONSIDERATIONS IN RELATION TO DECEASED CHILDREN

In cases involving infants and young children, or where child abuse is suspected, a paediatric pathologist may assist during the scene examination and at the autopsy.

For further information see Thomas, W.M. (ed) *Non-Accidental Injuries to Children* (Association of Police Surgeons (APS, see **www.afpweb.org.uk**) and Wilczynski, Ania (1997).

24.17 QUALIFICATIONS OF FORENSIC PATHOLOGISTS

Most forensic pathologists will possess the following specialist qualifications and memberships of professional bodies:

- Fellow of the Royal College of Pathologists;
- DMJ (Path) (Diploma in Medical Jurisprudence (Pathology));
- Plans are in hand for independent accreditation of forensic pathologists and their eventual inclusion in the CRFP Register.

REFERENCES

Association of Chief Police Officers (Crime Committee) (2000) *The Manual of Standard Operating Procedures for Scientific Support Personnel at Major Incident Scenes* (1st edn).

Byrd, J.J. & Castner J.L. (1998) *Forensic Entomology; The Utility of Arthropods in Legal Investigations*, CRC Press.

Dutra, F. (1944) 'Identifications of person and determination of cause of death from skeletal remains', *Archives of Pathology* (38) 399.

Erzinclioglu, Z. (2000) *Maggots, Murder and Men; Memories and Reflections of a Forensic Entomologist*, Thomas Dunne Books.

Gaule, M. (2002) *The Basic Guide to Forensic Awareness*, New Police Bookshop.

Goff, M.L. (2000) *A Fly for the Prosecution: How Insect Evidence Helps Solve Crime*, Harvard University Press.

Knight, B. (1991) *Forensic Pathology,* Arnold, pp. 9, 31–3.

Springer, F. (1999) 'Collection of Fibre Evidence from Crime Scenes' in Robertson, J. & Grieve, M. (eds) *Forensic Examination of Fibres* (2nd edn), Taylor and Francis, pp. 108–9.

Thomas, W.M. (ed) *Non-Accidental Injuries in Children* (APS: see **www.afpweb.org.uk**).

Wilczynski, A. (1997) *Child Homicide*, Greenwich Medical Media.

CHAPTER 25

Forensic psychiatry and forensic psychology

25.1 INTRODUCTION

The purpose of this chapter is to give a brief overview of the role of the forensic psychiatrist and the forensic psychologist in criminal proceedings. In the limited space available it is impossible to do these complex disciplines justice. The reader is alerted to the need to seek specialist advice or look, in the first instance, to the specialist literature referred to in the chapter and listed in the Further Reading section.

25.2 WHAT IS FORENSIC PSYCHIATRY?

Forensic psychiatry is a psychiatric speciality which has evolved its current practice in the UK over the last 35 years. Consultant forensic psychiatrist, Professor Robert Bluglass, notes that the field of operation is the overlap, interface and interaction of psychiatry and the law in all aspects, including criminal behaviour and the diagnosis, care and treatment of psychiatric patients where the disorder is associated with abnormalities of behaviour. Forensic psychiatry continues to be concerned primarily with mentally disordered offenders, but it now encompasses a wide range of offences and gives much more prominence to diagnosis, management, and treatment, in prison, in hospital or the community, using the skills of psychologists, nurses, social workers and probation officers in addition to psychiatrists.

25.3 THE ROLE OF THE FORENSIC PSYCHIATRIST AS AN EXPERT WITNESS

Throughout the 1990s it was estimated that about two per cent of persons appearing before magistrates' courts were remanded for psychiatric reports. In addition, individuals charged with certain crimes (e.g. murder, neglect of children, rape and arson) who are remanded in custody before trial are routinely seen by prison medical officers who will make an assessment of mental condition as part of a screening procedure.

In general terms, the opinion of a forensic psychiatrist should be sought in all cases where the accused appears to be suffering from a mental disorder either at the time of the committal of the offence or at the time of the trial.

In practice, psychiatric assessments (or indeed assessments by two physicians approved under Mental Health Act 1983, s.12 (see **para 22.4.3**) and ultimately two psychiatrists) will be required in the following situations:

1. Where a mental condition defence is being raised (e.g., fitness to plead; automatism, including feigned automatism and amnesia (while the medical use of this term is normally restricted to epilepsy, it is well recognised amongst psychiatrists that a person's normal state of consciousness and awareness may be interfered with by a whole host of other factors); where a plea of diminished responsibility is entered in a murder case; where the defence of insanity is raised (although this is a purely legal and not a psychiatric concept – the most apt medical equivalent for insanity is perhaps 'functional psychoses', which include schizophrenia and the affective disorders such as manic depression).

2. Where a psychiatric disposal (e.g. psychiatric probation order, hospital order, interim hospital order, restriction order, hospital and limitation direction, transfer from prison or guardianship order) is being considered.

In practice, a forensic psychiatrist will first meet an accused or other subject for the purpose of providing an opinion to assist the legal process. The accused should be made aware that the examination is not confidential insofar as the opinion will be disclosed to a third party.

25.4   THE CONTENTS OF THE FORENSIC PSYCHIATRIST'S REPORT

When preparing a report for legal proceedings it is good practice for a psychiatrist to carry out a comprehensive interview on as many occasions as are necessary in order to complete a full assessment. It is also recommended that relevant relatives or friends of the subject should also be interviewed. In addition, the psychiatrist should ensure that all relevant documentation about the subject has been received and is studied (e.g. previous hospital records, criminal record, school reports, probation reports, and similar material). Necessary evaluations and tests should be completed. Current textbooks, published works and other data should be consulted as necessary. The psychiatrist's report should detail the interviewing process, all scientific methods employed, and scientific materials consulted. A second opinion may also be sought at this stage. The psychiatrist should keep detailed notes of his or her work, including a record of the interview with the subject (should this need to be referred to in any pre-trial conferences or in court). Additionally, a psychological assessment may be carried out independently or be incorporated in the report, depending upon the case and local arrangements.

Professor Robert Bluglass has suggested that the forensic psychiatrist's report should contain the following information:

1. Details of assessment.
2. Sources of information.
3. Informants.
4. Offence in subject's words.
5. Personal history.
6. Family history.
7. Past medical and psychiatric history.
8. Mental and physical examination.
9. Tests.
10. Opinion.

(See Robert Bluglass 'The Psychiatrist as an Expert Witness' and Paul Bowden 'The Written Report and Sentences' in Bluglass, Robert and Paul Bowden (1990).)

25.5 QUALIFICATIONS OF FORENSIC PSYCHIATRISTS

Forensic psychiatry is a specialised field of medical practice (the professional body is the Royal College of Psychiatrists). There are currently about 150 forensic psychiatrists practising in the UK. A forensic psychiatrist is not eligible to apply to become a consultant forensic psychiatrist until after the completion of three years' specialist work with a consultant forensic psychiatrist.

25.6 WHAT IS FORENSIC PSYCHOLOGY?

Psychology is the science of human behaviour and experience. In the words of chartered forensic psychologist, Dr Eric Shepherd, these are an interplay of *cognitive factors* (attention, perception, comprehension, memory, language, reasoning) and *non-cognitive factors* (emotion, disposition, motivation). For all practical intents and purposes, forensic psychology is coming to be seen as an applied area of psychology which relates to crime, the criminal justice system, and the judicial process.

25.7 THE ROLE OF THE FORENSIC PSYCHOLOGIST AS AN EXPERT WITNESS

Dr Eric Shepherd notes that lawyers should not limit themselves to requesting a psychological report on their client or, in cases involving children or young persons, on the interview behaviour of the complainant or the 'specialist' interviewer (e.g. a police officer). He is of the view that lawyers should have a basic understanding of psychological issues and be able to identify potential factors so that an appropriate expert can be instructed. The range of factors which he identifies include:

1. Vulnerabilities in an individual's psychological make up, e.g. personality traits, particularly disposition to suggestibility, compliance, acquiescence, extreme levels of anxiety, low self esteem; psychological disorders (diagnosed, or potentially diagnosable, clinical conditions) e.g. psychotic and neurotic states and illnesses, personality disorders, acute stress disorder and post traumatic stress disorder; intellectual disadvantage and limitations in social functioning; specific learning difficulties and communications deficits, e.g. illiteracy.

2. Specific psychological stresses in the light of identified vulnerabilities, including being in detention and the conduct and effects of interviewing by police officers and others (particularly inappropriate conversational and listening behaviour; constraining, suggestive and 'shaping' questions; inappropriate questioning behaviour, i.e. how the questions are posed); mismatch between any advanced or specialist training received by the interviewer and the interviewee's performance; the psychological influence of inappropriate, pressurising and partial behaviours by appropriate adults, interpreters, and legal advisers.

3. The status of assertions made in witness conversations and statements, relative to what is known about: the psychological capabilities, limitations and vulnerabilities, particularly in terms of fallibility of memory and disclosure of people in general; individuals at a particular stage of development, under the influence of drugs (e.g. sleeping tablets, antidepressants, tranquillisers, steroids, and 'recreational' drugs), with a particular mental disorder, in a particular state of consciousness, or with a particular physical condition (e.g. epilepsy); the specific capabilities, limitations and vulnerabilities of the individual in question; the distortion and contamination of witness testimony that occurs through exposure to post-event information, particularly during the processes of investigation or counselling and treatment; points at which distortion and contamination actually or potentially occurred in respect of a particular individual.

4. Additional factors bearing upon the status of assertions made by suspects: the risk of partially or completely false admissions; the likely nature of the confession – voluntary, coerced, compliant, or internalised; potentially precipitating psychological factors.

See Ede, R. and Shepherd, E. (2000).

25.8 THE CONTENTS OF THE FORENSIC PSYCHOLOGIST'S REPORT

Consultant forensic psychologist, Dr Gusli H. Gudjonsson, points out that any psychological report prepared for criminal proceedings should contain a brief description of any psychometric tests that have been carried out upon the subject (detailed notes should be kept of any such procedures and all tests should be properly administered, scored, and interpreted). The results of any such tests should be corroborated by other sources (e.g. parallel tests, previous reports, school performance, other informants). When preparing a court report, the psychologist should have access to all relevant documents (e.g. previous reports) and be properly instructed as to the purpose of the psychological report. The salient legal issues should be made known to the psychologist. While most legal representatives will be interested only in the main conclusions, the body of the report should contain the basic data used to substantiate the conclusions.

(See Gusli H. Gudjonsson 'The psychologist as an expert witness' in Bluglass, Robert and Bowden, Paul (1990).

25.9 QUALIFICATIONS OF FORENSIC PSYCHOLOGISTS

Forensic psychologists should have Charter status conferred by the Division of Forensic Psychology of the British Psychological Society (BPS). Three minimum requirements must be completed:

(i) the candidate must obtain graduate basis for registration (GBR);
(ii) the candidate must complete an accredited master's course in forensic psychology;
(iii) the candidate must undergo two years' supervised experience.

(See Crighton, D., Cudby, T. and Horn, R. 'Joining the Division' *Forensic Update* 57, pp. 7–10.)

There are currently eight forensic psychology postgraduate courses in the UK which are accredited by the BPS (at the following universities: University of Liverpool, University of Surrey, Glasgow Caledonian University, Manchester Metropolitan University, University of Leicester, University of Kent at Canterbury, University of Birmingham, and University of Leicester). Applicants for places on such courses will be required to hold an undergraduate degree in psychology which entitles the candidate to the GBR with the BPS.

For further information see **www.bps.org.uk/sub-syst/dfp/index.cfm** (homepage of the BPS, Division of Forensic Psychology).

REFERENCES

Baird, J. & Evans, J. 'Psychiatric Disorder' in McLay, W.D.S. (ed.) (1997) *Clinical Forensic Medicine*, Greenwich Medical Media, pp. 181–92.

Bluglass, R. & Bowden, P. (eds) (1990) *The Principles and Practice of Forensic Psychiatry*, Chapman and Hall, pp. 161–6, 167–9, 183–97.

Crighton, D., Cudby, T. & Horn, R. 'Joining the division', *Forensic Update* 57, pp. 7–10.

Ede, R. & Shepherd, E. (2000) 'Psychological Factors' in *Active Defence* Law Society Publishing, pp. 457–9.

MacKay, R., Colman, A. & Thornton QC, P. 'The Admissibility of Expert Psychological and Psychiatric Testimony' in Heaton-Armstrong, A., Shepherd, E. & Wolchover, D. (1999) *Analysing Witness Testimony: A Guide for Legal Practitioners and Other Professionals*, Blackstone Press, pp. 321–34.

MacKay, R. 'Mentally Abnormal Offenders' in McConville, M. & Wilson, G. (eds) (2002) *The Handbook of the Criminal Justice Process*, Oxford University Press, pp. 447–1.

CHAPTER 26

Forensic linguistics

26.1 BACKGROUND

Linguistics is an academic discipline concerned with the analysis of language and speech. It embraces, in its broadest sense, a number of sub-disciplines, including phonetics (the specialised study of speech and voice patterns), and handwriting analysis (traditionally concerned with the deciphering of text illegible to the layman). This chapter briefly considers the role of:

(i) general forensic linguists; and
(ii) forensic phoneticians in the context of criminal proceedings.

This subject is highly specialised and complex. For those seeking further information, a comprehensive online bibliography of sources of material on forensic linguistics, compiled by the Department of English at the University of Birmingham, is available on the website of the International Association of Forensic Linguistics. See 'bibliography' on the homepage of the website: **www.iafl.org**

In addition, a periodical journal is available: *Forensic Linguistics: The International Journal of Speech, Language and the Law* (edited by Professor Malcolm Coulthard and Dr Peter French, published by University of Birmingham Press, ISSN: 1350–1771). The journal can be consulted online at: **www.builder.bham.ac.uk/forensiclinguistics/title.asp**.

26.2 THE ROLE OF THE GENERAL FORENSIC LINGUIST

General forensic linguistics is primarily concerned with, but not confined to, the determination of the authorship of written texts through the use of lexico-grammatical and semantic methodologies.

Examples of texts encountered in criminal proceedings that a forensic linguist can advise on include threatening letters, ransom demands, hate mail and, in recent times, mobile telephone text messages.

26.2.1 Attributing authorship to disputed texts

In order to assess whether a particular suspect is the author of a given text, the disputed text will be compared with a known sample of text produced by this suspect.

The rationale underlying this type of textual analysis is that individuals will adopt their own personalised set of rules in relation to the language construction that they use. This particular construction can, in turn, act as a kind of 'linguistic fingerprint' by which the individual can be identified from their use of language.

Examples of individual characteristics which are used to attribute a text to a particular individual include:

(i)   layout conventions;
(ii) non-standard punctuation;
(iii) unusual non-standard spellings;
(iv) repetition of certain favoured words or expressions.

While each of these characteristics may be unremarkable when considered in isolation, a number of such characteristics present in the same text can provide persuasive evidence of authorship.

Professor Malcolm Coulthard illustrates the evidential significance of the use of particular words, which at first appeared to be insignificant in themselves, with reference to the case of the 'Unabomber' in the USA. He notes that linguists instructed on behalf of the prosecution linked the well-known 30,000 word 'Unabomber Manifesto' with a 15-year-old, 300 word, document recovered from the defendant Kaczynski's premises. The two documents shared the following set of items – *'at any rate; clearly; gotten; more or less; presumably; thereabouts; in practice; moreover; on the other hand; propaganda*; and the word roots – *argue* and *propose'*. It was suggested that these items proved common authorship. In response to defence arguments that the choice of such unremarkable words and phrases could not in any way be diagnostic of common authorship, the linguists searched the internet for all documents which contained those words and phrases. While over three million documents contained one or more of those words and phrases, only 69 documents contained all of them and all 69 of those documents turned out to be a version of the 'Unabomber' manifesto. In other words, whereas anyone can use any word at any time, co-selection of words is individual.

26.2.2 Practical difficulties in establishing authorship of disputed text

The 'Unabomber' case is unusual in that the questioned and known texts were both of some considerable length. Most disputed texts, by their very nature, tend to be short and there may not be any known text compiled by the suspect available for comparison. It follows that a linguist will often not have sufficient data available in a given case from which to make any meaningful comparison. However, it should be appreciated that the availability of only a small amount of data will not necessarily preclude the identification of the author. Evidence of authorship is strengthened if the disputed text and the known text share a high number of non-standard features. Occasionally, such features may be apparent even in short texts.

26.2.3 The contextual meaning of words and phrases

In certain cases linguists may be able to assist with the meaning of words and phrases in a particular context (e.g. on whether the use of certain words equates to a threat) or with perceived communication problems (e.g. in cases of non-native speakers). It should be noted, however, that judges will generally rule expert evidence inadmissible insofar as it relates to the defining of the meaning of words and phrases because this is something which traditionally has been considered to be a question of fact within the common knowledge of the jurors (or the notion 'why do we need a language expert? We have 12 jurors who all speak English. Let them decide.').

In the appeal of Derek Bentley (Bentley was convicted of murder in 1952 and hanged), his conviction, on a reference by the Criminal Cases Review Commission (CCRC), was overturned by the Court of Appeal on the ground of material misdirections in the summing up, see *R.* v. *Bentley* [2001] 1 Cr App R 21. The court received linguistic evidence as fresh evidence on the ground that it would not have been available at the time of the trial. The court accepted that there was evidence (based on narrative analysis and research into the textual use of negatives) to support Bentley's claim that his interview had not been recorded accurately and that it was, at least in part, the product of a question and answer exchange converted into a monologue.

The reason for referring to the case at this point, however, is because it provides a famous example of the use of words and phrases where the meaning of those words amounted (or could have amounted) to a crucial issue in the case. In the event, due to the nature of Bentley's defence, the meaning of the disputed words was not fully explored either at trial or on the subsequent reference by the CCRC. The note of the case below is included by way of example to illustrate how the meaning of words and phrases may become a crucial issue in a particular case.

Bentley and his co-accused, Chris Craig, were jointly charged with the murder of a policeman who had been shot by Craig. The prosecution, in order to prove its case against Bentley, set out to establish that Bentley and Craig had, in the course of warehouse-breaking, agreed to use such violence as necessary in order to avoid arrest. Three police officers gave evidence that they had heard Bentley shout 'Let him have it, Chris'. It was part of Bentley's case that he had not known that Craig had had a gun until it had been fired and he (and also Craig) denied that the words attributed to him had ever been used.

The same expression 'let him have it' had been used by two professional criminals who were found guilty of the murder of a policeman in a case in 1940 (*R.* v. *Appleby* (1940) 28 Cr App R 1) and it was also a popular phrase (meaning 'kill him' or 'shoot him') used in contemporary gangster movies. It was suggested at the trial that it was a remarkable coincidence that Bentley should have used those exact words. The meaning of the words was, on the face of it, also clearly contentious (for instance, by saying 'let him have *it*' Bentley could have meant 'let him have [the gun]' meaning that he wanted Craig to hand over the gun to the policeman). In his closing speech, defence counsel referred to the possibility that the disputed words may have been open to interpretations other than the one suggested by the prosecution. Counsel did not suggest any alternative interpretation, perhaps because of Bentley's complete denial that the words had been used.

In relation to that issue the judge, in summing up, directed the jury to consider whether Bentley had shouted the disputed words and, if he had, what did he intend by the words used. It can be assumed that the jury accepted the prosecution interpretation.

The Court of Appeal accepted the police officers' version of events insofar as they related to the fact that the words had been said and no further consideration was given to the meaning of the words. The interpretation of the words used by Bentley have, however, been a source of debate over the years. This leaves open the question as to whether the true meaning of words, in certain circumstances, is necessarily something upon which the jury require no expert guidance.

The reluctance of courts to admit evidence on this general issue accepted, individual cases may arise where expert opinion can be of assistance to a jury, particularly if the issue of interpretation is a particularly complex one (for instance, if the speaker is in some way disadvantaged, e.g. by being a non-native speaker, or is vulnerable in other ways, like Derek Bentley) and it relates to a crucial issue in the case. Consideration should therefore be given to the potential significance of linguistic evidence in this context where the circumstances of the case so dictate.

An article which makes reference to the reluctance of American courts to admit linguistic evidence on so called 'ultimate issues' of what a speaker meant, puts the case for a limited role for discourse analysis in the legal system as follows:

> Linguistic experts can . . . point out a pattern of discourse markers that would have otherwise gone unnoticed, or inform jurors about the nature of Gricean implicature in appropriate cases. Once the jurors are aware of this information, they will be on the same footing as the expert (more or less), and able to draw their

own inferences based on their intuitions as enhanced by linguistic analysis that the expert has presented.

(See Tiersma, Peter and Solan, Lawrence M.)

As in the *Bentley* case, linguistic evidence has been employed in a number of well known cases involving disputed interview records and records of confessions. While most of these cases pre-date the Police and Criminal Evidence Act 1984 (PACE) when police interviews and confessions of suspects were not routinely tape-recorded, a number of cases raising these issues continue to come before the Court of Appeal upon referrals by the CCRC (see for example, *R* v. *Hakala* [2002] All ER (D) 277 (Mar)).

Linguists may make use of electrostatic detection apparatus (ESDA) in cases involving disputed interview and police records. For instance, ESDA evidence has been used to demonstrate non-contemporaneous alterations to police interview notes (see *R.* v. *McIlkenny* [1992] 2 All ER 417, the 'Birmingham Six' case and Davies, T. (1994)). For further information on ESDA evidence see **Chapter 20**.

26.3 THE ROLE OF THE FORENSIC PHONETICIAN

In the context of criminal proceedings, forensic phoneticians are primarily concerned with issues in relation to identification of suspects through voice recognition. They can also give an opinion on the following:

1. Disputed transcriptions of audio tapes and the integrity of tapes (such as whether a tape has been interfered with either physically or instrumentally, whether it is an original or a copy, and the type of machine that the tape was originally recorded on).
2. Speaker profiling (the use of phonetic, sociolinguistic and dialect data in determining the background, e.g. regional and social, of unknown speakers in recordings).

26.3.1 Voice recognition

In order to attribute an unknown voice to a particular individual, the unknown (or disguised) voice will be compared with tape recorded samples of known voices.

This work is not carried out by ear, but rather with the aid of sophisticated computer programs which can offer, amongst other things, real time analysis and accurate visual comparison of spectrographical prints through a split screen presentation.

The availability of sophisticated technology notwithstanding, recent research has highlighted a number of issues of difficulty arising with regard to the identification of tape recorded voices. Where the voice at issue has been recorded over the telephone line (e.g. obscene telephone calls, bomb threats or death threats) it has been demonstrated that the telephone can have a significant effect on the pitch contours of certain vowels. This may cast doubt on the veracity of some voice matching criteria.

26.3.2 Disputed transcriptions of audio tapes

In cases involving disputed transcriptions of tape recorded evidence (e.g. clandestine police recordings or recordings of police interviews) a forensic phonetician can be called upon to give an opinion on the accuracy of the transcription.

Mistranscriptions may occur as a result of interference or background noise which make the voice or voice(s) on a tape difficult to decipher. The success of the transcription process itself is also dependent on the ability of the transcriber to decipher and record the tape contents accurately.

In cases where the tape recording is unclear and the transcript raises issues of concern, e.g. it contains potentially incriminating utterances, an auditory and acoustic analysis of the voice(s) on the tape may resolve what may turn out to be an issue of vital importance in the case.

Professor Malcolm Coulthard gives the following example of a mistranscription made by a transcriber in a drugs cases – the transcriber heard 'but if it's as you say it's *hallucinogenic*, it's in the Sigma catalogue'; whereas what was actually said was 'but if it's as you say it's *German*, it's in the Sigma catalogue'.

26.3.3 Voice line-ups

The police have developed a system of 'voice line-ups' based on the identification parade model. These line-ups usually take the form of the lay witness being asked to listen to a tape recording consisting of a series of randomly sequenced voices speaking the same words or phrases as uttered by the perpetrator of the particular crime.

Such line-ups are riddled with problems due to the number of variables that can potentially adversely affect the fairness of such parades. For example research has demonstrated that factors such as accent, deliberate disguise, or a voice speaking in a foreign language can frustrate a voice line-up. Where there is an issue as to the fairness of a voice line-up, a phonetician may be able to offer a considered opinion.

In relation to the organisation of speaker identification parades and voice line-ups generally: see *R. v. Hersey* [1998] Crim LR 281; Laubstein, Ann Stuart (1997); and Schlichting, Frank and Sullivan, Kirk P.H. (1997).

26.4 QUALIFICATIONS OF FORENSIC LINGUISTS

Undergraduate and postgraduate courses are available in forensic linguistics. Generally forensic linguists who undertake consultancy work for the purposes of criminal proceedings should be practising members of the International Association of Forensic Linguistics. The Association criterion for admission is the possession of a postgraduate qualification in linguistics (there are also other grades of membership for those who do not want to practise as forensic linguists). The International Association of Phoneticians also operates strict criteria for membership and maintains a rigorous code of practice. Information in relation to those practising in both disciplines is available on the website of the International Association of Forensic Linguistics: **www.iafl.org**.

REFERENCES

Davies, T. (1994) 'ESDA and the analysis of contested contemporaneous notes of police interviews', *Forensic Linguistics*.

Gibbons, J. (2003) *Forensic Linguistics: An introduction to language in the justice system*, Blackwell.

Laubstein, A. (1997) 'Problems of voice line-ups', *Forensic Linguistics* 4.2, 262–79.

Rose, P. (2002) *Forensic Speaker Identification*, Taylor and Francis.

Schlichting, F. & Kirk P.H. Sullivan (1997) 'The imitated voice – A problem for voice line-ups?', *Forensic Linguistics* 4.1, 148–66.

Tiersma, P. & Solan, L. 'The Linguist on the Witness Stand: Forensic Linguistics in American Courts', *Language* 78:2, pp. 221ff.

CHAPTER 27

Veterinary science

27.1 INTRODUCTION

Forensic veterinary science, sometimes termed 'forensic veterinary medicine' or 'comparative forensic medicine' is, per se, a relatively young discipline that has attracted increasing attention and importance in recent years.

Human forensic medicine is a well-recognised and highly developed speciality, and for many decades, members of the medical profession in Britain and elsewhere, have been able to undertake training, obtain postgraduate recognition and find full-time employment in this field. There have been no such developments in veterinary medicine: in most Anglophone countries there is no recognised path to specialisation in forensic veterinary medicine, and those veterinarians who become involved are usually self-taught or, in a few cases, have attained a qualification based on training for human medicine. The continued absence of such a speciality is surprising, bearing in mind that members of the veterinary profession have traditionally appeared and often played a key role as expert witnesses in court cases concerning animals. As legislation relating to animal welfare, conservation and allied subjects increases, and as society becomes more litigious, the demand for veterinary specialists is likely to grow (see M.E. Cooper (1987)).

Relatively little has been published on forensic veterinary medicine, although some texts furnish information relevant to the provision of evidence in legal cases regarding domestic livestock and many medical books offer valuable assistance in certain fields. Surprisingly, forensic work concerning animals attracts relatively little attention in human medical texts, except for those cases in which animals cause injury or death. Even then, incorrect terminology is often used and rarely are scientific names of animals given.

Since 1982 the role that could be played by appropriately motivated and experienced veterinarians in legal cases involving wild birds has been recognised (see P. Robinson (1982); J.E. Cooper and M.E. Cooper (1986); J.E. Cooper and M.E. Cooper (1997); J.E. Cooper and M.E. Cooper (1991)). In the USA, the establishment of a wildlife forensic laboratory resulted in the provision of a service to wildlife law enforcement bodies and others. In Canada, Wobeser (1996) discussed the forensic post-mortem examination of wildlife and provided guidance on techniques and reporting. Other relevant data are scattered widely in the literature but the appearance of a special issue of *Seminars in Avian and Exotic Pet Medicine* (Cooper and Cooper (1998)), provided an opportunity to bring together much of the available information about veterinary forensics in one volume.

When taken in its broadest sense of activities linking animals with the law, forensic veterinary medicine encompasses two distinct situations. The first of these is when the animal is the victim (i.e. the object) of an assault or similar incident. Injuries and assaults can be inflicted on animals either maliciously or accidentally and include attacks, perversions, and mutilations. Death, injury, ill health, pain, or distress may result. There are often parallels with human forensic work: a 'battered pet' syndrome has been described, and its recognition is leading to closer collaboration between veterinarians, paediatricians, social workers and the police (see H.M.C. Munro (1996)).

The other situation is when the animal causes the incident. Injuries from animals include bites from both wild and domestic species, stings, trauma, electrocution, and hypersensitivity reactions. Wild and domestic animals may mutilate human bodies after death. This second area, when animals cause the incident is, arguably, an area of forensic veterinary (rather than human) medicine because any ensuing legal case will probably require expert evidence from a veterinarian.

27.2 SPECIAL FEATURES OF FORENSIC VETERINARY MEDICINE

Forensic veterinary work differs in many ways from routine diagnosis and treatment. The word 'forensic' is derived from the Latin 'forensis', meaning 'public', a pertinent reminder that forensic work is subject to open debate; the person providing evidence is likely to be open to interrogation, criticism, and attempts to discredit. Forensic veterinary medicine, therefore, needs a special approach and not all practitioners are comfortable with this.

The public nature of forensic work, especially if a court appearance is required, means that any veterinarian likely to be involved must be fully aware of the background and implications. Some important considerations are outlined below.

27.3 ROLE OF THE VETERINARIAN

Any veterinarian may become involved in a legal case in various ways. He or she may be a 'witness of fact' on account of, for example, observing an offence. Alternatively, the veterinarian may be a 'professional witness': for instance, because he or she examined as part of his or her work an animal that subsequently became the subject of litigation because it failed to recover from anaesthetic. The third situation is when expert opinion is required, for example, concerning the death of an animal in another practice or a wildlife poisoning incident; the veterinarian in this case is an 'expert witness' and is expected to provide specialist, objective, knowledge and opinion. A fourth possibility, which can on occasion be linked with serving as an expert witness, arises when a veterinarian is asked to be an adviser to an individual or organisation that is prosecuting or defending a case in court.

Practitioners may fall into any of the above categories but increasingly veterinary staff of universities or research institutes (some of them specialists in their own field), or suitably qualified private consultants, are involved in forensic cases.

27.4   FIELDS OF FORENSIC INVESTIGATION

As is in other fields, veterinary forensic work can encompass anything relating to the law and the approach needed may even be relevant to other matters such as insurance of animals or allegations of (veterinary) malpractice. However, the following areas are the ones in which a member of the veterinary profession is most likely to become involved as an expert witness:

1. Determination of the cause, time, and circumstances of death of an animal.
2. Verification of the origin (provenance) and history of live or dead animals and/or their derivatives. Many of these cases fall into the category of possible 'wildlife crime', and the legal case may rest on whether or not there has been a breach of national or international conservation legislation. There has been an increased involvement in this field by the veterinary profession, particularly regarding international legislation such as the Convention on International Trade in Endangered Species of Wild Fauna and Flora (CITES).
3. Assessment of welfare (pain, discomfort, or distress) and provision of an opinion as to whether an animal may be 'suffering' or have 'suffered' in the past.

Both clinicians and pathologists may be involved in such cases and, as in human forensic medicine, other specialists, including toxicologists, parasitologists and immunologists, play an important role.

27.5   FUTURE DEVELOPMENTS

The next decade is likely to see an exponential increase in legislation relating to animals, including wildlife. This is due to a number of factors, among them the escalating financial value of many animals, the global trade (some of it illegal) in exotic species, greater public concern over conservation and environmental issues, and an increased tendency for owners of animals to resort to litigation (see W.J. Adrian (1992)).

At the same time, there are likely to be more contested insurance claims and a greater tendency to bring disciplinary proceedings against those who appear to provide inadequate or unprofessional services. These developments mean that the veterinarian, especially the practitioner, will need to be better prepared and more knowledgeable on legal matters.

As 'wildlife crime' becomes more widespread, more lucrative, and more linked with other criminal activities, governmental and non-governmental organisations become more willing and able to tackle it. Some such efforts are at a national level, for example, in the UK the government-sponsored Partnership for Action against Wildlife Crime (PAW).

Public concern over conservation and environmental issues also encompasses unease about damage to ecosystems by, for example, chemical pollutants, radioactivity, or pathogens. There is often a demand that the parties responsible for such acts, whether malicious or not, should be brought to task. This in turn means investigations, enquiries, and legal (criminal or civil) action. Because animals are often affected, either as individuals or populations, there is a need for veterinary input.

Animal welfare considerations are very likely to play a major part in the increased involvement of the veterinary profession in legal matters, certainly in Britain. Many countries have animal welfare legislation, and, in the richer parts of the world, litigation to prosecute those who harm animals is becoming increasingly common. If is often very difficult to define 'suffering' and parameters for assessment of welfare, or even stress, are generally far from reliable.

Owners of animals are already becoming more litigious, and this trait is not confined to those who keep dogs, cats, horses, or farm livestock. Collections of exotic birds, mammals, reptiles, fish, or invertebrates, can be worth large sums of money. At the other end of the scale, the loss of one relatively inexpensive animal may prompt a lawsuit against a veterinarian. Such cases can embroil not only the practitioner who dealt with the animal but also other veterinarians called to be expert witnesses or to advise the prosecution or defence. Simultaneously, there is likely to be an increase in insurance claims, challenging professional opinions and certification, and reporting actions and attitudes to disciplinary bodies.

One aspect of greater involvement in legal work that may test the profession is how far the veterinarian should align himself or herself with one side of the dispute. Traditionally, the expert witness has been impartial, with his or her function being to assist the court. However, in recent years, veterinarians, in common with other specialists, have been called on to advise in the preparation of cases (for the prosecution or the defence) and to collect and present evidence. A step further on is the involvement of veterinarians in law enforcement, including crime scene investigation and execution of search warrants ('raids') on premises where animals or their derivatives are kept. In such instances, the veterinarian becomes part of a team and there is the risk of divided loyalties – between that of an impartial professional and that of assisting the team to win its case. Forbes ('Clinical examination of the avian forensic case' in J.E. and M.E. Cooper (1998)) discussed this dilemma and drew attention to the need for the veterinarian to adhere strictly to the law and to retain professional integrity. Veterinary involvement in law enforcement is not, of course, a new development and some of the implications were previously discussed by Davies (1989).

All of this means that the veterinarian of this millennium cannot afford to be complacent. Whether interested in legal cases or not, he or she is likely to become involved. The question that has to be asked is, 'How prepared is the veterinarian?' This is discussed in more detail later.

The disadvantages, sometimes futility, of working alone on only a national level have already prompted extensive cooperation between different countries, and included many of the poorer nations of Africa, Asia and South America as well as the richer 'developed' parts of the world. Many examples concern species and products covered by CITES, for example, rhino horn and ivory (collaboration between Europe, Africa, and Asia) and threatened psittacine birds (USA, Mexico and South America). Whether at a national, regional or international level, such activities will require veterinary input.

27.6 FUTURE NEEDS OF FORENSIC VETERINARY MEDICINE

1. Increasing the awareness of the veterinary profession.
2. Teaching and specialised training.
3. Access to information.
4. Establishment and use of systems and protocols.
5. Research and development of new techniques.

Each of these will be discussed in turn.

27.6.1 Increasing the awareness of the veterinary profession

Few practising veterinarians fully appreciate the need to be prepared for legal cases and the special challenges of such work. Some are remarkably unaware of their own vulnerability, especially when working with valuable animals. Academics and consultants, on the other hand, have recognised the new challenges, and training courses in (for example) forensic veterinary pathology are beginning to be arranged (see below).

27.6.2   Teaching and specialised training

'Teaching' here is defined as part of the education of any qualified veterinarian (Member of the Royal College of Veterinary Surgeons (MRCVS), in the UK) and 'specialised training' as postgraduate study. Although most veterinary students are taught jurisprudence, including a little on the very important subject of appearing in court as a witness, scant attention is usually paid to the role of an expert or adviser. There are moves in the UK to rectify this situation by incorporating into the veterinary course more relevant lectures and practical demonstrations.

At present, specialised postgraduate training in veterinary forensic medicine does not seem to be available, other than short courses and workshops (see above). This is a serious omission and means that most veterinarians rely still on experience rather than training in seeking recognition as specialists.

Wobeser (1996), emphasised that forensic post mortem examination of wildlife should be performed by 'pathologists with formal training and experience', and the same may reasonably be said of other veterinary disciplines that contribute to the legal process.

There is a clear need for veterinarians to be able to undergo postgraduate training and obtain recognition in forensic medicine. In view of the relatively small numbers involved at present, there may be merit in considering the development of courses (programmes) run in collaboration with the medical profession. In the UK, for example, The Royal College of Pathologists (RCPath) has a Specialist Committee on Forensic Pathology that is charged with advising the college on training and standards in forensic pathology. RCPath already includes veterinarians among its members and fellows, and there would appear to be merit in pursuing collaboration as a means of providing veterinary forensic training and specialisation. Moves have also started towards the development of an assessment and registration scheme that would bring specialists in forensic veterinary science within the scope of the CRFP register.

27.6.3   Access to information

Access to information is complementary to teaching and specialised training. However, even before improved teaching and specialised training are available, it is imperative – and possible – to start providing veterinarians with relevant information. Articles have been published on veterinary forensic work but they are generally widely scattered in the literature. Publications which are directed primarily at forensic work involving humans, or specialised publications concerning, for example, DNA (Deoxyribonucleic acid) and forensic genetics, are also valuable. Many medico-legal journals are available in English and other languages, and these can prove helpful, regardless of whether the reader is primarily concerned with *Homo sapiens* or other species of animals. A book on veterinary and comparative forensic medicine has been commissioned by Blackwell Science and is likely to appear in 2004 (Cooper, Cooper and Fegan-Earl, in preparation).

Veterinarians with an interest in the subject find it useful to join some of the many forensic societies and organisations, membership of which often comprises lawyers as well as medical and biomedical scientists. These associations hold meetings that provide contacts, and produce publications and guidelines, some which can be valuable to the veterinarian.

27.6.4 Establishment and use of systems and protocols

One of the hurdles to the development of veterinary forensic science and its acceptance as a speciality is the absence of standard systems and protocols.

There are as yet few tested guidelines as to which samples should be taken from animals destined for legal cases or even how they are best labelled, transported, and stored. Many veterinarians not working regularly in the forensic field are unaware of the importance of maintaining a 'chain of custody' and some do not know of the existence of, for example, 'tamper-evident' boxes for transporting evidence.

The virtual absence of defined and tested systems and protocols needs to be rectified as a matter of urgency. The special issue of *Forensic Veterinary Medicine*, seminars in Avian and Exotic Pet Medicine (edited by Cooper and Cooper (1998)), was intended to encourage the establishment of sound protocols that, in turn, would serve the veterinarian well when dealing with forensic cases. As countless cases show, it is often easier to find a fault with technical work (e.g. procedures, delegated duties, or record keeping) than to challenge an expert's opinion. Forensic veterinary medicine is, however, an evolving discipline and it is important that those who use or develop protocols disseminate relevant information widely. In turn, others should provide feedback so that appropriate changes and improvements can be made.

Coupled with the lack of systems and protocols described above is the need to establish databases. Databases include not only the relevant written literature (records, reports, books, and journals) but also material such as pathological specimens, blood smears, parasites, hides and skins, and electromicrographs of relevant tissues; together, these comprise a valuable resource – a 'reference collection'.

27.6.5 Research and development of new techniques

There has been little research in the field of veterinary forensic science and often extrapolation from human work is necessary, but not always ideal. The situation is slowly changing as more veterinarians become active in forensic work and disseminate, by virtue of papers, lectures, and legal evidence, their findings. A field in which research is needed is that of ballistics (see Munro, H.M.C. (1996) and Stroud in J.E. and M.E. Cooper (1998)). Post mortem change and methods of determining time of death also require proper study and evaluation although some data are available, for example, on birds and rodents. Advances in forensic veterinary medicine will be of more value, and the work facilitated, if done in collaboration with scientists from other disciplines – especially the medical and dental professions where many of the techniques used, especially pathology, are similar to those used in animal work.

27.7 CONCLUSIONS

Forensic veterinary medicine is a rapidly evolving subject. To date, it has been primarily concerned with issues relating to causes of death of animals, welfare, and conservation. New fields of activity are likely to emerge, for example, on account of concern over global pollution and decline in biodiversity and the public's insistence that action should be taken regarding illegal and irresponsible damage to the planet. In all these fields, the veterinarian will need to be prepared to work closely with professionals from other disciplines and to learn from them.

Although forensic veterinary medicine offers exciting challenges, it is as yet not a bona fide discipline within the veterinary curriculum and has not been given recognition as a post graduate specialist subject. This lack of status, coupled with a paucity and scattering of literature and data, often hampers the ability of the veterinarian to contribute skills and knowledge to the judicial process.

It is important that the members of the veterinary profession, even if they are not particularly interested in forensic work, are aware of the potential of litigation and that they orientate their day-to-day activities, especially the examination of suspect or particularly valuable animals, accordingly. Concurrently, increased pressure must be put on professional and regulatory authorities to recognise forensic veterinary medicine as a discipline and to provide adequate funding and support for its development. The police, the judiciary and the legal profession should also be made aware of the contribution that veterinary scientists, many of whom have specialist training in appropriate disciplines, can make to forensic science.

REFERENCES

Adrian, W.J. (1992) *Wildlife Forensic Manual,* Association of Midwest Fish and Game Law Enforcement Officers.
Cooper, M.E. (1987) *An Introduction to Animal Law,* Academic Press.

Cooper, J.E. & Cooper M.E. (1986) 'Is this eagle legal? A veterinary approaches to litigation involving birds' in Chapman M.J. (ed) (1986) Proceedings Forensic Zoology Discussion Group. London, UK, Zootechnology, pp. 27–80.

Cooper, J.E. & Cooper, M.E. (1997) 'Avian forensic work: Guidelines for practitioners', in Proceedings of the European Committee of the Association of Avian Veterinarians, London, England, pp. 75–9.

Cooper, J.E. & Cooper, M.E. (1991) 'Legal cases involving birds: The role of the veterinary surgeon', *Veterinary Record* 129, 505–7.

Cooper, J.E. and Cooper, M.E. (1998) Guest editors. *Forensic Veterinary Medicine.* Seminars in Avian and Exotic Pet Medicine 7 (4).

Cooper, M.E. (1996) *Community responsibility and legal issues*, Seminars in Avian and Exotic Pet Medicine 5:37–45.

Davies, E.B. (1989) 'The veterinary surgeon as a law enforcement officer', *Veterinary Record* 124, 101–102.

Munro, H.M.C. (1996) 'Battered pets', *Veterinary Record* 198, 576.

Munro, R. (1998) 'Forensic necropsy' in Cooper, J.E. & Cooper, M.E. (eds) *Forensic Veterinary Medicine.* Seminars in Avian and Exotic Pet Medicine 7, 4.

Robinson, P. (1982) *Bird Detective*, Elm Tree Books.

Stroud, R.K. (1998) 'Wildlife forensics and the veterinary practitioner' in Cooper, J.E. & Cooper, M.E. (eds) *Forensic Veterinary Medicine.* Seminars in Avian and Exotic Pet Medicine 7, 4.

Wobeser, G. (1996) 'Forensic (medico-legal) necropsy of wildlife', *Journal of Wildlife Diseases* 32, 240–9.

CHAPTER 28

Fire investigators

28.1 INTRODUCTION

A fire investigator essentially determines the nature of a fire, its progress from the area of origin, and the cause of ignition. This determination is made by studying the effect of heat on various materials which have survived the fire. In conducting this study, the investigator will refer to scientific literature for the physical constants of various materials found at the fire scene because the conclusions should be reached using scientific methodology.

28.2 ARSON: UK FIRE STATISTICS

The Home Office Report of the Arson Scoping Study (1999) indicates (see paras. 1.5, 1.7, and 1.9):

1. That there has been a continued long-term increase in the number of deliberate fires attended by the fire service, particularly in metropolitan areas.
2. That the 76,500 deliberate fires recorded by the fire service in England and Wales constituted 44 per cent of all primary fires (meaning those fires involving building and structures and other property, including vehicles).

While there is no national measure of the number of deliberate secondary fires (broadly those involving derelict buildings or vehicles, grassland, gardens, and refuse containers), of the 207,800 secondary fires reported in 1997, around a half are thought to be of malicious ignition.

Some brigades estimate that as many as 80–90 per cent of the secondary fires attended were malicious.

The cost of arson to society has now reached over £1.3 billion a year. In the last 10 years there have been around 1.7 million incidents of arson. Between 1986 and 1996 the number of deliberately started fires increased every year. The latest arson statistics are available online via **www.safety. odpm.gov.uk/rds/stats2000/index.htm**.

28.3 GOVERNMENT INITIATIVES TO COMBAT ARSON

Due to the multi-faceted nature of arson, there are many agencies and organ-isations which come into contact with the arson problem or upon whom it has an impact. The main contributors are the Home Office, the police, the fire service, forensic scientists, insurers, and loss adjusters.

The success of any arson investigation can be dependent upon good com-munication between the various agencies involved. With regard to the inves-tigation of arson, the Home Office Report of the Arson Scoping Study (1999) found (see para. 2.11):

1. that the police were reluctant to devote significant resources for investi-gation purposes because arson is perceived a difficult crime on which to secure conviction;
2. that Home Office support for the Arson Prevention Bureau (established by the Home Office in 1991 to act as a pivotal agency in public efforts to combat arson) has withered in recent years.

28.4 THE RESPONSIBILITIES OF THE FIRE SERVICE AT THE FIRE SCENE

Under the Fire Services Act 1947, the fire service does not have a statutory obligation to investigate the origin and cause of fires. Brigades do, however, have a duty to notify the police in cases of suspicious fires and, in practice and in accordance with Home Office guidelines, will also be involved in the investigation of fires.

Fire officers are often at the scene before police and, in some cases, may be the only emergency service attending. It is the responsibility of the fire service to recognise whether and the point at which, the police should become involved. This is often the crucial first step in any arson investigation.

At the scene, the officer in charge (OIC) (usually a senior fire brigade officer or a first response officer) has sole charge of all operations for the extinction of the fire under the Fire Services Act 1947, s.30(3).

It is the responsibility of the OIC to make the initial assessment of the 'supposed cause' of the fire and to complete an FDR (fire data report) (FDR1 (94)). Any further or revised findings should be recorded in a separate report (FDR2).

The OIC should also make full and accurate contemporaneous notes (in particular the existence of any suspicious phenomena at the scene up until the point when the fire is extinguished should be recorded).

Any fire data report(s) and the contemporaneous notes made should be made available to the police and will be disclosable to the defence.

28.5 RELEVANCE OF THE FINDING OF 'SUPPOSED CAUSE' OF FIRE IN THE FDR (FDR1 (94))

The findings recorded on the FDR1 (94) should not be viewed as binding or in any way conclusive. Bear in mind that the conclusion as to 'supposed cause' of the fire as recorded on FDR1 (94) may have been reached in the absence of any scientific evidence or investigation.

One experienced fire investigator, Dr Roger Berrett, has commented:

> I have no problem with this concept of supposed, or most likely, cause of fire bearing in mind that many accidental fires start in the kitchen and are often 'self apparent'. But when it comes to more complex situations there can be a problem because the fire brigade first response officers (who carry out the vast majority of FDR1 (94) completion) have limited time available to carry out the necessary detailed examination that many fires require, particularly 'single seat' ones. Such fires require a meticulous investigation to be able to establish the cause and, if arson is suspected, eliminate all accidental causes.

The current FDR1 (94) form was originally designed primarily as a fire prevention tool and as a basis upon which to found the Home Office annual fire statistics. It was not designed to fulfil the purposes and requirements of a criminal investigation.

The Home Office Report of the Arson Scoping Study (1999) states (at para. 2.27):

> When the current Fire Report Form (FDR1 (94)) was drawn up, the law concerned with evidence disclosure was different and thus it was not envisaged that the Fire Report would be considered as evidence or that all items referred to in the report form would have to be disclosed. Consequently, the terminology does not follow that used by the police [and the Crown Prosecution Service] and is open to misinterpretation. There is no suggestion that the police move away from using the term 'arson' but better, consistent definitions need to be arrived at between the recording of police statistics and the fire statistics to narrow the discrepancy in the number of deliberate fires recorded by both agencies.

The fire service has tended to record non-accidental fires as being either 'malicious', 'deliberate', or 'doubtful'. For the cause of the fire to be recorded under those terms, deliberate ignition has to be suspected, but not proved, as would be required to record a charge of arson under the Criminal Damage Act 1971.

The use of the term 'malicious' on FDR1 (94) has also been problematic. It has been recommended that the term should not be used because it presupposes that fire officers know the state of mind of an individual at the time of starting a fire.

As a result of difficulties encountered with the terminology used by the fire service in FDR1 (94), the Home Office has issued guidelines on recording the 'most likely cause' and 'defect, act or omission' on the fire report form (FDR1 (94)) in cases where the supposed cause is not accidental (Fire Service Circular No 21/2000; Home Office Circular No 44/2000, Appendix 1).

These guidelines state:

- that the information on the most likely cause(s) of fire recorded on the FDR should be those assessed on the evidence available to the fire brigade at the time;
- that fire officers completing the form should bear in mind that the form and all items referred to in it (e.g. contemporaneous notes) are disclosable and that care should be taken to record only factual data on the form;
- that the terms 'malicious' and 'doubtful' should be avoided and the indication of a percentage likelihood of cause, where a supposed cause is 'deliberate', should no longer be given.

28.6 THE ROLE OF THE POLICE IN FIRE INVESTIGATION

The police service is responsible for the prevention and detection of any crime (arson) and for reporting to the coroner any death that results from a fire. It is the duty of the fire OIC to report, or to have reported, any suspicions to Fire Brigade Control – who will in turn immediately inform the police. Once the police arrive they will assume responsibility for the preservation of the scene. When called in by the fire service, the police should attend the scene to consider whether any crime has been committed.

Assistance from the Criminal Investigation Department (CID) will be normally requested in such circumstances.

Where crime is suspected at a fire scene the first officer attending (FOA) will assume initial responsibility for the investigation.

Where death or serious injury have been caused a senior investigating officer (SIO) is to be appointed. The police are solely responsible for the direction and control of any criminal investigation into the cause of any non-accidental fire. In order to facilitate such investigation, access to the scene of the fire post extinction should be at the discretion and direction of the SIO.

28.7 CALLING IN A SCENES OF CRIME OFFICER (SOCO)

Generally an SIO, having consulted with the fire brigade OIC, will decide whether to call for the assistance of a SOCO. SOCOs should have basic training in fire scene work and should be able to recognise indicators of deliberate ignition (e.g. multiple seats of fire (denoted by areas of severe burning) indicating deliberate fire setting).

A SOCO will generally only request that a fire investigator attend the scene if they are not satisfied with any part of the scene investigation or consider that further support is required.

The Home Office guidelines emphasise the importance of the preservation of the scene and the collection of evidence for subsequent scientific or technical testing.

The IO, in consultation with a SOCO and having taking into consideration any advice offered by the senior fire officer, is required to take any appropriate measures to preserve such evidence as may be needed for investigation by fire investigators.

When a fire scene is not attended by a fire investigator, it is the responsibility of the SOCO to collect and appropriately package any materials requiring forensic examination. However, no evidential material should be removed if the fire scene itself is to be scientifically examined.

The SOCO should also, where possible, photograph the scene in the exact condition that it was found after the fire. A scale plan of the premises should be produced. In investigating fires, the interior and exterior of the building should be photographed and a note should be taken of any points of entry into the building and the security of the building.

See further Tony Cafe 'Photographing the Fire Scene' online via **www.tcforensic.com.au/docs/article1.html**.

28.8 HOME OFFICE GUIDELINES ON THE INVESTIGATION OF FIRES WHERE THE SUPPOSED CAUSE IS NOT ACCIDENTAL

Following the findings of the Report of the Arson Scoping Study (1999), the Home Office issued guidelines (effective from 21 December 2000) on the procedures to be followed in the investigation of suspected non-accidental fires: Fire Circular 21/2000, Home Office Circular 44/2000, Appendix 2; available online via **www.safety.odpm.gov.uk/fire/fepd/fpu.htm**.

The guidelines state that in cases of primary fires, the senior fire officer at the scene and the police investigating officer (IO) should be aware of the potential contribution that forensic scientists can make to a fire investigation. It is the responsibility of the IO, in consultation with scientific support staff, to determine whether the scene should be examined by a SOCO and/or a fire investigator. It should be noted that there are specialist scene examiners who have particular expertise in examining fires (sometimes referred to as 'fire examiners') in addition to laboratory-based forensic fire investigators working at graduate/analytical level.

Ideally, and in order to accord with Home Office guidelines, the IO or SIO, acting in cooperation with the fire service, should arrange for the attendance of a SOCO and/or fire investigator at a scene as soon as possible after extinction of a fire (assuming that the scene is safe).

It is appreciated that sometimes police will not call on SOCO support to attend the fire/crime scene until the next day or several days later. By this time significant forensic evidence may be contaminated or no longer be apparent.

28.9 THE INTERACTION OF THE POLICE AND THE FIRE SERVICE AT THE FIRE SCENE

While some brigades (e.g. London) have arson liaison officers or have regular meetings with police to discuss strategy issues, and a few brigades (e.g. Cleveland, Tyne and Wear/Northumbria, and Mid and West Wales/Dyfed-Powys) work jointly with the police on some or all arson investigations, this is not yet the norm.

The Home Office Report of the Arson Scoping Study (1999) recommended that interaction between the fire service and the police be developed as a matter of urgency. It found:

1. That partnership initiatives between the police, fire service and insurers were few and far between. That there was no formalised structure for inter-agency working and that many agencies are simply duplicating effort and wasting precious resources doing so.
2. That the police and the fire service are often not adequately resourcing what is required to carry out effective fire-related criminal investigations.

In response to Home Office Circular No 44/2000 a memorandum of understanding has been put in place between the Metropolitan Police Service and the London Fire Brigade. It recognises the following principal areas of mutual interest between the fire service and the police:

- all fires involving fatalities;
- all fires involving serious injury;
- all fires where death occurs at a later stage but may be attributed to the fire or there is suspicion that death may result from injuries sustained in a fire and this is confirmed following consultation with a medical practitioner;
- all fires where the cause of the fire is suspected to be non-accidental;
- suspicion of criminal activity at a fire scene;
- statistical evidence and data collection of fire-related crime to enable patterns and trends to be analysed and identified;
- all hoax fire calls.

See London Fire and Emergency Planning Authority (LFEPA)/Metropolitan Police *Fire and Arson Investigation: Memorandum of understanding between the London Fire Brigade and The Metropolitan Police Service* (2000).

28.10   THE INTERACTION OF THE POLICE, FIRE AND SCIENTIFIC SUPPORT SERVICES, AT THE FIRE SCENE

Of the 67 fire brigades in the UK, currently only three in England and Wales have dedicated full time fire investigation teams (with a further team in Scotland). The majority of brigades have to rely on multifunction teams (with a background in fire safety) with fire investigation being a secondary role.

An investigator depends upon the emergency services for initial information about the fire, and it will fall upon those services to preserve the scene. Fire investigation must therefore be considered in the overall context of the respective responsibilities of, and relationships between, the fire service, the police, scientific support services and the forensic scientist/fire investigator.

The fullest possible liaison and flow of information between the police, fire services, and forensic scientists is desirable. A number of barriers to effective day-to-day liaison exist, such as the difference in geographical boundaries and organisational structures of the police and fire service.

Because a fire does not become the responsibility of the police until arson, in the legal sense, is suspected there is sometimes a 'no man's land' between the 'fire investigation' (the responsibility of the fire service) and the 'criminal investigation' (the responsibility of the police). This has obvious repercussions for the integrity of the crime scene.

28.11   ISSUES OF CONTAMINATION OF THE CRIME SCENE

In practice, due to difficulties in the interaction of the police and the fire service and because the investigator will inevitably arrive at the scene after the emergency services have been there, there is potential for contamination of the scene.

The investigation of fires is particularly difficult because of the destructive effect of the fire. Flammable items in the vicinity of the fire will have been destroyed and remote materials and surfaces will have been affected by heat or soot deposits.

Fire fighting techniques may result in damage to the scene.

Evidence from the scene may have been damaged, displaced or removed by fire fighters. Evidence may be lost during the clearing up or salvaging processes and during any unscientific preliminary investigations.

While the Home Office guidelines state that individual brigades should not only have the capability to recognise arson but also to know when and how to take appropriate steps to preserve the scene and maximise the potential for recovering forensic evidence, this can sometimes conflict with the primary duty of the fire service which is to ensure that the fire is extinguished.

Discharge of this duty can inevitably result in the fire/crime scene being destroyed or considerably altered as a result of the fire-fighting activity.

There needs to be a much closer working relationship between the police, fire service, and forensic scientists. Each agency should to be clear about its respective roles.

The merits of establishing joint fire service and police teams more widely should be examined.

Any documented information collated by the fire service and/or the police about the origin, growth and decay of the fire/the general investigation, and any recovered evidence should be made available to the investigator.

28.12   THE ROLE OF THE FIRE INVESTIGATOR AT THE SCENE

An investigator (usually from the Forensic Science Service (FSS)) will be called in by the police generally as a matter of course in cases of fires involving a death or serious injury (regardless of cause) where arson or arson with intent to endanger life is strongly suspected, and large fires.

While the Home Office guidelines state that the police should not hesitate in calling in forensic assistance, there is anecdotal evidence that the introduction of direct charging since the granting of agency status to the FSS in 1988 has had an impact on the number of times that FSS support is called upon in arson cases.

There has been a marked fall in the number of arson cases submitted to the FSS as a percentage of the overall number of arson offences recorded. Most brigades have now established some form of liaison with police and forensic scientists. At the most basic level this is achieved through joint attendance at fire scenes.

Anecdotal evidence from the FSS has suggested that, with the possible exception of cases in which a death has occurred, forensic scientists rarely meet the IO (or SIO) in suspected arson cases. The FSS has also tended to take the view that the police perceive arson as difficult to investigate/labour intensive, and therefore a poor return for resources, unless the incident was extremely serious.

28.13   INVESTIGATION OF FIRES WHERE THE SUPPOSED CAUSE IS NOT ACCIDENTAL

The work undertaken by the investigator will usually comprise the following.

28.13.1   Collection and handling of evidence

Exhibits removed from the scene should be properly labelled, recorded and packaged before being submitted to a laboratory for analysis.

A quantity of debris from the scene should be collected from the suspected point of origin of the fire. In addition samples from items that may have absorbed accelerants or flammable liquids (e.g. carpets, doormats) should be packaged and sent for laboratory testing.

Specimens and debris from a fire scene should be packaged in suitable containers (e.g. nylon bags which will retain hydrocarbon), or in a packaging which will preserve hydrocarbon vapours (e.g. polyester-polyolefin bags). In certain cases glass jars may also be used. Polythene bags are not suitable because they are porous.

The collection of all materials suspected of containing volatile liquids should be accompanied by a thorough sampling of similar but uncontaminated control specimens from another area of the fire scene.

Numerous scientific tests will be carried out on exhibits (e.g. in cases involving the use of petrol bombs any sequential shattered glass should be tested for petrol and fingerprinted – the order of the carrying out of such tests may be an important issue if there is a possibility that evidence may be lost as a result of certain types of tests being employed).

28.13.2 Scene examination

The primary purpose of a scene examination is to determine the origin and cause of fire.

In some cases there may be a delay of days or weeks in order to allow for a scene to be made safe. If the scene cannot be made safe a scene examination to determine the cause of the fire will not be possible.

In cases involving unsafe structures, the opinion of a surveyor will be sought in order to determine whether a scene investigation is possible.

The effect of any delay (due to safety or failure of the emergency services to call in an investigator) on the integrity of the crime scene/exhibits should always be taken into consideration in the investigation.

If possible, an investigator should make a visual observation of the scene paying particular attention to the extent and severity of the fire damage, and making an assessment of any possible location(s) where the fire may have started (seat(s) of fire).

The investigator will look for any physical evidence which indicates suspicious circumstances, e.g. the presence of multiple seats of fire indicative of deliberate ignition.

The presence of an accelerant may also be indicative of deliberate ignition, notwithstanding that no accelerant is found in over 50 per cent of all arson cases. Laboratory testing should be carried out in order to confirm whether an accelerant was present. A small number of fire brigades are now using dogs trained to detect hydrocarbon for the purpose of confirming or detecting the presence of certain accelerants. The use of detection dogs is relatively new and developing.

Having established any areas where the origin of the fire may have been, an investigator will carry out an excavation in order to make an assessment of what may have been the ignition source.

28.13.3 Scene reconstruction

Particularly in the cases of smaller fires, it is sometimes fire-fighting practice (particularly in difficult cases) to remove the entire contents of the premises or to throw certain items out of the building during the latter stages of fighting the fire in order to prevent 'reignition'. Where possible, any removed items (such as charred furniture) should be replaced as this may help to indicate the origin of the fire, what material was initially ignited, and the ignition source. A scene reconstruction may also be necessary in order to properly ascertain burning patterns and thus determine the origin of the fire.

Samples should also be taken from the scene for testing in cases where it is suspected that an accelerant has been used. A defence expert should check any data provided as a result of tests by the prosecution expert (as the scene may no longer be available for inspection by the time any defence expert is instructed).

The investigator will be reliant on information provided by the emergency services in relation to the fire scene pre-extinction.

The investigator will consider the information provided in the FDR1 (94) (including information on when the fire brigade were called, the time of their arrival, what was then observed, and how they fought the fire) and any subsequent fire reports.

Consideration may also be given to:

- any contemporaneous notes made by the fire OIC and any pictures or video recordings taken by the fire brigade;
- information available from eye witnesses/transcripts of interviews;
- whether any witness or suspect statements are consistent with any scientific findings;
- any available images from closed circuit television (CCTV) and digital cameras;
- if a suspect has been detained or any of the suspect's clothing has been recovered, any charring or burning of the clothes should be examined;
- information about any particular practices that may have occurred inside a building that may have caused or contributed to the fire, e.g. storage of flammable materials, electrical equipment, heating appliances, the habits (including smoking, use of candles, etc.) of occupants of domestic premises (in one particular case where an inhabitant of a flat in a high rise block was charged with arson, a fire investigator, through the study of photographs, and taking into consideration the practice of the suspect to use candles for lighting, was able to ascertain that the fire may have been accidentally caused by a candle);

- the nature of the structure of the building where the fire occurred including, e.g. whether it complied with the necessary building and fire regulations;
- in cases of fires in certain domestic buildings (e.g. purpose-built flats), whether there was fire separation between the flats in order to determine if any fire in a single unit had or could have endangered lives of persons in neighbouring dwellings. This information may be relevant as to whether a charge of reckless arson can rightly be sustained.

In relation to a charge of reckless arson, the test is whether the risk that property might be damaged would be obvious to a 'prudent bystander'. Expert evidence in relation to a potential hazard, including that from a fire officer, would appear to be inadmissible. However, if there was no real or perceived risk of damage, then there is an argument that the expert evidence should not be excluded from the jury. See *R. v. Caldwell* (1981) 73 Cr App R 13, *R. v. Dudley* [1989] Crim LR 57, *R. v. Sangha* [1988] Crim LR 371, *R. v. Gemmell; R. v. Richards* [2002] EWCA Crim 1992.

28.14 FIRE CAUSES

The following causes have been considered by experts to be possible indicators that the fire is accidental:

- defective or left on heating or cooking equipment;
- defective chimney;
- hot ashes or coals;
- combustibles near heaters;
- smoking or matches;
- electrical;
- rubbish fires;
- chimney or bushfire sparks on roof;
- welding and cutting;
- friction sparks from clashing metals;
- overheating of machinery;
- candles;
- poor storage of flammable liquids;
- lightning;
- children and matches;
- 'spontaneous ignition';
- gas and gas appliances.

The following causes have been considered by experts to be possible indicators that the fire is not accidental:

- presence of flammable liquids;
- multiple points of origin;

- use of trailers, timing devices;
- presence of explosion;
- sign of forced entry;
- sign of contents removed before the fire or replaced with inferior goods;
- signs of tampering with gas or electric appliances or sprinklers;
- signs of artificial drafts (e.g. holes in walls);
- rapid onset of fire, higher than normal temperatures closet fires;
- other crime (e.g. burglary, unlawful killing) committed.

See further: Tony Cafe 'Physical Constants for Investigators' online via **www.tcforensic.com.au/docs/article10.html**.

28.15 THE ROLE OF THE DEFENCE EXPERT

A fire investigator instructed by the defence should conduct an examination of the scene (the scene will usually be preserved in cases of serious fires) and, as necessary, view exhibits and conduct their own laboratory tests.

If scene examination is no longer possible, the investigator should view any photographs of the scene (including any sequential photos of the investigation if available) and obtain all documented evidence.

28.16 FIRE SERVICE TRAINING IN FIRE INVESTIGATION

There is a lack of nationally agreed training on fire investigation. The fire service is currently developing a more systematic approach to the training of its officers in investigative techniques.

Current training is not uniform and brigades have trained their fire investigation staff in a number of ways via a mixture of in-house courses, fire service college courses, and some privately run courses.

There is little standard guidance available on which competencies are required for effective fire investigation (although national vocational qualification (NVQ) qualifications, such as NVQ Forensic Science Level 4, are being developed).

The Home office Report of the Arson Scoping Study (1999) recommended:

1. The development of a requirement for national standards in fire investigation and training.
2. Further development of standardised fire investigation qualifications.
3. The encouragement of cross-service training courses for the police, forensic scientists and the fire service in order to ensure that each agency understands the investigative needs of the other.

In response to those findings, most brigades have trained, or are attempting to train, all officers in limited fire investigation to the point of being able to recognise suspected deliberate ignition.

There has also been a recent emergence of fire investigation courses for brigades (mainly stemming from the private sector) which have had an input from a selection of relevant agencies including the police, forensic scientists and the legal profession.

Despite current training initiatives, a lack of time generally means that the fire brigade can carry out no more than a cursory investigation. Many fires may therefore be deemed to be deliberate even though the quality of the evidence is deficient due to a defective investigation.

28.17 POLICE TRAINING IN FIRE INVESTIGATION

The police have little training in dealing specifically with the complexities of suspected arson.

Probationary officers receive only half a day of pertinent arson investigation/detection related work during their initial training.

Sergeant and CID training courses schedule about two days' training for arson investigation work, although not all officers will receive this training.

Because arson can be perceived as a difficult crime on which to secure a conviction, there may be a general reluctance on behalf of the police to commit significant resources to its investigation. The police response to arson also needs to be set within the context of the general expanding workload/policing priorities. The police are measured against performance indicators for volume crime. Several forces have indicated that if they had more resources they would prefer to channel them into other areas rather than prevention of arson which is not viewed as a priority.

28.18 QUALIFICATIONS AND TRAINING OF A FIRE INVESTIGATOR

In principle it does not matter who investigates fires provided that they possess an appropriate background, qualifications, and training to carry out a competent examination of the fire scene, and to present evidence in court. In practice, fire investigators often tend to have diverse backgrounds and training in diverse subjects, e.g. fire fighting, natural sciences (including analytical methods), engineering, etc.

Typically a trainee fire investigator will shadow an experienced investigator for a period of about 12 months before reporting on cases. Even experienced fire investigators will be subject to quality assurance checks and any reports should be checked by another experienced investigator.

Some fire brigades now employ dedicated teams of fire investigators. Investigators may also be employed by the FSS, private companies providing fire investigation services, or be in private practice.

The CRFP has opened its register to laboratory-based (usually graduate level forensic scientists) fire investigators specialising in the reconstruction of incidents such as fires and explosions. The register will soon become open to fire examiners who attend and examine scenes.

28.18.1 Related areas of expertise

Some fire investigators will also be qualified to investigate explosions (e.g. of gas or petrol vapour) and related areas. The study of condensed phase explosives (e.g. TNT (tinitrotoluene), Semtex) is a different expertise.

REFERENCES

Fire Service Circular No 10/1992; Home Office Circular 106/1992 *The investigation of fires where the supposed cause is not accidental* online via **www.safety.odpm.gov.uk/fire/fepd/fpu.htm**.

Home Office (1999) *Safer Communities: Towards Effective Arson Control* (The Report of the Arson Scoping Study) available online via **www.safety.odpm.gov.uk/fire/fepd/fpu.htm**.

Home Office (Fire Policy Unit) Fire Service Circular No 21/2000; Home Office Circular No 44/2000 *The investigation of fires where the supposed cause is not accidental* online via **www.safety.odpm.gov.uk/fire/fepd/fpu. htm**.

London Fire and Emergency Planning Authority (LFEPA)/Metropolitan Police *Fire and Arson Investigation: Memorandum of understanding between the London Fire Brigade and The Metropolitan Police Service* (2000)

Tony Cafe 'Photographing the Fire Scene' and 'Physical Constraints for Investigators' online via **www.tcforensic.com.au** (homepage of website of Tony Cafe B Appl Sc, M Appl Sc, Fire Investigator, includes resources and links)

CHAPTER 29

Forensic accountancy

29.1 FRAUD STATISTICS AND INVESTIGATION

Statistics show that fraud is on the increase and the cost to industry in the 1990s was on average about £5 billion a year.

The use of electronic commerce and internet trading has created new opportunities for fraudulent activities and necessitated the development of sophisticated investigative methods.

Criminal cases for financial crimes are instigated by a number of prosecuting authorities including the police, Customs and Excise, the Serious Fraud Office (SFO), the Department of Trade and Industry (DTI), or other regulatory bodies.

29.2 INSTRUCTING A FORENSIC ACCOUNTANT

An expert accountant is generally instructed for the purposes of establishing whether there has been a fraud and assisting with the quantification of any direct and consequential losses flowing from the criminal act, or to assist in the tracing and recovery of assets. In addition to having a duty to the court, an accountant will be expected to adhere to the code of ethics of their own professional body (e.g. Institute of Chartered Accountants).

It should be ascertained that the accountants instructed for the prosecution are free of any potential conflicts of interest, e.g. if investigating a business that has gone into liquidation they should not also be acting for the creditors in the liquidation.

It is now increasingly common for forensic accountants to work within multidisciplinary teams employed on an investigation which will include information technology (IT) specialists, financial investigators, and other support staff.

29.3 THE ROLE OF THE FORENSIC ACCOUNTANT IN THE INVESTIGATION OF FRAUD

An accountant may become involved from the early stages of a criminal investigation. It is common practice for the police or the SFO to call in a forensic accountant either to accompany them on a raid of premises to assist with recovery and identification of financial documents and records or to sit in on or to assist with a suspect interview in order to clarify financial matters. Accountants involved in undertaking such activities are bound by the provisions of the Police and Criminal Evidence Act 1984 (PACE) and the Codes of Practice thereto.

A raid of premises will usually include a search and seizure of financial documentation which can include the imaging of information contained on hard drives of computers and the system servers, as well as the recovery of deleted data from the hard drive (which can be done without turning on the computer and thus the 'last accessed records' will not be changed and the evidence trail is not compromised).

It should always be confirmed that the process of imaging the data on the hard drive has not contaminated the recovered data in any way. If there is any issue in relation to the integrity of the data on the hard drive, computer analysts should be asked to provide evidence to confirm that no corruption of that data occurred during the imaging process.

Software packages are commonly used for the purposes of searching for deleted data, ascertaining relationships between transactions, and asset tracing. Software has been developed to assist with the processing of high volume data and multiple transactions.

Examples of such software include WIN IDEA (a package that assists in the analysis of data) and I2 (assists in graphical detection of relationships between data on spreadsheets).

The accountant's report should indicate and identify any particular software used in the course of the investigation and any findings made as a result of the deployment of the software.

29.4 GENERAL GUIDELINES FOR THE LEGAL ADVISER IN RELATION TO THE INVESTIGATION OF FRAUD

There may be a number of explanations for the existence of an alleged fraud. Moreover, the precise origin of the fraudulent activity within an organisation or company may not be immediately apparent. The following general issues should always be considered and discussed with any suspect:

1. Are any staff properly trained (consider whether human error is a possible explanation for any apparent inconsistencies or shortfalls – e.g. manual errors made during input of data)?

338

2. Are suspicious practices explainable by the fact that an individual (either alone or with others) was diverting funds in order to disguise previous mistakes or ongoing institutionalised errors (where a particular practice is known not to be in accordance with the general policy or guidelines of the organisation concerned – but it continues nevertheless)?
3. Are financial controls regularly tested, developed and improved? (Question what, if any, financial controls are in place, and investigate whether there are any loopholes or faults in those controls that may have facilitated fraudulent activity, e.g. is there scope for human error in the input of data? Is there a proper system in place for the recording of outgoing funds? For instance, can a particular expenditure be linked to a legitimate business expense even though it was not properly recorded in the first instance as such?)
4. Are employee duties properly supervised and segregated?
5. Are authorisation, access and validity checks regularly reviewed and electronic passwords updated (for instance, if the fraud can be linked to a particular computer terminal, check who has legitimate access to that terminal and who may have knowledge of the password; also consider whether the software security has been compromised or whether the security system can be by-passed)?
6. Has all the company software been properly interrogated in order to ascertain the actual origin of particular documents if this is an issue (consider whether the documents could have originated outside the company)?
7. Are currency and physical assets regularly reconciled with accounting and other records (consider whether there is a possibility that certain practices operate within the company unknown to management which may account for missing stock, e.g. the passing on of certain unused stock to employees without making any record)?
8. Are suspense accounts, exceptional items, and variances properly scrutinised?
9. Are databases and computer systems working correctly?
10. Can an apparent fraud be explained by a computer or systems error? (The following scenario is illustrative of computer error which was initially thought to be evidence of an internal fraud: following a stocktake which indicated a shortfall in stock in hand, the company instructed accountants to investigate what it thought was employee theft – the investigation revealed that the software used to record the movement of stock was faulty and was causing cumulative overstatement in the stock record figures suggesting a shortfall of physical stock when stock counts were undertaken.)

29.5 THE FORENSIC ACCOUNTANT'S REPORT AND FINDINGS

The following issues should always be considered:

1. Has a proper protocol for the recording of data, written procedure, and inventory systems been implemented during the course of the investigation?
2. What quality controls have been employed during the investigation?
3. Does the report clearly record, list, and identify any documentation that has been the subject of any audit?
4. Has any documentary evidence referred to in the investigation work been properly identified?
5. Is the investigation work consistent in method and in the way that it refers to documentary data?
6. Has the investigation work been conducted properly – can the various figures be reconciled?
7. Does the report state the conclusions in a balanced manner (e.g. does it consider whether there are any potential legitimate explanations for any suspect activities/give reasons why any possible legitimate explanations have been dismissed)?
8. Is the report balanced (e.g. if only a selection of a large number of allegedly fraudulent transactions have been investigated, have these particular transactions been demonstrated to be representative of the transactions as a whole?)?

29.6 DISPUTING ANY CONCLUSIONS CONTAINED IN THE REPORT

It should be considered in consultation with any suspect:

- whether other potentially exculpatory material or documentation exists that has not been considered;
- whether other explanations for the transactions exist other than those found or suggested;
- if there is any issue about whether any of the material considered in the report is genuine, has the possibility that that material is forged or has been otherwise manipulated been considered?

Any accountant instructed for the defence should consider, in addition to the report of an accountant instructed by the prosecution, any unused material and the prosecution accountant's working papers, which are all disclosable.

29.7   BRIEFING OF THE FORENSIC ACCOUNTANT

Whether acting for the prosecution or for the defence, it is essential that the accountant is briefed by the lawyers conducting the case in relation to the exact charges being prosecuted and the particular legal requirements of these charges (e.g. whether proof of intent is required, or whether proof of the commission of the offence suffices).

29.8   QUALIFICATIONS OF THE FORENSIC ACCOUNTANT

In the UK, a number of professional qualifications and professional bodies (e.g. Institute of Chartered Accountants in England and Wales) exist.

Further, there is a qualification of Certified Fraud Examiners. The newly created Assets Recovery Agency (ARA) is also likely to be involved in the determination of a suitable qualification for fraud investigation. Some countries (e.g. Canada) already operate a system whereby a specific qualification in forensic accounting exists.

29.9   INVESTIGATION OF SERIOUS FRAUD

It should be noted that if the case is being investigated by the SFO, a number of investigative powers not available in the course of general fraud investigation may be deployed. The SFO will accept cases for investigation if the fraud is complex. In so deciding, a number of factors will be taken into account, including the following:

1. The value of the alleged fraud (including whether the alleged value exceeds £1 million – this consideration of itself is not, however, conclusive).
2. Any international dimension to the case (in addition, the SFO provides mutual legal assistance to countries that have problems with fraud, corruption and organised crime).
3. Widespread concern caused by the case.
4. Whether the case requires specialised knowledge (e.g. of financial markets).
5. Whether there is a need for the deployment of the SFO's special powers under the Criminal Justice Act 1987, s.2 (which are not available to the police).

See further: 'acceptance criterion', online via **www.sfo.gov.uk/cases/cases.asp**.

Under the Criminal Justice Act 1987, s.2 banks and financial institutions may be compelled, upon written notice, to produce documents or answer questions in relation to a suspected fraud (the powers are commonly used to obtain information from third parties, especially those who may be subject to an obligation of confidentiality which prevents them from providing the information voluntarily). Statements obtained pursuant to s.2 are only admissible in criminal proceedings in limited circumstances.

In deciding whether to prosecute the SFO will follow the principles contained in the Code for Crown Prosecutors.

Statistics in the SFO Annual Report for 2001–2 indicated the following most common categories of victims of fraud: investors, creditors of companies, banks and other financial institutions, central or local government, and financial markets (manipulation).

29.10   RECOVERY OF UNLAWFULLY HELD ASSETS AND THE ROLE OF THE ARA

Note that the newly created ARA has extensive and new investigatory powers in relation to confiscation orders. Two new orders, related to customer information and account monitoring, have been created for use in relation to confiscation and money laundering operations.

The ARA (an agency of the Home Office) was established by the Proceeds of Crime Act 2002 for the purpose of the more effective confiscation of unlawfully held assets.

The Proceeds of Crime Act, s.8 provides the following investigative powers (available to the Director of ARA but also to police constables, customs officers and other investigators, e.g. Inland Revenue investigators):

- production orders and search and seizure warrants;
- customer information and account monitoring orders;
- disclosure order (only available to the Director of ARA).

Any investigations carried out by the ARA pursuant to the Proceeds of Crime Act are subject to a Code of Practice (which will contain similar provisions to those in Codes B, C and E of the Codes of Practice under PACE). Available online via **www.homeoffice.gov.uk/atoz/consult_papers.htm** is a draft copy of the Code of Practice.

REFERENCE

Taub, M. et al. (1998) *Tolley's Accountancy Litigation Support* (looseleaf) Criminal matters 170/1 (issue 4).

CHAPTER 30

Computer crime and related matters

30.1 INTRODUCTION

Computer-related crime or cyber crime and the law governing investigations into the same is a vast, growing, and technically complex area. The related legislation and its impact upon investigatory powers falls outside the scope of this chapter which aims to give a brief, rather than an exhaustive, overview of some of the general investigative issues relating to the field of computers, software, and information technology. The reader is advised to seek technical and specialist advice when such issues arise in any given case.

30.2 THE GROWTH OF CYBER CRIME IN THE UK AND INTERNATIONALLY

It is now widely acknowledged that computer crime in one form or another will form a part of virtually every criminal investigation in the coming years (see further Peter Lilley (2002) p. 20).

Since the 1980s there has been growing concern over the threats posed by hacking and other computer-related crimes. The recent denial of service attacks on prominent commercial internet sites and the dissemination of the 'I Love You' virus have emphasised the international nature of the problem. A number of surveys have suggested that these types of computer crimes will continue both in number and severity over the coming years, particularly since cyber criminals often have access to state of the art technology, can reach vast numbers of victims, and can readily avoid detection.

Despite this growth, a recent survey conducted by the Communications Management Association (CMA) found that few cases involving cyber crime ever reached court because of the lack of technical knowledge within the legal profession. See further **www.theicaf.com** and *E biz* magazine (May 2001).

30.3 WHAT IS CYBER CRIME?

Due to the global and international potential of cyber crime, lack of harmonisation of international laws and perceptions of the subject, not least the fallout that resulted from the fact that the creator of the 'I Love You' virus in the Philippines could not be prosecuted because the country had no criminal charge that covered the dissemination of a destructive virus, the Council of Europe drafted the first ever international convention to combat electronic crime and to facilitate the harmonisation of criminal policy and procedure across all member states (The Council of Europe Convention on Cybercrime (adopted Budapest, 23 November 2001)).

The explanatory memorandum to the Convention notes:

- that technological developments in the field of information technology have given rise to new types of crime as well as to the commission of traditional crimes by means of new technologies;
- that the consequence of criminal behaviour is far-reaching because crimes of this kind are not restricted by geographical limitations or national boundaries;
- that new technologies challenge existing legal concepts because borders are no longer boundaries to the flow of information and communications around the world; and
- that because domestic laws are generally confined to a specific territory, the problems posed must be addressed by international law.

The Convention codifies nine relevant criminal offences: illegal access, illegal interception, data interference, system interference, misuse of devices, computer related forgery, computer related fraud, online child pornography, and offences related to copyright and related rights. It also distinguishes four separate categories of cyber crime:

(i)   offences against confidentiality, integrity and availability of computer data and systems,

(ii) computer-related offences (including computer-related forgery and fraud),

(iii) content-related offences, and

(iv) offences related to infringement of copyright.

The Convention also seeks to extend search and seizure laws.

30.4 THE ROLE OF THE EXPERT AT THE SCENE

The assistance of an expert in the area of information, communications and technologies (ICT) can assist in relation to the following aspects of an investigation:

- to advise police officers on issues of search and seizure in relation to computer equipment and peripherals;
- to search for and advise in relation to the seizure of other storage media (e.g. personal organisers, palmtop computers, key fobs (holding passwords to access computer systems)) which may not be recognised as sources of relevant information by non-specialists;
- to assist in the recovery of encrypted data and in the presentation of electronically stored data in a visible and legible form (in this regard, the police may also seek the advice of the National Technical Assistance Centre);
- to assist police in carrying out surveillance operations.

30.5 COLLECTION AND PRESERVATION OF EVIDENCE

Any items which may contain electronic data relevant to an investigation should be removed from the scene and taken for laboratory examination. The physical seizure should be conducted in such a way so as to ensure that:

(i) electronic data is not destroyed or lost;
(ii) the integrity of the data is maintained; and
(iii) there is no contamination of the data.

The following items are examples of what might be seized in order to reconstruct a computer system for examination purposes:

- computer (main unit, monitor/screen and keyboard);
- mouse;
- leads, cables and power supply units;
- external hard disks;
- dongles (connected either to printer or LPT1 sockets); and
- modems.

For the purpose of retrieval of electronic data, the following items should be seized:

- floppy disks;
- CD Roms;
- DVDs;
- Jaz/Zip cartridges;
- DAT tapes;
- external hard disks;
- PCMCIA cards, and other storage media (e.g. mobile telephones, palm organisers, pagers, landline telephones, answering machines, facsimile machines, dictating machines, and digital cameras).

It is also useful to seize items that may assist in the examination of the equipment (e.g. computer/software operating manuals, keyfobs holding passwords/notes of passwords, keys, circuit boards, etc.). Printers, printouts, and printer paper should be seized for comparison purposes.

All seized items should be packaged, where appropriate, in labelled evidence bags (labels should not be placed upon the items themselves).

During search and seizure operations, consideration should also be given to the preservation of other evidence, e.g. fingerprints on items/computer equipment. The manner in which items are handled may compromise or destroy physical evidence.

Lawyers should consider the following issues in relation to the chain of custody which have particular importance in relation to the integrity of the computer equipment and data:

1. Method of transportation – during transportation, items should be protected from magnetic fields (e.g. windows, police radios) and protected as appropriate (e.g. by belting larger items of equipment to a car seat or wrapping smaller items in anti-static or aerated bags).
2. Storage – all items should be stored at appropriate temperatures and in normal humidity conditions.

30.5.1 Specific considerations in relation to the seizure of computer equipment which is switched on when discovered

The advice of an expert should be obtained if the computer is switched on or is believed to be connected to a network.

If a computer is 'networked' at the time of seizure an expert should make an image of the hard drive at the scene in order to secure data in an uncontaminated form. 'Imaging' is technically complex and a number of software programs are currently in use. It is imperative that expert assistance is sought in this regard.

Two copies of the contents of any storage medium will be made (for the defence and the prosecution) and the original will be left intact.

If no specialist advice is available at the scene, the Association of Chief Police Officers (ACPO) Crime Committee (2000) *Good practice guide for the recovery of computer based evidence* recommends that the power supply should be switched off and removed from the socket without any programs being switched off. It is accepted that this action may cause the loss of any evidence not saved to the memory, but that the action in itself will not compromise the integrity of data already present in the memory.

If there is any issue in relation to the integrity of computer data in a particular case, lawyers should ascertain:

• whether the area containing the equipment was appropriately secured by the search team;

- whether data could have been deleted or altered by remote access;
- whether anyone involved in the investigation touched the computer or mouse;
- whether the computer screen was restored.

Notes, videos, or a scene plan should have been made to record the positioning of the equipment before it was removed. Records should have been made and photographs taken to record the condition of the computer screen(s). Photographs should also be taken of the screen before and after any restoration from blank or from a screen saver.

30.5.2 Specific considerations in relation to the seizure of computer equipment which is switched off when discovered

1. The area should be secured as for computers that are switched on (see above).
2. The computer should not be switched on and it should be ascertained that the equipment is actually switched off because some screen savers can give the appearance that the computer is switched off when it is not.
3. Laptops should not be opened as some models may 'power on' when the lid is opened.
4. Computers should be unplugged from sockets – note that it is possible to access computers in 'sleep mode' remotely in order to delete data.
5. The scene should be photographed or videoed with the equipment in its original position.
6. All actions taken in relation to the equipment should be recorded and all seized items packaged and labelled as detailed above.

30.6 LINKING OF COMPUTER-BASED EVIDENCE TO SUSPECT

Software programs may record information in relation to the creation of a particular document, including the author, time the document was last saved, and so on. However, this information does not necessarily indicate who the actual author of the document was or who the operator of the keyboard was at the material time. For the purposes of linking material to a particular person, it is therefore necessary to make enquiries in relation to a number of issues, including the security of the computer system (both internal and external); who had access to any particular file; whether a password was required to access the system; whether passwords were widely known by those with access to the system, and so on.

Other physical evidence, e.g. fingerprints, may link a particular person to certain pieces of equipment or items – but such evidence will not necessary link that person to any data contained on or generated from that system.

If it can be ascertained that certain material may be saved on the hard drive without the knowledge of the computer user this may be a defence – e.g. material from the internet may be automatically saved in a browser cache without the operator's knowledge. In such cases, the computer's default settings should be investigated – because if those settings have been changed it is an indication of knowledge.

30.7 INSTRUCTING AN EXPERT FOR THE DEFENCE

A defence expert should be instructed if it is necessary to review any aspects of the prosecution case, e.g. in relation to the contamination of data or in respect of any defences raised which may require technical expertise.

30.8 QUALIFICATIONS OF EXPERT

There is currently no formally recognised qualification for ICT experts specialising in forensic work. The Institute for Communications Arbitration and Forensics (ICAF) was set up in 2001 by the CMA in response to demands from senior ICT professionals in business, industry, and the public services, to promote best practice in the security of information, the resolution of ICT-related disputes, and the solution of ICT-related crime. It has also opened a register of experts and consultants in ICT to support the resolution of disputes in courts of law and through alternative dispute resolution. For further information see **www.theicaf.com**

The Council for the Registration of Forensic Practitioners (CRFP) is, at the time of writing, working with leading professionals in the field to develop an assessment scheme for forensic ICT professionals. This will set down criteria against which the current competence of digital evidence specialists can be assessed to decide who should be included in the Register of Forensic Practitioners. As with other parts of the CRFP register, this will enable those seeking to employ such specialists, or commission work from them, to distinguish those who, through peer review, have been assessed as currently competent in the speciality.

REFERENCES

Association of Chief Police Officers Crime Committee (2000) 'Good practice guide for the recovery of computer based evidence' in *The Manual of Standard Operating Procedures for Scientific Support Personnel at Major Incidents* (1st edn).

Lilley, P. (2002) *Hacked, Attacked and Abused: Digital Crime Exposed*, Kogan Page, p. 20.

CHAPTER 31

Facial mapping, closed circuit television (CCTV), video, and image enhancement

31.1 FACIAL MAPPING

Facial image comparison is a scientific method of assessment as to whether or not a facial image recorded at the scene of a crime is that of a particular suspect. A number of techniques are currently in use which employ morphological or anthropometrical methods or a combination of both. These methods have been placed under a generic term 'facial mapping'.

Facial mapping experts will undertake a visual study of images obtained from a crime scene or other sources (these may be either moving or still and can be in a variety of formats, e.g. video, digital, photographs, etc.) and make a scientific comparison of those images with the facial image of the suspect.

The expert will then formulate an opinion of similarity from these comparisons. As a basis for any such opinion, the expert should be able to present and demonstrate the significance of any areas/points of similarity and differences, presence or absence of a feature, any probability factors, and the likelihood of repetition.

31.2 THE GROWTH OF THE USE OF SECURITY CAMERAS AND CCTV

The science of facial mapping has to be viewed in the context of the growth of the use of CCTV in the UK and other western countries over the last decade. CCTV is now present in practically all large retail outlets and financial institutions, in streets and public areas, in city centres, and there is, accordingly, a vast amount of material which could be used for identification of crime suspects and a consequential need for identifications to be made from such material.

The quality of images on CCTV has led to arguments that the evidence is of insufficient visual quality to render it admissible in criminal proceedings. On average, a large amount of image recorded on current CCTV systems is lost. Of the 625 lines used by an average CCTV camera, only 576 are used for the actual image (the other lines support and maintain the framing sequences and teletext). In the case of multiplex recordings only one field is used for

349

each image; this is about half the information of one frame (about 288 lines are used to make each frame) – therefore a very small number of lines are used to record the image of the face. The implications for the quality of the facial image are obvious (while current CCTV systems are likely to be replaced by digitalised systems which will have a much higher resolution overall within the next few years, experts consider that this new technology will bring with it its own issues in relation to the integrity of the images – see the findings of the House of Lords Committee on Science and Technology (1997–98)).

CCTV systems also have to fulfil a number of roles and there are competing considerations in relation to its operation. This can result in the recorded images being less than ideal for forensic comparison purposes. The following issues have been identified as common difficulties:

1. The operational requirements of CCTV users often stipulate that wider areas of view are covered so that any occurrence which takes place is recorded, and tracking of individuals through streets is possible without obstructions coming in the way. High viewpoints are therefore favoured. This means that it is not possible to record facial images from the angle that would normally be seen or photographed and any subsequent identification process which requires a control image will in turn need to be at the same angle and orientation as the CCTV image. High-viewpoint positioning of CCTV may also result in focus or motion blurs with the image being too small for analysis.
2. Financial constraints often lead to the use of poor equipment which can result in technical problems such as tape skid (which can render an image useless). The re-use of tapes can also render images useless. CCTV systems generally use VHS tapes and in many cases it has been found that tapes are recorded and re-recorded over until the image becomes so poor that it is unusable because the oxide becomes completely worn away.
3. Individuals have become wise to the existence of CCTV – those involved in more serious crimes, e.g. armed robberies, favour wearing masks or otherwise hiding their features (this may not always preclude facial image comparison; see *R*. v. *Stockwell* (1993) 97 Cr App R 260).

31.3 ADMISSIBILITY OF EXPERT EVIDENCE IN RELATION TO FACIAL IMAGE COMPARISON

The admissibility of expert evidence in relation to facial image comparison has been considered on a number of occasions by the Court of Appeal and these cases should be considered against the background of the often fragile nature of identification generally. In *R*. v. *Stockwell* (1993) 97 Cr App R 260, and *R*. v. *Hookway* [1999] Crim LR 750 expert evidence in relation to facial mapping was considered admissible where the same would be of assistance to the jury. In *R. v. Clarke* (1994) *The Times,* 26 December, the court held that expert evidence in relation to facial mapping by way of video superimposition was admissible where the evidence in itself was not sufficiently intelligible to the jury (i.e. that the value of poor quality images could thereby be enhanced). The court further considered that the probative value of this kind of evidence had to be determined on a case-by-case basis and would always be dependent on the reliability of the scientific techniques used. In a recent case, *A-G's Ref. (No. 2 of 2002)* [2002] All ER (D) 73 (Oct), in which the court considered the situations where, subject to the discretion of the trial judge and to appropriate directions being given in the summing up, evidence was admissible from which a jury could be invited to conclude that a defendant committed an offence on the basis of images from a crime scene. The court accepted that a suitably qualified expert in facial mapping skills could give evidence in relation to photographic images from the scene and a contemporary photograph of the defendant, provided that the images and the contemporary photograph were made available to the jury.

See further *R. v. Caldwell; R. v. Dixon* (1994) 99 Cr App R 73 and *R. v. Clare; R. v. Peach* [1995] 2 Crim App R 333 in relation to the admissibility of identifications of suspects made by police officers from video recordings where the officers, having studied the video footage in detail, were considered to have acquired special knowledge that the court did not possess.

31.4 IDENTIFICATION AND THE USE OF FACIAL MAPPING TECHNIQUES

In criminal cases this will generally take the form of the comparison of an image from the scene of the crime (the suspect image) with a photograph of the suspect(s) (the control image). The suspect image is usually of lower quality than the control image which has been taken under controlled conditions.

Examples of techniques used to carry out comparisons of facial images include traditional physical fit methods (which may involve the overlaying of one picture on another) and video overlays (which enable two or more separate images to be imported into a single channel output and allow the images to be superimposed, dissolved or generally manipulated). For further information on facial image comparison using video superimposition, see P. Vanezis and C. Brierley (1996).

Forensic photographic and imaging consultant, Kenneth Linge, indicates that the first action when making an actual comparison between two images is to make a detailed study of the scene of crime image noting any distinctive characteristics. He indicates that it is always best policy for an expert to do this on the image of the unknown person rather than the reverse, because there is a danger that any area which is assumed to be a characteristic could,

351

in fact, be an artefact. He states that one method of determining an artefact from a characteristic is to examine more than one frame and, if it remains constant in the same position on the face, then it can be concluded that it is probably not an artefact. Expertise in image interpretation in order to determine the possibility of this occurring is of paramount importance at this stage, as is the ability to distinguish facial undulations and feature shapes while considering lighting conditions.

The next step in the process is to scale the control image to the same proportions as the suspect image using fixed reference points on the face (usually the main features). Once this is complete, a search should be made of the control image for matching characteristics. If such areas can be identified on the control image this should be duly noted and some means of illustrating the points should be taken. This can be done using arrows, pointers, grids, indicator lines, overline outlays, or any other suitable scientific method (these can be drawn by hand but modern computer technology is now being used for this purpose with software packages (e.g. Adobe Photoshop 5) increasingly being used by experts as interpretative aids).

Kenneth Linge is of the opinion that it is possible to detect differences between images even if the images are of poor quality. While he does not believe that it will always be possible to separate so-called identical twins when comparing poor images, he considers that it should always be possible to so distinguish when comparing good quality images as a result of the sophisticated nature of the available analytical technology.

Facial mapping as a science is developing rapidly and a number of computational facial recognition systems are currently being tested. Furthermore, law enforcement authorities around the world have already begun to use facial recognition systems as search tools.

31.5 CRITERIA FOR SUBMISSION OF MATERIAL FOR FACIAL IMAGE COMPARISON

The original material is best evidence and should, whenever possible, be available for examination.

Advice from an expert should be sought in relation to the collection of photographic material from the suspect because it is preferable, whenever possible, that suspect/perpetrator images be obtained from the same viewpoint as the questioned image (the procedure for the photographing of suspects – with or without their consent – and the retention and use of photographs or other images taken of detained suspects is now governed by the provisions of the Police and Criminal Evidence Act 1984, s.64A (PACE)).

31.6 CURRENT NATIONAL WORKING PRACTICES, THE CONTENTS OF THE EXPERT'S REPORT, AND PRESENTATION OF FACIAL IMAGE COMPARISON MATERIAL IN COURT

The expert's report should indicate the nature of the material that has been compared. It should specify, for instance, whether the material was original or whether the findings were based on a copy. If the originals were not available the report should indicate the whereabouts of the originals and the reasons for using a copy. It should be noted that working from copy material may compromise the integrity of a study.

The nature of the comparison material and any shortcomings of this material for the purposes of making a comparison should be noted. It is preferable that suspect/perpetrator images be obtained from the same viewpoint, i.e. to match any facial views and camera perspectives as that shown in the comparative material.

Images from both sources should be compared in a manner suitable for presentation in court, e.g. by scaling and alignment or by morphological comparison. Comparisons may also be illustrated by overlaying grid patterns which allows a study of (relative) facial geometry between two images, which viewpoints match, and when lighting conditions are similar.

The demonstration of areas/points of similarity/difference will include a feature-by-feature analysis involving a variety of methods. Examples of acceptable methods include the following:

- drawn or electronically produced indicators/grids;
- transposed outlines (produced by hand or by computer);
- split or composite images (one or any portion of an image is overlaid on the second image to check/confirm correlation);
- video overlays/wipes on a frame-by-frame basis;
- facial proportions/spatial distribution of features;
- observation and search for textural detail (e.g. scars or any other anomaly of the skin in a unique position) may be undertaken to identify comparative information (dependent on the quality of the material received).

There is no standard scale of conclusion adopted by all practitioners at the time of writing.

31.7 ISSUES IN RELATION TO IMAGE INTEGRITY

Issues in relation to the integrity of suspect images or images from the scene of crime have given some cause for concern. For this reason, experts advocate that there is a need for documentation identifying chain of custody from moment of image capture (as opposed to seizure). This is difficult in cases where the suspect images have been recorded on privately owned CCTV systems or on seized tapes because the audit trail will usually only begin at the point of seizure by which time modification could have already occurred.

The advent of digital imaging technology which is fast replacing conventional analogue systems raises additional concerns regarding integrity.

The House of Lord Select Committee on Science and Technology (1997–98) reported on digital images as evidence. In summary, the Committee found that:

- with the present widespread availability of digital technology it would be a low cost operation to produce an image in which modifications would be undetectable;
- the public and all those in the legal profession should be made more aware of the technology, what it can do, and what its limitations are;
- if defence lawyers were to begin to realise how vulnerable images captured by digital cameras are to manipulation, then criminal convictions dependent on such evidence should be open to scrutiny;
- when presented with an image the observer should have no more, and no less, faith than if the information had been text on a sheet of paper of questionable provenance.

31.8 QUALIFICATIONS OF EXPERTS

The Associations of Chief Police Officers (ACPO/ACPOS) National Working Practices in Facial Imaging recommends that any practitioner reporting on cases involving facial image comparison should possess the following:

- a sound knowledge of facial anatomy, anthropometry and physiology together with in-depth knowledge of photo interpretation/image analysis techniques;
- demonstrated ability to compare facial morphology with facial proportions, observing the spatial relationships of features and facial landmarks between images from more than one source;
- awareness of the significance of probability factors, likelihood of repetition, and likely range of variation in CCTV images, thus demonstrating an awareness and an ability to analyse the effects of distortion caused by perspective, camera angle, motion blur, lighting, and translation of data formats;
- familiarity with the Home Office Guidelines (*CCTV Operational Requirements Manual*) and current research in this field;
- demonstration of relevant experience, previous case work undertaken, and experience of having given evidence in court.

The Council for the Registration of Forensic Practitioners (CRFP) will be opening a register for practitioners in this field.

REFERENCES

Aldridge, J. (1994) *CCTV Operational Standards Manual,* PRSDB, Home Office.

ACPO/ACPOS (as updated) *National Working Practices in Facial Imaging – Facial Image Comparison – Facial Mapping.*

House of Lords Select Committee on Science and Technology (Session 1997–1998, 5th Report 'Digital Images as Evidence', February 1998) (HMSO).

Linge, Kenneth A. *Forensic Facial Identification By Image Comparison* (unpublished thesis submitted for the degree of MSc, Department of Electronic Systems Engineering, University of Essex, 2001).

Vanezis, P. & Brierley, C. (1996) 'Facial image comparison of crime suspects using video superimposition' *Science and Justice* 36(1) 27–33.

CHAPTER 32

Forensic anthropology

32.1 THE ROLE OF THE FORENSIC ANTHROPOLOGIST

Forensic anthropology is the application of the science of physical anthropology to the medico-legal process. Forensic anthropologists are primarily concerned with the identification of human remains.

The profile of forensic anthropologists has risen within the last 10 years due to:

(i) involvement in mass disasters and identification of disaster victims (such as the victims of the 11 September World Trade Center disaster);

(ii) investigation into war crimes, violations of human rights (e.g. Rwanda, Kosovo, Chile, and Peru); and

(iii) an increasing level of police awareness mainly through the National Crime and Operations Faculty (NCOF).

The expertise of a forensic anthropologist should be sought, in particular, in cases of decomposing remains, skeletonised remains, and remains altered by conditions such as fire or explosion, dismemberment, high impact trauma, etc.

Ideally in such cases, a forensic anthropologist should work alongside a forensic pathologist from the point when the remains are discovered.

Occasionally a forensic anthropologist will be required to examine complete remains with no, or minimal, decomposition, e.g. if there is an issue in relation to identity or if some of the usual identifying features have been removed (e.g. the head, hands, or feet have been severed).

In cases involving skeletonised, traumatised or severely altered remains lacking soft tissue and organs susceptible to pathological examination, it may be possible for the forensic anthropologist to determine the major biological characteristics of the deceased, such as age at death, sex, stature, and ethnicity.

Additionally, in appropriate cases, a forensic anthropologist can:

• reconstruct events leading to the crime scene;
• make findings in relation to the cause of death;
• make an estimation of time of death;
• identify whether more than one set of remains is present at the scene and,

356

in cases where there has been a commingling of remains, determine how many persons are present.

For the purpose of identifying remains a forensic anthropologist will often work as part of a highly specialised team of experts. In addition to the forensic pathologist, the forensic anthropologist's expertise can often complement, and be complemented by, the following experts: forensic archaeologist (search and recovery procedures), radiologist (X-raying of bones), forensic entomologist (determination of the post mortem interval), odontologist (bite mark analysis), forensic dentist (collection of post mortem dental evidence), and physician (determination of the ante mortem condition).

32.2 THE FORENSIC ANTHROPOLOGIST AT THE CRIME SCENE

'Always take the expert to the scene and never the scene to the expert', Dr Sue Black, Consultant Forensic Anthropologist.

Whenever possible, the forensic anthropologist should be called to a scene where remains are discovered. The forensic anthropologist can advise on appropriate methods of recovery and on the searching of the area around and surrounding the remains for evidence that may be pertinent to the investigation (e.g. artefacts, clothing, bullets, etc.). There is a risk that this type of evidence will be lost or compromised if specialist advice is not obtained.

Attendance at the scene may also enable the forensic anthropologist to do the following:

- ascertain whether any remains present are in fact bones;
- segregate human remains from animal remains (e.g. foetal bones can resemble chicken bones or small stones to the untrained eye);
- determine whether the remains are complete or whether something has been carried off (e.g. by scavengers);
- ascertain whether the remains are those of more than one individual, and recognise items that are not immediately apparent (e.g. cremated remains may be confused with pieces of plastic);
- make preliminary observations (such as whether there is any evidence to show that the death was suspicious, e.g. presence of bullets close to the remains, absence of the hyoid which can indicate strangulation);
- assist in the discovery of remains where it is suspected that remains may be buried in a certain area (environmental profilers and forensic palynologists (palynology is a sub-discipline of botanical ecology) may provide further specialist advice on locating human remains).

32.3 PRESERVATION OF A SCENE WHERE REMAINS ARE DISCOVERED

Whether or not a forensic anthropologist is present at the scene, the following steps should be taken by the police when remains are discovered:

(i) the scene should be secured as soon as possible and the number of people visiting the scene restricted;

(ii) if the police, forensic physician, or pathologist consider that a forensic anthropologist should be consulted, the body or bones should not be moved until the arrival of the anthropologist;

(iii) detailed photographs should be taken of the body or remains *in situ*;

(iv) the surrounding area should be sealed if it is anticipated that there will be a delay before a search of the area can be undertaken;

(v) the surrounding area should be searched for clues as to identity or how the remains came to be there, e.g. abandoned vehicles;

(vi) if either the anthropologist or archaeologist will not be attending the scene then all bones and other objects should be collected and labelled – bones should be packaged in separate paper evidence bags (plastic bags should not be used even for dry bones because this packaging can cause the bones to sweat and hamper any later attempts to retrieve DNA samples);

(vii) sift the ground immediately under the remains (it is recommended that this area be dug and sifted to a depth of at least 30 cm) and the surrounding area (this may reveal personal effects, teeth, etc.);

(viii) make detailed records of the recovery – including photographs, videos, detailed plans or sketches of the scene (detailing the position where remains and other items were found). If the body is still anatomically intact, the left and right hands and feet should be bagged separately.

32.4 ASCERTAINING WHETHER THE REMAINS ARE HUMAN, AND DETERMINATION OF OTHER CHARACTERISTICS OF THE REMAINS

A forensic anthropologist conducting an investigation of suspected skeletal remains will aim to determine the following issues:

1. Is it bone?
2. Is it human?
3. What is the post mortem interval?
4. What bones are present?
5. Is more than one person present?
6. Can ethnicity be determined?
7. What is the sex?
8. What is the age at death?
9. What is the stature?

10. What are the individual characteristics of the remains that can lead to a positive identification?

Individualised characteristics are those nuances particular to an individual, e.g. handedness, ante mortem fractures, congenital abnormalities, dentition, etc. See Robert B. Pickering and David C. Bachman (1997) pp. 69–96.

32.5 DETERMINATION OF POST MORTEM INTERVAL (TIME SINCE DEATH)

Determination of time since death in the case of decomposing or skeleton-ised remains is extremely difficult. The range estimation will be much wider than in cases of recent demise and, in some cases, may be no more than an educated guess. It has been recommended that eight main categories of infor-mation should be acquired and considered if the time of death is to be deter-mined with scientific validity and to a standard appropriate for criminal proceedings, namely:

(i) season of the year when the body was exposed with hours of daylight and darkness;

(ii) temperature ranges for daytime highs and nighttime lows for the entire period (a body will decompose more quickly in high temperatures);

(iii) humidity ranges for the entire period (high humidity will hasten decomposition);

(iv) clouds, precipitation, snow cover;

(v) pH of soil for buried bodies;

(vi) depth of burial;

(vii) whether or not the body was buried in a receptacle;

(viii) plant growth around body;

(ix) scavengers common to area and den sites (large scavengers can devour remains and may drag parts of the body to secluded areas for feeding; smaller scavengers can disarticulate and scatter remains far from the original body location). While some forensic anthropologists are of the opinion that it would be unusual to find bones exposed for more than a year that have not been attacked and gnawed upon by rodents, consult-ant forensic anthropologist, Dr Sue Black, indicates that she has had two cases involving exposed remains that have remained undisturbed by rodents for three years (and that the possibility of such disturbance will vary depending on the location);

(x) insects common to area at each season (this is the main factor which affects the rate of decomposition; necrophilous (dead flesh eating) insects arrive at an exposed body quickly and different insect species will attack the body in a predictable sequence).

See Robert B. Pickering and David C. Bachman (1997) pp. 97–103.

The following indicators may also be useful in calculating a range for the estimation of the post mortem interval:

- if hair or skin are still present on the remains, this may be an indication that the body is probably not from a historic period;
- if the remains have been embalmed, wrapped in heavy plastic, or contained within a coffin (a cast iron coffin will cause more delay than burial in a pine box), the decomposition process will be slowed down;
- presence of artefacts (e.g. dates on any coins or labels on clothes found with the body) can be indicative of a time period;
- dental changes (e.g. presence of fillings or reconstruction) indicate a more recent demise;
- size of the body (larger bodies take longer to decompose than smaller bodies);
- wounding of the body (if the body was wounded it will be more susceptible to attack from carnivores and insects which will speed decomposition);
- whether the body was naked or clothed (heavy clothing will slow decomposition).

32.6 IDENTIFICATION OF TRAUMA

In many cases it will not be possible to determine the cause of death by examining the remains because the most common cause of death is injury to the body's major organs.

The presence of skeletal trauma will not necessarily be related to the cause of death and it should be noted that skeletal trauma can occur at three distinct times – ante mortem, peri mortem, and post mortem. It is good practice to X-ray remains to look for evidence of trauma or disease.

32.6.1 Ante mortem trauma

Seldom relevant to cause of death, but it may be useful for identification purposes (e.g. fractures, congenital deformities, degenerative conditions, or surgically implanted devices). Post mortem X-rays of the unknown subject can be compared with those taken of a known subject during life for identification purposes.

32.6.2 Peri mortem trauma

This may sometimes pinpoint the cause of death (e.g. stab wounds where the ribs have been damaged; gunshot wounds to the head where evidence of penetration and fracture may be present; the presence of a bullet lodged in vertebrae, or found close to the body). Bullet fragments are not necessarily visible to the human eye and X-raying of the remains is recommended. The presence of a weapon close to the body may also be a clue that any trauma was sustained peri mortem.

32.6.3   Post mortem trauma

Old bones become brittle and are subject to fracture. Post mortem trauma is generally of two types – either that which has occurred during the discovery and recovery of the skeleton or incidental fractures unrelated to the case. If fractures occurred at the time of death, the colour of the fracture ends will generally match that of the bone and there may be soil contamination of the fracture ends. If the bones were broken during the recovery, the fracture ends will generally be cleaner and lighter in colour than the surrounding bone.

Post mortem damage can also be caused by animals and this should not be confused with peri mortem trauma. Scavenger damage is generally marked by the presence of parallel incisor marks or ragged edges on bones.

32.7   USE OF SPECIALIST TECHNIQUES

A number of specialist scientific techniques are currently available or in the process of being developed which have implications for the identification of human remains and determination of other issues in relation to the remains. A forensic anthropologist may suggest the use of the following techniques in order to assist in the identification of the remains:

32.7.1   Facial reconstruction

This involves artistic techniques in an attempt to determine whether a skull can be matched to a particular human face. This technique is not forensic because an accurate and consistent method for facial reconstruction has not yet been developed.

32.7.2   Direct facial reconstruction

The building of a face with wax or clay over an actual skull. Difficulties arise in defining landmarks on the skull for measurement and also in the measurement itself. Changes in tissue thickness that can occur before and after death are also difficult to account for. Since 1986, the Forensic Anthropology Data Bank (FDB), a database of cranial measurements and other biological data, has been developed by the University of Tennessee using data from modern cases.

For further information on the FDB and computerised facial reconstruction see **http://web.utk.edu/~anthrop/FACdatabank.html** or contact Forensic

Anthropology Centre, The University of Tennessee, 250 South Stadium Hall, Knoxville, TN 37996 0720.

32.7.3 Craniofacial superimposition and video superimposition

This involves creation of a photographic image of the skull that can be superimposed on an ante mortem photograph of a deceased person. Video superimposition develops this technique further with the use of video cameras. These techniques are limited and should not be relied upon, by themselves, to determine identity.

32.7.4 Bite mark analysis

Analysis of the shape and number of teeth and modifications made thereto can be used to determine the identity of a potential assailant by comparison with dental records. The more unusual the dentition, the more significant the bite mark to an identification.

32.7.5 Forensic toxicology

Trace amounts of drugs and other toxic elements can be detected in skeletal remains by means of chemical analysis (e.g., if toxic metals are ingested between 24 and 36 hours before death, permanent traces will be left in the bones as well as the hair, nails, and skin).

32.7.6 Radiocarbon dating

A specialised technique which can detect a post mortem interval of up to approximately 45,000 years. This is more often used by forensic archaeologists to date remains.

32.7.7 DNA testing

Several special techniques now make DNA typing possible for forensic identification:

- restriction fragment length polymorphism (RFLP) testing can distinguish between all individuals except identical twins;
- polymerase chain reaction (PCR) testing allows for a positive identification to be made from minuscule samples of body fluids and tissues, including bone marrow.

32.7.8 Trace element and stable isotope analysis to determine:

- post mortem interval;
- geographical location of deceased whilst living.

32.8 HUMAN IDENTIFICATION INFORMATION SYSTEMS

In the UK the National Missing Persons Helpline (NMPH) charity maintains records of missing persons and has a dedicated identification department run by two forensic artists. When working on unidentified remains, the resources and databases of the NMPH may be of assistance to forensic anthropologists, police, and investigators generally. See **www.missing persons.org**.

For further information on global human identification systems see Roger Clarke *Human Identification in Information Systems: Management Challenges and Public Policy Issues* online via **www.anu.edu.au/people/Roger.Clarke/DV/ HumanID**.

32.9 THE FORENSIC ANTHROPOLOGIST'S REPORT

Whatever the particular format of the report, the following are examples of the type of information that may be included:

1. Summary of physical characteristics of the remains (including sex, age, ethnicity, height, handedness, trauma (including ante and peri mortem trauma), distinguishing dental traits, pathology, and build). If any of these categories have not been determined this should be stated.
2. Details in relation to any post mortem disturbance.
3. Disposition of the body.
4. A detailed explanation for the findings in relation to the physical characteristics.
5. Estimation of time since death.
6. Cause of death.
7. Any other significant points relevant to the particular case, e.g. identification of probable cause of trauma.
8. Discussion of any scientific tests or techniques employed where this may be relevant or helpful.

32.10 QUALIFICATIONS OF FORENSIC ANTHROPOLOGISTS

There are as yet no recognised qualifications or dedicated training courses in forensic anthropology, but there are currently three courses in the UK that offer limited post-graduate education in the subject (also a diploma in forensic human identification (DFHID) is now being offered by the Worshipful Society of Apothecaries). Ideally forensic anthropologists will have a graduate level background in an analytical or medical science but, in reality, this is not always the case.

Practising forensic anthropologists do not currently operate under the guidelines of any academic body. The British Association for Human Identification (BAHID) was established in 2001 as a forum for the discussion and promotion of subjects of a common interest to members of all professions who choose to operate within the domain of human identification and to encourage the development of standards that will enhance the professional standing of any single or multiple factions within the association.

The Council for the Registration of Forensic Practitioners (CRFP) has worked with BAHID, and with practitioners within it, to develop appropriate criteria and assessment methods by which practitioners in the human identification specialities can enter the register of experts. The register opened in January 2003.

Application for registration will require information concerning:

(i)   history of forensic experience, including a list of all forensic cases undertaken within the last five years;
(ii) two professional references attesting to the professional quality of the work undertaken;
(iii) details of relevant academic qualifications; training workshops and conferences attended, and academic research/publications;
(iv) evidence of practical expertise in the field of forensic anthropology, independent practice, and sole responsibility for cases; competence in evaluations and experience in all stages of human decomposition; awareness of current techniques, ethics, and legal requirements.

For further information on the BAHID see **www.bahid.org**.

REFERENCES

Clarke, Roger *Human Identification in Information Systems: Management Challenges and Public Policy Issues* online via **www.anu.edu.au/people/ Roger.Clarke/DV/HumanID**.

Pickering, R. & Bachman, D. (1997) *The Use of Forensic Anthropology*, CRC Press, pp. 69–96, 97–103.

CHAPTER 33

Forensic archaeology

33.1 INTRODUCTION

Probably about one in 10 homicide cases in the UK involves human burials. In this context forensic archaeologists can assist primarily in relation to:

(i) the location of buried remains;
(ii) the recovery of buried remains and other buried items;
(iii) ensuring that the integrity of any recovered evidence is maintained to a standard acceptable in any future criminal proceedings; and
(iv) ensuring that the burial site and any related evidence are appropriately investigated in order to meet the needs of other experts who will become involved in the investigation, e.g. forensic pathologists and forensic anthropologists who may undertake an examination of any human remains and associated items recovered.

33.2 BACKGROUND

Forensic archaeology utilises the search and recovery techniques that were originally developed by archaeologists to investigate the past and applies them in a legal context. These techniques can be applied not only to the excavation and recovery of buried human remains and associated objects which may be important to issues in relation to the remains (such as identification (e.g. jewellery) and cause of death (e.g. bullets)), but also to the excavation and recovery of clandestinely buried objects (e.g. drugs, firearms, or stolen goods). Sophisticated techniques developed by archaeologists for locating burial sites have also been applied successfully in the forensic context.

Like forensic anthropology, forensic archaeology has only been recognised as a forensic discipline in recent years. It has gained notoriety due to the involvement of forensic archaeologists in high profile cases involving serial killings, human rights abuses, and the location of mass graves.

Forensic archaeology is essentially a crime scene, as opposed to a laboratory based, discipline. In most cases involving remains, a forensic archaeologist will work within a team comprising a number of individuals with a wide spectrum of expertise which, depending on the nature and location of the remains, may include experts in aerial interpretation, terrestrial geophysics, cadaver dog handling, pollen assemblages, soil analysis, entomology, taphonomy, facial reconstruction, forensic pathology, and forensic anthropology.

It should be appreciated that archaeological techniques can provide evidence in relation to buried remains regardless of the age of the burial, and that as much evidence can be gleaned from a burial a number of hours old as from a burial thousands of years old.

33.3   THE ROLE OF THE FORENSIC ARCHAEOLOGIST AT THE CRIME SCENE

In cases in which supposed human remains are located either by accident or following an investigation, the early involvement of a forensic archaeologist in the processing of the scene and recovery of the remains is important in order to maximise buried evidence which may identify whether any crime has been involved, the nature of the crime, and to provide evidence that may lead to the conviction of the perpetrator (a scene involving potential human remains will, in the first instance, usually be treated as a crime scene even if it later turns out that no crime has actually been committed).

The scene of a suspected burial should be cordoned off and access restricted by the crime scene manager (CSM). If possible, the remains should be left in situ until a forensic archaeologist is able to attend the scene to give initial advice in relation to the nature of the deposit (including whether there is any evidence of deliberate burial), and on a potential recovery.

Another key role of the forensic archaeologist is to ensure from the earliest possible opportunity that any remains and other evidence are preserved to a degree that will negate any suggestion that further associated investigation(s) by other forensic experts have been compromised or contaminated in any way.

In cases where it is not possible to leave the remains undisturbed, or if they have already been removed by the finder or by someone else subsequently, markers should be placed on the area of exposure in order to assist with the location of any further remains from the site.

If there is any doubt as to whether the remains are human (e.g. where there has been disarticulation or scatter), a forensic anthropologist should be consulted immediately. It is also preferable for the anthropologist to view the remains at the scene. See **Chapter 32**.

33.4 STRATIGRAPHY

The fundamental principles of archaeology are based on the laws of stratigraphy, namely the existence of an ordered strata of individual, sequentially superimposed soil layers under the ground surface. These layers occur as a result of different activities (e.g. building, burning, fertilising, levelling, and the accumulation of manmade deposits) that have occurred in the given area over time, or they may become formed by natural processes. It may be possible to date individual layers by reference to their properties and to the external activity that has apparently caused them (e.g. layers consisting of manmade deposits may be dated by reference to building records). The role of the archaeologist is to ascertain what the individual layers mean. This may, in turn, enable the archaeologist to reconstruct and, depending on the circumstances, relatively date the events that the layers represent.

The natural stratigraphy will remain unchanged save for natural erosion (which will vary depending on geographical area) or external intrusion. One such intrusion is the digging of a grave. The act of digging the grave will create a new layer which is, in turn, susceptible to stratigraphical interpretation. If human remains can be identified as belonging to the grave, information relating to the particular layer that the grave represents and surrounding layers will be of relevance or of assistance in ascertaining key issues in relation to the remains, such as the post mortem interval, identification, and cause of death.

33.5 EXCAVATION AND RECOVERY OF HUMAN REMAINS FOLLOWING ACCIDENTAL DISCOVERY

Before any destructive archaeological intervention takes place, steps should be taken in order to determine whether the remains have been deposited as a result of a deliberate burial or whether the burial was as a result of other natural processes following a surface deposit of remains.

The presence of a 'grave cut' (a change in the soil layers as a result of a burial, i.e. the digging of a hole, the depositing of a body, and the refilling of the grave, having taken place) is indicative of a deliberate burial.

In order to ascertain whether or not a grave cut is present the vertical face at which the remains were discovered and the surrounding area will be cleaned using a trowel. A grave cut will be denoted by a defined change in the layers of soil.

The position of any grave cut should be recorded by photograph and plan. The grave cut is of evidential significance for a number of reasons:

1. A grave cut which is established to have been cut through the present ground surface is considered to be very modern, whereas a grave cut

which has been sealed by layers running over the top of it is not so recent.

2. From the nature of the grave cut, it may be possible to give an opinion on whether the grave was carefully prepared (denoted by regular edges) or dug in a hurry (denoted by irregular edges – common in cases of clandestine graves).

3. If no grave cut is present, this may be an indication that the remains have become encapsulated in the particular layer by some other means. A number of possible explanations for the presence of the remains will be considered. The remains may represent a burial occurring through natural processes following the disposition of an individual on the surface (which may or may not represent a homicide). Animal activity may also have caused the remains to become scattered. Such deposits tend to be in the topsoil. Alternatively, the remains may be present as a result of the transference of soil or landfill from a burial ground. Loose bones contained in lower soil layers can often be attributed to such redispositions and will not normally give any cause for concern. It may be possible to locate the original burial site if the origin of the layer can be traced.

33.6 EXCAVATION PROCEDURES

Archaeological excavation essentially involves the removal of individual soil layers and the examination of the contents of each layer. Only evidence that is recovered within a defined stratigraphic context will be admissible in any criminal proceedings. Material ousted by a digger or by spading will lack stratigraphic integrity and will have little or no forensic value.

Ideally, an excavation should be undertaken by a forensic archaeologist and other trained personnel in conjunction with scenes of crime officers (SOCOs) and a forensic pathologist and/or forensic anthropologist (if the remains are partially or fully skeletonised).

The following basic procedures are recommended as good practice (further procedures may be necessary in the case of mass graves):

1. Due to the destructive and unrepeatable nature of the excavation procedure all steps taken should be recorded systematically by photography, comprehensive notes, and plans. A proper recording and archiving procedure is also important in order to satisfy the chain of custody of any retrieved evidence. All notes and records will be disclosed to the defence as unused material in the event that the evidence of a forensic archaeologist is to be relied on at any future criminal trial. The notes and records will be made available to any archaeologist instructed by the defence.

2. The general surface area surrounding the area of interest will be cleared of any vegetation and debris.

3. The projected grave area should be marked out. It is recommended that the location of the grave is marked by at least two fixed reference points in order to position the grave within its wider environment and to assist in the location of the grave in the future.

4. Any layers overlying the grave should be removed individually. The soil should be sieved and a soil sample taken from each layer because surrounding layers may be of relevance to dating the layer in which the remains are contained.

5. A grave will be marked by clear-cut edges and the fill may be of contrasting colour.

6. The infill of a grave is removed using a trowel. If the individual layers are not obvious the grave will be excavated using a series of 'spits' (a series of horizontal layers, each about 10 cm deep) in order to provide a controlled removal of the deposits.

7. The grave infill should be retained, bagged and labelled according to its particular layer or spit.

8. All layers or spits should be numbered and related to the grave profile in order to provide a direct cross reference for reconstruction purposes. The location from which any soil samples, objects, or remains were recovered should be recorded by reference to the number of the layer or spit.

9. Excavation should continue until the remains are fully exposed.

Given that all the crucial evidence in relation to the burial lies within the grave, care should be taken to maintain the integrity of the grave and to ensure that the physical boundaries between any human remains and associated materials remain constant. If an area wider than the original grave is excavated, this can result in the contamination of the grave with external materials. The integrity of the evidence will thus be compromised.

Any contact trace evidence or items of evidential significance contained in the grave or integral to the grave cut revealed during the excavation process should be preserved as applicable while awaiting further examination. Examples of such evidence include:

1. Marks or impressions in the grave wall or floor made by tools or implements used to dig the grave (it may be possible to match these marks or impressions to a particular tool or implement).

2. Evidence crucial to the cause and manner of death (e.g. bullets or traces of poisons).

3. Items which may lead to the identification of the remains or which have relevance to the issue of the post mortem interval (e.g. jewellery, clothing, coins).

4. Other contact trace evidence which may have been transferred from the perpetrator to the grave.

369

5. Before the remains are moved, soil samples may be taken in and around the remains for the purpose of ascertaining the post mortem interval on the basis of entomological evidence (this sampling is normally carried out by SOCOs as routine rather than by the archaeologist). The advice of an entomologist may be sought depending on the circumstances of the case.

6. The grave should be preserved until the completion of any autopsy examination. If the autopsy reveals that the deceased had either injuries caused by a firearm or was the victim of poisoning, further excavation of the grave floor may be necessary in order to detect whether any fired bullets are present or whether toxic substances have permeated floor level.

33.7 THE LOCATION OF ALLEGEDLY BURIED REMAINS

There have been a number of high profile cases in recent years involving the location of buried remains. Given that such searches can be time consuming and manpower intensive, the police have sought the advice of forensic archaeologists in a number of cases, for example in the reinvestigation of the Moors Murders on Saddleworth Moor between 1986 and 1988.

A number of specialised archaeological techniques for locating buried remains and surface scatters exist. These include the following:

33.7.1 Study of surface changes

The disturbance of soil caused by a burial will have implications for vegetation growing in and around the disturbance. In the short term a change in vegetation will be visible, but surface changes can still be detected even if the burial is old and has become established in a subsequent ground surface. The same disturbance of soil will also affect the topography of the grave both in the short and long term, and is often evident as a shallow depression.

33.7.2 Aerial reconnaissance

This is traditionally used for detecting archaeological sites on open locations by identifying vegetational, topographic, and soil differences.

33.7.3 Multispectral and thermal imaging

This exploits two phenomena related to a burial, namely:

(i) the differentiation of the loss of heat at the ground surface between soil in which buried features have been deposited and the surrounding undisturbed soil; and

(ii) the heat emitted from biological decay processes.

33.7.4 Landscape and geological factors

Information relevant to burial detection can be obtained from sources such as Ordnance Survey maps and the British Geological Survey (which contains information on drift and bedrock geology). This information can be used to ascertain the nature of surfaces in specific geographical areas. This, in turn, may indicate which areas are susceptible to spade penetration (for the digging of a grave) and which areas will be difficult to dig or are suitable for shallow burials only.

33.7.5 Geophysical surveys

These are used to detect shallow subsurface disturbances which may not be visible on the ground. The various methods each have their own advantages and limitations depending on environment and geology. They are best viewed as complementary rather than as options, and require specialist operation. The most commonly used are:

- earth resistance (detecting disturbance through moisture content);
- magnetometry (detecting disturbance through localised change in the earth's magnetic field);
- ground penetrating radar (GPR) (detecting disturbance through discontinuities in electrical properties of substrates, especially useful with dense materials, e.g. concrete).

33.8 DATING TIME OF DEATH

Archaeological techniques for dating the time of death are not suitable for ascertaining the post mortem interval of recent demises, but radiocarbon dating can be used to date skeletal remains which are between thousands and tens of thousands of years old. This technique has been successfully used to confirm that apparently well-preserved remains are not, in fact, modern (i.e. after around 1950 when atomic weapon testing produced high radiocarbon levels in human remains). More recently, work on lead isotope analysis (^{210}Pb) has been able to date more accurately within the period since 1950.

In addition, the specialist techniques of archaeological recovery ensure that any evidence present in the grave, which may be of use in the relative dating process, is located and recovered.

33.9 QUALIFICATIONS OF FORENSIC ARCHAEOLOGISTS

There are as yet no recognised qualifications or dedicated training courses in forensic archaeology, but forensic archaeologists will usually have a graduate or postgraduate qualification in archaeology. The British Association for Human Identification (BAHID) promotes the interests of forensic archaeologists and other professions involved in the domain of human identification. In February 2003 the Council for the Registration of Forensic Practitioners (CRFP), through the endeavours of the Forensic Search Advisory Group (FSAG), opened the register of forensic practitioners to forensic archaeologists. For further information on BAHID and on CRFP Registration see **Chapter 32**.

REFERENCES

Hunter, J., Roberts, C. & Martin, A. (1996) *Studies in Crime: An Introduction to Forensic Archaeology*, CRC Press.

Hunter, J. et al 'Forensic archaeology, forensic anthropology and Human Rights in Europe' *Science and Justice* (2001) 41(3) 173–178.

CHAPTER 34

Further reading and information

CHAPTER 14 – DRUGS, TOXICOLOGY, AND RELATED AREAS

Black, J. (2003) *Drink Driving Offences*, Law Society Publishing

Callow, P. (with Lion Laboratories) (2002) *Drink Driving Case Notes*, Callow Publishing

Cole, M. & Caddy, B. (1994) *The Analysis of the Drugs of Abuse: An Instruction Manual*, Taylor and Francis

Cordonnier, J., Heyndricks, A. & Piette, M. (1986) 'Drug levels in plasma, vitreous humour, bone marrow, liver and bile', *Police Surgeon* (30) 60–7

Denney, R. (1997) *None For The Road: Understanding Drink-Driving*, Shaw and Sons

Department of Health et al (1999) *Drug Misuse and Dependence: Guidelines on Clinical Management*

HSE & Home Office, *Drug Misuse at work: An employer's guide*, HSE Books available online via www.hse.gov.uk/pubns/indg91.pdf (contains guide to physical and psychological symptoms of illicit drug use and side effects)

Drummer, O. (2001) *The Forensic Pharmacology of Drugs of Abuse*, Arnold

Fortson, R. (2001) *Misuse of Drugs and Drug Trafficking Offences*, Sweet and Maxwell

Garriott, J. (1996) *Medicolegal Aspects of Alcohol* (3rd edn), Lawyers and Judges Publishing Company

Gough, T. (1991) *The Analysis of the Drugs of Abuse*, John Wiley and Sons

Hayes, A. (2001) *Principles and Methods of Toxicology* (4th edn), Taylor and Francis

Klatt, E., Beatie, C. & Noguchi, T. (1988) 'Evaluation of death from hypoglycaemia', *J Forens Med* (9) 122–5

Ley, J. (1997) *Drink Driving Law and Practice* (2nd edn), Sweet and Maxwell

Marquardt, H., Schafer, S., McClellan, R. & Welsch, F. (1999) *Toxicology*, Academic Press

McCurdy (1987) 'Postmortem specimen collection', *Forensic Sci Int* (35) 61–6

Paterson, S. (1985) 'Drug levels found in cases of fatal self-poisoning', *J Forens Med* (27) 129–33

Rockerbie, R. (2001) *Alcohol and Drug Intoxication* (2nd edn), AlcoTrace Publications

Salamones, S. (2001) *Benzodiazepines and GHB: Detection and Pharmacology*, Humana Press

Shapiro, H. (1953) 'The concept of fatal dose', *Journal of Forensic Medicine* (1) 129–31

Stead, A. & Moffat, A. (1983) 'A collection of therapeutic, toxic and fatal blood concentrations in man', *Human Toxicology* (3) 437–65

Trestrail, J. (2000) *Criminal Poisoning: An investigational guide for law enforcement, toxicologists, forensic scientists and attorneys*, Humana Press

CHAPTER 15 – FOOTWEAR IMPRESSIONS AND INSTRUMENT MARKS

Byrd, M. (2001) *Crime Scene Evidence*, Staggs Publishing

Fawcett, A. (1970) 'The Role of the Footmark Examiner', *J Forens Sci Soc* (10)

Hilderbrand, D. (1999) *Footwear, The Missing Evidence: A Field Guide to the Collection and Preservation of Forensic Footwear Impression Evidence*, Staggs Publishing

Saferstein, R. 'Firearms, Toolmarks and Other Impressions' in Saferstein, R. (1998) *Criminalistics: An Introduction to Forensic Science*, Prentice Hall, pp. 466–501

CHAPTER 16 – CONTACT TRACES

Bevel, T. & Gardner, R. (1997) *Bloodstain Pattern Analysis*, CRC Press

Bevel, T. & Gardner, R. (2001) *Bloodstain Pattern Analysis with an Introduction to Crime Scene Reconstruction* (2nd edn), CRC Press

Crown, D. (1968) *The Forensic Examination of Paints and Pigments*, Charles C Thomas Publishing

Curran, J., Hicks, N. & Buckleton, J. (2000) *Forensic Interpretation of Glass Evidence*, CRC Press

De Forest, P. 'What is trace evidence?' in Caddy, B. (ed.) (2001) *Forensic Examination of Glass and Paint: Analysis and Interpretation*, Taylor and Francis, pp. 1–25

Gallop, A. & Stockdale, R. 'Trace and contact evidence' in White, P. (1998) *Crime Scene to Court: The Essentials of Forensic Science*, The Royal Society of Chemistry

Gaule, M. (2002) *The Basic Guide to Forensic Awareness*, New Police Bookshop

Houck, M. (2001) *Mute Witnesses: Trace Evidence Analysis*, Academic Press

James, S. & Eckert, W. (eds.) (1998) *Interpretation of Bloodstain Evidence at Crime Scenes* (2nd edn), CRC Press

James, S. (1998) *Scientific and Legal Implications of Bloodstain Pattern Interpretation*, CRC Press

Kidd, C. & Robertson, J. (1982) 'The transfer of textile fibres during simulated contacts' *J Forens Sci Soc* (22) 301–8

Lowrie, C. & Jackson, G. (1991) 'Recovery of transferred fibres' *J Forens Sci Soc* (50) 111–19

Lowrie, C. and Jackson, G. (1994) 'Secondary transfer of fibres' *Forens Sci Int* (64) 73–82

MacDonnell, H. (1993) *Bloodstain Patterns*, Laboratory of Forensic Science

McDermott, S. & Willis, S. (1997) 'A survey of the evidential value of paint transfer evidence' *Journal of Forensic Sciences* (42) 1012–18

Moore, J., Jackson, G. & Firth, M. (1986) 'Movement of fibres between working areas as a result of routine examination of garments' *J Forens Sci Soc* (26) 433–40

Murray, R. & Tedrow, J. (1992) *Forensic Geology*, Prentice Hall

Pounds, C. & Smalldon, K. (1975) 'The transfer of fibres between clothing materials during simulated contacts and their persistence during wear: part 1 – fibre transference and part 2 – fibre persistence' *J Forens Sci Soc* (15) 17–27 and 29–37

Robertson, J. & Lloyd, A. (1984) 'Redistribution of textile fibres following transfer during simulated contacts' *J Forens Sci Soc* (24) 3–7

Robertson, J. & Olaniyan, D. (1986) 'Effect of garment cleaning on the recovery and redistribution of transferred fibres' *J Forens Sci* (31) 73–8

Saferstein, R. (1998) 'Physical properties: Glass and Soil' in *Criminalistics: An Introduction to Forensic Science* (6th edn), p. 66

Salter, M., Cook, R. & Jackson, A. (1995) 'Transfer of fibres to head hair, their persistence and retrieval' *Forens Sci Int* (81) 211–21

Willis, Sheila, McCullough, John and McDermott, Sean 'The Interpretation of Paint Evidence' in Caddy, Brian (ed) (2001) *Forensic Examination of Glass and Paint: Analysis and Interpretation*, p. 273

Wonder, Anita Y (2001) *Blood Dynamics*, Academic Press

www.bisfa.org (homepage of the website of the International Bureau of the Standardisation of Man-made fibres)

CHAPTER 17 – DNA, BLOOD AND HAIR

Alcamo, I. (2000) *DNA Technology: The Awesome Skill*, Academic Press

Balding, D. (1999) 'Can a DNA profile be regarded as unique', *Science and Justice* (39) 257

Balding, D. & Donnelly, P. (1996) 'Evaluating DNA profile evidence when the suspect is identified through a database search', *J Forensic Science* (14) 603

Bevel, T. & Gardner, R. (1997) *Bloodstain Pattern Analysis*, CRC Press

Bevel, T. & Gardner, R. (2001) *Bloodstain Pattern Analysis With an Introduction to Crime Scene Reconstruction*, CRC Press

Briggs, T. 'The probative value of bloodstains on clothing', *Med Sci and Law* (18) 323

Butler, J. (2000) *Forensic DNA Typing: The Biology and Technology Behind STR Markers*, Academic Press

Coleman, H. & Swenson, E. (1995) *DNA in the Courtroom: A Trial Watcher's Guide*, Genelex Corp

Epplen, J. & Lubjuhn, T. (1999) *DNA Profiling and DNA Fingerprinting: Methods and Tools in Biosciences and Medicine*, Birkhauser Verlag AG

Evett, I. 'DNA profiling' [2000] Crim LR 341

Evett, I. (1992) 'Evaluating DNA profiles where the defence is "it was my brother"', *J Forensic Sci Soc* (32) 5

Evett, I. & Weir, B. (1998) *Interpreting DNA Evidence: Statistical Genetics for Forensic Scientists*, Sinauer Associates Incorporated

Farkas, D. (1999) *DNA Simplified II: The Illustrated Hitchhikers Guide to DNA*, American Association for Clinical Chemistry

Farley, M. & Harrington, J. (1990) *Forensic DNA Technology*, CRC Press

Frank-Kamenetskii, M.D. (1993) *Unraveling DNA*, John Wiley and Sons

Gettinby, G. (1984) 'An empirical approach to estimating the probability of innocently acquiring bloodstains of different ABO groupings on clothing' *J Forensic Sci Soc* (24) 221

Grubb, A. & Pearl, D. (1990) *Blood testing, AIDS and DNA Profiling: Law and Policy*, Family Law

Herrmann, B. & Hummel, S. 'Ancient DNA: Recovery and Analysis of Genetic Material' in Herrmann, B. & Hummel, S. (1994) *Paleontological, Archaeological, Museum, Medical and Forensic Specimens*, Springer-Verlag and Heidelberg GmbH

Houck, M. (2001) *Mute Witnesses: Trace Evidence Analysis*, Academic Press

Inman, K. & Rudin, N. (1997) *An Introduction to Forensic DNA Analysis*, CRC Press

James, S. (1998) *Scientific and Legal Implications of Bloodstain Pattern Interpretation*, CRC Press

James, S. & Eckert, W. (1998) *Interpretation of Bloodstain Evidence at Crime Scene* (2nd edn), CRC Press

Jones, S. (1997) *In Blood: God, Genes and Destiny*, Flamingo

Koehler, J. (1996) 'On conveying the probative value of DNA evidence: frequencies, likelihood ratios and error rates', *U Col L Rev* (67) 89 (4)

Krawczak, M. & Schmidtke, J. (1998) *DNA Fingerprinting: Medical Perspectives* (2nd edn), BIOS Scientific Publishers

Kirby, L. (1997) *DNA Fingerprinting: An Introduction*, Oxford University Press

Lambert, J. & Evett, I. (1998) 'The impact of recent judgments on the presentation of DNA evidence', *Science and Justice* (38) 266

Lincoln, P. & Thomson, J. (1998) *Forensic DNA Profiling Protocols: Methods in Molecular Biology Series* (vol 98), Humana Press

McPherson, M. & Miller, S. (2000) *PCR: The Basics from Background to Bench*, BIOS Scientific Publishers

Preston, J. & Mohammed, A. (2001) *Clinical and Forensic Applications of Capillary Electrophoresis*, Humana Press

Redmayne, M. 'The DNA Database: Civil Liberty and the Evidential Issues' [1998] Crim LR 437

Redmayne, M. (2001) *Expert Evidence and Criminal Justice*, Oxford University Press

Robertson, B. & Vinaux, T. 'DNA evidence on appeal II' [1997] *NZLJ* 247

Temkin, J. (1998) 61 MLR 821 'Medical Evidence in Rape Cases: A Continuing Problem for Criminal Justice'

Thompson, W. (1996) 'DNA evidence in the OJ Simpson trial', *U Col L Rev* (67) 827

Wonder, A. (2001) *Blood Dynamics*, Academic Press

Zander, M. 'All the evidence suggest we should change our minds over DNA' *The Times*, 30 May 2000

CHAPTER 18 – FIREARMS

Brandt, J. (1998) *Manual of Pistol and Revolver Cartridges*, Verlag

Zhuk, A. (2000) *The Illustrated Encyclopaedia of Handguns, Pistols and Revolvers of the World 1870 to the Present*, Lewis International Inc.

CHAPTER 19 – TRAFFIC ACCIDENT INVESTIGATORS

www.trl.co.uk – homepage of the website of the Transport Research Laboratory

www.mira.co.uk – homepage of the website of the Motor Industries Research Agency

CHAPTER 20 – QUESTIONED DOCUMENTS

Huber, A. & Headrick, A. (1999) *Handwriting Identification: Facts and Fundamentals*, CRC Press

Koppenhaver, K. (2002) *Attorney's Guide to Document Examination*, Greenwood Press

Levinson, J. (2000) *Questioned Documents: A Lawyers Handbook*, Academic Press

Morris, R. (2000) *Forensic Handwriting Identification: Fundamental Concepts and Principles*, Academic Press

Nickell, J. (1996) *Detecting Forgery: Forensic Investigation of Documents*, Premier Book Marketing Limited

Wellingham-Jones, P. (1991) *Drugs and Handwriting*, Patricia Wellingham-Jones

www.asqde.org – website of the American Society of Questioned Document Examiners

CHAPTER 21 – FINGERPRINTS

Ashburgh, D. (1983) *Quantitative-qualitative Friction Ridge Analysis: An Introduction to Basic and Advanced Ridgeology*, Ridgeology Consulting Services

Bevan, C. (2002) *Fingerprints: Murder and the Race to uncover the Science of Identity*, Fourth Estate

Campbell, D. 'Fingerprints: A Review' [1985] Crim LR 195

Cole, S. (2001) *Suspect Identities: A History of Fingerprinting and Criminal Identification*, Harvard University Press

Cowgar, J. (1986) *Friction Ridge Skin: Comparison and Identification of Fingerprints*, Elsevier

'HMA v. Shirley McKie. The Fingerprint Bureau: Primary Inspection 2000' online via www.scotland.gov.uk/hmic/docs/fppi-15.asp

Lambourne, G. (1984) *The Fingerprint Story*, Harrap

Menzel, E. (1999) *Fingerprint Detection with Lasers* (2nd edn), Marcel Dekker

Lee, H. & Gaensslen, R. (2001) *Advances in Fingerprint Technology*, CRC Press

CHAPTER 22 – FORENSIC PHYSICIANS

Clinical Forensic Medicine (periodical journal of the Association of Police Surgeons)

Medico-Legal Journal (periodical journal of the Medico-Legal Society)

Knight, B. (1985) *Forensic Medicine: Pocket Picture Guides*, Mosby

Knight, B. (1991) *Simpson's Forensic Medicine*, Arnold

Knight, B. (1992) *Legal Aspects of Medical Practice*, Churchill Livingstone

Stark, M. Dr, Rogers, D. Dr & Norfolk, G. (2003) *Good Practice Guidelines for Forensic Medical Examiners*, Metropolitan Police

Summers, R. (1988) *History Of The Police Surgeon*, Association of Police Surgeons of Great Britain

CHAPTER 24 – FORENSIC PATHOLOGY

Asnaes, S. & Paaske, F. (1980) 'Uncertainty of determining mode of death in medico-legal material without autopsy: A systematic autopsy study' *Forensic Sci Int* (15) 3–10

Bookis, S. (1986) 'Repeat autopsies on corpses from abroad: a futile effort?' *Am J Forensic Med Pathol* (7) 216–18

Cordner, S. (1985) 'The role of the second post-mortem examination' *Med Leg J* (53) 24–28

Erzincliglu, Y. (1983) 'The application of entomology to forensic medicine' *Med Sci Law* (23) 57–63

Erzincliglu, Y. (1989) 'Protocol for collecting entomological evidence' *Forensic Sci Int* (43) 21–213

Karch, S. (2001) *Karch's Pathology of Drug Abuse* (3rd edn), CRC Press

Knight, B. (1998) *Lawyer's Guide to Forensic Medicine* (2nd edn), Cavendish Publishing

Lothe, F. (1964) 'The use of larval infestation in determining time of death' *Med Sci Law* (4) 113–16

Mason, J. & Purdue, B. (1999) *The Pathology of Trauma* (3rd edn), Arnold

Mason, J. (2000) *Forensic Medicine for Lawyers*, Butterworths Law

McKeehan, H. (1970) 'Restoration of desiccated cadaveric fingers for the purpose of identification' *J Forensic Sci Soc* (10) 115–17

Richardson, L. & Kade, H. (1971) 'Readable fingerprints from mummified or putrefied skeletons' *J Forensic Sci* (17) 325–27

Shattock, F.M. (1962) 'Injuries caused by wild animals' *Lancet* (ii) 412–14

CHAPTER 25 – FORENSIC PSYCHIATRY/PSYCHOLOGY

Journal of Forensic Psychiatry (periodical journal)

Legal and Criminological Psychology (periodical journal)

Bartlett, P. & Sandland, R. (1999) *Mental Health Law: Policy and Practice*, Blackstone Press

Blackburn, R. (1995) *The Psychology of Criminal Conduct: Theory, Research and Practice*, John Wiley and Sons

Britton, P. (1997) *The Jigsaw Man*, Bantam Press

Bull, R. & Carson, D. (1999) *Handbook of Psychology in Legal Contexts*, John Wiley and Sons

Canter, D. (1994) *Criminal Shadows: Inside the Mind of a Serial Killer*, Harper Collins

Chiswick, D. & Cope, R. (eds.) (1995) *Seminars in Practical Forensic Psychiatry*, Gaskell Publications

Gudjonsson, G. (2000) *The Psychology of Interrogation, Confessions and Testimony*, John Wiley and Sons

Gudjonsson, G. & Haward, L. (1998) *Forensic Psychology: A Practitioner's Guide*, Routledge

Gunn, J. & Taylor, P. (2002) *Forensic Psychiatry: Clinical, Legal and Ethnical Issues*, Butterworth Heinemann

Harrower, J. (1998) *Applying Psychology to Crime*, Hodder and Stoughton Educational

Hollin, C. (1992) *Criminal Behaviour: A Psychological Approach to Explanation and Prevention*, Garland Science

Heaton-Armstrong, A., Shepherd, E. & Wolchover, D. (eds.) (1999) *Analysing Witness Testimony: A Guide for Legal Practitioners and Other Professionals*, Blackstone Press

Howitt, D. (2002) *Forensic and Criminal Psychology*, Prentice Hall

Memon, A., Vrij, A. & Bull, R. (2003) *Psychology and Law: Truthfulness, Accuracy and Credibility*, John Wiley and Sons

Stevenson, G.M. (1992) *The Psychology of Criminal Conduct*, John Wiley and Sons

www.abfp.com – Homepage of the American Board of Forensic Psychology

CHAPTER 26 – FORENSIC LINGUISTICS

Ahuja, A. 'Linguistic Fingerprint taken to Court', *The Times*, 29 September 1997, p.19

Baldwin, J. (1977) 'The Forensic Application of Phonetics' *Police Review* (18 November) pp. 1609ff

Fox, G. 'A comparison of "policespeak" and "normalspeak", a preliminary study' in Sinclair, J., Hoey, M. & Fox, G. (eds.) (1993) *Techniques of Description*, Routledge

Gibbons, J. (1987) 'Police Interviews with People of Non-English Speaking Background: Some Legal Problems' *Legal Services Bulletin* [Australian] 12:4, 183–4

Hollien, H. (2001) *Forensic Voice Identification*, Academic Press

Jessen, M. (1997) 'Phonetic manifestations of cognitive and physical stress in trained and untrained police officers' *Forensic Linguistics* 4.1 125–47

Jones, A. 'The Limitations of Voice Identification' in Gibbons, John (ed) (1994) *Language and the Law*, Longman, pp.346–61

Moosmueller, S. (1997) 'Phonological variation in speaker identification' *Forensic Linguistics* 4.1, 29–47

Pisoni, D. & Martin, C. (1998) 'Effects of alcohol on acoustic-phonetic properties of speech: perceptual and acoustic analyses' *Alcoholism: Clinical and Experimental Research* 13:4, 577–87

Rogers, H. (1998) 'Foreign accent in voice discrimination: a case study' *Forensic Linguistics* 5.2, 203–8

Schiller, N. & Koester, O. (1998) 'The ability of expert witnesses to identify voices: a comparison between trained and untrained listeners' *Forensic Linguistics* 5.1, 1–9

Shuy, R. (1998) *The Language of Confession, Interrogation, and Deception*, Sage Publications

Shuy, R. (1993) *Language Crimes: The Use and Abuse of Language Evidence in the Courtroom*, Blackwell

Verity, Detective Constable Angela, Lancashire Constabulary (1997) *Police and Deaf People September 1997*, Home Office Police Policy Directorate

Watson, R. 'The presentation of victim and motive in discourse: the case of police interrogation and interviews' in Travers, M. & Manzo, J. (eds) (1997) *Law in Action: Ethnomethodological and Conversation Analytic Approaches to Law*, Ashgate Publishing Ltd, pp. 77–99

CHAPTER 27 – VETERINARY SCIENCE

Bradley, M. (ed) (1996) *Wildlife Crime*, The Stationery Office.

Cooper, J. & Jones, C. (1986) 'A reference collection of endangered Mascarene specimens.', *The Linnean* 2, 32–7.

Dabas, Y. & Saxena, O. (1994) *Veterinary Jurisprudence and Post-mortem*, International Book Distribution

DiMaio, D. & DiMaio, V. (1989) *Forensic Pathology*, Elsevier

Fain, S. & LeMay, J. (1995) 'DNA analysis and wildlife forensic genetics: Identifying species, gender and individuals' in Farley, M. & Kobilinsky, I. (eds) (1995) *Forensic DNA Technology*, Vol 11.

Froede, R. (1990) *Handbook of Forensic Pathology*, College of American Pathologists

Forbes, N. (1998) 'Clinical examination of the avian forensic case' in Cooper, J. & Cooper, M. (eds.) *Forensic Veterinary Medicine: Seminars in Avian and Exotic Pet Medicine* 7, 4.

Green, P. (1979) 'Protocols in medicolegal veterinary medicine: identification of cases and preparation for court' *Canadian Veterinary Journal* 20, 8–12.

Guglich, E., Wilson, P. & White, B. (1994) 'Forensic application of repetitive DNA markets to the species identification of animal tissues', *Journal of Forensic Science* 39, 353–61.

Imrie, F. & Lord, J. (1998) 'Biologists in the witness box', *Biologist* 25, 62–6.

Jansen, W. (1984) *Forensic Histopathology*, Springer-Verlag

Mason, J. (1978) *The Pathology of Violent Injury*, Edward Arnold

Munger, I. & McGavin, M. (1972) 'Sequential post-mortem changes in chicken liver at 4, 20 or 37° C', *Avian Diseases* 16, 587–605.

Quadros, J. & Monteiro-Filho, E. (1998) 'Effects of digestion, putrefaction, and taxidermy processes on *Didelphis albiventris* hair morphology', *Journal of Zoology (Lond)* 244, 331–4.

Rothschild, M. & Schneider V. (1997) 'On the temporal onset of post-mortem animal scavenging: "Motivation" of the animal', *Forensic Science International* 89, 57–84

Royal Society for the Protection of Birds (1997) *Birdcrime '97*, Royal Society for the Protection of Birds

Seaman, W. (1987) *Post-mortem Change in the Rat: A Histological Characterisation*, Iowa State University Press

Simpson, K. & Knight, B. (1985) *Forensic Medicine* (9th edn), Edward Arnold

Stroud, R. & Adrian, W. 'Forensic investigational techniques for wildlife law enforcement investigations' in Fairbrother, A., Locke, L. & Hoff, G. (eds.) (1996) *Non-Infectious Diseases of Wildlife*, Iowa State University Press, pp.3–18

Stroud, R. (1995) 'Wildlife forensics: A new and challenging role for the comparative pathologist' *Comparative Pathology Bulletin* 27, 1–2

The Veterinary Association for Arbitration and Jurisprudence, C/o British Veterinary Association, 7 Mansfield Street, London, W1G 9NQ, UK

British Museum of Natural History (Veterinary & Forensic Services), Cromwell Road, South Kensington, London SW7 5BD, UK

United States Fish and Wildlife Service, Wildlife Forensic Laboratory, Ashland, OR 97520, USA

CHAPTER 28 – FIRE INVESTIGATION

Cardoulis, J. (1990) *The Art and Science of Fire Investigation*, Breakwater

Cooke, R. & Ide, R. (1985) *Principles of Fire Investigation*, Institute of Fire Engineers

Daeid, N. (2003) *Fire Investigation*, Taylor and Francis

Ide, R. 'Fire Investigation' in White, P. (ed.) (1998) *Crime Scene to Court; The Essentials of Forensic Science*, The Royal Society of Chemistry

Roby, R. & Carpenter, D. (2002) *Fire Investigation*, McGraw-Hill

Leitch, D. *A Guide to Fatal Fire Investigations*, Institute of Fire Engineers available online at ife.org.uk

Saferstein, R. 'Forensic Aspects of Arson and Explosion Investigations' in Saferstein, R. (1998) *Criminalistics, An Introduction to Forensic Science*, Prentice Hall

DeHaan, J. (2002) *Kirk's Fire Investigation* (5th edn), Prentice Hall

Jones, J. (2000) *Fire Investigator*, Oklahoma State University

O'Connor, J. & Redsicher, R. (eds.) (1996) *Practical Fire and Arson Investigation*, CRC Press

www.fire.org.uk (homepage of FireNet International – a special interest and resource network for the fire service and fire investigators) and www.fire.org.uk/fibooks.htm (links to books, journals, courses, and contact addresses)

www.ife.org.uk (homepage of the website of the Institute of Fire Engineers)

CHAPTER 29 – FORENSIC ACCOUNTANCY

City of London Police Fraud Desk (in conjunction with Coopers & Lybrand Forensic Accountancy) *Fraudsto* (contains practical information on preserving evidence)

City of London Police Fraud Desk (in conjunction with Ernst & Young and the Federal Bureau of Investigation) *A Meeting of Minds* (video presentation for financial institutions)

www.met.police.uk/so/so6.htm – Metropolitan Police Fraud Squad – Includes specific information on SO6 specialist fraud units, including Cheque and Credit Card; Computer Crime; Arts and Antiques; Extradition and International Assistance, and Money Laundering Investigation

www.sfo.gov.uk – Serious Fraud Office

www.homeoffice.gov.uk – links to information on Proceeds of Crime Act 2002 and Assets Recovery Agency via www.homeoffice.gov.uk/proceeds/index.htm and www.assetsrecovery.gov.uk

www.cityoflondon.police.uk/crime/fraud.htm – City of London Police Fraud Desk. A significant proportion of the City of London police officers are devoted to addressing particular issues in relation to fraud occasioned by the financial markets. The force also actively promotes fraud awareness throughout the City

CHAPTER 30 – COMPUTER CRIME

Bainbridge, D. (1999) *Introduction to Computer Law* (4th edn), Longman

British Computer Society (2001) *A Glossary of Computing Terms* (10th edn), Addison-Wesley

Casey, E. (2000) *Digital Evidence and Computer Crime: Forensic Science, Computers and the Internet*, Academic Press

Casey, E. (ed.) (2001) *Handbook of Computer Crime Investigation: Forensic Tools and Techniques*, Academic Press

Thomas, D. & Loader, B. (eds.) (2000) *Cybercrime: Law Enforcement, Security and Surveillance in the Information Age*, Routledge

United Kingdom Audit Commission (1994) *Opportunity Makes a Thief: An Analysis of Computer Abuse*, Audit Commission Publications

United Kingdom Audit Commission (1998) *Ghost in the Machine: An Analysis of IT Fraud and Abuse*, Audit Commission Publications

Wilding, E. (1996) *Computer Evidence: A Forensic Investigations Handbook*, Sweet and Maxwell

www.bcs.org.uk (homepage of the website of the British Computer Society)

www.icc-ccs.org.uk (homepage of the Cybercrime Unit of International Commercial Crime Services (a division of the International Chamber of Commerce))

CHAPTER 31 – FACIAL MAPPING: CCTV, VIDEO, AND IMAGE ENHANCEMENT

Barker QC, B. (September 1998 – unpublished) *The Legal Implications of Experts: The Practice, The Way Forward*, Presentation to the Second National Conference on Craniofacial Identification, Windsor.

Bruce, V., Burton, M. & Dench, N. (1994) 'What's distinctive about a face?', *The Quarterly Journal of Experimental Psychology* 47A (1) 119–41.

Bruce, V. (1988) *Recognising Faces*, Psychology Press

Bruce, V. & Humphries, G. (1994) *Object and Facial Recognition*, Psychology Press

Graham, S., Brookes, J. & Heery, D. *Towns on the Television, Closed Circuit Television Surveillance in British Towns and Cities* (Working Paper 50, Dept of Town and Country Planning, University of Newcastle upon Tyne, 1996)

Kanade, T. (1977) *Computer Recognition of Human Faces*, Birkhauser Verlag

Mardia, K., Coombes, A., Kirkbride, J., Linney, A. & Bowie, J. (1996) 'On statistical problems with facial identification from photographs' *Journal of Applied Statistics* 23 (6) 655–75

Nelson, A. (1998) *Shopper Behaviour, Crime and Perception of Risk in Cardiff City Centre* (unpublished PhD thesis, submitted for the degree of PhD, University of Wales, Swansea)

Pinker, S. (1985) *Visual Recognition*, MIT Press

Ullman, S. (1996) *High Level Vision: Object Recognition and Visual Cognition*, MIT Press

Valentine, T. (ed) (1994) *Cognitive and Computational Aspects of Facial Recognition*, Routledge

Watt, R. (1990) *Visual Processing*, Psychology Press

Wilcox, R. (1994) *The need for a facial feature database*, Home Office

Wilcox, R. (1996) *Facial feature database*, Home Office

CHAPTER 32 – FORENSIC ANTHROPOLOGY

American Journal of Physical Anthropology (periodical scientific journal)

International Journal of Osteoarchaeology (periodical scientific journal)

Bass, W. 'Time Interval since death' in Rathbun, T. & Buikstra, J. (eds.) (1984) *Human Identification*, Charles C Thomas Pub Ltd

Bass, W. (1987) *Human Osteology*, Missouri Archaeological Society

Byers, S. (2002) *Introduction to Forensic Anthropology: A textbook*, Allyn and Bacon

Fairgrave, S. & Thomas, C. (1999) *Forensic Osteological Analysis*, Charles C Thomas Pub Ltd

Galloway, A. (1999) *Broken Bones: Anthropological Analysis of Blunt Force Trauma*, Charles C Thomas Pub Ltd

Haglund, W. & Sorg, M. (eds.) (2001) *Advances in Forensic Taphonomy: Method, Theory, and Archaeological Perspectives*, CRC Press

Krogman, W. & Yasar Iscan, M. (1986) *The Human Skeleton in Forensic Medicine* (2nd edn), Charles C Thomas Pub Ltd

Maples, W. & Browning, M. (1996) *Dead Men Do Tell Tales: The Strange and Fascinating Cases of a Forensic Anthropologist*, Arrow

Nafte, M (2000) *Flesh and Bone: An Introduction to Forensic Anthropology*, Carolina Academic Press

Rebmann, A., David, E. & Sorg, M. (2000) *Cadaver Dog Handbook: Forensic Training and Tactics for the Recovery of Human Remains*, CRC Press

Schwartz, J. (1995) *Skeleton Keys: An Introduction to Human Skeletal Morphology, Development and Analysis*, Oxford University Press Inc (US)

Taylor, K. (2000) *Forensic Art and Illustration*, CRC Press

Thomas, P. (2003) *The Growing Science of Forensic Anthropology: Talking Bones*, Facts on File Inc

White, T. & Folkens, P. (1999) *Human Osteology* (2nd edn), Academic Press

www.csuchico.edu/anth/ABFA/ (homepage of the website of the American Board of Forensic Anthropology Inc (ABFA)

www.missingpersons.org (homepage of the National Missing Persons Helpline)

www.forensischinstituut.nl (homepage of the Netherlands Forensic Institute)

CHAPTER 33 – FORENSIC ARCHAEOLOGY

Boddington, A., Garland, A. & Janaway, R. (eds.) (1987) *Death, Decay and Reconstruction: Approaches to Archaeology and Forensic Science*, Manchester University Press

Brothwell, D. (1981) *Digging up Bones* (3rd edn), Cornell University Press

Clark, A. (1996) *Seeing Beneath the Soil: Prospecting Methods in Archaeology* (2nd edn), Routledge

Cox, M. & Mays, S. (eds.) (2000) *Human Osteology: In Archaeology and Forensic Science*, Greenwich Medical Media

Haglund, W. & Sorg, M. (eds.) (2001) *Advances in Forensic Taphonomy: Method, Theory, and Archaeological Perspectives*, CRC Press

Jensen, R. (2000) *Mass Fatality and Casualty Incidents: A Field Guide*, CRC Press

Killam, E. (1990) *The Detection of Human Remains*, Charles C Thomas Publishers

Komar, D. 'The use of cadaver dogs in locating scattered, scavenged human remains: preliminary filed test results', *Journal of Forensic Sciences* 44(2) 405–8

Mays, S. (1998) *The Archaeology of Human Bones*, Routledge

Miller, P. (1996) 'Disturbances in the soil: finding buried bodies and other evidence using ground penetrating radar' *Journal of Forensic Sciences* 41(4) 648–52

Pearson, M. (2003) *The Archaeology of Death and Burial*, Sutton Publishing

Spennemann & Franke (1995) 'Archaeological techniques for exhumations: a unique data source for crime scene investigations' *Forensic Science International* 74(1–2) 5–15

Ubelaker, D. (1999) *Human Skeletal Remains: Excavation, Analysis, Interpretation* (3rd edn), Taraxacum

Waldron, T. (2001) *Shadows In The Soil: Human Bones and Archaeology*, Tempus Publishing

www.forensicarchaeology.com – homepage of the website of Forensic Archaeology.Com

SECTION C

Appendices

Criminal Defence Service Form – CDS4

Application for Prior Authority to Incur Disbursements in Criminal Cases

CDS4

This form must be submitted to your processing office

Please complete in block capitals

Urgent? ☐ If so, please explain why on page 2

Please insert your firm's name and DX/Address in this box, for mailing purposes.
If address is not in this box, we cannot return this form.

Supplier number: | | | | | | | | |

Phone: _____

Client's details

UFN: | | | | | | | | | | | | Date of order: _____ / _____ / _____

Surname: _____

First name: _____

Solicitor's details

Name of Solicitor or Fellow of the Institute of Legal Executives instructed:

_____

Solicitor's reference: _____

Type of application

☐ Prior authority   ☐ Magistrates Court

☐ To instruct QC without junior   ☐ Crown Court

Details of proceedings

Main offence: _____ Date of offence: _____ / _____

Likely plea: ☐ Guilty   ☐ Not Guilty   ☐ Mixed plea

Date of next hearing: _____ / _____   Youth Court Matter: ☐ Yes

Purpose of next hearing: _____

CDS4   Page 1   Version 3 October 2003   (c) Criminal Defence Service

Details of application to instruct QC without a junior

a *For prior authority applications complete the box below and page 3*

Please give details of and reasons for the application:

Prior authority details

a *Complete if prior authority requested.*

a *You will need to establish that the steps are necessary for the proper conduct of the proceedings and that the amount to be incurred is reasonable.*

Tell us what authority you are seeking and why it is required. If you wish to obtain a medical report, state whether as to fitness to plead and/or plea and/or disposal:

Give a brief summary of the prosecution case. You may attach the copy advance disclosure or extracts:

Give a summary of the defence or mitigation. Attach a copy of your client's statement and details of any previous convictions, if available:

CDS4   Page 2

394

Expenditure details

a *Complete if prior authority requested*

Type of expenditure:
(e.g. medical report) _____

Name of expert: _____

Company name: _____

Type/status of expert: _____

Total authority: £_____   Maximum Authority: £_____
(before apportionment, if appropriate)   *(after apportionment, if appropriate)*

Preparation: £_____   Preparation-hourly rate: £_____
Cost of travel time: £_____   Travel - hourly rate: £_____

How many alternative quotes have been obtained? _____

If No, please give reasons for not getting alternatives:

If Yes, what were the amounts quoted?

If there are any other defendants who would benefit from the expenditure and with whom there is no conflict of interest, please confirm this will be a joint instruction:

☐ Yes   ☐ No

If not, why not?

Name(s) of other defendant(s): _____

CDS4   Page 3

395

Enclosures

a *Only copies should be sent.*

☐ Representation Order and any subsequent amendments

☐ Advance disclosure

☐ Client's statement

☐ Counsel's advice

☐ Other a *Give details*

Solicitor's certification

I certify that the information provided is correct.

Signed: _____ Date: ____ / ____ / ____

(A Solicitor or a Fellow of the Institute of Legal Executives)

Name: _____

For office use only

Amount allowed: £_____:_____   Hourly rate: £_____:_____

Reasons:

Signed Authority: _____

Experts' instruction notes

PUBLICLY FUNDED CASES

It is prudent in this publicly funded case to apply for an authority to the Legal Services Commission. A request for authority involves the calculation of the work to be carried out pursuant to the advocate's advice or our letter of instruction.

The LSC may grant an authority up to a maximum fee only. When deciding on a maximum fee carefully consider how much time you may spend on this case and build in a margin for error. This firm may only be paid sums up to the maximum fee by the LSC; further payments are discretionary and if we do not receive payment, neither will you!

A list of the documents provided by us to enable you to make an assessment is attached, marked Schedule A. When calculating your maximum fee, remember that your assessment should generally include the following:

(a) perusal of all documents listed in Schedule A;
(b) attendance on client if necessary;
(c) viewing prosecution exhibits at source;
(d) perusal of required scientific journals and authorities;
(e) preparation of report.

Your maximum fee should be calculated on Schedule B which we intend to submit to the LSC. Please make any further comments for the LSC in an accompanying letter. Please retain the papers referred to in Schedule A until we notify you of the LSC's decision. If our application is refused, please return them. If our application is accepted we will tell you the maximum fee allowed, which must not be exceeded.

If you receive formal notification from us to proceed and it is necessary to examine any prosecution exhibits, please contact us and we will ask the CPS to authorise you to make arrangements to do so with the laboratory and police officer in charge of the case.

Please send us three copies of your report including your *curriculum vitae* and let us have a note of your charges to date.

Please let us also have details of your availability for the next three months. If the case is not concluded within that period, we will request your availability dates at three-monthly intervals.

Please remember these terms of service requirements when calculating your maximum fee and contact us if you have any queries about them.

At the end of the case we will require all case papers to be returned to us.

SCHEDULE A: DOCUMENTS SENT TO EXPERT

Name of expert:

Name of client: File no:

CHARGE SHEET	[ ]
ADVANCE DISCLOSURE	[ ]
CUSTODY RECORD	[ ]
TAPE/TRANSCRIPT	[ ]
DEFENDANT'S STATEMENT	[ ]
MEDICAL REPORT	[ ]
PHOTOGRAPHS	[ ]
ADVOCATE'S OPINION	[ ]
WITNESS(ES) STATEMENT(S)	(LIST)
DEPOSITIONS	(LIST)
NOTICE(S) OF ADDITIONAL EVIDENCE	(LIST)

We confirm that the documents indicated have been forwarded to the expert.

Dated: Signed:

SCHEDULE B: EXPERT CALCULATION OF MAXIMUM FEE

Name of expert:

Qualifications:

Years of experience:

Calculation of fees: Specify under individual heading

Perusal documents: Schedule A

View prosecution exhibits
at source:

Attend client:

Perusal journals
and authorities:

Prepare report:

Maximum fee:

Dated: Signed:

CRFP good practice and registration

CRFP is the Council for the Registration of Forensic Practitioners. CRFP is an independent regulatory body. Our objective is to promote public confidence in forensic practice in the UK. We will achieve this by:

- publishing a register of competent forensic practitioners;
- ensuring through periodic revalidation that forensic practitioners keep up to date and maintain competence;
- dealing with registered practitioners who fail to meet the necessary standards.

Registration with CRFP, which is voluntary, will carry both privileges and responsibilities. The public will accept your registration as proof of your competence. Your responsibility is, in return, to maintain and develop your professional performance, adhering at all times to the standards in this code.

As a registered forensic practitioner you must:

1. Recognise that your overriding duty is to the court and to the administration of justice: it is your duty to present your findings and evidence, whether written or oral, in a fair and impartial manner.
2. Act with honesty, integrity, objectivity and impartiality: you will not discriminate on grounds of race, beliefs, gender, language, sexual orientation, social status, age, lifestyle or political persuasion.
3. Comply with the code of conduct of any professional body of which you are a member.
4. Provide expert advice and evidence only within the limits of your professional competence and only when fit to do so.
5. Inform a suitable person or authority, in confidence where appropriate, if you have good grounds for believing there is a situation which may result in a miscarriage of justice.

In all aspects of your work as a provider of expert advice and evidence you must:

6. Take all reasonable steps to maintain and develop your professional competence, taking account of material research and developments within the relevant field and practising techniques of quality assurance.
7. Declare to your client, patient, or employer if you have one, any prior involvement or personal interest which gives, or may give, rise to a conflict of interest, real or perceived; and act in such a case only with their explicit written consent.
8. Take all reasonable steps to ensure access to all available evidential materials which are relevant to the examinations requested; to establish, so far as reasonably practicable, whether any may have been compromised before coming into

your possession; and to ensure their integrity and security are maintained whilst in your possession.

9. Accept responsibility for all work done under your supervision, direct or indirect.

10. Conduct all work in accordance with the established principles of your profession, using methods of proven validity and appropriate equipment and materials.

11. Make and retain full, contemporaneous, clear and accurate records of the examinations you conduct, your methods and your results, in sufficient detail for another forensic practitioner competent in the same area of work to review your work independently.

12. Report clearly, comprehensively and impartially, setting out or stating:

   a. your terms of reference and the source of your instructions;
   b. the material upon which you based your investigation and conclusions;
   c. summaries of your and your team's work, results and conclusions;
   d. any ways in which your investigations or conclusions were limited by external factors, especially if your access to relevant material was restricted; or if you believe unreasonable limitations on your time, or on the human, physical or financial resources available to you, have significantly compromised the quality of your work;
   e. that you have carried out your work and prepared your report in accordance with this code.

13. Reconsider and, if necessary, be prepared to change your conclusions, opinions or advice and to reinterpret your findings in the light of new information or new developments in the relevant field; and take the initiative in informing your client or employer promptly of any such change.

14. Preserve confidentiality unless:

   a. the client or patient explicitly authorises you to disclose something;
   b. a court or tribunal orders disclosure;
   c. the law obliges disclosure; or
   d. your overriding duty to the court and to the administration of justice demands disclosure.

15. Preserve legal professional privilege: only the client may waive this. It protects communications, oral and written, between professional legal advisers and their clients; and between those advisers and expert witnesses in connection with the giving of legal advice, or in connection with, or in contemplation of, legal proceedings and for the purposes of those proceedings.

When you choose to register with CRFP, you accept these as the principles that must govern your professional practice. They are the standards against which CRFP would judge any information that called into question your fitness to stay on the register. You must therefore always be prepared to justify, in the light of this code, the actions and decisions you take in the course of your professional work.

To register log on to http://www.crfp.org.uk (see below for an example of the website).

401

REGISTER SEARCH

The register lists the practitioners CRFP have assessed as fit to practise a forensic specialty.

You can locate a registered practitioner, using the search facility below, in sever example, if you know their name or registration number or the region in which the can also search in two or more of the fields together – for example, if you are looking for a fingerprint examiner in the South East.

The details that appear on the register have been approved by the registrants them may be able to provide further information about themselves or their work upon request

First Name   [_____]

Surname: [_____]

Registration no: [_____]

Geographic location: **Select location** ▼

Show practitioners
who have indicated
availability to   ☐
undertake work
beyond their region

Specialties: **Choose specialty** ▼   ◉ and ○

[**Search**]

SEARCH RESULT:

Your search produced 1 results:

No:	Registration no:	Name	Specialty	Location
1.	00001	Ian Brewster	Scene Examination	Wales

REGISTERED PRACTITIONER DETAILS

Name: Ian Brewster

Sex: Male

Address: Gwent Police Headquarters
Croesyceiliog
Cwmbran
South Wales
NP44 2XJ

Region: Wales

Registration Number: 00001

Period of Registration: 19 June 2001 – 18 June 2005

Registered specialties: Scene Examination

Please click here to return to your search results.

FSS Manual of Guidance forms

ADVICE ON COMPLETING FORM MG/FSS(A)

7.26 Submission of case for scientific examination – MG/FSS(A)

7.26.1 To enable the Forensic Science Service (FSS) to process the case in the most efficient way, it is important that all relevant sections of the form are complete. The form should be completed in triplicate and all copies should accompany the laboratory submission.

7.26.2 This form should not be used in drink or drug driving cases. Use the MG/DD, D or E as appropriate.

7.26.3 **Day to Day contact number**

Please ensure that the person nominated is fully briefed and able to advise on all matters of the case. They will be contacted only on those occasions when the officer in the case is unavailable.

7.26.4 **Delivery date for receipt of statement**

The FSS representative should complete this box after discussion and agreement with the officer in the case/exhibits officer. Examples of the types of jobs falling within the urgent and critical categories are given below, at 7.26.7.

If the officer in the case/exhibits officer knows the custody or statutory time limit (where these are relevant), the delivery date for receipt should always be an agreed earlier date so as to allow time for the evidence to be processed and served on the defence and court within the relevant time limit. A period of two weeks before the time limit expiry should ideally be aimed for.

If the officer in the case/exhibits officer does not know the custody/statutory time limit, the FSS representative should insert the FSS target date in the box. Once the officer in the case knows the custody/statutory time limit, he/she should advise the FSS representative, together with the required delivery date, again aiming for delivery two weeks before the expiry of the time limit.

7.26.5 **Levels of Service**

To prioritise work and ensure that cases, particularly those with custody/statutory time limits defined in the relevant legislation, are completed on time, three levels of service have been defined. In complex cases, work should be prioritised so that the most relevant examinations are completed first.

7.26.6   Definition of job

A job can be considered as a portion of work needed to answer a specific question and which has a specific timeliness requirement. Jobs should be reflected in the wording of 'What is required to be established' section of the form.

7.26.7   ALL URGENT AND CRITICAL SUBMISSIONS MUST BE AUTHORISED BY AN INSPECTOR OR ABOVE. THIS IS IN ADDITION TO THE AUTHORISATION REQUIRED FOR PAYMENT THAT SHOULD CONFORM TO THE FORCE PROTOCOL (see below).

(i)   Urgent (jobs with agreed rapid requirement and guaranteed 100% delivery).

Examples of the types of jobs considered to be urgent include:

*   PACE requirements where the detention of persons without charge is an issue (PACE ss.41–44);

*   packages of work within a case where the results of the scientific examination are essential to inform the course of the investigation and where speed of response is imperative. For example:

    (a)   drugs test purchases;
    (b)   identification of shoe sole patterns left at the scene to identify the make of shoe;
    (c)   DNA samples from victim such as swabs taken from victims in rape cases, or alien bloodstains on victim's clothing;
    (d)   requests for scene visits where the scene is still 'live';
    (e)   fatal RTAs including scene visits and identification of vehicles from scene where the suspect has failed to stop.

Urgent jobs will also need to be identified on a case-to-case basis and agreement reached between nominated specific liaison staff representing both Police and FSS.

(ii)   Critical (essential cases with guaranteed 100% delivery on a specified date).

Examples include cases involving:

*   youth offenders;

*   adults remanded in custody;

*   sexual abuse of, or violence towards children or those that involve child witnesses.

Other individual cases may be classified as critical at the request of the CPS.

(iii)   Standard

This classification covers of all non-urgent jobs. The outcome of these examinations will be provided on the basis of a default delivery date reflecting the current FSS turn round times. Delivery to these dates will not be guaranteed in the same way as for urgent and critical cases, but would be in the nature of 'best endeavours'.

7.26.8 THE LABORATORY MUST BE NOTIFIED IMMEDIATELY OF ANY CHANGE IN STATUS OF THE CASE – See paragraph 7.8.13 re MG6.

7.26.9 Inclusion of suspect profile on the national DNA Database

If you wish the suspect profile to be included on the DNA database you must tick this box. The suspect must be informed that the sample will be used for a speculative search, prior to being charged. If you have a Phoenix number for the suspect this must be included.

7.26.10 Previous contact with the FSS

If you have contacted the FSS for any of the following reasons please ensure that the laboratory submission form is marked according to whichever of the following applies:

- there have been previous submissions relating to this offence. Include previous FSS case reference numbers and any police reference number;

- this case is thought to be linked with previously submitted cases i.e. it forms part of a series. Include all previous FSS case reference numbers and the operation name if relevant;

- you have contacted the FSS for advice prior to submission. Include the name of the contact and any reference number they have given you;

- a scientist has attended a scene prior to submission of items. Include the scientist's name and any FSS reference number given to you.

7.26.11 Authorisation of submission/payment

In addition to the authorisation for urgent and critical submissions please ensure that the submission bears the appropriate authority to comply with your Force Protocol. Unauthorised submissions cannot be accepted by the FSS.

7.26.12 Additional Information

Certain types of examination require additional information for the scientist to fully interpret their findings. Please ensure that the relevant additional FSS form(s) (e.g. the sexual offences form) is completed and attached at the time of submission. Failure to include all relevant information may delay the processing of your case.

7.26.13 Subjects

It is important to note whether the subject is a victim, suspect or witness in the case. It is also important to record the date and time of arrest and the relevant ethnicity code.

7.26.14 Circumstances of incident

These should be as full as possible and include all relevant details of the case, including the date and time that the offence took place and all information that will aid the scientist in the interpretation of scientific findings. If there is insufficient space please continue on a separate sheet.

7.26.15 What is required to be established

This should be worded to reflect the issues/uncertainties and matters in dispute that you would like the scientist to address. For example, in drugs cases you should consider whether you need drug identification only or identification plus purity determination. There will also be instances where it is imperative to establish whether there is a link between items.

Another example for a serious offence would be whether a weapon has been used to inflict injuries etc.

You should set the priority for the examination of each section of work and mark the priority of examination column accordingly. If necessary continue on a separate sheet.

7.26.16 It is important that forces do not use the old HOLAB form for submissions.

7.27 Items for forensic examination – MG/FSS (B)

7.27.1 The exhibit numbers recorded must correspond to those on the exhibit label. It is important to record full details including the date and time that these were taken, together with any identifying numbers on the packaging materials, such as drugs bags or exhibit bag numbers. Items should be packaged, to nationally agreed packaging guidelines, to ensure that the integrity of the evidence is preserved. Further information can be obtained from your scenes of crime section or from the FSS Scenes of Crime Handbook.

7.27.2 Sharp and hazardous items must be packaged to protect handlers and marked with the appropriate hazard label e.g. 'Biohazard'.

Form MG FSS A

SUBMISSION OF CASE FOR SCIENTIFIC EXAMINATION

(COMPLETE IN TRIPLICATE)   URN

1. POLICE CRIME REFERENCE NUMBER:	LABORATORY REFERENCE NUMBER: ....
2. Police Force: .... Address:	Division/Area: .... Code: .... Officer in Case: .... Telephone .... Fax: ....
3. **Day to day contact if other than the officer in the case:** Officer .... Address	Telephone .... Fax ....
4. **Dispatch date for receipt of statement (FSS ONLY)**	5. **Suspect Charged:** **YES/NO** Offence:..
6. Has this case been discussed with a representative from the FSS? If so **why, by whom** and **when**:	Offence type: Indictable-only YES/NO Triable either-way: YES/NO Summary: YES/NO Suspect in Custody: YES/NO Submission in Category: URGENT/CRITICAL/ STANDARD
7. Any previous submissions: If so: Laboratory Ref .... Police Ref.	**10. URGENT & CRITICAL SUBMISSIONS ONLY** **Urgent Submissions** (pre-charge) YES/NO (Agree priority with laboratory before submitting) Authorising signature; ....
8. Phoenix A/ S Number if known:	Name/Rank:..
9. Submit the following where appropriate <u>AND</u> indicate with tick ✓ in box Critical Success Factor Form ☐ Victims Statement ☐ Sexual Offences Form ☐ Voluntary Statement ☐ Firearms Safety Form ☐ Photographs ☐ Toxicology Form ☐ Plans ☐ Scene Examiners Report ☐ Other (specify) ☐	<u>Critical submissions</u> (post-charge); also complete form overleaf Adult in Custody, either way offence: YES/NO Indictable-only offence, adult in custody: YES/NO Indictable-only offence, adult on bail: YES/NO **Critical Submissions (Offender/victim Status)** Youth offender: YES/NO Persistent Young Offender: YES/NO
11. Authorisation of submission Date Stamp	Child Witness: Violent/Sexual Crime YES/NO Child Victim: Violent/Sexual Crime YES/NO Other, written requests from CPS YES/NO (Include copy of request) Authorising signature; .... Name/Rank:.. Method of delivery: By Hand ☐ Registered post ☐ Couriers ☐ Recorded delivery ☐
Seal Nos:	Rank:
Name of person delivering (block letters):	Signature:

2002(1)

Form MG FSS A

13. SUBJECTS

Laboratory Ref No. ....

Surname .... Forename(s) .... Sex ....

D.O.B. .... *Ethnicity Code .... Occupation ....

Deceased / Victim / Suspect / Subject for Elimination♦   Date and Time of Arrest ....

Surname .... Forename(s) .... Sex ....

D.O.B. .... *Ethnicity Code .... Occupation ....

Deceased / Victim / Suspect / Subject for Elimination♦   Date and Time of Arrest ....

Surname .... Forename(s) .... Sex ....

D.O.B. .... *Ethnicity Code .... Occupation ....

Deceased / Victim / Suspect / Subject for Elimination♦   Date and Time of Arrest ....

Surname .... Forename(s) .... Sex ....

D.O.B. .... *Ethnicity Code .... Occupation ....

Deceased / Victim / Suspect / Subject for Elimination♦   Date and Time of Arrest ....

14. CIRCUMSTANCES OF INCIDENT

Date... Time .... Location ....

....

....

....

....

....

....

....

....

....

....

....

....

....

....

....

....

....Continue on separate sheet if necessary

15. WHAT IS REQUIRED TO BE ESTABLISHED?

....

....

....

....

♦Delete as applicabl

2002(1)

Form MG FSS A

CRITICAL CASE KEY DATES FORM
(FOR FORENSIC WORK REQUIRED AFTER CHARGE)

You must complete Part 'A' **OR** Part 'B' as appropriate. If you fill in part A the FSS will fax back a dispatch date offering within 2 days of receipt of the MGFSS

Part A   Complete for *INDICTABLE ONLY* Offences

*Indictable-only cases must be pre-ordered by faxing the complete MGFSS form to the FSS **within 2 days of first appearance at Magistrates Court**. The FSS will fax back a guaranteed dispatch date within 2 days of receipt of the paperwork. The form should be faxed even if the items are not ready for submission so an appropriate date can be offered to the Crown Court preliminary hearing*

Defendant in Custody [ ]   Defendant on bail [ ]

Date Charged	/	/
Date first appeared at Magistrates Court	/	/
Date MGFSS faxed to FSS	/	/
Date of Preliminary hearing at Crown Court	/	/
Date items to be submitted to FSS	/	/

Other Key Dates if relevant (specify reason):

/	/
/	/

For FSS use only

Lab ref no:	/	/
Guaranteed dispatch date:	/	/

(Based on item submission date)

Part B   Complete for *EITHER WAY & SUMMARY* Offences

There is no pre-ordering requirement for these cases but consultation with the FSS to check whether key dates can be met is essential. Submission at the earliest opportunity will also be required

Date first appeared at Magistrates Court	/	/
Date fixed for Committal Hearing..	/	/
Date fixed for Plea and Directions..	/	/
Date fixed for trial	/	/
Police action date for file to CPS	/	/
Custody time limit expiry date...	/	/

For FSS use only

Lab ref no:	/	/
Guaranteed dispatch date:	/	/

Part C   If this section becomes relevant, you must fax this form to the FSS immediately

The circumstances in this case have changed OR the case has been discontinued and the forensic evidence is no longer required (please specify):

ITEMS FOR SCIENTIFIC EXAMINATION (Complete in triplicate)

All items must be properly packaged and labelled to preserve the integrity of the evidence
(The exhibit number and description given below must correspond with the exhibit label)

Laboratory Ref:..............

Item No.	Exhibit No.	Exhibit Bag No.	Description of Item(s)	This item relates to: (subject or location recovered from)	Date and time found/taken	Name of person seizing item

Continue overleaf if necessary

Specify any known health and safety risk eg Aids, Hepatitis, Scabies etc. NB Any sharp/hazardous items must be appropriately packaged and labelled. For advice contact any member of Scientific Support.

Method of Return: By hand ☐ Registered post ☐ Recorded delivery ☐ Courier ☐

Person receiving:

Print name: ....

Sign: ....

Date: ....

Laboratory personnel returning item(s):

Print name: ....

Sign: ....

Date: ....

Receipt at Laboratory

Date stamp

2002(1)

Laboratory returns

Date stamp

RESTRICTED – FOR POLICE AND PROSECUTION ONLY

CASE FILE INFORMATION

This document is for internal use only. It should be regarded as a memorandum between the police and CPS. It may well contain confidential information, and therefore must not be disclosed to the defence.

Name of Defendant: *ROBERTS, Lee* ....
(Surname first)

Is the investigation complete? ~~Yes~~/No

The following four questions **MUST** be completed in all cases

Medical Evidence

Are medical statements required? Yes/~~No~~. If **Yes**, have they been obtained? Yes/~~No~~

If **No**, target date to obtain: ....

Is obtaining medical evidence a problem? Yes/No. If **Yes**, give brief details: ....

....

....

Forensic Evidence

Have items been sent for examination? Yes/~~No~~. If **Yes**, delivery date for receipt for report (if known): *18th May 200?* Are extra items to be sent? Yes/~~No~~. If **Yes**, give brief details including reasons for later submission: *There are five outstanding items which have been sent for forensic examination. See over for full details* ....

....

Video Evidence (including child video evidence)

Has all evidence been viewed and copied? Yes/No. If **No**. target date for completion: ....

Is viewing and copying tapes a problem/ Yes/No. If **Yes**, give brief details: ....

....

Disclosure

Have all MG6C, D and E Schedules been completed and signed/ Yes/~~No~~

Are there any anticipated complications regarding unused material? ~~Yes~~/No. If **Yes**, give brief details:

....

In addition to any other confidential information supplied, the following questions must be considered and, where applicable, the box ticked. Details are then to be recorded on the reverse of this form.

		✓			✓
1	Victim personal statement taken/to be taken?		10	If no MF19 on file and compensation is an issue, enter victim's name and address	
2	Witness (including expert) statements still be taken?	✓	11	Previous convictions/allegations against defendant with similar MO?	
3	Photographs of the injuries? (include date when available)		12	Further persons to be arrested/interviewed/ID parade?	
4	Any vulnerable or intimidated adult witnesses. Is a strategy meeting required?		13	Others charged whose details do not appear on this file?	
5	Are there child witnesses/victims?		14	Other person(s) yet to be charged?	
6	Have any witnesses refused to make statements? (include names and evidence they could give)		15	Others cautioned out of the same incident? (include names, offences and reasons)	
7	Is an application required for video link evidence?		16	Matters of local/public interest?	
8	Strengths or weaknesses of evidence and/or witnesses?		17	Is this a financial investigation? (must apply to drug trafficking cases)	
9	Are there specific problems/needs of prosecution witnesses, eg interpreters?	✓	18	Are there any other applications required in this case?	

CASE FILE INFORMATION

There are protracted lines of enquiry in this case. Target dates for the receipt of reports and statement are as follows:

Forensic examination

1. *A knife block found at the scene (address) is being examined for DNA using an ultra-sensitive technique. Target date for this to be completed is 18th May 200?*

2. *A DNA technique is being carried out on samples taken from the washing machine at (address), and personal items (believed to be those of the victim) including a toothbrush and comb, are also being examind. Target date for completion 25th May 200?*

3. *Bin liners found in the trailer owned by (name) are being examined for fingerprints. Target date for completion 25th May 200?*

4. *Soil from the burial site is being analysed against footwear seized from the defendants (names). Target date for completion 25th May 200?*

5. *Samples taken from the body have been taken for toxicological examination. Target date for completion 28th May 200?*

Covert recording

300 audio tapes were used in the covert monitoring of the defendants home addresses (give addresses). All tapes need to be analysed for evidential purposes to present the fairest case. 32 tapes have been completed so far. Target date for completion – 11th June 200?

Telephone evidence

Itemised billing of the defendant's telephones has been requested. Cell site analysis is also being carried out. Target date for completion – 14th June 200?

Additional information

The murder investigation which commenced on 12th January 200? has generated 1670 actions, 534 statements, 480 reports and messages, 750 other documents and 1220 exhibits.

2. *Evidence from abroad*
   Plastic cable ties found on the victim at the burial site were similar in size, shape and material to those found in a motor vehicle owned by (name). An international letter of request has been sent to the manufacturer of the cables in Italy to obtain evidence of their origin. An estimated date for the availability of this evidence is 29th June 200? dependent upon the co-operation of the Italian Police.

A target date for submission of the file of evidence is 30th June 200?

9. *Prosecution witness no. 3 (name) requires a sign language interpreter. Mrs P Leversett assisted the witness in giving the three witness statements to date.*

Joint Operational Instructions (JOPI) 2003 Annexes

ANNEX H   SCIENTIFIC SUPPORT MATERIAL: FINGERMARKS AND PHOTOGRAPHS

1. All scientific support departments should follow procedures and working practices which ensure compliance with the requirements of the Code of Practice. Accurate and full records must be kept of all scene examinations, including details of any items retained as potential exhibits. Where such items are submitted for further examination, for example by the fingerprint bureau, the record should indicate that this has been done.
2. The Code of Practice requires the recording and retention of relevant material and information obtained in a criminal investigation. This will include negative information, for example where no fingermarks are found at a scene, or where the fingermark cannot be identified as belonging to a known suspect. The minimum periods of retention are set out in paragraphs 5.6 to 5.10 of the Code, but local force policy may determine longer periods.
3. The records of scientific support units in relation to a criminal investigation should be made available to the disclosure officer. This will ensure that the disclosure officer can carry out the task of scheduling unused material for the prosecutor. If necessary, scientific support staff should help the disclosure officer identify material which might undermine the prosecution case, or which might assist the defence.

Fingermarks and photographs

4. All fingermarks lifted or photographed at the scene must be recorded, retained and made available to the disclosure officer.
5. Where an exhibit is examined in the fingerprint laboratory, all relevant fingermarks must be recorded, and any lifts or photographic negatives retained. Again, this information should be made available to the disclosure officer.
6. If the fingerprint bureau decides that a fingermark is of insufficient value to determine identity, the mark should still be retained and the disclosure officer informed.
7. Where a fingermark is eliminated from the enquiry because it is identified as belonging to a person having legitimate access, it must still be retained. A record should be kept of the identity of the person eliminated from the enquiry. Once the elimination process has been completed, ten print elimination forms should be disposed of by either returning to the donor or by destruction.
8. Where photographs are taken, all the negatives or other media should be retained, even if the photographs are not intended to be used as evidence. A record should

be kept of the total number of photographs made, and if a statement is provided, this information should be included in the statement.

ANNEX I   DISCLOSURE OF UNUSED FORENSIC SCIENCE MATERIAL

Introduction

1.1   This annex provides guidance on how unused material in the possession or control of forensic science providers (FSPs) should be revealed to the police and then to the prosecutor. It also reflects the agreement reached between the CPS, ACPO, and the FSPs as to the best way to comply with the legal duties of disclosure to the defence imposed under the Criminal Procedure and Investigations Act 1996 (the Act).

1.2   Police and CPS should read this guidance in conjunction with the general instructions contained in the JOPI. FSPs should incorporate the guidance into their Quality Management Systems.

1.3   This document sets out:

- a brief explanation of the legal duties of disclosure arising at common law and under the Act;
- general principles regarding the preservation of material held by FSPs;
- agreed periods of retention for material held by FSPs;
- procedures agreed between FSPs, the police and CPS as to how the existence of material should be notified to the police and prosecutor.

1.4   The procedures set out in this annex have been agreed between CPS, the police, and FSPs in relation to work carried out by FSPs in criminal cases.

The duty of disclosure; general

2.1   The disclosure of material or information (e.g. records, tests, calculations, etc.) that support the opinion of the scientist giving evidence for the prosecution in cases tried at the Crown Court is governed by the Crown Court (Advance Notice of Expert Evidence) Rules 1987. Similar rules operate in respect of cases in the magistrates' courts (see Magistrates' Court (Advance Notice of Expert Evidence) Rules 1997).

2.2   The Act has been in force since 1 April 1997. It applies to all criminal investigations begun on or after that date. Those started prior to that date are still governed by the common law principles laid down in *R.* v. *Keane, R.* v. *Maguire* and *R.* v. *Ward*.

The common law duty

3.1   At common law, i.e. cases where the investigation began prior to 1 April 1997, 'the prosecution' will include the prosecutor; the investigator and any expert witness instructed by the prosecutor or the investigator e.g. forensic scientists, psychiatrists, pathologists, police surgeons, etc.

3.2   Disclosure principles will therefore apply equally to all members of the 'prosecution team' and all must reveal the existence of all unused material to the prosecutor. The prosecutor will then decide whether it needs to be disclosed to the accused.

3.3   It should be noted that the case of *R.* v. *Ward* placed a further important duty upon the expert:

'. . . an expert witness who has carried out or knows of experiments or tests which tend to cast doubt upon the opinion he is expressing is under a clear obligation to bring records of those tests to the attention of the solicitor instructing him. . . .'

This obligation remains upon the expert. When it applies, the experiment or test material should be supplied to the disclosure officer and prosecutor.

The Criminal Procedure and Investigations Act 1996

4.1   The Act places obligations upon the prosecutor and the police, but not upon the expert.
4.2   The Act's code of Practice does not apply to forensic scientists and other experts, although any material or information that they supply to or retain on behalf of the police will have to be recorded and retained in accordance with the provisions of the Code.
4.3   The Act's disclosure regime is explained in the main body of the JOPI.
4.4   Unused material retained by forensic science organisations and not copied to the police can only be acquired by the defence through the witness summons procedures (section 2 Criminal Procedure (Attendance of Witnesses) Act 1965 or section 97 Magistrates' Courts Act 1980) unless the information is volunteered.

Preservation of material

5.1   The Act and the Code do not impose any specific duties upon forensic experts regarding the preservation of material, but the guidance in this section sets out principles of good practice which should be followed.
5.2   It is vitally important that all material or information which may be relevant to the investigation and to the outcome of the case is recorded and retained.
5.3   When expert opinion is sought from the FSP not all the circumstances may be known. It would therefore be unwise to speculate on what the defence might be when deciding what to record or what to keep.
5.4   In particular, the FSP should always record the following:

- the results of any tests or calculations, whether positive or negative;
- any information obtained in connection with the forensic examination whether this points towards or away from the suspect;
- any information generated during the course of the examination that might have an impact on the investigation.

5.5   Notes and records of the above should always be retained by the FSP, together with the following items in particular:

- notes and draft versions of reports or witness statements (especially where these differ from the final version);
- any material gathered or generated in connection with the forensic examination, subject to specific arrangements to return material to the police following examination or to destroy it.

5.6   If there is any doubt as to whether material should be retained, or whether information should be recorded, discretion should be exercised in favour of the **preservation** of the item.

Retention periods

6.1 Detailed arrangements for the retention of case material are set out in a Memorandum of Understanding on the Retention of Case Material agreed between ACPO and the FSS. All FSPs should adopt these arrangements as best practice wherever possible.

Procedures: general

7.1 The police and the CPS procedures for the revelation and disclosure of unused material are contained in sections 2 and 3 of the JOPI.
7.2 The FSP should inform the police of all material retained in their possession in accordance with the procedure set out below.

FSP actions: preparation of the index

8.1 The FSP should provide to the police an index of all material in their possession. When the index is prepared, it will not necesarily be known what material is to be used as part of the prosecution case, and which will remain unused. Therefore the index should take the form of a list describing the material held by the FSP.
8.2 The scientific reporting officer should prepare the index and submit this to the police investigator when the report or statement is supplied in all cases except where an analyst's certificate is supplied in drink-drive cases.
8.3 All material should be individually listed on the index and described clearly and accurately so as to allow an informed decision on disclosure. (Where there are many documents or items of a similar type or repetitive nature, these may be described by quantity and a generic title. But, inappropriate use of generic listing may result in requests from the CPS or defence to see the items, with consequent delay and wasting of resources.)
8.4 Any single item which is known to be of particular significance should be separately listed.
8.5 If not mentioned in the report or statement, the reporting officer should indicate on the index any material that it is thought might undermine the prosecution case or reasonably assist the defence, so far as these are known. Wherever practicable, copies of material that might undermine or assist should be sent to the disclosure officer with the index.
8.6 The index must be kept up to date. Where material is generated or fresh material received after the initial preparation and submission of the index, a supplementary index should be supplied to the police disclosure officer.

Police actions: dealing with the forensic index

9.1 Where an investigator receives an index from the FSP, this must be retained, together with any other report, statement or document supplied. Any relevant oral information received by the investigator, or by the disclosure officer relating to material held by the FSP should be recorded and retained in accordance with the Code.
9.2 Upon submission of a full file, the disclosure officer should check the material listed on the forensic index. The index should list all material retained in the possession of the FSP. The disclosure officer should list the index itself on the MG6C. The index may be described generically; for example: 'Forensic Science Service Index – compiled 21 January 03 – list of all material in possession of

FSS'. The prosecutor should disclose the index to the defence in accordance with 10.2 below.

9.3 Where the disclosure officer believes that any of the material appearing on the index might undermine the prosecution case, or assist the defence, the item should be listed on form MG6E. The disclosure officer should consult the reporting officer where he or she is in any doubt.

9.4 The schedules, the index and any undermining or assisting material should be sent to the CPS with the full file in the usual way in accordance with section 2 of the JOPI.

9.5 Where the prosecutor indicates that unused material in the possession of FSP requires disclosure, the disclosure officer should send a copy of the index endorsed with the prosecutor's decision to the forensic scientist.

CPS actions: disclosure to the defence

10.1 Prosecutors should be alert to the distinctions between used and unused material, and to the different legal obligations of disclosure to the defence that arise under the Act, the Crown Court (Advance Notice of Expert Evidence) Rules, and the Magistrates' Courts (Advance Notice of Expert Evidence) Rules.

10.2 Upon receipt of the index, the prosecutor should review the listed items in the same way as he or she would for items on an MG6C schedule and record disclosure decisions '*D*' '*I*' or '*CND*' on the index itself. The prosecutor should then disclose the index itself to the defence at the same time the MG6C is disclosed. The FSP should be notified of the prosecutor's disclosure decisions via the disclosure officer.

10.3 Upon receipt of a defence statement, the prosecutor should consider with the disclosure officer whether any issues are raised which might have a bearing on any forensic examination carried out. Situations where this may occur are mentioned at paragraph 11.3 below. A copy of the defence statement should be sent to the polic for submission to the FSP where further advice is required as a result.

10.4 It will be important to maintain clear lines of communication between police, CPS and forensic scientist in any case where there is forensic material.

Police actions: defence statements

11.1 The defence statement should be provided to the FSP in all cases where the circumstances in 11.3 below arise, or where further work is required as a result, or where the forensic scientist requests it.

11.2 When a defence statement is received, or where information comes to light from any source which might affect any evidence supplied by a forensic expert, the disclosure officer should consider, in consultation with the investigator and the prosecutor, whether further enquiries need to be made.

11.3 The disclosure officer should send a copy of the defence statement to the forensic scientist together with instructions as to any further report or work required. A date should be given as to when a response is required. Situations where this should occur will include:

- where forensic evidence is challenged directly;
- where issues raised in the defence statement may have an impact on the interpretation of scientific evidence;
- where the scenario put forward by the defence statement differs significantly from that upon which expert opinion is based;

- whenever it is necessary to ask the FSP to review the forensic material or to conduct further tests in order to clarify the issues raised by the defence statement;
- where any issue is raised that might have an impact on forensic material, either used or unused;
- where a new line of enquiry is indicated, and the officer in the case considers that it should be pursued.

11.4 Where the disclosure officer is not clear whether the defence statement has any impact upon forensic material, the FSP should be contacted for advice on whether it may be desirable to review the material in the light of the defence statement.

11.5 In appropriate circumstances, it may be desirable to arrange consultation between the police investigators, the forensic scientist and the prosecutor to decide upon a suitable course of action. Whatever the nature of the case, it is important to maintain appropriate liaison between the FSP, the police and the CPS to ensure that the disclosure process is completed properly.

FSP actions: defence statements

12.1 If the defence statement reveals information that may have a bearing upon any opinion expressed by the forensic scientist, or which might affect the interpretation of any material held by the FSP, the disclosure officer should provide a copy of the defence statement to the scientist. This should be accompanied by further instructions, detailing any further work or report which may be required as a result.

CPS actions: defence requests for FSP material

13.1 Any requests received by the CPS for disclosure of unused material in the sole possession of FSP should be the subject of consultation between the prosecutor and the disclosure officer.

13.2 Consideration should be given to obtaining the material in accordance with JOPI paragraphs 3.139 et seq.

13.3 If, following such a request and consultation as outlined in the preceding paragraphs, the prosecutor decides not to seek access to the material, the defence should be asked to refer their request directly to the FSP concerned who will decide whether they will volunteer to provide access.

FSP actions: access arrangements for the defence

14.1 The FSP is a third party under the Act. The defence might make a direct approach to the FSP for access to case material, informally or by way of witness summons. The FSP will notify the police of such approaches. The FSP has discretion whether it will respond to informal requests for access, but obviously must comply strictly with the terms of any witness summons.

14.2 The following paragraphs represent the principles and the procedures to be adopted when making arrangements for defence access to, and examination of, retained FSP material.

14.3 Whenever access is sought by the defence to used or unused material, the FSP will:

- notify the police of any requests by the defence for access, and of any arrangements made;

- advise the police where the defence seek to carry out further tests which may alter, damage or destroy the material;
- make arrangements for ensuring that the integrity of exhibits is maintained and a continuity record is made where these are subject to defence examination;
- keep a record of any defence examination, including the nature and extent of the examination, and any views expressed;
- notify the police if the forensic scientist's views are likely to change as a result of the defence examination.

14.4 The prosecutor will have provided the defence with an endorsed copy of the index and the schedule of non-sensitive unused material (from MG6C). Where the prosecutor has indicated that unused material in the possession of the FSP should be disclosed, the disclosure officer will send a copy of the index, MG6C, and any letter at secondary stage to the forensic scientist.

14.5 The FSP should grant the defence access to the unused material that the prosecutor has indicated should be disclosed. This should be done on production of a copy of the MG6C schedule or index (or covering letter, if the latter refers to the material directly). The material to be disclosed will be marked upon the schedule or index by the prosecutor by a '*D*' or an '*I*' endorsed against an item in accordance with JOPI paragraph 3.33). Items that do not meet either disclosure test, and thus do not require disclosure to the defence will be marked by the prosecutor with '*CND*'. The FSP will use the copy MG6C supplied by the police as a checklist, and to identify material that does not require diclosure at that time.

14.6 Supervision of access to non-sensitive unused material by the FSP will be governed by way of local arrangements. As best practice, this should require that the investigator or disclosure officer is present wherever possible when the defence examine any forensic material.

14.7 It should be noted that the defence may also be entitled to access to material in the possession of forensic science organisations through the operation of the Crown Court (Advance Notice of Expert Evidence) Rules 1997 or the Magistrates' Courts (Advance Notice of Expert Evidence) Rules 1997. This will relate to the records of any tests, calculations, documents, or objects upon which the forensic scientist bases his expert opinion and which forms part of the prosecution case.

ANNEX J   AN EXPLANATORY LEAFLET ON THE PRINCIPLES AND PROCEDURES RELATING TO THIRD PARTIES UNDER THE CRIMINAL PROCEDURE AND INVESTIGATIONS ACT 1996 AND THE DISCLOSURE OF MATERIAL IN THEIR POSSESSION

Introduction

1. This document explains the procedures to be followed by the prosecution in seeking to obtain relevant material held by individuals and organisations that are regarded as third parties in criminal proceedings.
2. The law governing material held by third parties is contained in the Criminal Procedure and Investigations Act 1996 (CPIA) and the Attorney General's Guidelines published in November 2000.

Who are third parties?

3. In the course of an investigation to determine whether an offence has been committed, the police may become aware of relevant material in the possession of

persons or organisations which may have a bearing on the investigation. It is only the investigator and the prosecutor who have statutory duties of revelation and disclosure under the CPIA. All other categories of persons are third parties so far as the conduct of the case is concerned.

The legal requirements of the prosecution

4. Every accused person has a right to a fair trial, a right enshrined in our law and guaranteed under the European Convention on Human Rights. This right to a fair trial is fundamental and the accused's right to fair disclosure is an inseparable part of it.

5. The scheme set out in the CPIA is designed to ensure that there is fair disclosure of material to the accused which may be relevant to an investigation and which does not form part of the prosecution case. This is known as 'unused material'. Fairness does, however, recognise that there are other interests that need to be protected, including those of the victims and witnesses who might otherwise be exposed to harm. The CPIA protects those interests.

6. Investigators are under a duty to pursue all reasonable lines of enquiry, whether these point towards or away from the accused. What is reasonable in each case will depend on the particular circumstances. Investigators and prosecutors must do all they can to facilitate proper disclosure, as part of their general and professional responsibility to act fairly and impartially, in the interests of justice.

7. Where you possess material, which has not been obtained by the police, they are under a duty to inform you of the existence of the investigation and to invite you to retain the material in case they receive a request for its disclosure. Where the police inspect material with your agreement and do not retain it, they are under a duty to record details of that material and to reveal it to the prosecutor.

8. Where you do not allow the prosecution access to the material, the prosecution may apply to the court for a witness summons, and if granted would require you to attend court to produce the material to the court. Application for a witness summons will only be made where the prosecution considers that the material sought is likely to be material to the proceedings. You do have the right to make representations to the court against the issue of a witness summons.

9. Where the relevant material held by you or owned by you but in the possession of the prosecution is sensitive, in that it is not in the public interest to disclose, then the prosecution will treat that material in confidence. Where that material might undermine the prosecution case or might reasonably assist the defence case, a public interest immunity application must be made to prevent disclosure to the defence. Where you have an interest in that material, the prosecution is under a duty to notify you in writing of the time and place of any public interest immunity application. You have a right to make representations to the court.

10. Failure by the prosecution to take action that should have led to the disclosure of relevant material may result in a wrongful conviction or dismissal of the proceedings.

The prosecution procedures in dealing with third parties

11. In the course of an investigation, the investigator will write to you setting out the circumstances of the case and specifying the relevant material that he or she believes is in your possession.

12. Where you acknowledge that you hold relevant material which may have some bearing on the issues in the case, the investigator will requrest a copy from you or request to inspect the material.
13. Where you provide the material to the police in the course of the investigation, the police will discuss with you whether any sensitivity attaches to the material. Your view will be passed on to the Crown Prosecution Service.
14. Where the material is sensitive, and a public interest immunity application is made to withhold the material from the defence, you have a right to make representations to the court on issues of the sensitivity of the material. The Crown Prosecution Service will notify you of the time and place of the application.
15. Where you refuse to provide all or part of the material, or refuse to allow the police to inspect it, the police will request you to retain the material in case they receive a request for its disclosure or the court later requires the material to be disclosed.
16. Where an accused has been charged with an offence and you have refused to reveal the material to the police, or failed to respond to a request for the material, the Crown Prosecution Service may consider applying to the court for a witness summons. The procedure relating to witness summonses is set out below.

Rules relating to witness summonses in the Crown court (Criminal Procedure (Attendance of Witnesses) Act 1965)

17. Where the trial has not commenced, an application for a summons for a person to produce a document or thing to the court must be made in writing, to the appropriate officer of the Crown court. The application should contain:

- A brief description of the required document or thing;
- Reasons why the person will not voluntarily produce it;
- Reasons why the document or thing is likely to be material evidence;
- A supporting affidavit setting out the charge and specifying: the evidence which will enable the person to identify it; the grounds for believing that the person is likely to be able to produce the document or thing; and the grounds for believing that it will be material evidence.

18. A copy of the application and the supporting affidavit will be served on the person by the Crown Prosecution Service/police. It will inform the person of their right to make representations in writing and at the hearing, and that they have 7 days to inform the court if they wish to make representations.
19. If the person does not request a hearing, the appropriate officer of the Crown court will refer the papers to the judge. The judge will decide whether or not to issue a witness summons in the light of the information before him.
20. If the person requests a hearing, the court will set a time, place and date and will notify both the person and the Crown Prosecution Service. The hearing shall be in private unless the judge directs otherwise.
21. Where the person produces the document or thing prior to the hearing of the summons, the Crown Prosecution Service will notify the court that the requirements imposed by the summons are no longer needed.
22. A person may make an application to the Crown court to make a summons which has been issued ineffective on the grounds that he had not received a notice of application to issue the summons and that he had not been present or represented at any hearing of the application and would not be able to produce any document or thing likely to be material evidence.

Rules relating to witness summonses in the magistrates' court

23. If the proceedings are before the magistrates' court, an application can be made for a witness summons for a person to produce a document or thing under section 97 or 97A (committal proceedings) of the Magistrates' Court Act 1980.

24. Where an indictable only offence has been sent to the Crown court and before service of the prosecution case, an application can be made to the magistrates' court for a person to produce a document or other exhibit (Schedule 3, paragraph 4 of the Crime and Disorder Act 1998).

Draft letter to third parties

Dear Sir/Madam

REQUEST FOR DISCLOSURE OF MATERIAL HELD BY ....

(   ) Police are conducting a criminal investigation into allegations made against (*name and address, if appropriate, of the alleged offender*).

The allegations being investigated are, in general terms, that (*set out the nature of the allegations and the issues in the case*).

I believe that you hold material which may be relevant to the investigation, namely (*set out what material it is believed the third party holds*).

The reasons why I am seeking access to this material is because I believe that (*list the reasons which may include; material which might affect the credibility and reliability of a witness; material which might undermine the prosecution case; and material which might reasonably assist the defence case*).

I would be grateful if you would confirm whether or not you hold any such material and if so, whether you are prepared to disclose it for the purposes of the investigation. I would also be grateful if you could let me know whether you consider the material to be sensitive and the reasons for any sensitivity.

If you object to disclosing the material, I would be grateful if you could specify your reasons. I request that you retain the material in case the court requires you to disclose some or all of the material.

I enclose for your assistance, an explanatory leaflet that sets out the role of the prosecution in dealing with material in the possession of third parties. It explains what will happen with the material if you disclose it. Further, it explains what may happen if you refuse to disclose it.

It would be of great assistance if you could reply by (*insert date*).

If you wish to discuss this request, or any further information, please do not hesitate to contact me on (*insert contact number*).

Thank you in advance for your assistance.

Yours faithfully,

(*Officer in charge of the investigation/investigator/disclosure officer*).

APPENDIX 6

Drug influence recognition: aide memoire

Drug Influence Recognition - Expected Roadside Observations - Aide Memoir

Main Drug Groups

Expected Observations	CANNABIS Sativa, Indica	OPIATES Heroin, Morphine, Codeine, Methadone	STIMULANTS Cocaine, Ecstacy, Amphetamine, PCP	DEPRESSANTS Alcohol, GHB, Prescribed Drugs	HALLUCINOGENS LSD, Magic Mushrooms	INHALANTS Volatile Solvents, Paint, Glue etc
	Possible dilated Pupils	Constricted Pupils	Dilated Pupils	Possible dilated Pupils	Possible dilated Pupils	Normal Pupils
	Reddish whites of eyes Smell	Sleepy appearance Facial itching	Eyelid tremors Grinding teeth	Watery eyes	Dazed appearance Sweating/Goosebumps	Bloodshot/watery eyes Smell
	Poor co-ordination & balance	Possible euphoria	Restlessness Euphoria	Unco-ordinated Slow sluggish reactions	Unco-ordinated Poor balance	Flushed/sweaty appearance Dizzy/lightheaded
	Impaired time & distance	Slow reflexes	Fast internal clock Anxiety	Drowsiness	Distorted time & distance	Distorted time & distance
	Disorientation Relaxed inhibitions	Low slow speech Dry mouth	Won't keep quiet Easily irritated	Thick, slurred slow speech	Paranoia Hallucinations Synesthesia	Non-communicative/ Slurred speech Nausea, Headache
Pupil Exam	Possible Dilated	Constricted	Dilated	Possible Dilated	Possible Dilated	Normal
Romberg	Fast/slow	Slow	Fast	Slow	Fast	Normal
Walk & Turn	Impaired	Impaired	Fast	Impaired	Impaired	Impaired
One Leg Stand	Impaired	Impaired	Fast	Impaired	Impaired	Impaired
Finger to Nose	Impaired	Impaired	Fast	Impaired	Impaired	Impaired

DRUG GROUP

ALWAYS SAY NEVER, NEVER SAY ALWAYS

Section 23(2) Misuse of Drugs Act 1971

SEARCH that person and DETAIN him for the purpose of searching him.

SEARCH any vehicle in which the Constable suspects that the drug may be found and for that purpose require the person in control of this vehicle/vessel to stop it.

SEIZE and DETAIN anything found in the course of the search which appears to the Constable to be evidence of an offence under the act.

Section 4 Road Traffic Act - Field Impairment Testing Process

When considering carrying out an FIT, the following process will be followed:-

1. Breath Test (Negates presence of alcohol)
2. Read Additional Warning from aide memoir or MG/DD/F
3. Pupillary Examination
4. Romberg Test
5. Walk & Turn Test
6. One Leg Stand Test
7. Finger to Nose Test
8. Take results of all tests to determine impairment
9. Arrest (if impaired)
10. Consult with Police Surgeon in Custody

All Instructions for tests MUST be read from either the Aide Memoir or the MG/DD/F

Remember a SYSTEMATIC STANDARDISED ASSESSMENT is the key

Section 4 - Road Traffic Act 1988

Any person who drives, attempt to drive or is in charge of a mechanically propelled vehicle on a road or other public place, and at the time when he is driving is UNFIT to drive through drink or drugs, commits an offence.

IMPAIRMENT - a combination of all three of the following:

1. Manner of driving
2. Physical condition of the driver
3. A toxicological sample (blood or urine)

DRUG RECOGNITION

If a Constable has reasonable grounds to suspect that any person is in possession of a controlled drug the Constable may:-

---

Drug Search Plan

Before going out on patrol, search the rear seat of the police vehicle to confirm there are no substances previously hidden.

When you stop a suspect, has the driver or passenger anything in their mouth?

Check sun visor, (envelope), spills in particular (are there any tears, or splits in material)?

Pull down lever for bonnet, or column adjuster. (Drugs stuck to tape in the hollow).

Under the front part of the drivers seat.

Under the carpet, to the right of the driver, in the area of the chassis number.

Check cassette cases, or cigarette packets in vehicles.

Headrest area of driver.

Do the interior lights work? Are there drugs in place of the bulb?

Check ashtrays and cigarette lighter holder.

APPENDIX 7

London fire brigade forms

FS/FIT/1

LONDON FIRE BRIGADE LIAISON REPORT

"FOR POLICE ACTION - SEE OVER"

To be completed in all cases where the
fire requires the attendance of POLICE or
LFB FIT and involves:- SERIOUS INJURY ☐
                FATALITY ☐
or is of a SUSPICIOUS NATURE ☐

| SECTION ONE | Tick relevant box

CIRCULATION

PINK:	FB OiC	GREEN:	POLICE OiC
BLUE:	Id.O/SOCO	YELLOW:	FB FIT

LFB OFFICER COMPLETING

NAME ....

DATE .... TIME ....

SIGNATURE ....

A. ADDRESS ....   DATE OF CALL ....

....   TIME OF DISCOVERY ....

    TYPE/USE of PROPERTY ....   TIME OF CALL ....

    FB STATION GROUND ....   TIME OF ARRIVAL ....

    OIC FIRE .... Tel: ....   TIME UNDER CONTROL ....

    OIC FDR1 .... Tel: ....   MEDIA RESOURCES   YES/NO

    WATCH .... R ... W .... B .... G .... (circle)   PHOTOS or VIDEOS (delete as necessary)

FIT ATTENDED? YES/NO   Tel: ....*   1st POLICE OFFICER.   DIV NO. ....
LFB AREA .... FIT OFFICER ....   NAME ....   STATION ....

B. **FIRE BRIGADE OBSERVATIONS:**

    SUSPECTED AREA OF ORIGIN ....

    RELEVANT REMARKS (e.g., ANY ABNORMAL FIRE BEHAVIOUR, REASON for SUSPICION, plan if necessary)

    ....

    ....

C. **FIRE FIGHTING ACTIONS:**

    EXTINGUISHED BY (include installations) ....

    RELEVANT TURNING OVER OF SCENE ....

    OTHER ACTION (movement of BODIES, FURNITURE, etc.) ....

SERVICES)	ELEC:-	ON	OFF	N/A	UNKNOWN	BRIGADE SWITCHED:-	ON	OFF	N/A
ON ARRIVAL)	GAS:-	ON	OFF	N/A	UNKNOWN	BRIGADE SWITCHED:-	ON	OFF	N/A

D. **SECURITY OF BUILDING:**

    ON ARRIVAL WAS ALARM SOUNDING?   YES/NO   FIRE/INTRUDER

    FB ACTIONS TO GAIN ACCESS/VENTILATE ....

    DOORS BROKEN BY FB ....

    WINDOWS BROKEN BY FB ....

    OTHER RELEVANT ACTIONS ....

    OTHER RELEVANT SECURITY OBSERVATIONS ....

DID ANY FB OFFICER BLEED AT SCENE?   YES/NO   NAME .... STN ....
WHERE WAS BLOOD LEFT AT SCENE? ....

E. REPORT HANDED TO POLICE OFFICER : DIV NO. .... NAME .... STN ....

    LOCATION: ON SITE - POLICE STATION - OTHER ....

| * FOR POLICE ACTION AND CONCLUSION SEE REVERSE SIDE (GREEN AND YELLOW COPIES ONLY) *

FORM 9283

POLICE LIAISON REPORT

Form to be handed to officer in charge of the CRIME DESK for
distribution to Investigating Officer and Id.O/SOCO.

**When the Crime Desk is unmanned, the form must be handed to the
Station Officer, who will be responsible for forwarding it direct to
the OIC Crime Desk.**

Investigating Officers to complete when the crime is classified and
in all cases inform London Fire Brigade Investigation Team by telephone or copy.

SECTION TWO

F. CRIME BOOK NUMBER/O.B. REFERENCE   :   ....

   CLASSIFICATION (TYPE)   :   ....

   POLICE INVESTIGATING OFFICER   :   NAME ....RANK ....

                                                   STATION ....TEL NO. ....

   Id.O/SOCO/LAB SGT. ATTENDED   :   YES/NO

                                                   NAME ....TEL NO. ....

   MP LAB FIU ATTENDED   :   YES/NO

                                                   NAME ....

   FIRE RELATED ITEMS TAKEN   :   YES/NO

G. **RELEVANT INFORMATION FOR TRANSMISSION TO LFB FIT:**

   e.g. (Statements required, progress, etc.) ─────────────────────────────────

   ───

   ───

   ───

   ───

   ───

   ───

   ───

H. **FIRE BRIGADE FIT INFORMED OF RESULT:**   **ON AUTHORITY OF:**

   DATE TELEPHONED/COPY SENT ....   NAME ....

   BY WHOM ....   RANK ....

   TO WHOM ....   SIGNATURE

   FIT TEL NOS: SEE (A)*

   NORTH WEST - ACTON:-   0181-992 1256   Fire Station, Gunnersbury Lane, W3 8EA
   NORTH   - CLERKENWELL:- 0171-837 6354   42/44 Roseberry Avenue, EC1 4RN
   NORTH EAST - EAST HAM:-   0171-587 2119   210 High Street South, E6 3RS
   SOUTH EAST - NEW CROSS:-   0171-587 4995   266 Queens Road, SE14 5JN
   SOUTH WEST - CLAPHAM:-   0171-587 4235   2 Braidwood Court, Grafton Square, SW4 0JS

   IF URGENT, ANY BRIGADE FIT CAN BE PAGED BY CALLING 0171-587 4444 (FB OPERATIONS ROOM)

SECTION THREE

   FOR ADDITIONAL FIRE BRIGADE USE
J.

   FIRE STATION INFORMED OF RESULT BY BRIGADE FIT

   DATE   ....

   BY WHOM ....

   TO WHOM ....

427

Report of Fire

Date: Day | Month | Year

KEY

Tick the appropriate box ☑
(or boxes)

Insert code from codelist ☐
or enter number

Brigade use ☐

Write in details ☐

1. Brigade information

1.1 Brigade incident number

1.2 Brigade Area where fire started — Station ground

1.3 Brigade and Home Office Call number — Fire spread box ☐

2. Incident information

2.1 Address of fire

2.2 Postcode (for buildings) or grid reference

OS national grid reference

2.3 Risk category

☐ A ☐ B ☐ C ☐ D ☐ R — ☐ Also ✓ if Special risk within area

2.4 Name(s) of occupier(s)/owner(s)

Times

2.5 Estimated interval from

a) Ignition to discovery

☐ Immediately ☐ Under 5 mins ☐ 5 to 30 mins ☐ 30 mins to 2 hours ☐ Over 2 hours ☐ Not known

b) Discovery to first call

☐ Immediately ☐ Under 5 mins ☐ 5 to 30 mins ☐ 30 mins to 2 hours ☐ Over 2 hours ☐ Not known

(use 24 hour clock)

hour | mins | day* | month* | year*

2.6 .... First call to brigade

2.7 .... Mobilising time

2.8 .... Arrival of brigade

2.9 ..... Under control

2.10 Last appliance returned

* Only complete 2.7 to 2.10 if different from 2.6

2.11 Was this a late fire call?

☐ No ☐ Yes

2.12 Discovery and call

a) Discovered by

☐ Person ☐ Automatic system ☐ Other - specify in Section 7

b) Method of call by

☐ Person ☐ Automatic system ☐ Other - specify in Section 7

2.13 Was there an automatic fire alarm system in area affected by fire?

☐ Go to 3.1 No ☐ Yes

2.14 Alarm activation method

☐ Heat ☐ Smoke ☐ Flame ☐ Other - specify in 2.18 ☐ Not known

2.15 Powered by

☐ Battery ☐ Mains ☐ Mains & battery back up ☐ Other - specify in 2.18 ☐ Not known

2.16 Did it operate?

☐ No ☐ Yes but did not raise alarm ☐ Yes and raised alarm — Go to 2.18 or 3.1

2.17 Reason for not operating/not raising alarm

2.18 Other details of automatic fire alarm

FDR1 (94)

3. Location of Fire

3.1 a) Type of property where fire started

b) If mobile property, give location

3.2 Residential accommodation affected by fire?

☐ No   ☐ Yes, where fire started only   ☐ Yes, spread to residential   ☐ Yes, where both started and spread to residential   ☐ Not known

3.3 Main trade or business carried on where fire started
If none ✓ box ☐ eg wholly residential, and go to 3.4

3.4 Multiseated fire

☐ No   ☐ Yes

Fires in buildings and ships

If not ✓ box ☐ and go to 3.10

3.5 Occupancy of building where fire started
(leave blank for ship)

☐ Single   ☐ Multiple same use   ☐ Multiple different use   ☐ Under construction   ☐ Under demolition

☐ Derelict   ☐ Unoccupied   ☐ Other - specify below eg - under refurbishment   ☐ Not known

3.6 Place where fire started

3.7 Use of room, cabin or roof space where fire started

3.8 Floor, deck of origin

Number ☐ if above ground/main deck

✓ if ground/main deck

Number ☐ if below ground/main deck

✓ if other, specify below

3.9 Total number of floors in building where fire started

☐ (leave blank for ship)

Fires starting in motor vehicles

If not ✓ box ☐ and go to Section 4

3.10 Make/Model

3.11 Fuel of vehicle

☐ Petrol (not fuel injected)   ☐ Petrol fuel injected   ☐ Petrol (not known)   ☐ Diesel/ other oil   ☐ Electric   ☐ LPG   ☐ Other - specify in 3.17

3.12 Was vehicle turbo/supercharged?

☐ No   ☐ Yes   ☐ Not known

3.13 Registration number (if available)

3.14 Year of manufacture (if available)

3.15 Part of vehicle where fire started

3.16 Was engine running? (immediately before fire)

☐ No   ☐ Yes   ☐ Not known

3.17 Other information available eg VIN No,Chassis No etc

4. Extinction of fire

Fixed firefighting/venting systems
(in area where fire started)

If none ✓ box ☐ and go to 4.6

	Type 1	Type 2	Type 3
4.1 Type of system (code up to 3) See Code list 4.1	☐	☐	☐
4.2 Manual or automatic M = Manual A = Automatic Z = Not known	☐	☐	☐
4.3 Did it operate A = Yes and extinguished fire B = Yes and contained (controlled) fire C = Yes but did not contain, (control) fire N = No	☐	☐	☐
4.4 Number of heads actuated	☐	☐	☐

4.5 Reason(s) for not operating/containing/controlling
(Leave blank if answer to question 4.3 is A or B)

Type 1

2

3

Method of fighting the fire

4.6 Before arrival of brigade

4.7 By brigade up to stop

4.8 Number of main jets used ☐

4.9 Number of local authority appliances attending up to time of stop ☐ ☐
Pumping   Other

(If further details required by brigade - use Section 7)

5. Supposed cause, damage and other fire details

5.1 Most likely cause

a) ☐ Accidental   ☐ Malicious   ☐ Deliberate   ☐ Doubtful   ☐ Not known

b) caused by

☐ Child   ☐ Youth   ☐ Adult   ☐ Animal   ☐ Other (not a person or animal)   ☐ Not known

Give additional details of person (if known)

c) Defect, act, or omission giving rise to ignition

5.2 Source of ignition

a) Appliance/installation and other sources

b) Powered by

c) If source is an appliance, enter the make or model, if known below

5.3 Material or item ignited first

a) Description

b) Composition

5.4 Material or item mainly responsible for development of fire

a) Description

b) Composition

5.5 Dangerous substances affecting firefighting or development of fire (Specify up to 2 in order of priority)

If none ✓ box ☐ and go to 5.6

a) Material	b) Circs.
1	
2	

Circumstance codes:- M = being Made S = in Storage T = in Transit
U = being Used W = combination of circumstances Z = not known

c) Main effect of substance on fire and/or firefighting

5.6 Explosion

a) ☐ Yes occurred   ☐ First   ☐ During fire   ☐ First and during fire   ☐ Not known

☐ No   go to 5.7

b) Materials involved in explosion (Specify up to 2)

1	
2	

c) Containers involved in explosion (Specify up to 2)

1	
2	

5.7 Abnormal rapid fire development

No ☐   Give additional details (if known)

Yes ☐

5.8 Damage caused to:

i) item ignited first
ii) room, cabin, compartment etc of origin
   (buildings, ships & vehicles only)
iii) elsewhere on floor, deck, other compartments of origin
   (buildings, ships & vehicles only)
iv) elsewhere in/on property of origin
v) outdoors beyond property; beyond building, ship, plant, vehicle etc

a) %: enter percentage of item/room etc damaged
eg. 25 = quarter, 50 = half etc

b) Severity: enter code to show severity of damage
L = Light,   M = Moderate   S = Severe

Damage caused by	to i) a %	b	to ii) a %	b	to iii) a %	b	to iv) a %	b	to v) box(es) if affected
fire									☐
heat									☐
smoke									☐
other									☐
Total not to exceed 100%									buildings
% of structure damaged	%		%		%		%		vehicles
Number of additional:			rooms cabins c'partment etc		floors				other locations
			damaged						
			total						

If further description required by brigade use Section 7

5.9 Estimate of horizontal area damaged

a)		Area - sq m		b)
	☐	under 1 sq m	☐	
	☐	1-2	☐	
	☐	3-4	☐	
Area	☐	5-9	☐	Total area
damaged	☐	10-19	☐	damaged
by direct	☐	20-49	☐	by fire heat
burning	☐	50-99	☐	smoke etc.
	☐	100-199	☐	
	☐	200 +	☐	
		If over 200 write in to nearest 50 sq m		

5.10 Animals killed

If none ✓ box ☐ and go to Section 6
if yes record up to 3 main species

	Species	Number
1		
2		
3		

6. Life Risk

Involvement of persons (as known to brigade)

If none ✓ box ☐ and go to Section 7

6.1 Number of non-fatal casualties
(including those who were rescued)

6.2 Number of fatal casualties

6.3 Number of rescues only (exclude those who were casualties)

6.4 Approximate number of persons at discovery of fire in room, cabin, compartment, etc., of origin

6.5 Approximate number of persons at discovery of fire in other parts of building, vehicle, etc.

6.6 Approximate number who left the affected property (including any who were casualties)

6.7 Fatalities, other casualties and rescues:
Complete one line for each person.
Refer to guidance notes for codes.
Use single code in each column 2 to 7

if no injury leave blank
if not rescued leave blank

	Name of person	Age Yrs	Sex	Location	Main Circum-stance	Status	Nature of injury	Rescued by	Rescue methods up to 2	Brigade use
A										
B										
C										
D										
E										
F										
G										
H										
		1	2	3	4	5	6	7	8	9

7. More detailed description of fire/further information (if applicable)

Section/question

7.1 Further investigation to be carried out

☐ No   Yes by ──── ☐ Fire brigade ☐ Police ☐ Others ☐ Fire of special interest

7.2 Further information to follow

☐ No/Not known   ☐ Yes

Special study boxes

7.3	7.4	7.5	7.6	7.7

Name & rank of person in charge at first attendance (IN CAPITALS)

Name & rank of person in charge of the fire (if different from above) (IN CAPITALS)

Signature

Form completed by (IN CAPITALS)

Rank

Date

The Stationery Office (FM) Ref. 602740 Feb 97

431

Association of Police Surgeons Forms

PROFORMA TO ASSESS SEXUAL ASSAULT

Complainant's Name   Date   1

<u>PROFORMA FOR POST-PUBERTAL FEMALE AND</u>
<u>MALE FORENSIC SEXUAL ASSAULT EXAMINATION</u>

> **Note:** This form has been designed for use by Police Surgeons (also known as Forensic Medical Examiners, Forensic Physicians or Sexual Offence Examiners). It is provided to assist the examining doctor in the assessment of an adult complainant of sexual assault. It is to be regarded as an aide-memoire and it is therefore not necessary for all parts of the proforma to be completed. On completion this form is the personal property of the examining doctor.

1. EXAMINATION DETAILS

Location ....Date of examination ....

Time of arrival.........................Time introduced to complainant....................

2. DOCTOR DETAILS

Name of FME..

Other doctors (if present) ....

GP details ....

3. POLICE DETAILS

Name of attending police officer ....

Name of investigating officer ....

4. OTHERS PRESENT

Social worker / Care worker ....

Others (relationship to examinee) ....

Prepared by Dr Jeanne Herring & Dr Debbi J. Rogers on behalf of the Education and Research Committee of The Association of Police Surgeons August 2002

Complainant's Name   **Date**   **2**

5. PATIENT DETAILS

Name ....

Date of Birth .... Age ....

Gender   FEMALE / MALE   Ethnicity...

Marital status ....Lives with....................................

Occupation ....

6. CONSENT TO EXAMINATION AND REPORT

I .... consent to a medical

examination as explained to me by Dr.............................. to include:

- a. Full medical examination from top to toe
- b. Collection of forensic specimens / clothing
- c. Taking of photographs for record and evidential purposes
- d. Slides / videocolposcopic recording / diagnostic / training via a colposcope
- e. Consent for the use of anonymised data from this proforma to be used for medical research

I understand that Dr ....may have to produce a report based on the examination and that details of the examination may have to be revealed in court.

I have been advised that I may strike out any of the above before I sign and halt the examination at any time.

I understand that the information recorded on this form and any photographs taken may be later required by the court.

Signed .... Date ....

Signed .... Date ....

Name (& relationship of person with parental authority)................................

Witnessed...

Name of Witness...

Relationship of witness..

Prepared by Dr Jeanne Herring & Dr Debbi J. Rogers on behalf of the Education and Research Committee of The Association of Police Surgeons August 2002

Complainant's Name   **Date**   3

7. HISTORY of ASSAULT

Briefing taken from ....

Contact details ....

Location of assault ....

History of events ....

....

....

....

....

....

....

....

....

....

Confirmation / additions from complainant (verbatim & recorded contemporaneously)

....

....

Are you aware of any injuries? (Details)

....

....

Are you aware of any ano-genital bleeding? ....

....

Weapon Used?   YES / NO :   (Details)

....

Damage to clothing? YES / NO : (Details)

....

Prepared by Dr Jeanne Herring & Dr Debbi J. Rogers on behalf of the Education and Research Committee of The Association of Police Surgeons August 2002

Complainant's Name   Date   4

8. OTHER SEXUAL ACTIVITIES
(details e.g. urinating, sucking or biting, spitting or ejaculating over body)

....

....

Penis to mouth   yes/no   Penis to anus   yes/no

9. DRUG AND ALCOHOL USE IN RELATION TO ASSAULT

	DATE	TIME	ALCOHOL	DRUG
5 days pre assault				
12 hrs pre assault				
Post assault				

10. POST ASSAULT – ask if relevant

                                                    YES   NO

Eaten

Drank

Wiped (specify site and disposal of e.g. cloth / tissue)

Bowels open

Passed urine (*note time*)

Changed clothes (*specify*)

Self harm (*sites*)

Complaints of pain / soreness / bleeding post assault

    Details ....

    ....

Prepared by Dr Jeanne Herring & Dr Debbi J. Rogers on behalf of the Education and Research Committee of The Association of Police Surgeons August 2002

Complainant's Name   **Date**   5

Brushed teeth / gums/ dentures (*circle*) Mouth wash / spray used (*circle*)

Washed / Bathed / Showered / Douched (*circle*)

Changed tampon / pad / sponge / diaphragm (*circle*)

Forensic samples taken before examination started:

Details..

....

By whom taken ....

11. MEDICAL HISTORY

Past medical / surgical history / hospital admissions

....

....

....

....

....

....

....

....

....

....

....

....

....

Major psychiatric diagnoses..

Learning difficulties...

Suicidal / DSH..

Prepared by Dr Jeanne Herring & Dr Debbi J. Rogers on behalf of the Education and Research Committee of The Association of Police Surgeons August 2002

Complainant's Name   **Date**   6

Obstetric and gynaecological history

Present contraception .... TAMPON / PAD USER ?

LMP .... Cycle .... Menarche if relevant ....

Children .... Modes of delivery ....

Current genito-urinary symptoms

....

....

Past history vulvo-vaginal trauma / surgery

....

Current vulvo-vaginal skin disease / infection

....

Past history of anal trauma / surgery / bleeding on defecation

....

Current anal skin disease / infection

....

Sexual history

SI prior to assault in last 14 days : YES / NO

If yes, note date : ....

If yes, was condom used : ....

If yes, was lubricant used (*note type*) : ....

SI post assault : YES / NO

Types of intercourse in last 14 days only

....

....

Prepared by Dr Jeanne Herring & Dr Debbi J. Rogers on behalf of the Education and Research Committee of The Association of Police Surgeons August 2002

Complainant's Name   **Date**   7

Current drug history (this is defined as drugs used in last 5 days)
If recorded elsewhere e.g. 'scenesafe form' no need to duplicate
Note strength and dosage and when medication was last taken

Prescribed...

....

....

....

OTC ....

....

....

Illicit...

....

....

12. EXAMINATION

Name(s) of persons present ....

....

Height ....

Weight ....

Skin Colour ....

Hair Colour ....

Demeanour ....

Disability (*note type*)

....

....

Prepared by Dr Jeanne Herring & Dr Debbi J. Rogers on behalf of the Education and Research Committee of The Association of Police Surgeons August 2002

Complainant's Name   **Date**   **8**

Head to Toe Survey (detail below and on APS body diagrams when appropriate)

Notes inc. measurements, colour, shape, site, type of injury etc.

Document negative findings

Scalp / Hair

Face

Eyes

Ears

Lips

Inside mouth / Palate

Teeth

Neck

Back

Buttocks

Arms R /L

Hands / Wrists R / L

Fingers and Nails R / L (note if cut / broken / false / bitten)

Front of Chest

Breasts

Abdomen

Legs R / L

Feet / Ankles / Soles R / L

Additional details e.g. jewellery injuries, items lost at scene, injection sites / self harm

Other findings

Prepared by Dr Jeanne Herring & Dr Debbi J. Rogers on behalf of the Education and Research Committee of The Association of Police Surgeons August 2002

439

Complainant's Name   Date   9

SYSTEMS EXAMINATION

CVS

Pulse rate / character .... BP ....

Heart sounds ....

Other findings ....

RS

Trachea / Air entry / PN etc ....

Breath sounds .... PEFR (if indicated).................

Abdomen

L.K.K.S..... ....

Tenderness / Masses ....

Bowel sounds ....

Diagram (if indicated)

CNS

Pupil size and reactions ....

Eye movement / nystagmus ....

Conjunctivae ....

Conscious level ... .

Balance / Coordination ....

Reflexes ....

Prepared by Dr Jeanne Herring & Dr Debbi J. Rogers on behalf of the Education and Research Committee of The Association of Police Surgeons August 2002

Complainant's Name   **Date**   **10**

Genital Examination – tick as indicated

Extra lighting   Colposcope   Additional magnification

Position used – clarify:...

Details of Female Genital Findings (and recorded on APS body diagrams)

Thighs

Pubic area

Pubic hair

Labia majora

Labia minora

Fourchette

Fossa Navicularis

Vestibule

Hymen (diagram when indicated)

Internal findings

Vaginal wall

Cervix

Size of speculum used : SMALL / MEDIUM / LARGE

Foley catheter used YES / NO

Sterile water used : YES / NO   Lubricant used YES / NO Type:

Prepared by Dr Jeanne Herring & Dr Debbi J. Rogers on behalf of the Education and Research Committee of The Association of Police Surgeons August 2002

441

Complainant's Name   Date   11

Details of Male Genital Findings (and recorded on APS body diagrams)

Thighs
Pubic Area
Pubic Hair
Scrotum
Testes
Penis
Foreskin

Details of Anal findings

Natal fold
Perianal / Anal margin
Internal findings
Proctoscope used : size and type :
Sterile water used : YES / NO   Lubricant used YES / NO   Type
Diagram (if indicated)

Prepared by Dr Jeanne Herring & Dr Debbi J. Rogers on behalf of the Education and Research Committee of The Association of Police Surgeons August 2002

Complainant's Name   **Date**   **12**

FORENSIC SAMPLES (If Scenesafe form or similar not used)

Identification number	Description of sample	Moistened Yes / No	Time taken

To whom handed ....

Date and Time samples handed over ....

Prepared by Dr Jeanne Herring & Dr Debbi J. Rogers on behalf of the Education and Research Committee of The Association of Police Surgeons August 2002

Complainant's Name   **Date**   **13**

After Care – include details

                                          YES   NO   DETAILS

STD screening referral   ....

PCC given / referral for IUCD   ....

Antibiotics given   ....

Other medication given   ....

Referral for Hep B immunisation / PEP   ....

Referral to GP   ....

Referral to other support services   ....

Post sexual assault leaflet given   ....

Advice given to complainant   ....

....

....

Time examination concluded...

Time notes concluded...

Dated and signed by FME..

Witnessed notes made at time of examination..

Conclusions / Advice given to police:

Prepared by Dr Jeanne Herring & Dr Debbi J. Rogers on behalf of the Education and Research Committee of The Association of Police Surgeons August 2002

SAMPLE CONSENT FORM FOR FMEs

CONSENT.

Verbal Consent Obtained   Yes ☐   No ☐   Special features............................

I consent to a medical examination, including the taking of samples if appropriate on

myself or my .... as explained to me by Dr ....

I understand that Dr .... may have to produce a report based on the examination and that details of the examination may have to be revealed in court.

Signed .... Date ....

Witnessed .... Date ....

Name of Witness .... Relationship of witness ....

Prepared by Dr Guy A. Norfolk, on behalf of the Education and Research Committee, January 2002©

SECTION 4 RTA ASSESSMENT FORM

 ASSOCIATION OF POLICE SURGEONS
SECTION 4 RTA ASSESSMENT FORM (Version 5.1 9/02)

1 | INTRODUCTION AND GENERAL GUIDANCE

Note: This form has been designed by Dr Ian F Wall on behalf of the Education and Research Committee of the Association of Police Surgeons for use by Police Surgeons (also known as Forensic Medical Examiners or Forensic Physicians) who have been trained in the use of Standardised Impairment Tests. The form is provided to assist Police Surgeons in determining whether a person has a condition, which may be due to drink or drugs and not necessarily due to 'impairment'. It is to be regarded as an aide-memoire and it is therefore not necessary for all parts of the form to be completed. Some details are included so as to aid possible subsequent assessment of fitness for detention in custody. Where a test is abandoned the reasons should be recorded in Additional Particulars at 12. If the questions are read from a card, the wording should be identical to those used in this form and the card must remain available for production at court. On completion this form is the personal property of the examining doctor.
    Whilst this form is designed to provide for the recording of findings following the examination of a subject to determine both the persons general medical condition and the degree of any impairment present, it is important to stress that the primary question police require to be answered is 'Has the person a condition which might be due to some drug?' It is not necessary to determine impairment or unfitness to drive.

2 | GENERAL DETAILS

Name:	Police station:
Address:	Custody record No:
	Date of birth:
	Occupation:
Arrest date:	Arrest time:
PNC warnings:	
Time Called:	Time Arrived:
Time examination started:	Time examination completed:

3 | BACKGROUND INFORMATION

Road side breath test:	Intoximeter readings:

Information from arresting officer (PC.......................)...........................

....

....

Field impairment test results...

....

....

Information from Custody Officer (PS....................)..........................

....

....

Dr's name.....................Date................   * Delete as Applicable   Page 1

ASSOCIATION OF POLICE SURGEONS
SECTION 4 RTA ASSESSMENT FORM (Version 5.1 9/02)

4	**CONSENT**

Consent witnessed by:

"My name is Dr. .... and I have been asked to examine you to ascertain whether in my opinion, you have a condition which might be due to drink or drugs. You should be aware that any conversation with me might not be treated confidentially"

"Do you agree to a medical examination?" ***YES/NO**

If **NO** make observations of accused's behaviour:.................................
....
....
....

If **YES**, consider written consent:

I consent to a medical examination as explained to me above:

Signed..

5	**MEDICAL CONSULTATION**

Consultation commenced at: hours

History of recent events:...
....
....

Current medical problems...
....
....

Past medical history:..
....
....
....

Dr's name......................Date................   * Delete as Applicable   Page 2

ASSOCIATION OF POLICE SURGEONS
SECTION 4 RTA ASSESSMENT FORM (Version 5.1 9/02)

HEARING PROBLEMS		BALANCE PROBLEMS	
VISUAL PROBLEMS		ASTHMA	
DIABETES RENAL IMPAIRMENT		EPILEPSY HEPATIC IMPAIRMENT	

Alcohol intake and times in last 24 hours:...

....

WEEKLY ALCOHOL INTAKE | Units per week |

TIME LAST ATE | | **TIME LAST SLEPT** | |

Past psychiatric

history:...

....

....

Previous self harm attempts:...

....

Social history:...

....

Relevant educational history (to assess if learning disability etc):...............

....

MEDICATION	DOSE	DURATION	ROUTE	LAST TAKEN
Prescribed				
OTC medicines				
Non-prescribed				

Dr's name......................Date................   * Delete as Applicable   Page 3

ASSOCIATION OF POLICE SURGEONS
SECTION 4 RTA ASSESSMENT FORM (Version 5.1 9/02)

6 | **MEDICAL EXAMINATION**

EXAMINED IN PRESENCE OF:

General demeanour:..

....

State of clothing:..

....

Mental state:..

....

....

....

Specimen of handwriting:...

....

....

Areas of body examined:..

....

| **SPEECH** | | **MOUTH** | |
| **BREATH** | | **BLOOD SUGAR** | |

DRUG MISUSE	**CVS**	**RS**	**GIT**
Needle marks:	Initial pulse:	PN:	Soft:
Shivering:	BP:	BS:	Tender:
Yawning:	Temp:	Added sounds:	LKKS:
Rhinorrhoea:	Heart sounds:	VR:	BS:
Gooseflesh:		PEFR:	
Lachrymation:			

Other abnormal findings:...

....

....

Dr's name......................Date...............   * Delete as Applicable   Page 4

ASSOCIATION OF POLICE SURGEONS
SECTION 4 RTA ASSESSMENT FORM (Version 5.1 9/02)

EYE EXAMINATION

Use the gauge below or a printed laminated card to assess pupil size:

1.0 1.5 2.0 2.5 3.0 3.5 4.0 4.5 5.0 5.5 8.0 8.5 7.0 7.5 8.0 8.5 9.0

EYE SIGNS	RIGHT	LEFT
Conjunctiva		
Pupil Size		
Direct reflex		
Indirect reflex		
Visual acuity:		
Visual fields:		
Horizontal gaze nystagmus		
Lack of smooth pursuit		

Vertical gaze nystagmus: *YES/NO   Convergence: *YES/NO

Spectacles: *YES/NO   Contact lens: *YES/NO

Other abnormal eye findings:..

....

7   **IMPAIRMENT TESTS**

"I would like you to perform a series of tests to enable me to ascertain whether you have a condition which might be due to drink or drugs, or whether your ability to drive is impaired by drink or drugs. The tests are simple and part of my evaluation will be based on your ability to follow instructions. If you do not understand any of the instructions, please tell me so that I can clarify them."

ASSOCIATION OF POLICE SURGEONS
SECTION 4 RTA ASSESSMENT FORM (Version 5.1 9/02)

8	ROMBERG TEST

"Stand up straight with your feet together and your arms down by your sides. Maintain that position while I give you the remaining instructions. Do not begin until I tell you to do so. When I tell you to start, you must tilt your head back slightly and close your eyes (demonstrate but do not close your eyes). Keep your head tilted backwards with your eyes closed until you think that 30 seconds have passed, then bring your head forward and say 'Stop'".

"Do you understand?" YES/NO*

ABLE TO STAND STILL DURING INSTRUCTIONS: *YES/NO

EXCESSIVE BODY SWAY SEEN: *YES/NO

INTERNAL BODY CLOCK: 30SECONDS AT ....SECS

"How long was that?"............................

ABLE TO COMPLETE TEST: *YES/NO

COMMENTS:

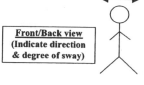

| Front/Back view (Indicate direction & degree of sway) | Side view (Indicate direction & degree of sway) |

9	WALK AND TURN TEST

Identify a real or imaginary line.
"Place your left foot on the line. Place your right foot on the line in front of your left touching heel to toe demonstrate). Put your arms down by your sides and keep them there throughout the entire test. Maintain that position whilst I give you the remaining instructions".

"Do you understand?" YES/NO*

"When I say start, you must take nine heel to toe steps along the line. On each step the heel of the foot must be placed against the toe of the other foot demonstrate). When the ninth step has been taken, you must leave the front foot on the line and turn around using a series of small steps with the other foot. After turning you must take another nine heel to toe steps along the line. You must watch your feet at all times and count each step out loud. Once you start walking do not stop until you have completed the test".

"Do you understand?" YES/NO*

Dr's name.....................Date................ * Delete as Applicable Page 6

ASSOCIATION OF POLICE SURGEONS
SECTION 4 RTA ASSESSMENT FORM (Version 5.1 9/02)

Any deviation from the instructions and any observations should be indicated below and on the diagram above

Able to stand still during instructions: *YES/NO

Start too soon: *YES/NO   Stops walking: *YES/NO

Turn: *Correct/Incorrect

Misses heel/toe: *YES/NO   Steps off line: *YES/NO

Raises arms: *YES/NO   Correct step count: *YES/NO

Notes:

---

10 | **ONE LEG STAND TEST**
"Stand with your feet together with your arms by your sides. Maintain that position while I give you the remaining instructions. Do not begin until I tell you to start."

"Do you understand?"   *YES/NO

"When I tell you to start you must raise your right foot six to eight inches off the ground, keeping your leg straight and your toes pointing forward, with your foot parallel to the ground (demonstrate). You must keep your arms by your sides and keep looking at your elevated foot while counting out loud in the following manner, 'one thousand and one, one thousand and two' and so on until I tell you to stop."

"Do you understand?"   *YES/NO

Repeat procedure with each foot

	LEFT	RIGHT			LEFT	RIGHT
SWAYS	YES/NO	YES/NO	HOPS		YES/NO	YES/NO
	*	*			*	*

PUTS FOOT DOWN	YES/NO	YES/NO	RAISES ARMS	YES/NO	YES/NO
	*	*		*	*

- If YES –
record at what point(s) in the count that it occurred i.e. one thousand and six (1006)

Dr's name.......................Date................   * Delete as Applicable   Page 7

ASSOCIATION OF POLICE SURGEONS
SECTION 4 RTA ASSESSMENT FORM (Version 5.1 9/02)

11 | FINGER AND NOSE TEST

"Stand with your feet together and your arms in this position. (Demonstrate extending both hands out in front, palms side up and closed with the index finger of both hands extended). Maintain that position while I give you the remaining instructions. Do not begin until I tell you to start. When I tell you to start you must tilt your head back slightly (demonstrate) and close your eyes. When I tell you which hand to move, you must touch the tip of your nose with the tip of that finger and lower your hand once you have done so (demonstrate).
"Do you understand?"   ***YES/NO**

Call out the hands in the following order, left, right, left, right, right, left.

EXCESSIVE BODY SWAY:	YES/NO
CORRECT HAND USE:	YES/NO
ADDITIONAL COMMENTS :	

```
2           1
4           3
5           6
```

Draw lines to spots touched

12 | ADDITIONAL PARTICULARS (see notes at 1).

....
....
....
....
....
....
....
....
....
....
....
....

| FINAL PULSE: | | CONSULTATION ENDED AT: | hours |

Dr's name.......................Date................   * Delete as Applicable   Page 8

453

ASSOCIATION OF POLICE SURGEONS
SECTION 4 RTA ASSESSMENT FORM (Version 5.1 9/02)

13	**CONCLUSIONS**

Is the person fit to be detained?   ***YES/NO***

If **NO** make note of reasons and subsequent action.................................
....

Is there a condition present which might be due to a drug?"   ***YES/NO***

If **YES** make note of conditions:..
....
....

**POLICE OFFICER ADVISED THAT A CONDITION
PRESENT THAT MIGHT BE DUE TO A DRUG AT:**   [   ]
                                                                                        hours

Is there impairment present?"   ***YES/NO***

If **YES** make note of reasons:..
....
....

**If there is a condition present which might be due to a drug the police
officer will proceed as on Form MG DD/B at B18.**

14	**SUBSEQUENT PROCEDURES**

Blood or Urine decision

Are there medical reasons for the sample not to be of blood?   ***YES/NO***

If **YES** make note of reasons (Officer will then proceed to require Urine)
....

15	**CONSENT FOR BLOOD SAMPLE**

Consent witnessed by: [   ]

*"My name is Dr.   .... and I have been asked to take a sample of blood
from you which will be tested for alcohol and/or drugs"*

"Do you agree to a blood test?"   ***YES/NO***

Dr's name.......................Date................   * Delete as Applicable   Page 9

ASSOCIATION OF POLICE SURGEONS
SECTION 4 RTA ASSESSMENT FORM (Version 5.1 9/02)

If **NO ask:** *"Is there any medical reason why I should not obtain a sample of blood from you?"*

Make notes of accused's reasons:...

....

....

....

If **YES,** details as below:

Blood specimen successfully taken at...........................hours

Site............................... Venting needle used?   ***YES/NO**

Blood specimen given to .... at................hours

If venepuncture unsuccessful, reasons:...

....

.............(Police can still proceed with a urine requirement on form MG DD/B).

It is also useful to assist the Police Officer in completion of Form MG DD/E Drugs Sample Information Form.

Dr's name.....................Date................   * Delete as Applicable   Page 10

SCENE OF SUSPICIOUS DEATH FORM

**Proforma for the FME at the Scene of a Suspicious Death/Death
in Custody.**

Name of deceased ....

Age ....   D.O.B ....   Date of examination ....

Address of scene ....

Time called ....   Time of arrival ....   Time death confirmed ....

Time left scene ....

History

Briefed by: ....

Last seen alive: ....   Name of GP if known: ....

History:

Has the body been moved?   Yes ☐   No ☐

If yes, why and by whom?

Significant features of scene:
(Include all relevant information such as medication, drug paraphernalia, alcohol,
bloodstains etc.)

Sketch/photography if necessary:

**Prepared by Dr Guy Norfolk on behalf of the Education and Research Committee of
The Association of Police Surgeons ©**

Examination of Body.

(Only examine the body after being briefed by the officer in charge. Do not move the body or disturb the locus without prior permission)

Ambient temperature (ask SOCO to record) ....

Body temperature[1] ....   **Site temperature recorded** ....

Rigor Mortis:

    Small muscles (jaw, hands)   Absent ☐   Present ☐

    Large muscles (arms, legs)   Absent ☐   Present ☐

As a rough guide in average temperatures[2]:
A *warm* and *flaccid* body has been dead for less than 3 hours
A *warm* and *stiff* body has been dead for 3–8 hours
A *cold* and *stiff* body has been dead for 8–36 hours
A *cold* and *flaccid* body has been dead for more than 36 hours.

Hypostasis   Absent ☐   Present ☐

Colour of hypostasis .... Site ....

External Examination
(Notes on state of dress, pupillary size, presence of any body fluids, injuries etc.)

---

[1] The advice of the local Home Office Pathologist should be sought regarding the taking of body temperatures. When appropriate, temperatures should be taken with a low reading chemical (not clinical) thermometer, which ideally reads from 0–50 degrees centigrade. The temperature should be recorded from the rectum if this can be done safely without loss/contamination of any trace evidence. If in any doubt, and particularly if there is any suspicion of sexual assault, record the temperature from deep inside the external auditory meatus. The thermometer should be left in situ for at least 5 minutes before being read.
[2] Knight B. (1996) Forensic Pathology, Second Edition, London; Arnold at page 61.

Prepared by Dr Guy Norfolk on behalf of the Education and Research Committee of The Association of Police Surgeons ©

DEATH SCENE ALGORITHM

Association of Police Surgeons
Death Scene Algorithm

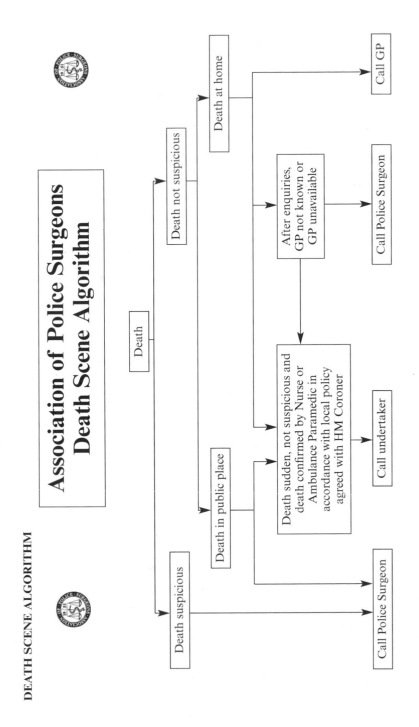

Death

Death suspicious

Death not suspicious

Death in public place

Death at home

Death sudden, not suspicious and death confirmed by Nurse or Ambulance Paramedic in accordance with local policy agreed with HM Coroner

After enquiries, GP not known or GP unavailable

Call Police Surgeon

Call undertaker

Call Police Surgeon

Call GP

This algorithm has been designed by Dr Ian F. Wall on behalf of the Education and Research Committee of the Association of Police Surgeons. August 2002

INTIMATE SAMPLES TABLE

THE FORENSIC SCIENCE SERVICE

© The Forensic Science Service, the Association of Police Surgeons and the Association of Chief Police Officers. 2000.

GUIDELINES FOR THE COLLECTION OF SPECIMENS

SAMPLE TYPE	REASON FOR ANALYSIS	METHOD OF SAMPLING	PACKAGING AND STORAGE
Saliva	Detection of semen if oral penetration within 2 days. *First sample*	Take 10 ml (if possible) of liquid saliva.	Plastic bottle placed in tamper evident bag. **Freeze**
Mouth swab	Detection of semen if oral penetration within 2 days. *Second sample*	Take 2 sequential samples by rubbing swab around inside of mouth, under tongue and gum margins or over dentures or dental fixtures.	Plain sterile swab returned immediately to appropriate swab sleeve/tube and placed in a tamper evident bag. **Freeze**
Mouth washings	Detection of semen if oral penetration within 2 days. *Third sample*	Rinse mouth with 10ml of sterile water and retain washings in bottle.	Plastic bottle placed in tamper evident bag. **Freeze** (place empty water vial with exhibit)
Skin swabs	Detection of body fluids and lubricant.	If stain is moist, recover on a dry swab. If stain is dry, dampen swab with sterile distilled water. Recover on more than one swab if staining remains visible after initial sampling.	Plain sterile swab returned immediately to appropriate swab sleeve/tube and placed in a tamper evident bag. **Freeze**
Control skin swab	Recovery of background DNA for mitochondrial analysis.	Dampen swab with sterile distilled water and swab adjacent unstained area of skin.	Plain sterile swab returned immediately to appropriate swab sleeve/tube and placed in a tamper evident bag. **Freeze**
Unused swab	Control for low copy number DNA analysis.	Submit unopened swab from appropriate module in every case where swabs have been taken.	Submit residual water and container in pot with swab in tamper evident bag. **Freeze**
Head hair	A. Detection of body fluids, e.g. semen. B. Identification of foreign particles or fibres (only where something is visible or an item has been placed over the head). C. Control sample from *suspect* only. Microscopic hair comparison.	A. Cut or swab relevant area. B. Remove visible foreign particles with disposable forceps and collect in plain paper. Tape head using low adhesive tape or comb hair with a *primed* comb if an item has been placed over the head. C. Cut a representative sample of 10-20 hairs close to the skin.	Place unused swab in tamper evident bag and store with other swabs taken. Place in tamper evident bag. Freeze In tamper evident bag. (Submit scissors in bag if used to cut hair.) Place in tamper evident bag.
Pubic hair	A. Detection of body fluids e.g. semen. B. Identification of foreign hairs or fibres.	A. Cut or swab relevant area. B. Comb hair and collect debris on paper.	As for swabs or place in tamper evident bag. **Freeze**
Vulval swab	A. Detection of body fluids if vaginal intercourse within 7 days or if anal intercourse within 3 days, or ejaculation on to perineum. *First sample* B. Detection of lubricant, if used, or if condom used within 30 hours.	Rub 2 sequential swabs over whole of vulval area. Number the swabs in the order taken. (Moisten swabs with distilled water if required.)	Plain sterile swab returned immediately to appropriate swab sleeve/tube and placed in a tamper evident bag. (Submit distilled water vial if used.) **Freeze**
Vaginal swab - Low	A. Detection of body fluids if vaginal intercourse within 7 days or if anal intercourse within 3 days. *Second sample* B. Detection of lubricant, if used, or if condom used within 30 hours.	Take 2 sequential swabs under direct vision before speculum is passed. Number the swabs in the order taken.	As above
Vaginal swab - High	A. Detection of body fluids if vaginal intercourse within 7 days or if anal intercourse within 3 days. *Third sample* B. Detection of lubricant, if used, or if condom used within 30 hours.	Take 2 sequential swabs using unlubricated speculum (moisten with sterile distilled water if necessary). Number the swabs in the order taken.	As above
Endocervical swab	Only necessary if vaginal intercourse more than 48 hours previously. *Final sample*	Take 1 swab via the speculum.	As above

459

THE FORENSIC SCIENCE SERVICE

© The Forensic Science Service, the Association of Police Surgeons and the Association of Chief Police Officers. 2000.

GUIDELINES FOR THE COLLECTION OF SPECIMENS

SAMPLE TYPE	REASON FOR ANALYSIS	METHOD OF SAMPLING	PACKAGING AND STORAGE
Penile swab - Coronal sulcus Glans / Shaft	A. Detection of body fluids if intercourse within 2 days. B. Detection of lubricant, if used, or if condom used within 30 hours.	Take 2 sequential swabs from coronal sulcus and 2 sequential swabs from shaft and glans. Moisten swabs with sterile distilled water. Number the swabs in the order taken.	Plain sterile swab returned immediately to appropriate swab sleeve/tube and placed in a tamper evident bag. (Submit used distilled water vial.) **Freeze**
Perianal swab	A. Detection of body fluids if intercourse within 3 days. *first sample* B. Detection of lubricant, if used, or if condom used within 30 hours.	Take 2 sequential swabs from the perianal area using swabs moistened with sterile distilled water. Number the swabs in the order taken.	As above
Rectal swab	A. Detection of body fluids if anal intercourse within 3 days. B. Detection of lubricant, if used, or if condom used within 30 hours.	Take swab lower rectum after passing proctoscope 2-3cm into the anal canal. Moisten proctoscope with sterile water if necessary.)	As above
Anal canal swab	A. Detection of body fluids if anal intercourse within 3 days. *Second sample* B. Detection of lubricant, if used, or if condom used within 30 hours.	Take swab as proctoscope withdrawn.	As above
Fingernails	Recovery of trace evidence (e.g. bodyfluid, possible fibres) or connection with fingernail broken at scene (if the circumstances suggest this as a possibility.)	Preferably cut nails. If the nails are too short or cutting is unacceptable, take scrapings for debris using fingernail quills into a paper wrapping.	Place in tamper evident bag **Freeze**
Buccal scrapes	Reference sample for DNA profiling.	Take 2 buccal scrapes from inside each side of the mouth (in cases involving oral sex between persons of the same gender; take an additional sample at least 2 days after incident).	Place plastic tubes into a tamper evident bag. **Freeze**
Condoms	Detection of body fluids and seminal fluid, if used during intercourse.	Secure the open end with a freezer clip or knot.	Place in a plastic container/pot in tamper evident bag. **Freeze**
Ground sheet/Couch cover	To identify foreign particles which may fall from clothing or body during examination.	Stand examinee on ground sheet.	Place in tamper evident bag. **Store dry**
Sanitary towels/Tampons	Detection of body fluids, e.g. semen, if in situ or after vaginal intercourse.	Retain intact.	Place in tamper evident bag or in a plastic container in a tamper evident bag. **Freeze**
Blood preserved (sodium fluoride & potassium oxalate)	Analysis for alcohol, drugs (drugs of abuse & medicinal) and volatiles. **NB:** Take blood and urine in every case, unless the incident was more than 4 days prior to the examination when a urine specimen only is required. If in doubt, consult the Laboratory for advice.	Take 10ml of venous blood into blood container. Insert septum securely and screw cap on firmly. Invert several times to mix with preservative. **NB:** If volatiles are suspected (i.e. solvent abuse) then a portion of the blood sample must be taken into a RTA vial with septum and aluminium cap (this vial is not supplied in the kit). The RTA vial must be filled approximately half full and the remaining blood placed in the container supplied.	Place glass container inside Securitainer and then place in a tamper evident bag. **Refrigerate**
Urine preserved (sodium fluoride)	Analysis for alcohol and drugs (drugs of abuse & medicinal.) **NB:** Take blood and urine in every case, unless the incident was more than 4 days prior to the examination when a urine specimen only is required.	Urine is passed into a collection vessel and approximately 20ml decanted into the urine container (fill to line; do not exceed). Screw cap on firmly. Invert several times. (Do not remove preservative tablet). **NB:** Take a urine specimen as soon as practically possible; urine can be taken prior to full medical examination.	Place glass container inside Securitainer and then place in tamper evident bag. **Refrigerate**

Body fluids = Blood, saliva, semen, seminal fluid, vaginal secretions, (faeces and urine).

Index

Questioned document examiners
(continued)
paper examination 20.15
qualifications and training 20.17
sequential testing of documents
20.12
suppliers of services 20.19
Questioning evidence 9.2

Radiocarbon dating 32.7.6, 33.8
Reconstruction of crime 11.3
fire scenes 28.13.3
Reconstruction of faces 32.7.1–2
Reference samples 4.9.1
Research, forensic veterinary science
27.6.2

Samples
from autopsy subject 14.3
consent issues 22.2.2
destruction of 12.1
taken without consent 12.1
taking from suspect 4.16
testing for drugs/alcohol 14.3–5
types of 4.9
see also **Blood; Urine**
Scene release documentation 5.4
Scenes of crime officers (SOCOs) 1.2,
2.1.4, 2.2.2, 8.4
attendance at crime scenes 3.4.5
briefing of 4.8
communication with 4.12
fingerprints and 21.2
fire scenes 28.7
management of 3.3
policy book 5.1.4
report 5.1.3
selection of evidence for forensic
testing 6.2
training 3.2, 3.3, 21.2.1
Science
use of forensic science 3.1
see also **Forensic scientist**
Scientific support coordinator's notes 5.7
Scientific support department (SSD) 2.3.2
disclosure by scientific support
department to disclosure officer
12.2.1
fires and 28.10
Search for evidence 4.2, 4.7
Security cameras *see* **Closed circuit
television (CCTV)**

Selection of items for forensic testing 6.2
Self-inflicted injuries 24.14.3
Semen, collection and preservation of
semen stains 17.6.2
Senior investigating officer (SIO) 2.3.1
Sensitive material, disclosure of 12.8
Sexual abuse cases 22.7
Sexual assault
role of forensic physician 22.6
samples from victims/suspects 17.6.5
Shoeprints *see* **Footmarks and shoeprints**
Signatures 20.5
assisted or guided hand 20.5.2
simulated 20.5.1
traced 20.5.1
vulnerable 20.5.3
Sketching crime scene 4.8, 5.2.3
Skid marks 19.3
Speech
contextual meaning of words and
phrases 26.2.3
role of forensic phonetician 26.3
voice recognition 26.3.1–3
Stab wounds 24.14.1
Stable isotope analysis 32.7.8
Statistics
arson 28.2
cyber crime 30.2
drink/drug driving 14.2.1
expression of conclusions on cloth
fibres 16.2.11
fraud 29.1
probabilities of evidence 13.4
traffic accidents 19.1
Stimulants, symptoms of use 14.11.1
Stomach contents, from autopsy subject
14.3
Submissions, management of 3.4.1
Suicidal injuries 24.14.3
Surveillance, training in 3.3.4
Suspect
examination and taking samples
4.11, 4.16
fingerprints from 21.5.1
samples from 17.6.5–6

Technical support unit 2.3.6
Third parties, disclosure of material in
hands of 12.9
Time limits, custody time limits 12.10
Toolmarks *see* **Instrument marks
(toolmarks)**